Motiv'Plicati

"Champions Live for Challenges!"

Fyrial (The Writing Dame)

Amazon.com., 2020
ISBN 9798504755199
410 Terry Avenue North Seattle, WA 98109 United States, Seattle, wa
www.amazon.com

Contents

Acknowledgments

All praises go to God—The Lord Jesus Christ, who left The Comforter(The Holy Spirit) to inspire every word, in Motiv'Plication. This book is dedicated to the victims of the 2018 Parkland shooting, and other families/school staff/individuals impacted by gun misuse due to treachery or the impact of mental health instability. My prayers are with the families, who went through the pain and terror. I also acknowledge my mother, Patricia MY INSPIRATION—who lost her life, for inspiring me, in another realm. I will love you forever and always. A special thank you to my father, Max, and stepmother Meryl. Due to your words of encouragement, I always put God first, remain humble, and disregard negativity. I love you with all my heart. Educators, we do not need to stop, yield or go according to dictators disconnected from reality. Taking a stand is crucial if we want gun violence and regulation to change. Use the voice God gave you to encourage who is right, shun what is wrong, and fight for justice. Mental health issues, should not be taboo, ignoring them leads to evil manifestations. If you are suffering from a cognitive imbalance, do not be ashamed to seek professional help. Champions admit there is a problem and do what it takes to find a solution.

Champions live for challenges!

Disclaimer

This is a work of fiction. Names, characters, businesses, places, events, locales, and incidents are either the products of the author's imagination or used in a fictitious manner. Any resemblance to actual persons/events is coincidental.

One
Setting the Stage

Casey Coper sat starry-eyed on stage, next to the podium. What could she say that would impact her fellow graduates to raise their motivational standards?

"Casey … Casey," as she snapped out of the daze, the echo of her name got louder. Immediately, she wobbled toward the dean, in six-inch stiletto heels. She brushed the long brunette ringlet curls out of her face. Shaking, she attempted to speak but nothing came out.

"Remember what you rehearsed," she mumbled.

Casey was tall with a toned body and idealistic features. Her beauty was enough to captivate, any audience but she wanted them to pay attention to her words, not her great looks.

As she stood before hundreds of graduates, she got a glimpse of what her teaching experience would be like. It caused an adrenal rush.

"Casey, please …" said the dean.

"I apologize," she said.

Dark circles under her eyes reflected six hours of sleep, she lost the night before. She was about to speak words that would influence the perspective of her classmates' lives, forever. She tossed the sweat-stained speech cards and the words began to flow.

"We did it! As you know, I earned the title of Valedictorian. It wasn't easy to attain. Although my parents and husband are proud, my degree means nothing, if there is no application of what I learned, in the educational field. Therefore, I am asking our graduating class to rise. The dean looked at her, in bewilderment. She had no clue, what her plan was. The look on her classmates' faces, should be every educator's goal. Their expressions reflected sixty percent anticipation, twenty percent excitement, and twenty percent uncertainty.

The way we begin our journey is the only way to determine if the past two years were an investment or a joke. On the count of three, I would like everyone to think of their biggest fear, regarding the field of education. Once you pinpoint it, determine one strategy you learned, from this program that will help you, conquer it. I asked you all to stand up, because the situations we will face, cannot be tackled, sitting down. What good is running from our deepest fear? If we expect our students to fight their greatest fear, we need to lead by example. Let's stand up for justice and equality to acquire educational equilibrium. Since sitting in a classroom, didn't give us this opportunity, we must expect to deal with new situations, head-on. When negative people claim we're ridiculous for pursuing this field … stand, if parents mock your attempt to educate their children … stand and when administrators place you on the frontline without warning … stand. No one can win a battle, sitting down. The ability to stand will sift out our true motives.

Never forget, this is not the end of our learning process. We should deem this day, the starting point of our educational journey. It would be beneficial for you to view students and parents, in the same light. If we underestimate our students' capabilities, we will offset them. If we set unmodified goals, based on the performance of others, it will frustrate them. OAllow your academic plan of action to evolve. Unless we transform the words from our degree into useful methodologies, completing this program, was in vain. We must change the educational process, one action at a time. Thank you," she said. The audience could not stop, marveling, over her passion. She was so excited to teach her new class, in the fall.

The Process

Casey counted the days, hours, and minutes, until the first day of school. She never realized the hiring process would be a challenge.

"I'm so tired of going on interviews, lovecicle," she said.

"I know, ADORATION," said Rye, as he kissed her forehead, gently.

Rye Coper was 6"4" with brown eyes and dark brown hair, smooth skin, a crisp white smile, and handsome. He was built like a buff linebacker. He was Casey's husband. They were everything to each other.

"If I hear, "you're not the right fit one more time, I promise," she said.

"Don't worry, everything will work out," he said.

"Oh, or how about after the interview when they don't call back, I love that," she said.

"It'll be fine," he said.

"You always say that," she said.

"And I always mean it. Don't get discouraged," he said.

"I hope I get hired at We Will Thrive," she said.

"You will whatever you want you will get. Listen, I need to run to the office," he said.

"No, don't go," she said.

She peered into his eyes, pleading for him to interpret the desperation, she felt.

"Fine, I'll go tomorrow," he said.

As she was about to give up hope, the phone rang.

"Hello," said Casey.

"Yes, this is Ms. Zepps. May I speak with Mrs. Coper," she said.

"Speaking," she said.

It took everything for her not to drop the phone. Rye came close and held her hand.

"Um … yes, Mrs. Coper Principal Lazman would love for you to join the We Will Thrive Family," she said.

"That's great," she said.

"You were an intern so your background check is done," said Ms. Zepps.

"Yes, I was," she said.

"We'll need you here bright and early, Monday morning to fill out some paperwork before you start," she said.

"Absolutely," she said.

"Have a great day," she said.

"You too," she said.

After Casey hung up the phone, Rye swooped her up, in his arms.

"You see, I told you," he said.

"Yes, you did, I start Monday," she said.

"Yup, now on to the next easy part, passing that test," he said.

"Yeah ... right on time," she said. Casey looked at the ground trying not to second guess her capability of passing the test. He was familiar with that face.

"Yeah, I take it," Saturday, everything is happening, so fast," she said.

"You'll ace it," he said.

"Oh, I almost forgot, about Ava," she said.

"Man ... what about her," he said.

"She wanted me to tell her when I got hired," she said.

"Oh ... right ... her," he said.

"She's gonna be so happy for me," she said.

Rye put her down and looked away. Ava was her best friend that he never trusted. He believed she was jealous of his wife.

"Don't be like that," she said.

"She's not on my popularity list," he said.

"Please don't ruin the moment," she said.

"Okay, I'm going upstairs to finish some work," he said.

"Sounds intense," she said.

"I still and always will love you," he said.

"I still and always will love you, too," she said.

Rye stirred a passion in her. Every time he showed support, it reaffirmed the reason she loved him.

"Those Kids"

An academic adrenal rush overwhelmed Casey. It was time to be the change she spoke about. We Will Thrive Elementary was a
low-income school, where students were disadvantaged. She knew Ava would be supportive, considering she went on over fifty interviews, and finally got hired. It was time to call and tell her friend the great news.

"Ava," she exclaimed.

"Hey, what's up," she said

"I got the job," she said.

"That's great," she said.

"Yeah," she said.

"Wait ... where ... which school," she said.

"I am a fourth-grade teacher, at We Will Thrive Elementary," she said.

"Um ... did you hear me," she said.

"Yes, do you understand, the neighborhood you'll be working in," she said.

"What do you mean," she said.

"That's one of the roughest parts of town," she said.

"Um ... okay ... what's your point," she said.

"That school has "those kids," she said.

"Excuse me, who are **THOSE KIDS**," she said.

"You know, they have a hard time with speech and are like ... well ... ghetto," she said.

She tried to maintain her composure. Who in the world were "those kids?"

"Okay, does that mean "those kids" are not worth having a teacher," she said.

"Well, I didn't say that," she said.

"No, that's exactly what you're saying," she said.

"What does the neighborhood have to do with teaching "those kids," she said.

"I don't want you to think I'm not happy for you, Case.," she said.

"Of course not, you got a job at Stuck Up a.k.a. Remain an A School At Any Cost

Elementary," she said.

"Calm down," she said.

"Just because the neighborhood isn't the best and the kids are what you consider not "up to par," doesn't mean they're worthless," she said.

"That's not … what … I mean," she said.

"Anyway, I refuse to let negativity penetrate my cloud of happiness," she said.

"Don't get upset," said Ava.

"Whatever, I guess to you "those kids" don't deserve anything," she said.

"I'm happy for you Case, just be careful," she said.

"Thanks for the warning, I'll be fine, teaching "THOSE KIDS," she said.

"I meant no disrespect," she said.

"Fine, talk to you later," she said.

"Bye," she said.

Maybe she had a small point, about taking precautions. As Casey reflected on entering the school for her interview she recalled, the half-broken beer bottles and outed cigarette butts. The environment did not deter her, from the school, neither did the economic status of the students or their parents. Her first day of school was approaching. She was determined not to let anyone or anything ruin it.

Testing …

Casey was hired. All her eggs were in a safe knit basket. The test was the last facet to the beginning of her teaching journey. "Please place your bag, in this locker," said (Mr. Hez) the test proctor. She was a little worried but the anxiety did not overwhelm her. There were two portions she had left to complete, after her program. How hard could it be?

"Here's the restroom key," he said.

She took it and continued to listen to the testing protocol. The rules were simple. He escorted her into the room. She sat down, placed the restroom key next to her scrap paper, and started the test. Casey finished the language arts portion, in under thirty minutes. She laughed to herself. It was so easy. The math segment was next. She was slightly concerned but could not back out. She recalled the strategies from the test prep course. The first few questions were simple; however, as the test progressed the questions started to get arduous. She started to sweat, intensely. Her nerves engulfed all feelings of confidence and she started to guess. Finally, she raised her hand to indicate the test was complete. He came in and escorted her out. She received her belongings and was given the login code to access her test results. She logged in and saw she passed the language arts but missed the math portion by two points. "Two points," she whispered to herself.

She could not handle the embarrassment. Statistically, she was less likely to pass, the second time, around.

She walked to her car, in disbelief and turned her phone back on several texts were wishing good blessings, from her family, friends, and husband.

This made her cry, intensely. It was shameful. She put on depressing music and drove home. She sat in the driveway in disbelief, logging back into the system, from her phone to double-check the test results. She needed more time to register, what happened. Not even five, minutes later, Rye came running to the car. Quickly, she exited out of the website.

"Hey Mrs. Coper, how was your test," he said.

"It was good," she said.

"Are you sure," he said.

"Yes, don't ask me, again," she said.

"Okay …," he said.

"Sorry, it's just," she said.

He looked at her with admiration. She knew he would love her, no matter how many points she missed the test by, but embarrassment overshadowed his potential.

"Never mind, everything's fine," she said.

"Let's go inside, I made you something special," he said.

As they entered the house, she smelled something wonderful. He made her a cake. It read: congratulations to the best teacher, in the world.

She started to cry.

"ADORATION what's wrong," he said.

"Nothing, it's just so perfect, lovesicle," she said.

"Okay, you don't have to cry," he said.

She was happy about the thoughtful gesture but was crying for a different reason. He felt something was off but didn't want to press the matter.

"Here, have a slice of pizza," he said.

"I can't eat, right now," she said.

"Okay, well it's here when you're ready," he said.

"What are you doing," she said.

"Relax, You're tired," he said.

As he brushed a strand of hair, out of her face, he picked her up and walked upstairs. She was exhausted.

"Rest," he said.

He kissed her, closed the door, and left the room.

Feelings of failure drained her thoughts of capability. Her new job was starting soon. She did not want to start on a hypocritical note. She decided to combat them by remembering her speech. This test would not get in the way of her doing a great job, helping underprivileged kids, or impacting the students. She decided she had other portions of the test to take. No one would know the difference.

She would retry. Everything would work out. Her phone kept buzzing. It was her family and friends. She decided to send a mass text to them. It read:

Hello, everyone! The test went well. I have a few more portions to take. Thanks for your kind words. They meant the world. Love you guys.

She was exhausted. Normally, she would meditate on words of encouragement. The only word that stood out in her mind was FAILURE. Why couldn't she shake this feeling of inadequacy? Soon, she fell asleep.

Day 1

The next day was here, finally. Casey was still hurt, about failing her test but she pushed her feelings to the back of her mind. This was the first day. It was so exciting.

She ran downstairs to look for Rye.

"Good morning," he said.

"Hey, why are you up, so early," she said.

"It's your first day," he said.

"The banking world doesn't start, 'til 8:45 but I needed to get up, extra early for you," he said.

"I still and always will love you," she said.

"You're okay too," he said.

"Proper response please," she said.

"I still and always will love you, ADORATION," he said.

"Thanks, lovesicle," she said.

"Hurry, you don't want to be late," he said.

She rushed upstairs and took a shower. Forty-five minutes later, she was ready.

"Okay, I'm all set," she said.

"You need to eat," he said.

"I'm not hungry," she said.

"It's non-negotiable," he said.

She forced a piece of toast down her throat and kissed him goodbye.

"Take the rest with you," he said.

She had her rolling cart with the school materials. She was ready. He walked her to the car.

"I almost forgot, I asked the principal if I could set up my class and she said they were still finalizing things," she said.

"Okay, and…" he said.

"I'll need to stay back, after school to set my room up, or maybe by some miracle I could do it on a break," she said.

"Teachers usually get it done, in a week but I'm over the top," she said.

"True, I don't get off, till five," he said.

"I know, I was just telling you," she said.

"I still and always will love you," he said.

"I still and always will love you," she said.

"Text me, when you can," he said.

"Okay," she said.

As Casey drove, she felt a jolt of excitement and nerves hit the bottom of her stomach. What would the first day be like? Finally, she arrived. She took out her belongings and headed to the front office.

As she opened the door, she heard—"My child ain't going to that school," exclaimed an irate parent.

"Ms. B., I need you to calm down," said Principal Lazman.

"Majesty was reassigned, based on your new address," he said.

"I don't care, she ain't going, there," exclaimed the parent.

"Please keep your voice down, I don't want to call the police," said Principal Lazman.

"Mrs. Coper … hello," said a familiar voice.

Casey diverted her attention to the office manager's desk.

"Mrs. Coper, you made it," said Ms. Zepps.

"Yes, I did," she said.

"Don't worry about what's going on, over there," she said.

Casey thought the suggestion to ignore the heavy office traffic was a joke. It was busier than Wall Street.

"Here is the most important form, just sign the bottom and you're good to go," she said.

Casey tried not to pay attention to the screaming, irate parent in the corner but it was hard.

"Here you go," she said.

"Girl you know that lady was gone," said a loud voice.

"Ladies, please keep it down," she said.

At first, she thought the women were parents(of students) but they were teachers. Soon two police cars pulled up, in front of the office. As two officers entered to solve several issues, Casey looked alarmed.

"Naw, they tried my baby," said the irate parent.

"She ain't going to that c****er school," said the irate parent.

"Ma'am you will need to calm down," said the officers.

They escorted her to their car.

"Principal Lazman, Mrs. Coper is so excited to start her first day," she said. She looked embarrassed.

"Welcome things aren't usually this crazy," she said.

"Oh … that was no big deal," she said.

"Here's Mrs. Batet, your team leader, her class is connected to yours," she said.

"Hello, welcome to We Will Thrive," she said.

She seemed jovial. She was in her early thirties, tall, gorgeous and outspoken.

"It's nice to meet you," she said. As the educators walked off, she rushed behind them.

"You ladies make sure to thrive, every minute … today," she said.

"We will," she said.

"Yeah … we will," she said.

"Girl … the secretary's so seven dollar bill phony," she said.

Casey hated being put in awkward situations.

"Anyway … back to the office fiasco, sorry you saw that," she said.

"It's no problem," she said.

"Things can get crazy on the first day, heck on any day," she said.

"No, it's fine," she said.

She noticed Casey was trying to downplay her state of shock.

"I guess the school you came from was a little different, huh," she said.

"Maybe a little," she said.

"How long have you taught," she said.

"It's my first year," she said.

"Oh, fresh meat for the sharks," she said.

"I guess," she said.

"Here is the teacher's lounge," she said.

She pointed to a miniature room to the left of the cafeteria. Five minutes later, they arrived at her new classroom.

"If you need anything, I'm right next door," she said.

"Thanks so much," she said.

"Oh, our first team meeting, won't be until after a month," she said.

Casey was confused. During her internship, her team met, weekly.

"When do I get to meet the rest of the team," she said.

"Oh, hold on let me go get them," she said.

She walked out of the room and returned five seconds later.

"Here I am, it's just us girl, you will get used to my sense of humor," she said.

Or lack thereof thought Casey.

"Let me start setting up, time goes so fast," she said.

"Yeah," she said.

"Here are some important papers, about your class," she said.

Casey was wondering why she had her documents.

"Relax, Ms. Zepps just gave them to me," she said.

"Thanks," she said.

"I'm gone, settle into your new room and look over those documents," she said.

"Oh … wait … let me see your roster, wow, you have some of mine from last year," she said.

She did not understand why Mrs. Batet was rolling her eyes and shaking her head. It was important to start the new year with a new outlook.

"Girl, all I have to say is thou anoints my head with oil, my cup runneth over," she said.

"What," she said.

"You'll see, Oh yeah… go …. Motivators," she said.

"Motivators," said Casey. She looked confused.

"That's who we are The Motivators," she said.

"Yeah, I know," she said.

Casey looked at her roster. According to the birthdates, there were several retained students, in her class. At least five of them were twelve, in the fourth grade. Was this a mistake?

Under her roster were several Individual Education Plans. Several students had special needs. She put the paperwork down and took a look, at her new classroom. There was a heap of old books, in the corner, behind her desk and the Dry Erase Board was stained with a permanent marker. She decided to remain positive. Time was going fast. She looked, at her phone.

Text me later, you will do great, love Rye.

Thanks love, she replied.

The first bell rang.

"Hey, you good, remember, I'm right next door," she said.

"Okay, thanks," she said.

"You need to stand at the door to greet the students," she said.

"Oh … right," she said.

"It's all in the procedures, didn't you get the list," she said.

"Um … yes, sure," she said.

"Okay, so … let's get to greeting," she said.

Casey got up from her chair and opened the door. There were over twenty students, waiting. She was nervous.

"Nah I hate y'all," said a student.

Two students started to shove, each other.

"Um … excuse me we are not doing that," she said.

Casey did not like Mrs. Batet addressing the behavior of her students. She had a class to focus on. Also, what was with the terminology?

"Excuse me, what is your name," she said.

"Bow," said the student.

She looked bewildered.

"Okay, Bow please try to set an example," she said.

"Ms. Ma'am, he started it though," said Kaz.

"Stand by me," she said.

"But it ain't my fault," he said.

"Dang that's the teacher, she fine," said another student.

"Okay, sir what's your name," she said.

"My name Renald," he said.

"Please don't speak about me that way," she said.

"Sorry Miss," he said.

"Now, how about you each give me a high five before you come in," she said.

The students started laughing.

"Miss, you mean dap," said Kaz.

"Yeah, that's what I meant," said Casey. She never realized their comments could cut deep. It may seem silly to others but the jeering hurt. She was sensitive to the opinion of students. What was wrong with her?

"Here Miss, dis the way we do it," said Kaz.

He showed her the handshake and she was grateful. One by one the students entered.

"Please have a seat," she said.

The students ignored her request.

"Yo mama ain't nothin," said Renald (to another student).

"Okay, listen you can't talk like that," she said.

"Hold up y'all," he said.

"I'm finna be good dis year, she fine," he said.

She ignored his comment. It wasn't worth the confrontation. She saw the students on the announcements but the class was so rowdy, she gave up, trying to understand.

"Please take your seats," she said.

"Y'all be good for Miss She So Fine," said Renald.

"Shut up," said Kaz.

"Boys, stop it," she said.

As Casey approached the students, she could feel the presence of someone getting ready to address an issue that was not her concern.

"Excuse me, I don't know what y'all think this is but you're next to the right one," said Mrs. Batet.

"Please calm down, everyone," she said.

"Every last one of you, sit down," said Mrs. Batet.

Quickly, the students got quiet and sat down.

"If you need anything else, just come next door," she said.

She didn't know, how to feel. She was grateful for her intervention but this was not a good start to the year. When neighboring teachers intervene with behavioral issues, it sets unstable precedence. The students know, this teacher is there to enforce the rules. The action could cause a lack of respect for their teacher.

"Thanks," she said.

"It's not a problem," she said.

"Okay, my name is Mrs. Coper, I will be your teacher, this year," she said.

"Man … I want Mrs. B," said another student.

"Shut up you was bad for her, last year," said Kaz

"Okay, please don't use the words shut up," she said.

"Forget her," said another student.

"Excuse me, what is your name," she said.

"Who cares," said the student.

"Miss, her name Matique," said Kaz.

"I could tell you everybody name, in here," he said

"Boy shut up," she said

"Well, Matique we need to go over the rules," she said.

"Rule number 1 we are going to respect each other," she said.

"Yeah right," she said.

"That means you may not say things like shut up or I don't care, in this class," she said.

"I want my old teacher," she said.

Ring! Ring!

"Hello, Mrs. Coper speaking," she said.

"Yes, Mrs. Coper, we noticed you haven't taken the attendance yet," said Ms. Zepps. There was yelling in the background.

"Um … yes," she said.

"Is everything okay," she said.

"Yes, it's fine," she said.

"You dumb," said Renald.

"Please don't call people names," she said.

"Hello," she said.

"Yes," she said.

"Okay, just take roll and enter it, in the system, thanks," she said.

"Sure," she said.

"Thank you," she said.

She didn't want to reveal certain students refused to confirm their names. Also, attendance in the system did not reflect the six additional students in her class. How in the world was she supposed to pull this off?

She had no choice, she asked Kaz to assist her.

After she took the role. The students continued to disregard every request. The rest of the day was filled with name-calling, breaking up fights, and disrespectful gestures. Finally, it was time for dismissal. She did not get a break, because the lunch schedule was altered. They ended up eating in the room. Casey questioned leadership, at her new school. There were one hundred and seventy-nine days, left in the school year. She did not want to seem ungrateful but the rest of the year could not go like day one.

She went to the front office to clock out and entered through the back door.

"Girlfriend had no control of the class, you hear me," she said.

"Oh really, I knew it, when I heard the loud yelling, in the background," she said.

"I had to go over like seven times, the kids will run all over her," she said.

Casey couldn't believe it. They were gossiping freely. Their verbal daggers dug deep. Everything was so hurtful.

Quickly, she approached the time clock and punched out.

"Hey girl, I know things were crazy for you, today," said Mrs. Batet.

"It was fine," she said.

"If you need anything, remember we're here," she said. Mrs. Batet smirked at Ms. Zepps. Casey's face was blank. These women were dangerous. She didn't know, who to trust.

Except for the field trips, the school where she completed her internship was different. The people were real, students were relatable and leadership was superb.

"You okay," she said.

"Yeah," she said.

"See you tomorrow," she said.

She ignored her comment and walked toward her car. Ding! Ding! Ding!

ADORATION you never texted me. I know your first day went well. Text me when you can. I still and always will love you, Rye. That was one of many notifications, she missed on her phone.

She started to sob. Her speech was supposed to give her strength, no matter how bad things were. She never imagined her first class would be like this. What would she tell him? She drove home, in shock. After entering the car, she saw missed calls, from Ava. She was determined not to speak with her, about day one. This experience had to get better. The drive home was depressing. As she entered the driveway, Rye ran to the car.

"What are you doing home, so early," she said.

"I left early, it was your first day and I wanted to be here," he said.

"Um ... okay," she said.

"What's wrong and why didn't you answer any of my messages," he said.

"I can't handle an interrogation, right now," she said.

"I'm not interrogating you ..." he said.

He bent down to retrieve her belongings.

"I got it," she said.

After they walked inside, she dropped her things and started to cry. He held her, closely.

"I knew something was off, what happened," he said.

"Everything was horrible, the schedule the kids and everyone is two-faced," she said.

"Slow down," he said.

"I need to come up with a plan, quitting is not an option," she said.

"Are you sure, this's what you want to do," he said.

She gave him a look of uncertainty.

"Why would you question that," she said.

"Because you are so unhappy and it's only the first day," he said.

"Didn't you hear my speech," she said.

"Of course but I don't want anything pushing you over the edge," he said.

I can't give up," she said.

Her eyes filled with tears. He knew that look. It was an expression he could not bear to handle. This was a problem, he could not solve. No matter what he said, she would disregard it.

"Okay, you're really smart, come up with something the kids will respond to," he said.

"I need you to leave me alone, right now so I can think," she said.

He kissed her forehead.

"I'll be in the office," he said.

She didn't respond and started going through the pile of papers, from Mrs. Batet. She went through each one and began to construct incentive plans that would help each student.

Half an hour passed and she heard a knock, at the door.

"Here's something to eat, I'll leave it on the table," he said.

"Yeah, thanks," she said. She barely heard him.

There were papers everywhere. She was engulfed in constructing the plans.

Ding! Ding!

"Hello," she said.

"Monarch didn't you get messages from daddy and I," said Mrs. Peinst.

"Yes, sorry, I got caught up," she said.

"That's no excuse," she said.

"I'm sorry mom," she said.

"There's an emergency," she said.

"Really, what is it," she said.

"It's your father and I, we're concerned about that new school, after looking up the information—I'm safe and my first day went well," she interjected. Mrs. Peinst was a beautiful woman who always tried to dictate her daughter's life, she was married to Mr. Peinst. He was a tall, handsome man with a serious demeanor. Although they communicated, Casey distanced herself, due to their controlling ways. Monarch was her nickname, ever since she was a little girl. She earned it since she was obsessed with royalty and her mother thought princess was common, instead, she opted to use monarch. Her parents were the only people who could refer to her that way.

"It's fine, please tell dad not to worry," she said.

"I'm here, beautiful monarch," he said.

"Hey dad," she said.

"Okay, I wish you didn't have to work," she said.

"Please don't go there," she said.

"Well it's the truth, if you married Blaze you wouldn't need to work or-—I'm really busy, let's talk another time," she interjected.

"Wait, we love you, monarch," she said.

"I love you guys," she said.

"Are you eating," said Rye.

"Not yet—oh, you're on the phone," he interjected.

"Of course, with her parents," said Mrs. Peinst.

"Hey M.I.L., how are you F.I.L.," he said. Since she was an only child, Casey made some decisions, regarding their marriage, without consulting Rye. As a result, he had a tumultuous relationship with her parents. Instead of referring to them as mom and dad, they were called M.I.L(mother-in-law) and F.I.L.(father-in-law).

"I was telling your gorgeous wife about my concerns with that school," she said.

"I think she can handle it," he said.

"You hear that he believes in me," she said. Even though he did not want her stressed out, they agreed to always unify(regarding decisions), in front of others(especially her parents).

"I guess, it would be nice if she didn't need to work, right Rye," she said. He tried to maintain a peaceful state of mind.

"She wants to work, right ADORATION," he said.

"It's not working, like everyone heard in my speech, my degree was not earned in vain," she said.

"You're right," said Mr. Peinst.

"Anyway, goodbye and I love you," she said.

"Please call/text us, goodbye," said Mrs. Peinst.

"I can't stand when she makes those comments," he said.

"Lovesicle—ignore evil words," she said.

"I always do but it's hard," he said.

"Everything is fine, let me finish," she said.

"I still and always will love you," he said.

"I still and always will love you," she said.

She continued to work, steadily as the evening ended, she wrapped up the last document.

"It's nine o'clock, I don't mean to disturb you, but it's bedtime," he said.

"You only ate half of your dinner," he said.

"I wasn't hungry," she said.

"Okay, well let's go to bed," he said.

"Fine," she said.

She shut everything down, took a shower, and headed to bed.

Rye could not stand when her mind was preoccupied. He hated interacting with a percentage of her.

"I still and always will love you," he said.

"I still and always will love you," she said.

He attempted to gently rub the back of her neck and she pulled away.

"Okay, goodnight Case.," he said.

He turned in the opposite direction. She hated sleeping, back to back. It was unhealthy. She wanted to tap him and say, "I didn't mean it" but her energy was exerted.

Day 2

The next day, Casey went to work an hour early. She was determined to make sure, everything was ready. She refreshed her mind and focused on the lesson of the day.

Each incentive plan is aligned with the appropriate Individualized Education Plan. She also decided to construct plans for students who had prior issues, based on observation and information from other paperwork.

She adjusted the seating arrangement and kept working.

"Good morning," said Mrs. Batet.

Was it 7:15 a.m. already?

"Good morning," she said. She loathed having to respond.

"It's looking nice, in here," she said.

"Thanks," she said.

Casey was never a great actress. She took drama, in middle school and earned a C-. She tried to remember the strategies. It was no use.

"It's a new day, Mrs. Coper," she said.

"Please call me Casey," she said.

"Well … Casey, I like your new seating arrangement," she said.

"Thanks, I can't talk, now," she said.

"Okay, girl I see you're busy," she said.

"Yeah, that's me, so busy," she said.

"I'm next door if you need me," she said.

She felt forced to smile. After she left, she continued to work.

It was time to start the day. The sound of students talking, outside the classroom, caused her to shudder. What were they doing here, so early? She looked at her phone. It was 7:35 a.m. Why did the time go so fast? Slowly, she opened the door and waited for the students. They were sitting down and speaking, loudly. She clapped twice and motioned for them to stand.

"Mornin Miss, you remember how to give dap," okay," said Kaz.

"I do," she said. She met his greeting, fist to fist.

"I see you, Miss," said Phaze.

She gave each student dap and motioned for them to take a seat. She stood there with a straight face. Finally, all the students were seated.

"What's up wicha girl," said Phaze.

"She mad," said Kaz,

"Why ain't she talk-in," he said.

"I dunno," he said.

"Y'all scared her, yesterday," said Phaze.

"Nah she ain't scared, she back today," said Kaz.

As a result of the students being so loud, Mrs. Batet entered her class. Before she could address the issue, Casey blew her whistle. The students clogged their ears.

"I'm happy you are all seated, today we start fresh," she said.

"Okay girl, day two and you got this," she said.

"I do," she said.

"My voice was strained, I will not yell, today." She said. Quickly, she closed the door and returned to her class.

"Raise your hand if you understand, me," she said.

Everyone raised their hand.

"Good, let's start by watching the announcements," she said.

"Phaze please turn on the television," she said.

Davy and Abell started making faces, at each other. Quickly, she sat between them. They looked embarrassed.

The class did not know how to react. Her demeanor was completely different. They could not predict her actions.

"We are not speaking, during the announcements," she said.

The room was quiet. The students looked at her, in bewilderment.

"Good morning Motivators,

"This is Principal Lazman!

Welcome back! I hope you had a restful summer. We have some new teachers on campus. Please remember to respect yourselves and each other, be kind, try your best, and always mo---ti--vate," she said.

"Let's recite our creed," she said.

"Motivate! Motivate! It's never too late to motivate!"

"Save the date, don't be late, never forget to motivate!"

"Positive things are coming our way!"

"Negativity … Go away!"

"We will never accept defeat!"

"The Big Wig Test is under our feet," said announcer one.

"Motivate, motivate, it's never too late to motivate," cheered the students.

"It will be a great day, at We Deserve it, Elementary," said announcer two.

She noticed how engaged the students were, during the school creed. After the announcements, she approached the board and started to write numbers.

"Today, we are going to talk about rules. I will be calling each student to my desk," said Casey. We will respect each other. That starts with having respect for time," said Casey.

"Who cares about time," said Kaz.

"You do," she said.

"Listen, time is very important," she said.

"I want to get to know each one of you, that takes time," she said.

Mrs. Batet peeked her head in and noticed it was quiet.

"Everything good," she said.

"Yes, everything's fine with my class, how's yours," she said.

"Oh big try …. she good …," said the students.

Quickly, she closed the door.

"Let's start by recognizing how important time is. I want you to write about the time we wasted yesterday," she said.

"Remember … I am here for you," she said.

"Every time you waste one minute, it makes it hard for you to learn what I need to teach you," she said.

"Sorry Miss," said Kaz.

"Yeah we sorry," said Renald.

"Don't worry about apologies, just do better," she said.

"Miss, I'm Genereese," she said.

"It's so nice to see you, again," she said. She was a quiet and polite student.

"I'm good, yes," she said.

"Of course," she said.

"You tell my mom," she said.

"Yes, if you would like me too," she said.

"Can I give you a hug," she said.

"Yes," she said. Moments like these made her happy.

 One by one she allowed each student to come to her desk, daily. The routine was not in conjunction with the schedule but she was willing to take the risk. It was essential for them to understand each other. Although she had a long way to go, now there was a baseline for control.

Unraveling

 After attending meetings with jaded colleagues, following an inconsistent curriculum, and splitting herself constantly, Casey's academic adrenaline started to deplete. Instead of an ideal class of eighteen, she ended up with twenty-two special students. Was this a class or a football team? She had a range of students, who did not understand why slapping was not a permissive pastime, cursed constantly, and displayed manipulative actions. They also struggled with academic/behavioral challenges. At the last faculty meeting, her principal kept reiterating "copies are a rare commodity." How would she stop making them, when the curriculum required printouts of each book's content? She made the mistake of asking a question, during that faculty meeting and if looks were bullets, her body would have been full of holes. It was challenging for her to stay abreast of the last-minute updates. Colleagues, parents(of her students), and administration suffered from mood swings. She wondered if happiness in this field was a mirage.

"Good morning," said Ms. Pink.

"What's so good, about it," she said.

"Are you okay? We noticed a change, in you," she said.

"I'm fine," she said.

"Are you sure," she said.

"Yes, now leave me alone," she said.

"Okay, I won't bother you, again," she said.

The nerve, asking about my wellbeing, she doesn't care. she thought. Where do you need to go to get the real deal, in this school? People are so seven-dollar bill phony," she said. Why wasn't she concerned, last week when Casey looked irate(in the cafeteria) and kept quiet. Ms. Pink was not concerned about anyone. While she chaperoned(the students) in the cafeteria they could have swallowed silverware for all she cared.

The bell rang, it was time to carry out the tasks on another mundane Monday. Casey welcomed students, every morning. She had to put on that plastic smile and say, "Hello"_____. "How was your weekend?" They would ask her the same question. She wanted to have a heart-to-heart to explain, she does not know how to relax. Her day was comprised of the usual challenges, students cursing, bloody fingers, addressing their irate parents, and putting her voice on instant replay.

"Everyone please sit, we're about to begin," she said.

"Miss you in trouble," said Kaz.

"What do you mean," she said.

As she opened her plan book, there was a screechy noise, from the door closing.

Her principal entered the class and sat at her desk. Why was this the day she would be observed? She took and deep breath and prayed for God's grace.

"Okay class, let's start with our routine," she said. She made a hand motion and they stood up.

"Our objective is to learn, about rainforest animals," they said.

"Nice, you make be seated," she said.

"Please place your head down and hold up the number of fingers based on our I Already Know Chart," she said.

"Remember, no peeking, she said.

"Now place the numbers down and pick your head up," she said.

"Oh … miss pick me," said Davy.

"Thanks for raising your hand, Abell go ahead," she said.

"Miss I know bout the forest, I watched it before," he said.

"Awesome, try to focus on the details, again," she said.

Every stroke of Principal Lazman's keyboard made her shutter.

"Oh, and my mama got me the new video game," he said. The class laughed.

"Don't forget what the topic is," she said.

"Please pay attention to this short video clip," she said.

As they watched the clip, she walked around to ensure everyone was paying attention.

Creak! She left. Ding! The observation feedback notification caused an even mix of anxiety and hope.

"Keep working, please," she said.

Quickly, she took a deep breath and opened the message.

Good morning,

I would like to start by writing you did a great job redirecting the students, actively monitoring them, and using evaluation tools. My only suggestion is not to ignore a student who directly addresses you. Great job! Keep up the Motiv'Plication.

Principal Lazman,

We Will Thrive Elementary School

"We need to step it up!"

She appreciated her feedback; however, she wondered … if ignoring was not a strategy(she would utilize) to eliminate poor behavior what would she suggest? She continued to instruct the students on twenty percent. It was time to recharge. Mundane Monday finally came to a horrific end. As she started to pack up, she heard a notification. Who was emailing me this time, she thought.

Good afternoon,

This is Ms. Spoils, your Union Representative. Unfortunately, the news I am about to provide may cause a shock. Before you continue to read this email, please have a seat. Employees of schools who scored a C or below, the past year, will take a major pay cut, by next May. All educators in this category will make fifteen thousand dollars, yearly. Unfortunately, we are one of the schools. This is a substantial decrease. Additionally, the petition we signed to increase school security personnel/equipment and mental health services remains unaddressed. This is a huge concern, considering most school shootings that occurred during the past month were impactful. Educators plan on doing something, about these decisions. I am coming around with a petition, if you are interested in obtaining more further details, please inform me.

Thank you.

Ms. Spoils

Union Representative

P:1212555 ext. 280

-Union Reps Unite!

Was this a sick joke? How did the powers that be concoct this? The pressure was too much. She heard several teachers, in the hallway, voicing discontent. The whole school was a mess. She wanted to voice her feelings but figured it would not change anything. Although she did not want to walk away, from her class, Casey needed to do something.

"Ava," she said.

"I heard the news," said Ava.

"I can't believe this," she said.

"I know," she said.

"How in the world, do they expect us to survive," she said.

"They compromised our security and income," she said. She sobbed, bitterly.

"Please don't cry," she said.

"I'm trying not to," she said.

"I will speak with my principal to ask if the first-grade opening is filled, at my school," she said.

"No," she said.

"Why not," she said.

"I can't give up on my students," she said.

"You'd rather watch your paycheck get smaller," she said.

"I mean … I can't quit on them," she said.

"Thankfully, your husband has a great career," she said.

"You still deserve more, " she said.

"I know, we need to figure out how to solve this," she said.

"I'll call you with an update when I find out," she said.

"Okay, thanks," she said.

Three sob-filled hours later, she tried to prepare dinner, before her husband came home. Thus far, she only prepared the salad, but exhaustion won the battle. She plopped on the couch and pulled up her traveling case that held the educational tools for her livelihood. She cracked open the large bin and began grading papers. They mounted into a blanket of comfort and she fell asleep.

"H ... hello," she said.

"Hey, Case were you sleeping," she said.

"Yeah, just a quick nap, what's up," she said.

"Well, I spoke to my boss and all he needed was pompoms," she said.

"Wow," she said.

"He is thrilled, about the idea of a low-income teacher, joining our network," she said.

"Really," she said.

"Yes," she said.

"That's amazing," she said.

"I think it has something to do with your resilience," she said.

"Maybe he figures you will work harder, based on the situation, who cares," she said.

"Um ... I do," she said.

"The point is, after you meet Principal Just, you will be hired," she said.

"Hurray," said Casey.

"Come by at three, dressed in all white," she said.

"All white ... Um ... okay," she said.

Casey had one hour to get ready. She was so excited. She wore a lacy white dress with her hair tightly pulled back and seven-inch white stilettos; she looked sharp. After she got dressed and grabbed a copy of her resume and headed out to Inspire Me Elementary. She felt a strange lump, in her throat. She was so nervous. After heading north for thirty minutes, she saw a narrow pathway, surrounded by trees. The G.P.S. led her in the correct direction. She saw a black and white sign that read Inspire Me Elementary straight ahead. There were numerous Alpine Trees, the crisp smell of fresh air was amazing. Finally, she arrived.

As she approached her destination she pulled into an extended driveway. Slowly, she approached the entrance. There were several people, dressed in all white, standing outside what looked like a mounted castle. This place was not a school, it was an educational haven. Four muscle-bound tall men(dressed in white suits), greeted her, one approached her and asked for her keys.

"Which school has a valet," she said.

The man did not respond, he only smiled, slightly.

She got out of the car and handed him the keys. As the handsome tall man drove away, her car vanished. She thought it was a bit odd but was consumed by the beauty of her environment. The remaining three men escorted her to the office, (also named the sanctuary). The decor reminded her of an ideal environment, every student should have. Each step was gold accented with inspirational phrases. As she read the phrases, one, in particular, stood out, DREAMS DRAG TIRED FEET. She loved it.

The three men left her, in the sanctuary, as she approached a young woman with platinum hair, sitting at the front desk.

"Mrs. Coper, I'm the secretary here. Principal Just is waiting for you," said Ms. Luna.

"Thanks," she said.

"So, you must be the miracle, we've been waiting for," said Principal Just.

Casey looked around, in bewilderment.

"Miracle …" she said.

"Yes, you remained inspired, despite your circumstances that means you are a miracle," he said.

"Oh, okay," she said.

"Come with me," he said.

The duo left the sanctuary and headed toward the cafe. She could not believe her eyes. Pathways leading to every entrance were gold. Every teacher, student, and staff member looked like high-end celebrities.

"Do you mind, me asking when we are going to have our interview," she said.

He chuckled.

"Conforming to normal interview posture is mundane," he said.

"Yes, that's true," she said.

"I understand, this may not be the traditional school, you're used to," he said.

"To be honest, it's not" … she said.

"That's because we are not just a school," he said.

"Once you have the privilege of viewing the unique activities each student does here, you will see, this is not a school, it is an equal opportunity haven that sharpens the appeal of each student, and fine-tunes their capabilities by diminishing negative perspectives," he said.

"This school seems like the acme of success," she said.

"It is," he said.

"At Inspirational Elementary we understand life is driven by choices, this helps eliminate victimized mentalities and encourage true unique learning opportunities," he said.

"It's so unique, how did the idea for the organization come about," she said.

" This educational haven came into existence, several years ago. Ms. Ava Lane told me such great things, about you and the situation you are facing," he said.

Casey hung her head, sadly. She did not want her situation advertised, but it was beyond her control.

"Before you join our network, I have one question," he said.

"What's that," she said

"Are you ready," he said.

"Absolutely," she said.

"Why did you remain in such a disadvantaged system," he said.

"I never viewed it that way," she said.

"Students were always so grateful, regardless of their living conditions or horrific circumstances, this meant the world to me," she said.

"I see, please continue …" he said.

"After I pitched ideas and realized certain educators were in this field to keep a roof over their head, I gave up," she said.

"The system is tarnished, but I can't fight alone," she said.

"Interesting," he said.

"Do you have any questions/comments for me," he said.

"Yes, what are the benefits of being in charge, of such a unique school," she said.

"I don't like the term, in charge," he said.

"My apologies," she said.

"Not necessary, the term defeats the purpose of why our school came into existence," he said.

"We believe in supporting the unique needs of each child, strongly," he said.

"Administration leads by example," he said.

"Thant's amazing," she said.

"Thanks, our network of educators feel valued, every minute of every day," he said.

"Interesting," she said.

"Differentiation starts in the heart, not during instruction," he said.

"Wow, I have never heard that explanation before," she said.

"We are first at a lot of things," he said.

Casey smiled.

"We veer away from learning environments with no personalization," he said.

"Do you mind disclosing salary information," she said.

"Not at all, our teachers start at one-hundred thousand dollars, yearly," he said.

"Interesting, that's different from what we're going through," she said.

"Of course, there's that first time pattern, again," he said.

"So true," she said.

"If teachers earned advanced degrees, they get an additional one hundred thousand dollars," he said.

"Oh really, tell me more," she said.

"We don't believe in insulting the capabilities of our teachers by diminishing pay scales," he said.

"Diminishing pay scales," she said.

"All teachers pay eighty dollars a month for health coverage(regardless of preexisting conditions)," he said.

"Sounds like a miracle," she said.

"It is the field has changed for the better, since implementing this new approach," he said.

"I would love to teach here," she said.

"If you believe traditionalism and deadwood mentalities are not trending, we would love you to join our team," he said.

"I don't support stale mentalities," she said.

"Perfect, are you available to start, tomorrow," he said.

She felt so comfortable with him but something made her reluctant to commit.

"Um … sure," she said.

"Great, I have some advice," he said.

"Really, what's that," she said.

"Don't stop dreaming, or you'll end up in the negative abyss," he said.

"The negative abyss," she said.

"Yes," he said.

Before she could ask, what he meant, she found herself falling down a dark bottomless pit.

Reality?

"I won't …" she exclaimed.

"ADORATION, are you okay," he said.

Casey was so happy to see the face of her tall and handsome husband.

"I knew I should have turned off the news while you were sleeping," he said.

"No wonder you had a nightmare, hold on … before you explain what the nightmare was about, let me turn it off," he said.

"No," she said.

"Okay, sheeze … don't have a heart attack," he said.

"Just be quiet," she said.

She reached for the remote control and turned up the volume. She saw protestors alongside one of education's bigwigs, Ms. Zebedee. She was well renowned for her advocacy work and a big mouth. Casey needed to hear what cause she was protesting for.

"This is Reporter Sight, coming to you live from the outside of The Crescent Building," said Reporter Sight.

"I am standing with the mother of Aristocrat Stems, the parent of the five-year-old child who was gunned down, three days ago, and Ms. Zebedee the educational activist," she said.

"Could you tell us why you and others are protesting," she said.

"Yes, well I'm well known for fighting injustice. Parents and educators are so tired. A child was killed on this road, due to negligence. Our leaders need to wake up and provide what we need to keep these kids, safe," she said.

"I see," she said.

"He was five and died because of these lax safety laws and sick murderer, said the child's mother.

She consoled her. The pain in her eyes was piercing.

"I understand your concern," she said.

"We are tired of being trampled on. This protest is nothing. Our objective was to get signatures and volunteers to participate in the huge protest, we are planning, soon. If you are interested in helping us take a stand, call 000-000-0000 or willyouevermakeachangesittingonyourbehind?.com," she said.

"Well there you have it, members of this community are upset, this loss was tragic," said Reporter Sight.

"Please continue to watch our channel for updates, regarding policy changes and the next protest, this is Selah Sight, Reporting live from Max it Out News," she said.

"That is so sad; I need to help," she said.

"No, I don't want you getting caught up in that," he said.

"What," she said.

"A little child was killed, because of slack laws and you want me to sit down," she said.

"You can't take on changing everything," he said.

"Take a seat in the back of the class, and put your head down, you need a timeout," she said.

"Whatever, you're not getting caught up in that," he said.

"Oh really, drill sergeant," she said.

She looked at Rye, in disgust.

"I need to get ready," she said.

"Look, I love you," he said.

"What if something happens to you, at this protest thing," he said.

"It's not some protest thing," she said.

"We are a community, I am an educator that could have been one of my students," she said.

"But It wasn't," he said.

"I had a dream--no … it was a nightmare, Case—I woke you up," he said.

"Please don't cut me off," she said.

"Fine," he said.

"Listen, this guy in the dream said I need to change things, not to get lost in the negative abyss," she said.

"Here you go with the sign stuff," he said.

Why couldn't Rye understand—the passion she had to change policies?

Wake up, Call

The next morning, Casey fixed her green tea and opened up her email.

Good afternoon,

Our assistant principal, Ms. Rat Race, and I decided to hire a Lead Motivator to assist you.

Please join us, in the library, after dismissal, today.

Your Principal,

Ms. Lazman-We Need to Step it Up!

Normally, she would complain, about this last-minute email, but last night's dream was at the forefront of her mind. Who has time for complaints? As Casey approached the library, she heard teachers singing the M-O-T-I-V-A-T-I-O-N Song. What in the world, was going on? The library was packed. Half of the teachers were stuffing their faces with free refreshments and the other half looked disengaged. Casey sat down(behind the negativity crew).

"I hope they don't have annoying icebreakers," said Ms. Pink.

"The last thing we need after a seven and a half hour day, is an ice breaker to make the process longer," said Ms. V. they had so many questions/concerns, about this Lead Motivator. How would she impact such a tough crowd?

"Good afternoon," My name is Ms. Motivation. I am a leader specialized in helping people pinpoint motivation deficiencies, here to help you practice Motiv'Plication" she said.

"I know what you're thinking, what in the world is that? Despite what you believe, each one of you has capabilities, beyond your wildest dreams. The reason I am here is to help you, highlight them. If you don't believe me, look, at how many teachers quit, so far, this school year. The screen projected resignation papers with confidential information blacked out. The number of teachers who quit was in the triple-digit range. The teachers were concerned," she said.

"You are still here for a reason. Please take a moment to reflect and think about the resignation papers you see on the screen. What is the difference between you and the educators who walked? After you reflect, recall the day you decided to pursue this profession. You each have a clipboard and a pen, under your seats. After you deeply reflect on what ignited your pursuit of this profession, please document reasons you feel cheated, unsupported, and boxed in.

It's hard to feel free, in a mental prison. Today is your day to break free of it, to teach effectively,"she said.

Every teacher in the room was speechless and hard at work. Casey wrote about the disappointments she faced, as an educator. It was disheartening since she was a first-year teacher. She notated the negative comments, unrealistic demands, and verbal prison she felt was real. The activity reminded her of why she wanted to pursue this field, and why professionalism is important. Why did she jumped to defend the caliber of students in this demographic and experience excitement, despite the half-broken beer bottles and outed cigarette buts she passed driving into school every day? Showing up as a shell of a person was a huge disservice to students, administrators, colleagues, and herself. This realization set her over the edge, the stinging from the corners of her eyes was unbearable. Without warning, tears engulfed her face and her mascara looked like warpaint. you are teachers, people undervalue your capabilities and overuse your time, I refuse to fall into that statistic. Negativity triggers a deadly division. Positivity triggers the release of Motiv'Plication. What in the world does the term mean? It's ensuring a positive mentality is always added to and never taken away from a mission/vision. Keep all segregating comments to yourself. Unchecked negativity is a flesh-eating virus that triggers a carcinogenic cultish mentality. The division is emotional cancer that spreads, at a fast pace. Getting back to the reason that ignites your professional desire, is crucial," she said. As she was speaking, Casey had a revelation, she would reread her graduation speech. Each segment(of it), held relevance to the situation she faced. Ms. Motivation opened the floor for questions. The teachers were all emotionally drained and ready. When the floor was opened, everyone gave each other looks of death not to raise their hands.

"My name is Casey Coper, I have a question," she said.

The negativity crew whipped their heads around, in disgust.

If looks could cause injuries, she would have broken legs. Regardless, she took a deep breath and asked her questions.

"What do you do, when people accuse you of not doing your job," she said.

"I have several friends, who are teachers and hold support positions, it seems like a group of people always accuse them of doing nothing," said Casey. Phew! She got the words out and her limbs were still intact.

"That's a great question," she said.

"I hold a support position. My job is to help educators, parents, and students, unbury their potential and give them ways to cope with stress, among other things. People accuse me of the same thing and guess what … I could care less. As educators, you need to remember, why we are here, no matter what role we play, it is relevant. Your energy is for the students, once you know they are not being shortchanged, anyone else's thoughts on your job description are irrelevant. Bitter people who make these accusations are jealous of the person, in the position. Remember … Motiv'Plication is a way of being. Multiply positivity and diminish negativity. Oh … and hating carries a 1:3 ratio. If you're doing one good thing, three people will likely envy and hate you for trying."

"Did that help," she said.

"Yes, thank you," she said.

"Let's practice, what we learned, today," she said.

"Principal Lazman and Assistant Principal Rat Race thanks for allowing me to help edify the staff's mentalities," she said. She had the gift of expression.

"Okay, then, you are dismissed," she said.

Casey began sprinting up the hallway, back to her classroom. She dug in her desk, under some conference forms, was her journal. June seemed like such a long time ago. She opened it and turned to the coffee-stained page. Slowly, she revisited the words that inspired her to teach. Although her entire speech was profound, certain quotes, held major relevance.

"We must stand up for justice and equality to acquire educational equilibrium."

Who said, any career was perfect?

"The way we initiate change is the only way to determine if the past two years were investment or a joke," she said.

Although her attempts seemed unsuccessful, she knew giving up was not an option. She wanted to invest, in education. True investments take time. "If we expect our students to fight their greatest fear, we need to lead by example," she said.

Her deepest fear was not impacting the lives of her students. She never wanted to be the teacher who got lost, in the thick of negativity. Casey put little relevance on how she got there, it did not matter. From this day forth, she would focus on fortitude.

Her strategy to attain educational equilibrium would include Ms. Zebedee. She would help her organize the next groundbreaking protest. These budget cuts were not going to happen, without a fight.

Casey took a deep breath and opened her computer. She pulled up the search engine and typed in the website she believed would get her on the right track. She dialed the number, nervously.

"Hello, Ms. Zebedee's Office," said Ms. Nance.

Ms. Nance answered the phone. She was her secretary and assistant coordinator. Her tone was soothing yet professional.

"How may I assist," said Ms. Nance.

"Um … yes," she said.

"My name is Mrs. Coper," she said.

"I am an elementary teacher," she said.

"Yes, how may I assist," said Ms. Nance.

"I would like to help Ms. Zebedee's team with the upcoming protest," she said.

"Absolutely," she said.

"What grade do you teach," she said.

"Fourth grade … I teach …," she said.

"Please hold," she said.

Casey took a deep breath. Did she say something wrong? What if they viewed her grade level, as irrelevant. She was so nervous.

"Hello," she said.

"Yes," she said.

"Ms. Zebedee speaking," she said.

"Hello … I … you are …" she said.

"Yes, I am an educator who happens to be human, just like you," she said.

The two chuckled, at her comment.

"Well, my name is Mrs… Coper … Casey Coper," she said.

"Mrs. Coper, would you like to assist us with the protest," she said.

"Sure," she said.

"Please come by tomorrow, at five-thirty, we would love to have you," she said.

 "I will be there tomorrow," she said.

She could not believe Ms. Zebedee wanted her to join the team. The experience would be amazing. She was naturally innovative and broke ground on many levels.

The Meeting

The next day, Casey was enthusiastic. She approached the packed parking lot with a stomach full of anxiety and anticipation. Normally, this combination would cause her to faint; however, she knew she would help strike a change the world would feel for years to come. She parked her car and rush toward the door, jam-packed with passionate people fueled with determination. It was hard to fit through the door. There were many people of every race, gender, and title. The crowd consisted of leaders, teachers(of all levels), security guards, and support staff members.

"Could I have your attention, please," she said.

"Thank you all for attending our protest organization meeting. The new bill states the plan to decrease our salaries to pennies. This protest will be a demonstration of why we are not accepting change for hard work or excuses, regarding the security of students or ourselves. We need financial and safety assurance," she said. She wanted an explanation of how there was enough funding for numerous activities and the salaries of other stakeholders but ensuring a secure environment, providing mental health services and proper pay compensation were impossible. These key elements were non-negotiable. She had the support of superintendents, principals, assistant principals, and other key players, in her field. She would use this protest, as a platform to explain why these deficits needed to be filled. They were working to make the world understand their role in society and why it is crucial to get compensated, beyond what they were offered. Participants needed to ensure their objective matched the goal of why they worked to demonstrate unity. Unification could not be a front, it had to be real. Otherwise, people they were trying to convince may think twice to listen, or take their requests, seriously. Divided protestors are a walking paradox. Ms. Zebedee looked outstanding. She wore a formfitting pencil skirt, her hair was tucked in a bun, and her top flowed perfectly. She made walking around on stilettos look like a breeze. Casey spaced out. She wanted to know how she demanded the attention of everyone in the room, silently.

"Are we all on the same page,

"Yes," yelled the educators.

"Do we want the same thing,

"Yes," yelled the educators.

"Okay, then let's make our demands known. We are no longer requesting politely. This is a protest and we are more than bleachers," she said.

As the crowd applauded, she walked toward Casey.

"How was that," she said.

"Great," she said.

"How can I help," she said.

"You can finish making the signs, over in the corner, or help pass out refreshments," she said.

"How long have people been here," she said.

"Some came right after work, others took the day off," she said.

"Are we going to do this," she said.

"Do what," she said.

"Protest for the same salaries as N.F.L. Players mental health support and security measures," she said.

The unshakable look in her eyes provided the answer before the words left her lips. She went onto explain what made her make his correlation and how relevant it was to the situation at hand. Her tenacity was beyond admirable, and the correlation made all the sense worldwide. We could see how this protest made sense. Hopefully, stakeholders would share the same viewpoint, after tomorrow.

Casey knew participating in this protest could cause job termination; she didn't care. If she expected students to take the lessons on Rosa Parks and Martin Luther King Jr. seriously, an example needed to be set. Finally, she could display her passion with a group of people who shared her perspective. The feeling was surreal. She was one of the last people to drive off. On her way home, she wondered how this event would pan out. Ms. Zebedee had several strategies, up her sleeve.

They would be the key to opening the ears of stakeholders who refuse to listen to concerns, below their pay grade. Finally, she was home. She lost track of time, the clock read eight-thirty.

Slowly, she opened the door and tried hard not to make a sound.

"Where were you," he said. She decided to creep in, but her effort was pure vanity.

"Hey," she said.

"Don't hey me, where were you," he said.

"Where was I," said Casey. She smirked purposefully to irritate Rye.

"I told you, helping with the protest," he said.

"Really," he said.

"Yes," she said.

"I need you to hop aboard the honesty train," he said.

"Who speaks like that," she said.

"I do," he said.

"I need to use elementary terms, maybe then you will pay me attention," he said.

"You're hilarious," she said.

"I'm so sick of taking a backseat to lesson plans, team meetings and now protest planning," he said.

"You're sick of taking a backseat to my agenda, yet you're complaining about my compensation," she said.

"They don't pay you guys, enough," he said.

"Okay Mr. Hypocrite," she said.

"Which one is it, stop speaking in contradictory circles," she said.

"Whatever," he said.

"You better not have been with anyone else," he said.

"I was, her name is Ms. Zebedee and she is going to help make history, soon," she said.

"So funny," he said.

"Everyone can't work a traditional nine to five and truly check out," when they clock out," she said.

"They should learn to," he said.

"That is hard for some educators to do, especially, if they are fighting for a cause," she said.

"I don't want to fight," she said.

"I'm going to bed," he said.

"I don't understand how you are non-confrontational, yet start arguments you refuse to finish; it is so irritating," she said.

"Goodnight ADORATION, I still and always will love you," he said.

"I still and always will love you, Detective Rye," she said.

She moved her hair and allowed him to place his hand on the back of her neck.

"Thank you," he said.

"You're welcome," she said.

Their love was stronger than ever but would his support level(of her passion) increase?

Two
"Teachers Aren't Bleachers!"

Eerie smog does not exceed the suspense, educators are exuding, tonight. Deafening shoe to concrete pounding, outweigh any historical protest. Numerous reporters yearn to speak with the leader of the protest, but only one is successful.

"This is Selah Sight, reporting live, from Max it Out News. Thousands of educators are protesting, in response to the impassive attitude of officials, regarding low pay compensation, insufficient funds for security(despite recent mass shootings), budget cuts for mental health services, and more," she said.

"Teachers Aren't Bleachers, teachers aren't bleachers, teachers aren't bleachers," yelled masses of frustrated educators.

Bill 90001 caused upheaval. Educators were demanding the implementation of a new methodology. They were tired of budget cuts, compromised safety laws, and being brushed aside. As a result of mental health service deficits and slack gun regulation, there were a number of mass shootings, throughout the district. When did funeral attendance become a common pastime? Supporters signed petitions advocating for an increase of social workers, mental health counselors, guidance counselors, and stability coaches. The response of the powers that be was to cut funding and choke out the only lifeline, accessible to students. Each person(who committed recent shootings) had a mental health imbalance. Unfortunately, one worker from each psychological wellness category to service masses of students is unacceptable. People who refuse new ideas and are defensive, of philosophies based on expired educational standards.

" Let's hear the input of one of education's biggest moguls, Ms. Zara Zebedee," she said.

"How are you," asked Reporter Sight.

"Disturbed but well," she said.

"What prompted this protest," she said.

"I called an emergency meeting and received tons of signatures, opposing the bill," she said.

"What does it entail," she said.

"Safety issues, pay compensation and unfair policies should be addressed, immediately. Sadly, based on board meetings, uniform policies are the main focus. Priorities are flipped. A brief overview of the bill included: millions of dollars funneled to educational institutions that already have a surplus of funds, at least three weekly mandated early release days, due to teacher pay cuts, no additional academic assistance for students that have low economic status, payouts of security guards systems necessary to ensure school shootings halt and mental health are top priority and more," she said.

"We are requesting the following":

1.) All schools will have active security cameras with monitors.

2.) All schools will review security measures and procedures, in an innovative and fun way.

3.) All schools will maintain open communication with administrators, regarding possible threats/violent acts that may occur.

4.) All schools will be required to have metal detectors.

5.) All schools will have a one-way entry and exit.

6.) All schools will ensure security equipment is in working condition, daily.

7.) All schools will ensure students have the opportunity to voice their opinion.

8.) All schools will provide a way for students to inform personnel of possible harm their peer/s may carry out. The identity of students who provide the warning will remain confidential.

9.) All schools will carry out an extensive investigation to ensure Possible Harm Reports are valid.

10.) All schools will implement a No Tolerance Policy, regarding all forms of bullying.

11.) All educators who participate in each safety training, monthly will receive a one thousand dollar bonus, yearly.

12.) All teachers and students who implement safety procedures accurately will receive a five thousand dollar award for their school.

13.) All schools will provide positive reinforcement for every student, teacher/parent without it's not my problem mentality. The evidence provided will be rewarded and recognized by the superintendent of each district.

14.) All schools will have Security Resource Officers, full-time on campus. The numbers will be based on enrollment.

15.) All schools will pay everyone, helping to ensure students are safe, a yearly bonus for every safety measure implemented and proven effective.

16.) All schools will hire several individuals, specialized in mental health to check-in, track and update administration and security personnel, regarding potential threats.

17,) All schools will implement a no-tolerance policy, regarding threats that include but are not limited to: threatening to harm another individual/their school

18.) All schools are required to have safety meetings both in the house and open to the public. Public safety information will be disseminated, at all Parent Awareness Meetings.

19.) All schools will hold safety and anti-violence training, monthly.

20.) All schools will implement strategies to reward students for making positive choices, despite what demographic the school is located in.

21.) All schools will implement a school-wide nonviolence plan that will correlate to the specified struggles of the population.

22.) All schools will implement the district's unified nonviolence plan and integrate aspects of it, during lessons, speeches, and activities. Teachers, students, and parents who prove the implementation of the plan will be rewarded.

23.) All salary increases contributed by stakeholders, as a result of the protest, will be equalized, bonuses and additional earnings are not included.

"Why didn't you organize this protest, right after the bill was passed," asked Reporter Sight.

"I know we're a couple of weeks behind, due to the administration of pretests; however, the process is over, and we need change," she said.

"Thanks for explaining," she said.

"Educators were coordinating, during that time. We are well-equipped to address each issue," she said.

Over the years, she had the privilege of meeting influential people, who strongly support her expertise.

"Could you explain, the correlation between football players and education, from your blog," she said.

"My detailed breakdown will explain details," she said.

"I look forward to reading details," she said.

"What's the driving force, behind this process," she said.

"I'm not diminishing their achievements, accumulated yards, or compromised safety(during games). This is not a teardown fest for athletes, but we help prepare the future of tomorrow. This bill proposes teachers make fifteen thousand dollars, a year," she said.

Misconception

"People oblivious to the field of education may think we babysit. Their definition is inaccurate. Players earned titles, within the system, who deserve six-figure salaries. We are not watching the game, we are part of it. Power comes from individuals, who believe their actions strike a reaction," she said.

"The motto of this protest is, "Teachers Aren't Bleachers," could you explain, what it means," she said.

"We wanted a motto that represents how the political educational realm views us, based on proposed and affirmed policies. Bleachers are inanimate objects, used to provide a place for fans to sit, at sports events. Individuals who write and approve policies without taking educators, parents, and students into consideration, do not view us, as human beings. We are lifeless objects used to propel stakeholders, who are not well-versed on the frontline of education to sit on our backs—while viewing the game. This warrants our motto," she said.

"What's the driving force, motivating you, during this process," asked Reporter Sight.

"It's time for educators to come out from hiding, within indifferent domains. We aren't inanimate objects. She pointed out callous people, disregarding the point of education. Students should be afforded equal access to academic tools. This was not a "teacher's union issue" or an "It's not my problem, thing." Uniting for the greater good, was the only option for us," she said.

"You hit several major points," she said.

"We are more than complaints, without action!"If you'll excuse me, it's time to ignite change," she said.

"Welcome, as a result of your commitment, we are gathered here, today. Countless signatures and prior objections made us newsworthy. Please welcome Ms. Sight, a Max it Out News Reporter," she said.

The protest was the hook that caught the attention of higher arch educational representatives, they needed to accomplish the goal of helping attentive officials understand the rules of the game, which they call education.

Gaps of Expectance

Stakeholders want teachers to run as fast as they can, down the field while helping students acquire the skills for grade promotion. These expectations come with many tasks. Teachers must meet formal/informal observation criteria, complete academic and behavioral referrals, prepare lesson plans, ensure the academic, social/behavioral well-being of each student has not been compromised, communicate with parents throughout the year, and maintain a level of professionalism, (regardless of how the parent chooses to voice their questions/concerns), keep an accurate record of students' progress, implement the effective strategic intervention, notate early warning signs of possible academic failure, administer frequent testing, attend workshops, stay on schedule, stay abreast of policy changes via their team leader/union representative/administration, correlate all material/delivery to state standards, stay updated regarding state regulations and privacy policies deliver explicit corrective feedback, modify work according to the students' level and complete components to maintain a valid teaching certificate. Teachers must avoid being tackled by misconstrued concepts of who they are perceived to be. Education is a mentality that morphs into a lifestyle.

"In our game, the priority is to help students, win!"

"Mediocrity will no longer be tolerated. We are demanding not only to regain our original financial support but to earn the same salaries as beloved Pro-football Players. About one month ago, I met with Mr. No, a reputable educational representative. When he expressed why the low salaries of educators and funding for educational enhancements should match, the salaries of Pro-football Players, they laughed saying, if you can show me the hard work educators put in, compared to pro-athletes, I will triple their financial support. How many of you know, true educators live for a challenge," she exclaimed.

"Whoo, we do," yelled the protestors.

"Do we live for challenges, Ms. Spoils our fabulous union rep.," she said.

"You already know we do," she exclaimed.

"Mr. No, get your pen and notepad ready. As educators, we request your acknowledgment of our contribution to our game. Players feel like lifeless bleachers, who cannot take the weight of one more unjust policy, resting on their backs," she said.

"Yeah! Teachers aren't bleachers," exclaimed protestors.

"We are on the front lines, just as a defensive and offensive lineman. Changes are never personal but always necessary. Congruence between education and football is evident," she said.

She constructed the detailed correlation that went viral, explaining the frontline duties(of educators), in the game. The breakdown of the proposal read:

The Proposition for Change

Any group can wear helmets and collide. Football is an in-depth game that has a greater goal. Education holds the same stance. Some people think we provide minimal diligence until summer vacation, sit behind a desk and have little to no contact with students. In contrast, our mission is not superficial. The objective of any game is to win; however, strategies utilized by both teams, are different. Educators use strategic intervention to win. Please continue reading you are in for a journey of reality.

Football(Students)

The prized possession in any game is the ball. Ironically, one definition of football is an object treated harshly, as the subject of extensive abuse. This addresses the pulse of education, students. Taking time to understand each complexity(the students face) is an investment, a considerable amount of people are not willing to make. This hosts a myriad of problems for us. We do not dismiss or choose not to sign up to solve them. No disrespect to any team, as I hold each pro-athlete in high regard. Students do not derive from the National Student League Draft Pick. The functionality of our game sets on the premise of who attains the ball. Students without a functional internal/external environment, are disadvantaged. Would playing the Super Bowl with a half-inflated ball suffice? The answer is no! Ensuring we are granted the proper environment compensation, and support services for them to learn should be a regularity throughout all districts. The displacement of funding allocation is a consistent form of prejudice educators tackle. Regardless of barriers, we are expected to win the game.

Coin Toss

Three minutes before the football game begins, the referee meets with team captains for a coin toss. Based on the result, the following are determined:
1.) Which team will start with the ball?
2.) It determines the route the teams will take to score.
3.) Results verify which end zone teams will defend.

The beginning of the new school year represents the coin toss, in education. Every new year brings challenges. Schools that have the upper hand, (meaning increase a letter grade) gain leverage to kickoff, automatically. Schools whose letter grades declined do not get this advantage of starting with the ball(students). Poor test scores, living conditions, and a lack of materials contribute to how our game starts.

Kickoff

The kickoff determines where the offense will begin. The determination of if the kick returner will run the ball out or signal a touchback is made if it lands in the offense's end zone. We need the ball to land in our end zone. The beginning of the school year should reveal the starting point for where each student is and what strategic intervention will be utilized to help them, attain long and short-term goals. In many cases, that will not happen. As a result, the defense takes possession of the ball(our students). Providing vague information(through inaccurate Baseline Data) is harmful to the outcome of the game. A comprehensive understanding of who students are, helps us set realistic goals that will enhance success. Financial allocation is a part of the process. Decisions regarding financial allotment contribute to the premise of how the year will begin. Educators need to kick off each year by acknowledging the evolvement of methodologies and individualized views.

The Field

Before the annual Super Bowl, field designers guarantee each yard is in perfect alignment. Although I commend the individuals who invest hours ensuring each color, line, and measurement on the field is correct. I wonder why, all educational facilities are not afforded tools, furniture, and funds to secure a fair and thriving environment. Designers ensure the field is one hundred yards long and fifty-three yards wide. Hosting the Super Bowl in an environment less conducive to popular expectations would be unacceptable. Why should any educational environment, not be held to the same standard? Each student must acquire skills to help reach their academic end zone. If the environment lacks stimulation, they are less likely to thrive. Our supply list should not be based on the variance of funds. Ignoring educational equilibrium tells one student they are worth less than their counterpart. This causes a skewed scale of equality.

Halftime

Halftime consists of players taking a few minutes to rest/regroup. This time for us does not consist of a talented renowned singer performing. It takes place right before winter break, it entails grading papers, inputting grades, retesting students, and informing parents of their child's progression/regression. During this time educators tend to burn out. The feeling is triggered by certain educators reaping the impact of procrastination. As professionals, we do not have the option of entering grades late, not communicating, or administering tests, incorrectly. Although I encourage parental involvement any time of year, December should not be the starting point of holding students accountable. Closing the gap between what we feel versus what needs to get done is crucial. If students are not performing, correctly, educators need to follow up with why it occurs and how to fix it. Clear communication is the key to producing positive results. Educators should not address baseline scores with clear objectives and quarterly goals(for the first time), midway through the year. Academic scores set the tone of strategic intervention. If the individualized needs of each student are met, in a timely fashion, we will have no choice but to tackle daily struggles.

The Downs

A Down is the distance(measured by yards) utilized in the game. It begins when the ball is snapped. If the offensive team progresses the ball, at least ten yards within four downs the team earns a new set(of downs). This grants an opportunity to either kick a field goal score a touchdown or propel the ball an additional ten yards to earn more downs. In the event offense does not score or propel the ball tens yards after three tries there are two options. They can use their last down(the fourth one) to try for an extra play. If the team decides to go for it and is successful, it attains a fresh set of downs. When the offense does not make it to the first down marker, their rival gets the ball, in its position, at the line of scrimmage. Educational advancement is measured by percentage points. We are given three opportunities to gain yardage. The opportunities include a baseline, midyear, assessment, and end-of-year exam(known as the state test). There are other times we can assess students, informally; however, these are not game-changer tests. The Big Wig State Test is our last chance to assess yards to win. Unlike football, we do not get the opportunity to earn a new set of downs. That is the reason adequate support and financial equilibrium are crucial.

End Zone

The End Zone is defined as the area where scoring takes place. Our End Zone in the field of education is determined by performance. We score when students learn information and display knowledge, through testing. Test scores determine if we make it to the End Zone or not. Scores that are considered low cause the team to lose. This is because scoring is performance-based. Through deliberate intervention, players can get the ball to its proper destination and earn their team points. We need to identify our role/s, in the field of education. Football maps out the position of each player and coaches implement effective plays to ensure defense does not gain enough leverage to defeat offense. We implement effective strategies that correlate with plays. As time goes on, we tend to overlook which team educators play on. Either we are offense, helping our students gain necessary yardage or tools for their success or we are defensive, in direct opposition of it. If funding is cut, the result will lead to a decrease parental involvement meetings and provide fewer materials for academic enhancement, we take the defensive stance, triggering the detriment of student success. Why would you care about the impact budget cuts have on low-income schools, when your child is not enrolled in one? Caring starts at the top. If you cannot relate to students who go to bed and wake up hungry why should you be compassionate? I've been in that position that's why I fight until my stomach is full. At my sister's Super Bowl Party attendants live by the term "no shame". When the receiver rolled into the End Zone, they danced and cried; fans on television roll down bleachers, when the team(they supported) scored. I imagined reacting similarly if all educators were compensated for the touchdowns, they help students accomplish. Parents, students, and educators should come together to construct effective plays that beat opposing forces of education. Our fight is not personal. We need to ensure students are well equipped with weapons of knowledge to enhance society for centuries to come.

Line of Scrimmage

Under NFL Guidelines there are two lines of scrimmage, one restricts the offense and the other restricts the defense. Educators are dealing with selective administrators, students, and parents who place little to no conceptional value on our lines of scrimmage. We undergo verbal, emotional, and socioeconomic challenges that make winning the game of education, a challenge. The union(known as our referees) is limited, regarding the loss of funding. Whenever we have unexplained budget cuts our line of scrimmage is crossed. How in the world do we get funds cut but higher officials get pay increases? This is the ultimate slap in the face. As demands raise our salaries are lowered. This needs to be changed!

Tackles

Tackles take place when the defense prevents the offense from advancing the ball by bringing its carrier to the ground. Several negative barriers try to tackle us when attempting to make it to the End Zone. We undergo financial, physical, and emotional opposition that heightens the chances of us losing, the game. Imagine taking an extra job, just to acquire money for gas. Once your paycheck from your second job comes through, it is devoured by a negative bank account balance. After facing numerous disputes, you throw on shock-absorbent sneakers to sprint past an irate parent. This is one example of how educators get tackled. Persistent educators refuse to forfeit the game.

Touchdown

Football fans tend to scream, salivate, and roll down bleachers, when their team, makes a touchdown. This is the most important aspect of the outcome. Since each touchdown is the result of a strategy, players who achieve victory are praised. In the game of education, we do everything short of hold our breath to achieve them. Educational touchdowns are achieved, when students master skills that cause an increase, in their school's letter grade. Our six-point victory is contingent on consistency, efficiency, and strategic configuration.

Interception

An interception occurs when a player on defense catches a pass the quarterback propels. Conceding that a defensive player is not down the individual can run towards the opposing team's end zone. Educators are intercepted, when we intend to raise the scores of our students by explaining effective strategies but miss the mark. Whenever we fail to assess students, correctly our opposing team has the advantage. The past is a clear indication that no system is perfect. Educators in the game for years could state an entire list of acronyms that represent prior initiatives that were a partial or complete failure. These individuals make mistakes from the past and run with them. Unfortunately, certain curriculums and strategies did not work. That does not mean leadership teams should stop attempting to address learning deficits. Defensive players want the offense to give up and let them gain complete control over the ball(students) by eliminating assessment tools. We cannot do that. I do not agree with unreasonable tests, being the beginning and end game but instead of making the process arduous, working as a unit to modify these measurement tools, is critical for students to succeed.

Vince Lombardi Trophy

Every year football fans experience bubble guts, thinking about which championship team will utilize their best skills to win the Super Bowl. The National Football League Championship demonstrates which team will implement strategies to earn The Vince Lombardi Trophy, named after the former NFL Coach, who helped his team, gain victory. It is the biggest honor for Super Bowl Winners. Our Vince Lombardi Trophy is attained, once state test scores increase. We are trying to maintain or exceed prior strategic intervention. Excellent performance must be maintained, if not, we will feel the breath of stakeholders, down our necks. Either way, the Super Bowl of Education is no joke. The reward correlation is an intangible measure of accomplishment, we experience when scores/learning gains exceed expectations.

Football Coach(Superintendent)

Every good team has a coach. An effective individual who perseveres through times of hardship and develops strategic plans to help their team win. Our superintendent representative supports our mission to enhance our educational community. The person in this role ensures administrators, educators and students are justified, on all spectrums. Coaches and superintendents do not retreat when challenges arise. These architects of the game work to ensure the vision of their team is implemented, effectively. They need to make hard decisions for the well-being of the team, likewise, our superintendent chose to maneuver educators, according to their area of expertise. After every game, the coach should analyze effective versus ineffective plays. Superintendents work with their leadership team to carry out the same practice by overseeing which leaders are suitable for specific roles. The offensive line consists of administration, selective non-instructional employees, and teachers. Similar to football, every player in education has the designated role to help the greater good of the team.

Quarterback(Principal)

This player is the leader of the offensive line—responsible for communicating the plays, leading the team down the field, and managing the snap(from the center). The quarterback is considered the lifeline of the game who possesses exceptional emotional, physical, and cognitive abilities. When an administrator is given directives, (from their coach to the superintendent), the player must demonstrate emotional resilience, physical strength, and superb cognitive abilities to help carry out the play. As policies and academic interventions are put into action, the principal must determine which type of play will benefit their team. Effective communication(for this player) is paramount regardless of how loud it gets, during the game. The quarterback must convey play specifications to the offense, likewise, the principal must express reliable information(from the superintendent), for the staff to function, effectively. This contender needs to determine if the play will be carried out or altered.

Center(Assistant Principal)

The center is responsible for beginning each play by hiking the ball(students) to the quarterback(principal), blocking hits that would cause the regression of their leader's mission/vision not to thrive, and organizing the offensive line. Assistant principals(who play this position) are responsible for formulating events/team meetings meant to enhance the staff that will impact efficient intervention. This player is considered the foundational protector of the quarterback for the offensive line and makes contact, during every play. In our game, this contender is responsible for taking preventative measures correlated to the quarterback(principal). Once accomplished, the outcome will be to affect students, positively. The center has the advantage of viewing everyone on the defensive front, making credible communication mandatory. An assistant principal communicates to team leaders, parents, and students how to implement the School Improvement Plan. This position requires parent training, lesson plans, data charts, and school events to run smoothly and align with the vision of the principal. This competitor is on top of the ball(students). Keeping up with their status is necessary for any play to run effectively.

Wide Receiver(Team Leader)

The wide receiver is expected to catch passes(pertinent information for students to thrive) from the quarterback(principal). The team leader can choose to run with information to disseminate or focus on blocking out negativity, regarding new policies/procedures that are not conducive to helping students but rather stifle the learning process. When the receiver is in a passing play their goal is to outrun defenders. Information given by the principal must be documented and carried out for the well-being of the school. The team leader is considered to be a threat, based on speed/their ability to hold onto passes(pertinent information for students to thrive). This player collaborates with teammates to determine what type of pass will be carried out and communicates with the quarterback(principal), frequently.

Guard 1 (Guidance Counselor)

Guidance counselors who line up between the center(assistant principal) and tackle(social worker) on the offensive line, used for blocking(mostly), require a high level of strength. Guards have a keen way of helping students deal with tragic events(like recent shootings) and function despite demands expected of them. Our state requires students to perform, amidst tragedy. Many of them mask anger which feeds into a vicious cycle of resentment and bitterness. A great guidance counselor helps identify problems and target ways to manage/ eliminate negative emotions. The player of this position helps students, guard their hopes when tragic events emerge. The guard provides an emotional haven of embrace. This link in the team blocks negativity from outside sources meant to influence students.

Guard 2 (The Office Manager)

The Office manager blocks for the quarterback(principal) and is taken for granted(by some stakeholders). This is a disappointment since guards utilize a large amount of strength to regulate the school's office climate. This player's duties are not limited to taking messages. The role requires the guard to organize/document pertinent information for the principal(quarterback). This connection in the team manages the functionality of the front office that impacts the school. Their tasks also include communicating with the data processor, guidance(guard 1) counselor, social worker, behavioral specialist, academic specialist/s, parents of students/their parents, and school staff, regarding significant issues. Several educators submitted positive reviews about their office managers. When the proposal was submitted to terminate the position (a few years ago) our union fought and the suggestion was disregarded.

Left Tackle(Social Worker)

There are two tackles on a football team the position of left tackle requires a sharp mentality and agility. Social workers must have the ability to thwart the pass rush of defensive ends(selfishness that feeds into indifference). The essence of this player's mission is to end selfish mentalities by providing resources to families and helping to edify the community. Misconceptions regarding them are vast. People hear the title and cringe. This player provides students and their families with resources to help function during chaotic situations. Sadly, the school social worker is overlooked or frowned upon, because of the requirement to report students who experience emotional/physical deterioration. Our left tackle guards the principal against violating policies and conveys information. This helps to emotionally safeguard the principal(quarterback) from allowing the defense to gain leverage. Understanding the temperament of students that have parent/s struggling with living circumstances, custody battles, mental health issues/other sensitive topics, feeds into cognitive productivity.

Right Tackle(E.S.E. Specialist)

This player is the team's star run blocker, who needs a tight grip, to create space for the running back(academic coach/teachers) to go through. Exceptional Special Education Specialists work hard to keep abreast of laws that help teachers provide the best services for students with special needs. Right tackles also host meetings for students who may have disabilities, inform teachers of policy changes and implementation, provide resources for parents, students, and teachers, and create Special Education Reports, to track academic/ behavioral progress. Educators depend on this player to run through times of uncertainty. The E.S.E. Specialist may also hold positions of leadership and provide coping mechanisms. This player also runs plays gearing to the strong side of the offense. The defense tries to stop players from carrying out runs, specialists help teachers persevere by explaining tactics to assist with challenging situations. Educators administer tests, throughout the year. Test scores may be discouraging for teachers/students. The right tackle comes up with incentive plans for teachers to implement with students with special needs/students at risk of failing their grade level.

Tight End(Supportive Parents(of Students We Teach)

Supportive parent/s who fit this role are lined up on the offensive line and are large enough to be effective blockers, usually. The player of this position helps create a functional mentality for students to excel at long and shorter-term goals. This is mandatory for teachers, trying to help them understand new concepts. After being in the educational field for years, Ms. Zebedee had the privilege of crossing paths with supportive parents, who wanted to ensure students excel. The tight end may also receive the football(students). Parents who participate end up impacting the lives of the student's mentality that helps with an increase in scores.

The Running Back(Teacher/Academic Coach)

An academic coach (who can also fulfill the role of a teacher) plays this position, based on the formation. This is one of the toughest jobs, in football. The player's duties include taking handoffs from the quarterback(principal) on rushing plays. This member of the instructional staff receives directives from the principal, based on the school's performance data. Our players train teachers to help students increase test scores and their mentality regarding academic performance. They also model how to deliver lessons, correctly. The contender of this position is given the responsibility of running with a positive state of mind, staying abreast of policies, and ensuring students/teachers perform, optimally. If the quarterback(principal) does not feel the academic coach is effective, may recommend returning to the classroom. The player in this position cannot lose touch with their purpose.

Fullback(Kindergarten-Second Grade Primary Teacher)

This player executes power running, catch passes or block for the running back/quarterback. Some stakeholders believe the fullback is paid to wipe noses and tie shoes; however, this is a misconception. If you research synonyms for the word(primary) you will find associations like paramount, original, etc. Every scholar needs a good primer before moving onto the next grade level. Dismissing the pertinence of a primary teacher constitutes heavyweight ignorance. This link in the team blocks for the quarterback(principal) by helping to ensure students gain knowledge and master skills for them to thrive in higher grades. If they are not attained latent issues are bound to emerge. This competitor is expected to keep up with curriculum changes, certification requirements, parent conferences, district changes, developmental variances, behavioral issues. Additional expectancies are helping their students grasp information, despite behavioral issues, poor adjustment skills, undetected learning difficulties, lack of parental involvement, and safety issues. In addition, the fullback is required to explain horrific occurrences, in the community. This is taxing since developmentally the students are wrapping their minds around so much. The recent tragedies inflicted fear on educators, students, and parents. The primary teacher assists with blocking the halfback(an intermediate teacher). Whenever I hear criticism from any teacher(based on their level), I explain the concept that one blocks for the other.

Halfback(An Intermediate Teacher)

The halfback lines up in the backfield. The quarterback(principal) and fullback(primary teacher) are responsible for carrying the ball(students) on running plays. This player can also block for players, carrying the ball(students). The role of an intermediate teacher fits this position since the school's grade is contingent on them avoiding roadblocks to help students attain information and increase the school's scores. This team link needs to block for quarterbacks(principals) when negative situations emerge that would hinder the student's performance. The player of this position may receive the ball(students). Intermediate teachers are under immense pressure to produce results. The halfback faces difficulties that impact the way students process information. Barriers may include and are not limited to students with displaced anger, poor self-image, poor reasoning skills, undetected learning disabilities that could impact performance, oppositional parents(with defensive mentalities), behavioral issues, low parent involvement, truancy, early onset of puberty, miscommunication between guardians and their teacher/s, disconnection between the teacher and student due to a miscommunication and negative factors. Elementary school students struggle with the idea of not feeling safe. There were massive high school shootings that continue to increase. Young children do not understand how to deal with grief and why anyone would express anger, by taking the lives of others. Intermediate teachers need to explain terrible occurrences on the level the student understands.

The Middle School Teacher/Academic Coaches(Also Plays Halfback)

Teachers that play this position work to increase the scores of their school to help attain a better school letter grade. Middle school teachers are unique. This player is responsible to carry the ball(students), during the game. Students in middle school are ages eleven to fourteen. This age range brings many challenges. If left unaddressed, the defense could tackle players of this position making scoring in the End Zone next to impossible. The middle school teacher has the task of dealing with social and emotional issues, unique to their intense students. This educator is responsible for integrating unique information, in the curriculum, based on state standards that will help students, gain and demonstrate knowledge on the Bigwig Statewide Test. This link in our team is expected to help integrate the curricular theme, for students to fully understand, content. Our halfback faces issues including drug/alcohol experimentation/heavy usage, pregnancy, increased violent acts, verbal/emotional/physical bullying, poor behavioral choices(based on hormonal changes), suicide attempts, choking, eating disorders, peer pressure, premature sexual activity, performance indifference due to low self-esteem, social displacement, poor communication, low parent involvement, truancy, willingness to participate in risky behavior and monitoring a large number of students. At this stage, hormones speak for students. The lifeline(of these students) consists of friends and reputation. If either is infringed upon, they could act out, irrationally. This challenger struggles with ineffective safety policies. Several of them lost older siblings, in recent shootings. They are petrified a mass shootings will continue if policies do not change. Safety remains a constant struggle.

High School Teacher (Tailback)

The teacher/s that play this position can be interchangeable with halfbacks, based on the formation. Our tailback teaches students ranging from ages 15-18 or older while fulfilling the duties of a tailback. This competitor specializes in one subject and conveys the information to students. This instructor is at risk of feeling short-circuited, due to the increased number of students, extensive hours, and life-changing challenges that occur with students in this category. Life-changing events high school teachers deal with include but are not limited to eating disorders, peer pressure, unsafe sexual activity, performance indifference due to low self-esteem, social displacement, poor communication, low parent involvement, drug/alcohol experimentation/heavy usage, pregnancy, increased violent acts, verbal/emotional/physical bullying, disrespectful behavior(based on a sense of entitlement), suicide attempts, choking, teenage pregnancy, sexual disease transmission, increased violent tendencies, grading papers and monitoring students in the triple-digit number category and more. This educator is expected to master the dissemination of their subject area, despite external factors. Players of this position feel uneasy, about effective safety measures. Recent school shootings caused an additional emotional and mental strain on students, they are petrified to show up and have a hard time, remaining engaged. The High school teacher needs to maintain a calm and collected demeanor for students not to fall apart. Meanwhile, they are about to crash and burn.

Defense

Defensive players make our objective, next to impossible to attain. When educators receive less funding, the defensive line is in the lead. It is comprised of negative mentalities that are a huge barrier to the outcome of each educational investor. Defensive players are always trying to prevent offensive players, from scoring. They attempt this unjust act by concocting unrealistic policies that are inconsistent with effective learning. How in the world, do you expect educators to survive by paying them, bus fare? Certain policies are in opposition to practices for students to thrive. Policyholders who have an impassive attitude regarding education, stand with individuals who try to highlight nonexistent issues. Particular stakeholders fail to realize unjust policies trickle down to impact the classroom, negatively.

Defensive End(Selfishness) 1

The defensive end restrains the running back(teachers/academic coach), from running plays to the outside or plundering the quarterback on passing plays. This position equates to selfishness. One of the biggest obstacles, in obtaining a positive environment to win the game. Anyone who possesses this horrible trait risks blocking innovation and opens themselves up to a loss. Selfishness is an unhealthy mentality that needs to stop. Claiming any situation is not your problem when you are directly affiliated with it, is a breeding ground for loss. This position restrains running backs(teachers/academic coaches) from accomplishing the goals of the quarterback(principal) and inhibits academic and professional growth. Unification brings edification in times where circumstances are stagnant. Educators must remember an unselfish mentality is the only way to help their team, score points.

Defensive End(Laziness) 2

Defensive ends cover the edges of the field. A good tactic of a player in this position is to create barriers to impede the teacher/s/the academic coach from running down the field. Laziness is a nasty habit that engulfs educators that entertain it. This practice is unproductive and causes instability in and out of the classroom. I witnessed people who fed into this useless routine by informing parents(of students) they were in danger of grade retention pass the deadline, entering grade percentages late, showing up to work late, and more. Unfortunately, some of their administrators increased their behavior by lowering accountability. This defensive end sets players up for failure.

Defensive Tackle(Displacement of Funding Allocation) 1

One duty of the defensive tackle includes stopping the running back(teachers/academic coaches) on running plays. This happens when funding allocation takes a turn for the worse. Defensive tackles are also responsible for getting pressure up the middle on passing plays and occupying blockers so the linebacker can roam free. We are inhabited in vain when ridicule bills are proposed and accepted. Every moment spent in constructing signs to protest, against these ridiculous ideas, is taken away from students. Just as defensive linemen are ready to prevent offensive lineman(educators) from gaining yardage, through effective plays, front liners of education, need to annihilate insubordination. Refusing to implement effective directives is one of the largest penalties, we acquire. Effective change emerges from purposeful strategic intervention.

Defensive Tackle (Degradation) 2

If this challenger realizes the offense is carrying out a running play the player will pursue the runner and tackle or force a fumble. Degradation is the dismal reality of a lot of students. Fighting against the ones who suffer from circumstances beyond their control is prejudicial. Sadly, the amount of funding per scholar is based on a rich versus poor status. Lower property values impact funding and skew our game. If we intend to make it to the end zone, effectively we cannot get tackled by this giant. Equilibrium for all students, teachers, and parents(of students) should be enforced. Every day we encourage educators to tell students how special they are, regardless of how hopeless their environment seems, government officials refuse to back us up. Our salaries are being cut, funds are not allocated fairly, security is minimal, extracurricular activities are in danger and people are tired of painting on a happy face and acting as if everything is fine. This system is breached.

Linebacker(MLB—Spitefulness) 1

The linebacker lines up in the middle of the defense(positioned in the back of the defensive line) and makes the calls for the team. This player is in communication with the coach to convey commands to his teammates. The Middle linebacker needs to impede wide receivers, stop runs, and monitor the quarterback's actions simultaneously. Mental health services should be extended to all educators and students. Some people do not know how to overcome being hurt, as a result, they become spiteful. The MLB poses a threat to the functionality of our team by inhibiting creativity, endangering career security, and altering the temperament of our affiliates. This linebacker is a hindrance that spreads, easily.

Linebacker(OLB—Low Self-worth) 2

The outside linebacker lines up against tight ends and have the task of covering short passes and raid the quarterback(principal). The player of this position observes the offenses' Adaptability is a requirement. Low self-worth bounces from one misconceived notion to the next. This mentality stops players from running plays. If our self-esteem stems from a distorted viewpoint, the chances of winning decline. Great linebackers know if they can find breaches in the mentality of the quarterback, it benefits defense. Educators need to avoid being tackled by foolish mentalities imposed by people who decide our stance is insignificant. Encouragement, genuine positive intentions, and feeling secure in your purpose results in winning the game. Insufficiency triggers low self-esteem which leads to low self-worth. Teachers tackled by this giant, submit to a fear-driven lifestyle. Fearful educators informed of the recent bill cried and went home. Our dignity would not permit us to do that. This linebacker will not tackle us.

Cornerback(Gossip) 1

This position is one of if not the fastest position on the field, based on play awareness. Gossip represents it, perfectly. Educators need to be aware of what information to run with versus what to throw away. Submitting to gossip inhibits a sound mind that causes the play to nosedive. Sadly, many educators believe lies, deceit, and slanderous details, regarding different people. This is unhealthy for a player's mental state. I need all refs on board to annihilate this defensive player. Cornerbacks need to read the actions of the quarterback(principal), to act./deal with grown adults, in catfights as a result of foolish rumors. This contender should not get attention if our focus is on the ball. Gossip can cause power depletion that will result in our team losing the game.

Cornerbacks(Arrogance) 2

The cornerback lines up head to head with the receiver(team leader) to prevent the quarterback(principal), from completing a pass(learning gain in the best interest of the student) or tries to make the quarterback(principal) pay for attempting to pass the ball(students). Arrogance is never a complimenting attribute; it is one of the worst emotions, players succumb to. If the player is corrected(in a tasteful manner) it is for the edification of the team. The receiver(team leader) infiltrated with this emotion, can cause a rift, in the game. Any contender who discourages explicit corrective feedback may cause the team to have penalties. Amid policy changes, rule implementation, and measuring student goals, arrogance tends to emerge. Comments like, "This school is nothing, without me, I am the team and this place is a joke" lead to tackles.

Strong Safety(Negativity) 1

Negativity should not tackle a teacher, who has experience in the field; however, it can. Anyone who does not remain in a positive state of mind is subject to being tackled. Many educators cannot take unwarranted criticism while trying to increase the progress of their class. A negative mindset classifies as a weak point that can delay scores for the offensive line. The defense can derail the thread of any well-thought-out play, if negativity engulfs the running back, causing the player of the position not to operate with a sound mind. A clear and positive perspective is the first step to keeping your mentality fixated on your role in the game. Educators who find it difficult to remain this way, impact students, and could cause the team to lose. Yearly, realism is diminished and heightened expectations weaken our offensive line. This is part of the irritant that triggered our protest.

Free Safety(Instigation) 2

Free safety is the subordinate line of defense. Whenever offense is gaining leverage instigation will emerge. This player will watch the play develop and attack where it is supposed to take place. An instigator will sit in the background and try to spread their negative mentality. People who engage in this behavior are a hindrance. Making it our duty to figure out where a play will end up to attack with harmful words, is a horrible end goal. Anyone engaged in this behavior should ride the bench.

Special Teams(Individuals/Mentalities)

Football has special teams formatted for specific objectives, during segments of the game. Individuals in this formation are responsible for kickoffs, goals, and punts.

Long Snapper(Protestors)

This player starts the game for the kicker and punter by snapping the football onward to earn a field goal/punt. The long snapper assumes the role of a player on offense after the task is finished. Educational protestors(comprised of anyone who fights against injustice for us) This player can snap the ball to the holder or punter. Why would this player decide to snap the ball to the holder(stakeholders) when the best interest of the ball(students) does not matter? Elements of the job description include: monitoring students, helping to run/running small academic groups in the classroom, setting up for special visits from higher officials, helping educators implement effective behavioral plans, and assisting with the learning process and additional duties. Thankfully, we have a strong support system of passionate people who are not intimidated by stakeholders in higher positions.

Kicker(Funding Allocation)

This player has strong leg skills that increase his ability to score the goal for any position in the game. The kicker is responsible for field goals and kickoffs. Players of this position represent funding allocation, in education. The amount of money provided to each school(based on performance) is what determines the staff, enrollment, budget/performance. This is a hard position since no school year starts from financial complacencies. I refuse to listen to suggestions from uncooperative stakeholders about making it work. We did that for an extended period, our objection is nonnegotiable.

The Punter-(Title I Liaison/Their Supervisor)

This player ensures financial allocation, supplies, additional staff salaries, parent involvement training, detailed budgets, and staff strengthening funds are utilized, correctly. Our punter kicks the ball away if the offense does not achieve a first down/score. In our system funds were allocated based on the school's disadvantaged status. Several locations used to receive funding that was the determining factor of our students' success. These funds are now in question/in the process of being eliminated.

Holder(Any Stakeholder)

Players of this position determine the amount of money that is allotted to each school. The funding proposal is unjust and will impact students, teachers/staff members. These individuals hold the key to starting the game. The holder is the backup for the quarterback. Sadly, the player of this position struggles with funding allocation, fairly and as a result, several schools will shut down. This cannot happen. When stakeholders determine a principal regressed academically, they step in and close the institution or supplement people in leadership. The nerve of this player in this position is alarming. I witnessed principals request budget approvals that were denied, based on favoritism or a myriad of insufficiencies beyond their control. Thankfully, we are standing up against unethical methodologies and will not back down.

Return Specialists

— Kick returner(Budget Keeper/Overseer)

The player of this position represents anyone who oversees their school's budget. The individual needs to figure out if returning the ball is the best option. These players struggle with the best choices to make regarding our students. I understand fear of losing your income can induce terror sedation; however, submitting incorrect budgets will only prolong the process of getting caught. Do not allow people who claim to be leaders bully you into this action. Several players did not report suspicious activity, regarding financial displacement. This caused schools that had a surplus of funds to get additional monetary support. It makes me nauseous to think schools in our district(not considered up to par) will close because of inequity. Kick returners, if your leaders are mishandling funds do not hesitate to complete an anonymous report. Your actions will alter the destiny of our students.

—Punt returner(Persistence)

This competitor catches the punt and sprints down the field to benefit the offense. Persistence represents the punt returner, in our game. We need to stay strong by refusing to allow stakeholders to strip our dignity and down play what we deserve. Protestors invested time and energy into fighting for change. Principals, teachers, parents of students(we teach), and several other supporters, experience sleepless nights ruminating on unjust occurrences. Persistence encourages us to continue to fight against evil.

Gunner-(Disappointment)

This player sprints to try and tackle the kick/punt returner. Disappointment represents this position; however, we refuse to get tackled. Our voices will get louder and the attempts to gain yardage by tackling persistence within us will fail.

"Well, there you have it, the education to football comparison," she said.

"That was one serious comparison," said Reporter Sight.

"It took a while but after—Sorry to interrupt… this just in, stakeholders have decided to grant the request of protestors," she said.

"Did you hear that teachers aren't bleachers," she said.

"Hurray," screamed protestors.

"The teachers aren't bleachers, teachers aren't bleachers, teachers aren't bleachers," they exclaimed.

The new proposal was projected on the screen, everyone could see the horrific decisions that were overturned and salary increases.

"Details of the new Bill proposition are in," she said.

"It looks like everything was granted, except one detail," she said.

"Stakeholders are requesting primary teachers get four million dollars less on their increase," said Ms. Zebedee. The crowd started to scream, in disagreement. Reporter Sight looked concerned. As emotions ran high police officers drew near.

"We are adults, I don't think we need to be prompted to maintain professionalism," she said.

"Speak for yourself," said Ms. Po(a kindergarten teacher).

"I'm not taking less money, because I teach snot-nosed brats," said Ms. Po.

"Excuse me, Ms. Po, that's inappropriate," said Ms. Zebedee.

"I deserve more money than the snot nose instruction crew," said Mr. Wu. He was a teacher, at The Best High School, who was a short stalky man with a serious demeanor and stubborn attitude. He resisted policies that seemed unjust.

"You think you deserve more ... why," she said.

"I teach eleventh graders. I have a challenging group of kids with special needs, who have real issues. I need to follow their Individual Education Plans or I get the lovely gift of a lawsuit," he said.

"Wait ... you think we don't have kids with special needs, in elementary. Did your students pop out the womb and land in eleven grade," she said.

"I wouldn't trade teaching Special Education Students for the world, but the challenges are way more than teaching babies. I should be compensated, based on those challenges, I face," he said.

"Contrary to their claim, It looks like educators are not in unison, unfortunately, this doesn't appear to look promising. This is a huge problem, if they don't get on the same page, no funds will be released," she said.

It seemed as if she was instigating the issue. Ms. Zebedee did not like it. She approached the podium mike.

"Excuse me, we could schedule a meeting to discuss logistics. This is not the time or place," she said.

They disregarded the comment and continued to debate.

"Her speech made sense, but I bust my behind, every day," he said.

"Me too," said Mr. Wu. As the educators argued, Casey saw someone she was acquainted with, in the crowd.

"Hey Ava," she whispered. The air was stiff, as mounds of pressure built up. Every protestor was on edge.

"Hey, what a mess," she whispered.

"It's such a shame, this same debate escalated. During my internship, there was a huge divide, between the teachers and staff regarding bonuses, based on performance," whispered Casey.

"I know, we had the same issue, at my school," whispered Ava.

"We all bust our behinds," said Ms. Po.

Ms. Zebedee, Casey, and Ava looked worried. This was not the original plan. People all over were watching this. It did not look good.

"There's no way, wiping snotty noses and gagging tattle tales compares to pregnant teenagers and issues with older kids period," he said.

"Okay, you switched teams, what defensive player are you," she said.

The crowd chuckled.

"It seems as if an altercation is brewing," said Reporter Sight.

"Come closer," said Mr. Wu.

"Excuse me," said Ms. Zebedee.

"You're excused," he said.

She was alarmed.

When she was getting ready to announce to meet, at a later time, Ms. Po leaped over several signs to attack Mr. Wu.

"Let's zoom in on officers in the middle of breaking up an altercation, as we speak," said Reporter Sight.

"Break it up, people," said several officers.

"This is disgraceful. Turn the cameras off, please," she said.

"Unfortunately, we can't turn the cameras off, at a whim," she said.

"Of course you can't," she said. She tried to maintain her composure and keen sense of professionalism. The ulterior motive of this journalist was predictable.

"There are several mini-riots on the rise, make sure we get this," said Reporter Sight.

"Why don't you shut the heck up, you don't know my struggle," she said.

"What in the world do kindergarten teachers struggle with, timing bathroom breaks," he said.

"Police are on the scene and just in time, we never knew, the protest would take such an unfortunate turn. This is a big disgrace, not only for Ms. Zebedee but for all peaceful protestors who want to make a difference. Reporting live, I'm Selah Sight from Max it Out News," she said.

Middle/High vs. Elementary Debate

"May I start by saying how disgraceful we looked on national television," said Ms. Zebedee. She highlighted several key points. There were over three million viewers, watching the segment. The educators started in perfect unison and ended up divided and physically fighting.

"I still think, high school teachers should be paid the most. What the heck do primary teachers do, wipe noses and tie shoes," said Mr. Wu.

"Every teacher has challenges, regardless of the grade, they teach," said Ms. Zebedee. What about elementary kids, we teach that get pregnant," said Ms. Po.

"Could someone please get old lady outlier, to acknowledge accurate statistics? You may have one or two elementary school pregnancies, compared to how many in middle and high," said Mr. Wu.

"Somebody better get this man," said Ms. Po.

"I have a billion papers to grade and deal with students who face life and death situations," said Mr. Wu.

"Don't you get it, intermediate elementary students take the Bigwig Statewide Test," said Casey.

"Ouch," she said. Ava pinched her while trying to place her index finger over her mouth.

"Quit it," said Casey.

"Now who wants to give another weak opinion," he said.

"Our students have hard lives too, we feed into the middle school that feeds into your high school you teach at," said Casey.

"Oh really," he said.

"Yes, really," she said.

"What grade do you teach, Ms. Know it All," he said.

"Sir, I would appreciate it if you didn't call me names. I'm Casey" she said.

"Who cares," he said.

"To answer your question, I teach fourth at We Will Thrive Elementary School," she said.

"When was the last time, one of your fourth graders told you she was pregnant, or dropping out of school," he said.

"Excuse me, we are all adults, here. Please watch your tone. We should be able to have an educated discussion, without getting nasty," she said.

"I'm not getting nasty, just being real," he said.

"Enough! Financial contributors are seriously reconsidering obliging our requests, as a result of this pettiness," said Ms. Zebedee.

"With all due respect, middle and high school teachers deserve higher salaries," he said.

"Says who," said Casey and Ms. Po.

"All pro football players are not paid the same," he said.

Ms. Zebedee looked, in disgust. She fought so hard for unification. The protestors could not see how horrible, this made them, appear. After breaking ground to potentially get paid, in the millions, there was still discontent. Greed can never be satisfied. She could not believe, protestors could be the cause of educators making fifteen thousand dollars, a year. The potential increase of millions of dollars lied in the entire group deciding to stick together for the best interest of education.

"I have a suggestion, why not do a trial run," he said.

"You come and take the cakewalk, you're so certain about and I will take on your role, as a high school teacher," she said.

"What are you doing," said Ava.

"Don't worry, I think teachers will go for it, they'll see a day in fourth grade is no walk in the park," she said.

"Bad idea Case.," she said.

"Besides it will be good for me to experience teaching high school," she said.

"You have no idea what you are in for, especially in such a rough neighborhood," she said.

"What does it matter, I'll be teaching "those kids" only they'll be older," she said.

"When are you going to let that go and why are your eyes closed," she said.

"I need to go to my happy place," she said.

She recalled details of the Motiv'Plication Training and it inspired her not to fly off the handle. She was trying to remain in a positive state of mind.

"If you mention the neighborhood I work in, one more time as if the kids I teach are multiplying bacteria, we're going to have a problem," she said.

"Case … I'm looking out for you, you look like a high schooler," she said.

"Really," she said.

"You remember the movies we watched, in school," she said.

"Yes," she said.

"Well, you aren't Mrs. Save a School," she said.

"I'm a big girl, who can take care of myself," she said.

"Okay, have it your way," she said.

"Hello … are you going to explain or whisper to your friend, time is ticking," he said.

"I'd love for you to walk in my shoes for a second, Ms. Elementary," he said.

"Great, I accept the challenge," she said.

"You do," she said.

"That's right," she said.

"What challenge," he said.

"I'll teach, at your school," she said. Mr. Wu looked shocked but refused to back down. Bewildered, Ava looked at her, as she yanked her arm.

"Quit it," she said.

"Um … you don't have to go that far," she said.

"Sure I do. These educators claim I can't speak on levels I haven't taught," she said.

"Are you forgetting you still have the last parts of your test to study for," she said.

"Here we go," she said.

"You're not one hundred percent legit," she said.

"I get it," she said.

"They only give new teachers a year to get certified," she said.

"I know," she said.

"Why are you taking on this crazy responsibility on a temporary certificate," she said.

"Tests don't make teachers," she said.

"How many people do we know that passed a test, yet they have no clue how to relate to kids or teach a lesson," she said.

"This is a lot," she said.

"Everything will be fine," she said.

"You need to focus and study," she said.

Casey wanted to experience the challenges he faced, before speaking about unfamiliar issues. In addition to providing her with a new sense of empathy—it would broaden her teaching experience.

"Are you sure you want to do this," she said.

"Of course," she said.

The plan was for her to spend the remainder of the year teaching high school after she weathered all storms, no one could say she had no clue, about teaching older students, in their demographic. Mr. Wu and Casey would trade places. This would make history. Everyone in the room looked shocked, especially her friend. She appeared to be very young. She didn't want the students undressing her with their eyes or carrying out worse actions. One of the main concerns addressed during the protest was a lack of safety measures. The school Mr. Wu taught at had one security guard and malfunctioning surveillance cameras. This was unacceptable, especially for a school with a population of over five thousand.

"You don't need to prove yourself," whispered Ava.

"We ask our students to prove themselves, all the time, shouldn't I lead by example," she said.

She knew initiating the challenge of working with high schoolers, from a low-income neighborhood that lacked resources, would be no easy task, regardless, she was determined to switch places with Mr. Wu.

"We can make arrangements, first thing tomorrow," she said.

"No, I don't want you sleeping on this, let's do it, now," he said.

"We can call this The Teacher Switch Challenge," he said.

Beads of sweat mounted on her forehead.

"After we switch places, let's share our experiences. Based on our encounters, we will vote on if all teachers should receive the same amount of funds, after the switch," he said.

"Sounds like a plan," she said.

"Our experience will determine who is right and wrong and how we vote," he said.

Finally, stakeholders were willing to compensate educators on a million-dollar scale; however, the contingencies were so unique.

"If I experience challenges (at a primary level) that are the same or worse, during our switch, I will vote for the salary increases to be equal," he said.

"That sounds fair," she said.

"If you realize problems at my level are more, I expect you to compliment my request for more funds," he said.

"That's fair," she said.

"Do we have an understanding," he said.

"Yes, wait … what about the rest of the policy changes we are protesting for," she said.

"Everything else will have to wait," he said.

"Ms. Z., will the challenge go against any district policies," she said.

"No, keep in mind policy changes won't address anything until we are on the same page," she said.

Casey was not sure, how she felt about that but apparently, everyone wanted the switch to take place. She needed to do this for herself and others. Although the policy change aspect bothered her, she decided to prolong addressing it, until the switch was over.

"Should we tell our students goodbye," she said.

"Not in person, you can send an email or video message, also, I will formulate a letter for you to send home to parents," she said.

Principal Waggenport(the principal of The Best High School and Principal Lazman(the principal of We Will Thrive Elementary School agreed with Ms. Zebedee.

The educators exchanged contact information. During the remainder of the meeting, they discussed specifics pertinent to the switch. Once details were provided, they shook hands and agreed not to back out.

"The Best High would love to have you," he said.

"My work address is 987 SW Lane, the neighborhood is so bad your G. P. S. may reject it," he said. He chuckled.

"I'll be there," she said.

"Make sure you're on time, this isn't elementary, you need to check-in by 6:00 a.m.," he said.

"In that case, I'll be there by 5:45," she said.

"This will be the challenge of the decade," he said.

"Let's make history," she said.

Everyone at the meeting cheered as the educators shook hands. When they parted ways, Casey was able to register the commitment to this. Fear started to grip her decision but there was no going back.

Rye In Shining Armor?

"What are you doing here," said Casey.

"I saw the mess on t.v. and came," said Rye.

"Why do you always think I'm in danger," she said.

"Think … you mean know," he said.

"I'm fine," she said

"Thank God," he said.

"You do realize I drove right," she said.

"Just follow me," he said. As they headed home, she rehearsed how to tell him about The Teacher Switch agreement, which she made off-air. Finally, they reached their destination.

"Let's hurry inside," he said.

"Fine," she said.

"You were in the middle of a possible riot, I don't feel comfortable with any of this," he said.

"You're being dramatic," she said.

"Oh really, check out channel ten … oh here's channel seven and my favorite clip on channel three," he said.

"Turn that off," she said.

"Teachers aren't Bleachers," he exclaimed.

"We made history, sure there were some bumps but we pulled through," she said.

"Bumps, you mean a few train wrecks," he said.

"What happened to support," she said.

"I do but I can't support you walking off a cliff," he said.

"Well … I may as well tell you— I'm doing The Teacher Switch," she said.

"What's that," he said.

"I'll be trading places with a high school teacher for the rest of the year," she said.

"High school—what are you saying, you teach babies," he said.

"Technically, I teach elementary kids that are older," she said.

"Keep dreaming that's dangerous," he said.

"I committed and can't go back," she said

"So you're doing this," he said.

"Yes, of course," she said.

"Those adults are ruthless," she said.

"What do you mean, they're teens," she said.

"They're grown," he said.

"Some of them may look that way but they aren't," she said.

"I know about the other side of town, it's challenging," he said.

"Duh … that's why they need my help," she said.

"Do you think that's the best decision, considering the stress it'll put on your body, he said.

"It's my body," she said.

"Yeah but it's our child that we are trying to have," he said.

"Just respect my decision," she said.

"Narsh said your body should not be under a lot of stress, during this process," he said.

"I know, we were there, together," she said.

Ding! Ding!

"What is happening, can't I catch a break," she said.

"Hello," she said.

"Casey Peinst—it's Coper mom," she said.

"We saw that horrible mess on the t.v., we've been calling nonstop," she said.

"I know, you texted and called a billion times," she said.

"Why didn't you call back," she said.

"I was busy, I just got home," she said.

"Before we keep going, I'm spreading the news, I'm doing The Teacher Switch," she said.

"What's that," she said.

"I'm trading places to teach at a high school for the rest of the year," she said.

"You can't be serious with this craziness," she said.

"Um … I am and it's not craziness for the teachers to get all the pay raise money, I said yes to it," she said.

"Why do you need to be the test dummy for this thing," she said.

"I volunteered and want to do it," she said.

"We're coming to talk sense into you," said Mr. Peinst.

"Dad, don't do that," she said.

"Where's Rye," he said.

"Here, oh and he tried to talk me out of it, already, " she said.

"Let us speak to him," he said.

"Here you go," she said.

"What's this outlandish decision about," she said.

"Hey guys, I have no clue," he said.

"You aren't going to let her do this, right," he said.

"It's out of my hands," he said.

"This is dangerous," she said.

"I'm aware," he said.

"Could we speak with monarch," she said.

"She's right here," he said.

"Oh, well I can't talk, I just got home and need to prep for tomorrow," she said.

"Those big kids are going to swallow you whole," she said.

"Wow, thanks for the support, I need to go," she said.

"Monarch, listen to your mother," she said.

"I love you guys," she said.

"Honestly, I'm tired of listening, hear me-this is my decision, since you can't support that, there's no more communication until I contact you guys," she said.

"You can't be serious monarch," she said.

"I am, you never support my decisions," she said.

"How can you say that," she said.

"Because it's true," she said.

"Breathing down my neck to marry someone else," she said.

"That barely happened," she said.

"Oh really, how about asking when we're going to have a child when you know I'm going through fertility treatments," she said.

"Adoration calm down," said Rye.

"No, you stay out of this," she said.

"We didn't mean it, like that," they said.

"Look, I can't argue with you, respect my decision or you'll push me away, completely," she said.

"Hello," she said. Her parents were quiet. They never saw this side of her. It was not worth taking the chance.

"Okay," said Mr. Peinst. Her mother was crying, they were shocked.

"Mom, there's no need to cry, we need a break from each other," she said.

"Okay, we hear you, monarch," he said.

"We will talk soon, hopefully," he said.

"Love you and be careful," she said.

"I love you guys, bye," she said.

"Wow, was that necessary," said Rye.

"Yes, it was," she said.

"So you're really not speaking to your parents because they're warning you," he said.

"I need support," she said.

"Right off a cliff, okay fine," he said.

They ate dinner and got ready for bed. As they were lying down, he pulled her close.

"I still and always will love you," he said.

"I still and always will love you," she said.

"I hope you know what you're doing," he said.

"Of course," she said.

"Don't tell me not to worry, it's no use," he said.

"It's because you care, trust me I get it," she said.

As he rubbed the back of her neck, she fell asleep.

Three
The Teacher Switch

"Good morning or should I even say that," said Rye.

"It's too early to be facetious," said Casey.

"The argument yesterday was scary for all of us," he said.

"Yeah … well … thanks for showing up," she said.

"Of course," he said.

"Why are you up so early," she said.

"I need to show support and by the way, the protest went viral," he said. He handed her the phone and she could not believe how many replays there were.

"Ah! This is amazing, we're trending," she exclaimed.

"Yeah, something else to increase your stress level—always hypes me up," he said.

"The vibes need to be modified," she said.

"There's no negativity coming from me," he said.

"Oh … it seems that way," she said.

"I'm concerned about your well-being, that's all," he said.

"We got home late and you blew up on your parents," he said.

"The point is I'm sitting in the control seat, from now on," she said.

"Don't get mad but I don't want you doing this," he said.

"Of course not that's no surprise," she said.

"You know how much this switch will eat up your time," he said.

"It'll be an investment," she said.

"Then why would you take on this switch thing," he said.

"Switch thing … we went viral for a reason," she said.

"Yes, you looked like sharks ready to kill each other," he said.

"Okay, it wasn't all peaceful but at least we got the attention of stakeholders," she said.

"I tried coming in earlier, but the area was barricaded off," he said.

"Quit trying to follow me and trust—I'm okay," she said.

"How can I trust that, when you're on the news in the middle of a huge crowd, looking petrified," he said.

"I can't argue with you, this morning," she said.

"Or any morning, I'm concerned," he said.

"We're trying to create a new life, your body needs limited stress," he said.

"Look, we spoke about this already, I'm leaving," she said.

"Could we talk about it later," he said.

"Yeah … I guess," she said.

"Hold on," he said. Quickly, he started to get dressed.

"Where are you going," she said.

"To walk you out and you need to eat," he said.

"There's no time for that," she said.

"Please at least take the protein shake—I made you," he said.

"This is heavy," she said. She had a suitcase full of materials to decorate her new classroom.

"Let me help you," he said.

"Fine, hurry please, I can't be late," she said.

"I've got it," she said.

"Oh … so I'm not good enough to open your door," he said.

"Go back and try to get some sleep Mr. Dramatic, before you need to get ready," she said.

"Don't worry about me," he said.

"I don't want to bother you but are you working late," he said.

"I may need to stay after to set up my room. You know how I am about decorations" she said.

"I know," he said.

"Have a great day, I still and always will love you," he said.

"Likewise, I still and always will love you, too," she said.

As she drove to her new school she tried to reset her peace of mind. Why did he insist on altering her mood? Was it because he cared or to place her in a bad state of mind so she could dwell on their argument? She couldn't figure it out. As she approached The Best High School —she heard a notification. I still and always will love you. No matter what happens we need to be there for each other. I did not mean to ruin your morning. Quickly she stopped reading the text and altered her phone setting to an I can't right now, status. After praying and listening to one of her favorite songs, she was ready.

The New School

She entered the front office and saw three ladies.

Casey was greeted by Ms. Tooks the office manager. She was a beautiful, tall, middle-aged woman with no-nonsense written on her forehead. She wore her hair in a tight bun with tendrils that fell on either side of her large bangs.

"Hello, how may I help you," she said.

"Good morning! My name is—Yeah, I know, the whole world knows … Casey Coper," she said. Rolling her eyes, she gave a look of disgust that made it apparent, The Teacher Switch was not a venture she supported.

"You're one of the guinea pigs for The Teacher Challenge," she said.

"I wouldn't compare myself to a rodent," she said.

"That's subjective," she said.

Her look of skepticism would trigger anyone to respond, negatively; but Casey was determined not to humor her.

"You'll be in room 207," she said. Smirking she gave her the classroom key.

"Thanks," she said.

"I should warn you, Mr. Wu has some tough students," she said.

"I'm aware of the challenges, they don't bother me," she said.

"Well, Ms. Know It All … knows it all … don't you," she said.

"I guess hazing has begun," she whispered.

"What was that," she said.

"Nothing, just a thought," she said.

"Here's your roster, rules and regulations, map of the school with the route to your new room, bathroom key … and … she cut her off.

"We need a key for the bathroom, here," she said.

"This ain't the elementary land of candy and bubblegum, you're used to … but you already know that," she said.

Although her blood started to boil. She disregarded the snide comments and smiled.

"Sure, thanks," she said.

"If you have any questions, just contact me, at extension 1727," she said.

"Extension 1727 got it," she said.

"I added you to the in-house email and phone system, welcome to your new school family," she said.

Although Ms. Tooks was sarcastic she appreciated the information. She headed up to the classroom and opened the door. Desks were disheveled, several textbooks were used to prop up desks and the classroom odor was sinful. Mr. Wu had two posters on the wall. One was a smiley face, the other was the school rules ripped in half. There were alternate decoration options, in her car. After school, she planned on remodeling. For now, she would focus on her rosters and the new environment. She sat down at her new desk and opened her second husband(her laptop). She decided to email him. The email read:

Good morning,

I hope you have a great day. My students are special. I left all the pertinent information, in an organized folder on my former desk. If you need anything, don't hesitate to contact me, via email or phone, I think you know the extension, lol. Again, I hope you have a great day. Keep up the Motiv'Plication!

Sincerely,

Mrs. Coper

Phenomenal Teacher

The Best High School

-Loveless learning is lifeless learning.-Casey Coper

As she finished typing, she heard a loud knock at the door.

"Come in," she said.

"Hey … my name is Zed Zee," he said. He was a handsome man, about 6'6, muscular with big broad shoulders, his eyes were mysterious. She found him attractive.

"I remember you, from the meeting," he said.

"I apologize, your face isn't familiar," she said.

"You nervous to be one of the first teachers to do The Teacher Switch," he said.

"Maybe a little … actually … I'm nervous but it will be worth it for equilibrium purposes," she said.

"Equilibrium purposes fancy words …," he said.

"You're funny," she said.

"You have a beautiful smile," he said. She lost for a moment.

"Take my number, in case of an emergency," he said.

She looked reluctant to take his number. He noticed her apprehensiveness.

"Trust me, you'll need it, don't worry—I see the ring on your finger," he said. She smiled.

"In this environment, we need to stay tight-knit," he said.

"Okay," she said.

"My number is … 777 … as she proceeded to take his phone number, she thought of Rye's reaction. Hopefully, it would not be an issue. Quickly, she started looking at the rosters, rules, and regulations of the school.

"Well, let me get going, I need to set up, it was nice meeting you," he said.

"It was great speaking with you," she said.

"Same here—I'm next door if you need anything," he said.

Unbeknownst to her, he lingered, in the doorway. There was at least a two-minute intermission of staring and silence.

"Thanks," she said.

"Oh, just one thing," she said.

"What's up," he said. Unaware, he was still there, she started smiling.

"What extension is 9121," she said.

"It's written, in huge red letters, at the top of my rosters," she said.

"That's the extension for security," he said.

"Gotcha," she said.

"Oh, yeah, please avoid the phrase, I'll wait to get the students' attention," he said.

She lowered her head slightly smirking, in agreement.

"I can't stand when educators say that," he said.

"Make that mistake here and you'll be waiting, forever," he said.

"Oddly, they get even more upset, when students proceed to ignore them," she said.

"Okay, I'm going, this time," he said.

"Later," she said.

Ding! Ding!

This better not be Rye, she thought.

Good morning monarch,

Your father and I love you, so much. We apologize for making you feel like we don't support you. Please be careful and whenever you feel comfortable, reach out. Mom

Casey replied:

Good morning mom,

Thanks for checking on me. I appreciate it. Please respect my decision, not to correspond. I need to sort things out. I love you and dad. Again, I'm safe and a genuine adult, who can handle herself. Have a great day.

Introductions

The first bell rang and she felt like her stomach was in her mouth. She was petrified. Students started to enter. They were loud and some looked twenty-one.

"Excuse me, could you take your seats," she said.

"Yes, a sub., dis finna be an easy day," said Lanson.

"Right, right, right," said Sanrell.

"Dis man stay speak-in in threes," said Lanson.

"Good morning, please take your proper seats, once you do, and I will explain who I am and why I'm here," she said.

The students acted as if she was speaking aimlessly. In complete disregard, they continued to converse, laugh, and play fight. They were out of control.

Honk! Honk! Casey had a backup plan. She blew the field horn, she picked up, a while back. The students clogged their ears and stopped talking.

"Okay, as I said, could everyone please take their seats," she said.

Slowly, students sat down and stared at her. She noticed there were three pregnant girls, in the class. Along with students who appeared to be retained.

"As I said before, my name is Mrs. Coper, I'll be your teacher for the remainder of the year," she said.

"Mr. Wu took over my fourth-grade elementary class," she said.

"Man ... what, this lady funny," said Lanson.

"He sent you guys a video message to say goodbye. Let's take a look," she said.

"Hey guys, I decided to switch places with Mrs. Coper for the rest of the year, please make sure to listen and follow directions. Fighting is not a pastime. There are more ways to express yourself without using your fists. Remember all the things I taught you. I will see you, at the end of the year. Bye," he said.

"Miss you joke—in right? How you goin teach juniors when you look like us," said Lanson.

"Okay, that's inappropriate," she said.

"Sorry, ... you look so young, though," said Lanson.

"Me looking young or old isn't your concern," she said.

"Oh ... miss tried you," said several students.

"I have a seating chart, please get to your proper desk or I will be forced to take off points," she said.

"Hey miss, my name Smithna you want me to help you," she said. She had a blue wig, a beautiful face, and a white smile.

"That is a beautiful name and yes I would appreciate your help," she said.

"If the noise level does not come down, I'm taking off points," she said.

"Mrs. C. Points from what," she said.

"I'll explain after you get to your proper seats," she said.

"Y'all get where y'all need to be, I want my points," she said.

"Miss I could go use the restroom," said Sanrell.

"Okay," she said.

"Miss he can't go, alone, you gotta call security," she said.

"That girl a snitch," said Lanson.

"So ... she a nice lady, I don't care what y'all say," she said.

"Hey, we're not using language, like that," she said.

"Y'all best stop," she said.

She dialed the extension for security; the call was forwarded to the front office.

"Ms. Tooks speaking," she said.

"Hello, yes this is Mrs. Coper," she said.

"Oh ... is everything okay," said Ms. Tooks.

"Everything's fine, A student needs to use the restroom," she said.

"I forgot to inform you, they can't go alone," she said.

"It's fine," she said.

"I hate forgetting things that are big but seem little," she said. This was not the time for a philosophical moment.

"We just need security, it's an emergency," she said.

"Our security guard Mr. Veftel just came to the front office, give me a second," she said.

"She claims a student needs to use the restroom that's probably her call for help," she said.

"Why she has us in this switch thing, confuses me," he said.

"The poor thing looks twelve," she said.

"Oh no ... those kids must be in heaven," he said.

"I don't know, why she's fooling herself," she said.

"Hopefully, she survives the year," he said.

"The year ... you mean the day," she said.

Ms. Tooks thought she put the call on hold but she was wrong. She heard every word.

The two laughed, as he grabbed a donut, from a box on her desk.

"Alright let me head up there," he said.

He entered the room with an indifferent expression on his face. He was a short, stalky man, with a salt and pepper beard and mustache.

"You called for security," he said.

"Yes, this student needs to use the restroom," she said.

"More like the vending machine," he said. The class laughed.

"Let's go, Sanrell," he said.

"Okay, back to what I was saying," she said.

"Miss how they got that man, teach-in babies," said Lakes.

"Mr. Wu is fine," she said.

"Let's start with introductions," she said.

"My name Anfel and I like tell-in jokes and make people laugh," he said.

"Please continue, do you have a nickname," she said.

"They tried call-in me one but it ain't stick, my momma was so loud call-in me inside from play--in, wit the man's name, it just stuck," he said.

"The man's name," she said.

"Yeah, that government name, he da man," he said.

"Anyway my wife is my world, people be hate-in cuz we in love," he said.

"You're married," she said in an inquiring voice.

"Naw, not yet but we basically, like married it's like we say that if we wit somebody serious," he said.

"Oh really, you was just with a freshman, let me not out this boy," said Smithna.

"Too late, mouthy," he said.

"No names please," she said.

"Sorry," he said.

"It's nice to meet you, Anfel," she said.

"You too," he said.

"Alright, let's take a look here, next is—"Swoon, nice to meet you," he interjected.

"What's the name your mother gave you," she said.

"No disrespect but it's on the paper with the other names, please don't say it," he said.

"May I ask ... why not," she said.

"I don't use my government name, it's a tricky system," he said.

"Oh really," she said.

"Yes," said Swoon. Slowly, he went up to her and said his name, in a low voice.

"I know it, from the seating chart," she said.

"So why you, ask," he said.

"I wanted you to introduce yourself by it, not a nickname," she said.

"My name Swoon," he said.

"Boy why you eat-in time, we went to middle school witchu, Spenez," said Stiltz.

"Man … quiet," he said.

"Okay nice to meet you, please try not to speak out of turn," she said.

"Anyway, before I was rudely interrupted," said Swoon.

"They call me Swoon because my emotions run deep wit pretty ladies, like you, Mrs. C.," he said.

"Not appropriate, that's enough," she said.

They started talking about her beauty. She had to pull the attention reins back in.

"My fault, I got a weakness miss," he said.

"No problem, it's going to be a strength, soon," she said.

"Oh … miss tried you," said Garnell.

"It's not a try, I'm here to teach you how to show respect, regardless of how you feel, that's necessary for life," she said.

"She takin us to church, already," said Lanson.

"Amen & amen," said Swoon. She tried not to smile but it was difficult.

"Alright, who would like to introduce themselves, next," she said.

Ramirez raised his hand. She wanted to continue, in order but he looked so excited, she had to call on him.

"Go ahead," she said.

"Mi name Rimez, nice to meet you," he said.

"Tell me a little bit about yourself," she said.

"No problem," he said.

He got up and walked to the front of the class.

"Here this man go," said Stilts.

"Let's not be rude, go ahead," she said.

"I hope you hundastand, mi accent," he said.

"Yes, I understand perfectly," she said.

"Mi from the great island, Jamaica," he said.

"Interesting, I noticed how hard you were working," she said.

"This likkle work a notin," he said.

"It's still admirable," she said.

"Anyway, Jamaica is the land I love, mi barn hand raise deer" he said.

"Everyday mi wear mi belt to let these hate-as know, where the best place in the world is," he said.

"Oh, for the ladies," out there, I cook curry chicken and rice and peas/white rice," he said.

"That sounds delicious, do you have a nickname, also," she said.

"Mi nickname Rat," he said.

"Why do they call you to Rat," she said.

"When mi did small mi did need glasses and mi teet did big so dem seyh mi fava rat," he said.

"Thanks for sharing," she said.

"You may have a seat," she said.

"Who's next," she said.

"Me, my name's Deider," he said.

"It's wonderful to meet you, Deider," she said.

"Nice to meet you, they call me Do," he said.

"These are such interesting nicknames," she said.

"People ask me for help—they say," Deider do this and Deider do that, and I never say no, so, they started call--in me Do," he said.

"You seem like a generous person," she said.

"Life ain't bout me it's about other people," he said.

"That's the sweetest mentality to have," she said.

"No credit necessary, it's me," he said.

"Your humility is amazing. A lot of adults aren't that way," she said.

"Don't make me shy," he said.

"Thanks for being awesome," she said.

"My name Denny. They call me DenJ for Denny Junior," he said.

"Nice to meet you, Denny," she said.

"My daddy died when I was two," he said.

"I'm sorry to hear that," she said.

"Don't be, Mrs. C.," he said.

"I always like to rap and make up songs about all kinds of stuff," he said.

"One day, Imma be a rapper and a singer," he said.

"I believe you will," she said.

"All y'all are in a very special class with a very special person," he said.

"Man … please," said Stilts.

"Can I finish, though it's so rude— interrupt-in people, right miss," he said.

"I do, please continue," she said.

"Like I was saying, Imma blow up and get my mama fifty mansions wit fifty toilets on fifty-billion acres of land," he said.

"Fifty-billion acres, huh, you have really good intentions," she said.

"Thank you, she everything to me," he said.

"That's a beautiful statement," she said.

"Next in line is Rezline," she said.

"You could skip me," she said. She noticed her facial expression and decided not to ask why.

"Okay … I guess up next is Miken," she said.

"They call me Money," he said.

"Ah-ha, I guess I can figure out what that nickname means," she said.

"Yup, I'm about that paper, dough, dinero dreams make me happy …" he said.

The class laughed.

"Everything goes back to money, God and time are the only things worth more," he said.

"God is worth the most, though," he said

"God is worth more than money," said Sanrell.

"Yup, God can't be spent or lost," he said.

"I can't argue with that, short and sweet, who's next," she said.

"That would be me, Ms. fine, I mean Mrs. gorgeous," said Lanson.

"Let's not rename each other," she said.

"Naw Mrs. C., I'm renam-in you," he said.

The class chuckled and the boys were staring hard to see her reaction. She approached him with a stern face.

"Please don't, call me any name, other than the one I would like to be called," she said.

"Relax miss …. I was just play-in," he said.

"Have I disrespected you," she said.

"No," said Lanson.

"Then please—show me the same respect and don't play like that," she said.

"My bad, sorry," he said.

"Apology accepted, let's continue, why do they call you, Lakes," she said.

"I can't say, it's not class appropriate," he said. The girls turned and nudged each other, laughing.

"I respect that Lanson, may I call you by your name," she said.

"Yeah," he said.

"Football one of my favorite things to play and—ask dis man if he made the team miss, please …," Stiltz interjected.

"Man, forget that fak-coach that team, they can't take all this talent," he said.

"Wait, what's a fak-coach," she said.

"A fake coach, that's what they got out here," he said. The class laughed.

"Oh … wow … um … okay … I'm sure you're a great player," she said.

"Don't listen to him, he swear cuz I ain't make the team that broke me, yeah right," he said.

"This man face got so long, he was salty fa days," he said. The class continued to laugh and make comments.

"Man quiet," he said

"Everyone calm down and please don't interrupt," she said.

"Yeah don't interrupt," he said.

"I don't need help," she said.

"Okay, calm down, It's nice to meet you, Lanson," she said.

"Nice to meet you, miss," he said.

"Next is Nazaire, please introduce yourself," she said.

"Hey, they call me Zaire, short for my name," he said.

"That's a nice name, it's great to meet you," she said.

"Thanks," he said.

"We got nice names, too," said Sanrell and Lanson.

"Of course you guys do," she said.

"Enough, let him finish," she said.

"Sorry," they said.

"Imma keep go--in… I like to help my family, write verses and sing … I could sing some-thin for you," he said.

"Okay, let's hear it," she said.

"Hello …. Mrs. C., no one can deny your infinite beauty … you a great teacher to me …," she started to get emotional.

"He fine and he could sing," said a group of girls, fanning themselves. Casey smiled.

"That was beyond beautiful," she said.

"Thanks," he said.

"Imma take him on tour wit me," said DenJ.

"Boy shut up on tour where, to da bathroom," said Smithna.

"Please don't say shut up and be respectful," she said.

"Sorry, miss," she said.

"Thanks for sharing your beautiful voice with the class," she said.

"Okay, Da'Zay you're up next," she said.

"As everybody know … it's yo girl—the first and last … Da'Zay oh … fun fact I love school and I be getting all A's," she said.

"She a lie-yad," said Rat.

"Manners everyone," she said.

"Oh … and I think I'm really pretty and everybody think I look good, even the cats and dogs, at this school," she said. Several people started to laugh.

"Yeah right, Mrs. C. could I vote on what she said," said Sanrell.

"No and please stop interrupting, you're up next," she said.

"Thanks for sharing, Da'Zay, " she said.

"Next is Sanrell, go ahead," she said.

"Aye … oh yeah … Mrs. C. my name Sanrell," he said.

"Yeah … yeah … here he go," said the class, in unison. She was grateful to have such energetic and entertaining students.

"Nice to meet you," she said.

"They call me Stilts cuz I got lanky legs, ever since I was a jit," he said.

"That's interesting," she said.

"My mama would say it look like I was stand-in on stilts so that was my nickname," he said. The class chuckled.

"I'm real good so I started playing football and made the team, not like some haters, we know Lakes," he said his name while pretending to clear his throat and the class laughed, loudly.

"Miss I'm not gonna choke this man, cuz you here," he said.

"Settle down, everyone, aggressive language is not okay, either," she said.

"My fault," said Lanson.

"Back to me, you gonna come to my games, miss," he said.

"I don't see, why not," she said.

"We everything—GO NUMBER 1'S," he said. The class started to cheer.

"Settle down, I know everyone's excited," she said.

"And I like to teach elementary kids how to shoot and help them, a lot," he said.

"That's awesome," she said.

"Yup," he said.

"Thanks so much for telling me, about your great talent," she said.

"Ain't noth--in," he said.

"I'll take you up on the football game invitation," she said.

He had a huge smile on his face and was happy, about his new teacher.

"Next is—-I'm Garnell, Greater than anybody out here," he said.

"Oh … the lies," said Da'Zay. He turned around acting like a device was in his hand.

"Is everything okay," she said.

"Yeah, I had to mute a hater," he said. She started to laugh. These students were so funny and full of life.

"It's great meeting you Garnell," she said.

The class started to shout. She had to calm them down.

"Please tell me about yourself and your fabulous nickname," she said.

"People call me Greater, cause I'm GREATER than everybody, at everything like … gettin girls, football, dance—in, rapping, anything you can think of," he said.

"Wow, what great confidence," she said.

"Man please, he ain't greater than me at football," said Lanson.

"Oh … miss he funny you mean like the field you don't play on, cuz you ain't on da team," he said.

"Yeah I'm on the team, here," he said.

"Quiet Lanson, please," she said. Biting his lip, he turned the other direction.

"Thank you," he said.

"Now back to Greater—you ain't greater than me, at reading," said Da'Zay.

"Girl I ain't unmute you," he said.

"Here we go," said Smithna.

"Please don't judge and wait for him to finish talking, it's rude," she said.

"Like I said ... I'm Greater," he said.

"It's great to meet you," she said.

"Mrs. C., they keep be-in on each other, in the back," she said.

Rezline and Biren seemed to be a cute couple. Casey wanted to enforce the no public display of affection rule but she did not want to disrupt the class introduction activity. If the couple was not blatantly inappropriate, she would look the other way. She wondered what Mr. Wu would do, in this case.

"Girl get this, we finna go viral," said Rezline.

Suddenly, she reached over and slammed Biren's face, against the desk. His nose was gushing blood; it appeared broken.

Casey was shocked. Quickly, she ran next door to get Mr. Zee.

"Didn't I tell yo behind, you would get caught," she said.

"Crazy baby what is you talk--in bout," he said.

"Don't Crazy Baby me, I saw you like dat girl picture," she said.

"Ah my nose, what's wrong witchu, girl what is you talk--in bout," he exclaimed.

"All yo accounts linked to my phone, I saw the like," she said.

"I ain't like no girl picture," he said.

"Now you wanna play like you don't know," she said.

"Imma hurt you," he said.

"No ... she ran to try and put a wedge between the couple. Suddenly, Mr. Zee came rushing in.

"Y'all better stop, not on your new teacher's first day," he said.

"This finna be so good," said Da'Zay.

"My nose," he said.

"Good, now yo nose match my heart, it hurt—don't it," she said.

"You crazy," he said.

"How you gonna do me like that, I'm carrying yo baby," she said,

"No you ain't, you say dat junk, every month and every month it ain't true," he said.

"Excuse me, this is not the place for fighting," she said.

"This ain't no fight new lady, it's about to be murder," she said.

The students started screaming to instigate the fight. Casey felt out of control. They had a look of delight in their eyes. It was troublesome.

"Quit," said Mr. Zee. She had no clue, he would come so quickly. Where was security?

Before the couple tried to attack each other, he made a swift move restraining them.

"The rest of you sit down," he exclaimed.

Everyone took their seats.

Police officers entered the classroom—along with Mr. V. and arrested them. They took three witnesses(from the class) for questioning. She looked deeply disturbed. How many fights were they subjected to, daily?

"Hey, I told you I'll be here, when you need me, you good," he said.

"Not really, but I will be," she said.

In the last ten minutes of the class, Casey shook, uncontrollably. Was she cut out for this?

"You gonna leave us-after this—huh miss," said Smithna. Casey looked bewildered. That would be a valid question is she was the type to give up.

"It's time to go, almost, Imma go to the vend-in machine," she said.

"Have a seat," he said.

"Aight," she said.

"Hey, you don't look good, go get some fresh air, I'll watch them," he said

"Fresh air," she said.

"Yeah, go take a walk to the office, you'll need to fill out an incident report," he said.

"Okay," she said. Shortly after she left, the bell rang.

"Aight y'all I got 20 on who gonna win da next fight, who want in," she said.

"Nothings happening again unless you want to be in the same boat—as your friends," he said.

Casey's next period was planning. On her way to the office, she was in deep thought. She went to the teacher's lounge, entered the restroom, closed the door, and began to cry.

She came out of the stall and washed her face, eventually. She would need to toughen up, to survive the switch. She tried to appear unbothered when entering the front office.

"We need you to fill out an incident report," said Ms. Tooks.

"Okay," she said. Her eyes were bloodshot red and the crying eye bags were evident.

Serves her right, she thought. This little teacher swears she's a real woman. Why would you drag our school into this? She thought to herself.

"It's been a rough first ... I mean ... the first half of the day, hasn't it," she said.

What was with people? Did she need to rub her face, in it? The snide comments and demeaning gestures were unnecessary. She knew Ms. Tooks was not thrilled about the setup; she would need to get over it.

"I'll fill out whatever you need me to, just show me the format," she said.

"Oh yeah ... it's different, for elementary teachers," she said.

She took the form, from her, and went back to her new classroom. She didn't want to harass Mr. Wu but he needed to know what happened.

Attention Mr. Wu,

The first period started, wonderfully but there was a fight. I cannot disclose names, via email for confidentiality purposes but it was bad. One of the students busted his nose; it may be broken. Honestly, I could not stop crying. Mr. Zee is the best neighbor. He was instrumental, in breaking it up. I will remain positive and look forward to a great rest of the week. I can't wait to hear, how things are going with my former students. Keep up the Motiv'Plication!

Sincerely,

Casey Coper

Phenomenal Teacher

The Best High School

-Loveless learning is lifeless learning.-Casey Coper

She filled it out and placed it, in Ms. Tooks' mailbox. It was lunchtime. Casey never lost her appetite or ate in the teacher's lounge(at her former school); lately, she was the queen of new adventures. As she opened the door, she saw a sweet yet familiar face.

"There's Ms. Brave," he said.

"Thanks for your help, earlier," she said.

"Would you like to join, me," he said.

His question caused a flashback. She recalled her mother(Mrs. Peinst) warning her of mistakes married people make when they feel misunderstood.

"Mommy, how did you and dad stay together—so long," she said.

"It wasn't easy monarch, but I realized never to take my feelings for granted," she said.

"What do you mean," she said.

"When a marriage is on rocky ground, the worst thing any partner should do is engage in meaningless conversations" with people they know are attracted to them," she said.

"I won't vent to anyone, like that," she said.

"Good, never pave the way for adultery," she said.

"I won't," she said.

"Now, you can always tell your mother any and everything," she said.

"Yeah ... I bet you would love that," she said. The two chuckled, as they got dressed for Casey's wedding ceremony.

"Yoo-hoo, anyone there, you can eat with me," he said.

"Sorry, I zone out—sometimes," she said.

"Okay ...," he said.

"I just came in the lounge to eat my lunch," she said.

"So does everyone who comes in here with food," he said.

"I need to get back to my room," she said.

"Are you okay, you still look a little dazed," he said.

"I'm fine, It's just ...everything happened so fast," she said.

Before she knew it, Casey felt the corners of her eyes heating up. She promised herself she would not cry, again. When she envisioned the students hurting each other and getting arrested, it caused her to break the promise.

Quickly, he got up and walked over to her.

"Hey, you'll be fine, these things happen," he said.

"This wasn't supposed to happen on day 1," she said.

"It's not your fault," he said.

"Under the tattoos and foul language they are sweet kids, yearning to learn," he said.

"I don't doubt that," she said.

"Well ... stop abusing yourself internally, I got that from my therapist," he said.

She smiled.

"I truly believe, every student is sweet and desires to learn, sorting through the dysfunction and distractions to get to the desire, is a challenging task," she said.

Casey continued to smile.

"You have a beautiful smile," he said.

"Thank you, my husband says that's one of my best features," she said.

He was unsure how to respond.

"Anyway ... if you need me to help with anything(other than breaking up fights), I'm here," he said.

"Wow ... such reality," she said.

"My bad, too soon," he asked.

As they spoke, she received a text:

ADORATION... I'll have dinner for you. Ditch the setup and come straight home. I still and always will love you!

Rye

What was his problem? Why couldn't he respect her decision to carry out The Teacher Switch? This was ridiculous.

"Everything okay," he said. It was hard for her to mask unhappiness. Rye would learn, she demanded respect. Since he wanted to make it hard—so be it.

"Actually... I could use your help, setting up later," she said.

"Later, you plan on staying," he said.

"Of course, did you think I would run away, because of a rough morning, try again," she said.

"Okay, Ms. Tenacious, what time are we setting up your class," he said.

" I thinking ... right after school," she said.

"Oh ... okay," he said.

"We need to treat this with urgency, the environment is a huge factor for students and teachers," she said.

"Yeah ... no offense to Wu but the walls in the class look bad," he said.

"Exactly, these kids need an inspirational environment," she said.

"Whatever you say," he said.

Although she was alarmed by the students' actions, Casey refused to give up. She was determined to break ground regardless of what anyone thought or said. She was very grateful, at least one genuine active line of support was available.

"So, I can count on you for sure, right," she said.

"Of Course," he said.

"Okay well ... see you right after school," she said.

"Cool," he said.

They left the lounge and headed back to class. She had a plan that would make sure the students understood fighting was not an afterthought or a plan b, it was not going to happen.

Meanwhile ... at We Will Thrive Elementary ...

Mr. Wu received his key, after checking in with Ms. Zepps. She was adamant about showing him around and explaining protocol.

When the two entered the teacher's lounge, he was welcomed by one of the best principals, in the district, Principal Lazmun. She was an attractive middle-aged woman, with long brown curly hair, heavyset, and the perfect smile. "We are very happy you are joining us for the rest of the year," she said.

Mr. Wu thought she was so supportive and polite.

"You're in great hands, she is the best office secretary, in the district," she said.

"You're too kind," she said.

"I need to go but we will be seeing each other, if you have any issues, don't hesitate to contact me," he said.

"Thank you," he said.

"Keep up the Motiv'Plication," she said.

He looked confused by the familiar statement, but his focus was on the sweet-smelling pancakes, syrup, and breakfast treats.

"We wanted to give you a proper welcome, a couple of members of the support staff, picked up some breakfast," she said.

"It smells delicious," he said.

"Would you like some," she said.

"That would be great," he said.

"Sit down, I'll share some out for you," she said.

Was this, some kind of prank? Mr. Wu could get used to this treatment. His welcome letter and the staff's positive attitude showed how grateful they were to have him as a recent addition to the team, the pancakes, tea, and bagels weren't bad either.

"Thanks so much," he said.

"No, Thank you," she said.

Elementary seemed more close-knit than high school.

"When you're finished, please stop by my office to get your room key," she said.

He could not eat another bite, he wanted to ensure, he did not fall asleep, during class. During breakfast, he remembered where he saw the statement, keep up the motivation. Casey wrote it, in her emails. He wanted to know the meaning behind it. He thought to himself, how hard could it be to teach, elementary?

After Mr. Wu finished, eating he went to the secretary's desk.

"Did you enjoy your breakfast," she said.

"Enjoy is an understatement, it was delicious," he said.

She handed home a key, roster, and folder with pertinent school information.

"You're in room 111, it will be a great day, today, keep up the Motiv'Plication," she said.

"One quick question, why do you guys say that phrase," he said.

"That's an easy one, we say the quote to remind each other of positive mindset oriented goals, we remain in a positive state of mind by keeping repetition, at the forefront, in case someone forgets," she said.

"Interesting," he said.

"We did a training, about it with Ms. Motivation," she said.

"You should speak to Principal Waggenport, about booking her," she said.

He was not sure about the idea. Certain people state they want ways to retain positive but at times the claim is untrue.

"All the elementary schools hired Ms. Motivation," she said.

"You are what you think," she said.

"That's a different way of looking at things," he said.

"I think it's sad when one part of the district is on one page, and the other part is in a whole other book, don't you," she said.

"Um ... I guess," he said.

She smiled. Sometimes, people do not know how to react to intense positivity or passion.

"It will be a great day," she said.

"I hope so," he said.

"We aren't hoping, it will be," she said.

Wu's New World

Mr. Wu headed toward Room 111 classroom. When he entered the floral fragrance, permeated his nostrils. The room looked like a professional, decorated it. The walls were covered, in cloud and sunshine bulletin board paper with mini drops of gold. There were several positive meme printouts attached to beautiful gold and silver backdrops. He favored the meme that read Leaders lead positively. Everything was in perfect order. He was scared to mess anything up.

He sat down popped open his email and started reviewing the policies and procedures. Certain details were similar to The Best High but others were drastically different. Walking students to dismissal and forty-five minutes for planning were all new concepts. He found tons of information, in the binder she left, neatly organized on the desk. He looked for the students' information, baseline scores(test results when students enrolled), lesson plans, and grade level information. As he read, there was a knock on the door.

"Come in," he said.

"Good morning, my name's Mrs. Batet," she said.

  She was in her early thirties, tall, gorgeous, and dedicated to serving the students. She could have been a model.

"Good morning, I'm Mr. Wu," he said.

"If you're taking over for Casey, you have big shoes to fill," she said.

"We'll see just how big those shoes are," he said.

"Anyway, welcome to the fourth-grade team," she said.

"Nice to meet you," he said.

"Thankfully, your location works, our classrooms are connected and I am team leader," she said.

"That should be beneficial," he said.

"If you have any questions/comments/concerns, don't be afraid to let me know," she said. We need our scores up, are you good at teaching writing," she said.

"I don't like to praise myself but yes, my writing skills, are definitely up to par," he said.

 "Great, let's see if your delivery matches your skills, it's one thing to be good at a subject, it's another thing to help students get on that level," she said.

He gave her a baffled look.

"My mouth has no limitations," she said.

Did she say that out loud, he thought.

"You do realize you're going to lose this challenge, correct," she said.

"We'll see," he said.

"One more thing, did you want me to print this out for you," she said.

"Sure thanks," he said.

"One, second … here you go, please read it to the students. I hear the kids, coming in," she said.

"Thanks again," he said.

"Have a great day and remember, stay positive and let me guess … Keep up the Motiv'Plication," he interjected.

"How'd you know, our famous line, you're officially part of the team," she said.

As he approached the door, his heart pounded. He could not wait to meet the students. Slowly, he took a deep breath and turned the door handle. When the students saw him, they were shocked. Casey was never absent. They thought Mr. Wu was a substitute.

"Who you," said Davy.

"I'm Mr. Wu, where my teacher," said Abell.

"I'll explain everything, after the announcements," he said.

"Good morning, Motivators, here are today's announcements," said announcer one.

"This is a reminder, field trip forms will not be collected, after today," said announcer one.

"Remind your parents to attend Super Science Night, we'll be learning about interesting science facts," said announcer two.

"Also, give a warm welcome to Mr. Wu," said announcer two. He chuckled, at the background applause.

"We're one of the first schools to participate in The Teacher Switch Challenge," said announcer one.

"If you see a new man on campus, it's not a stranger, it's Mr. Wu," said announcer one.

"That's all for today's announcements one more thing … let's stand and say our daily quote to motivate," said announcer two.

"Motivate, motivate, it's never too late to motivate!

Save the date, don't be late, never forget to motivate!

Positive things are coming our way,

Negativity … go away!

We will never accept defeat!

The Big Wig Test is under our feet," said announcer two.

"Motivate, motivate, it's never too late to motivate," cheered the students.

"It will be a great day, at We Will Thrive Elementary," said announcer one.

"Hmm …motivators … interesting," said Mr. Wu under his breath.

After the announcements, two students started to argue.

"You and yo mama are" … said Renald.

"Shut up," said Kaz.

"Do not say, shut up," he said.

"He was talk--in bout my mama," said Kaz.

"What's your name," said Mr. Wu.

"My name Renald," he said.

"Don't say anything, about his mother," he said.

"Aight, sir," he said.

The students put their backpacks away and sat down. After the morning announcements, he instructed them to write down the homework assignment,

"My name is Mr. Wu," he said.

"Mr. Who," said Kaz.

"It's Mr. Wu, I'll be your teacher for the rest of the year," he said.

"Mrs. Coper wrote you a message, listen carefully, as I read it," he said.

Good morning,

You all are awesome. I decided to take The Teacher Switch Challenge. It is an unselfish thing. Mr. Wu will be taking over my class for the rest of the year. Please be respectful and remember to practice, everything I taught you. He will give me reports on your behavior and grades. Please make yourselves proud. We have no time for excuses or fights. You'll do great on the Big Wig Test. Give yourself a big hug and remember I care so much about each of you.

Your Teacher,

Mrs. Coper

Certain students looked upset, others were in shock.

Reynold's (one of the students) mouth almost hit the floor.

"I'm guessing this is shocking for you," he said.

"Yes, Imma miss my other teacher, " he said.

Genareece was one of the students who took Casey's absence hard. She was a soft-spoken, withdrawn little girl. He felt so sorry for her.

"I could use the bathroom," she said.

"Sure," he said.

As she got up, tears rolled down her cheeks. She remained in the restroom for the next fifteen minutes, crying. He allowed her time to recuperate.

"Your teacher left information about all of you for me to read and I have the seating chart that tells me if you are where you are supposed to be," he said.

After he informed the students of the chart, four got up and went to their assigned seats.

"What she said, about me," said Kaz.

"We won't talk about it, now," he said.

There was no time to waste, they needed to get ready for The Big Wig Test. During the remainder of the day, students tried their hardest to adjust to Mr. Wu's teaching style. He did not have a warm and funny personality(like Casey), but his delivery was remarkable. They understood the writing process and were grateful for him chunking information. After lunch, he was informed a meeting would be held(during his planning period) about testing and the new behavioral matrix details. The teachers were not receptive to it. They were asked to implement it, before contacting support staff/administration to deal with any issues. There was concern with the high number of referrals and repetitive offenses causing the same students to remain in the office. Thankfully, it was time for dismissal.

"So, you survived day one," she said.

"I did more than survive, the students learned so much," he said.

"Great, let's hope it shows on The Big Wig," she said.

Mr. Wu hoped these kids were good test-takers. The baseline scores he saw were not the highest. Certain students are receptive and display knowledge on content independent of the test pressure. Others do not work well under the same circumstances.

In all, his first day went well.

Lesson One

Good afternoon and welcome back, " she said.

The students look shocked she was still there.

"Let me explain something to you, fighting is not an option, in this classroom. During this period, you will fill out this form and sign it. If I catch any of you, fighting or instigating, you will be written up and removed. Raise your hand, if you hear me," she said.

They raised their hands, in silence. "Now, we're going to read through this agreement, together," she said.

I_____, will not instigate(try to start an argument/fight), while my teacher is trying to explain important information to myself/classmates. This information will help me become a Senior and get into college/technical school, eventually. The steps I plan on taking to become a senior

are_____

_____

_____

_____.Whenever

I instigate an argument/fight it makes those steps, next to impossible

because_____

_____

_____

The reasons I come to school are not only to use the restroom, eat lunch and go to study hall. They

are_____

_____ _____. Disrespect is not a pastime, it is a choice. When I disrespect others, I am disrespecting myself, automatically. Today, I see myself, in a new way. I do not need to like everyone, but I owe them respect, especially if they have not said or done anything to disrespect me. Fighting solves nothing. This event will not be tolerated by any teacher, at The Best High School. By signing this agreement, I understand being removed from a classroom/getting suspended/getting arrested are bad choices for me. If I am not in class, I am not learning. Bad decisions will make passing tests and eventually graduating hard.

Trying my best is what I should expect from myself. My dreams, goals, and visions can all be accomplished.

Signature

_____

Date _____

Casey spent the class period going over each portion of the agreement. The students took responsibility for their actions, during the fight. Once details were explained, they reached a new level of understanding. She was happy.

The end of the day finally arrived. She had the same students for all four periods. On certain days, they had double subject periods. It was very interesting.

"Hey, champion, you made it to the end of the day," said Mr. Zee.

"If words and actions don't align, they're trash," she said.

"Wow, was that a recent post," he said.

"Actually … yes," she said. The duo laughed, as they walked to her classroom.

"This is a lot of stuff, you moving in," he said.

"Maybe," she said.

They brought the bags upstairs and started opening the supplies, full of items that read inspirational messages. Mr. Zee could not stop reading, them.

"Don't fumble Your Future, Winners Work Wisely, Dreams Drag Tired Feet …," he said.

"Did you know, I came up with those quotes," she said. As he read each quote, he became intrigued.

"The theme of my room rests on one of my favorite quotes, Dreams Drag Tired Feet," she

said.

"Hmm… Dreams Drag Tired Feet," he said.

"I like it, what does that mean," he said.

"It means … motivation comes from dreams you're trying to attain, despite how tired you are, the promise of dreams coming true, inspires you to keep pushing," she said.

"Nice, you related to a famous poet, by chance," he said.

"Don't be extra, could you grab the cloud paper," she said.

"Sure, you planning on decorating, in those shoes," he said.

"What's wrong with my shoes," she said.

"Um … normal people don't decorate, in high heels," he said.

"I guess you aren't talking to me," she said.

"Who else is here," he said.

"I strive to be exceptional, on purpose, Exhibit A(my heels) prove it," she said.

"Okay, Judge Coper, I guess you wear them everywhere," he said.

"Yes, the beach, the shower, in the rain, you know the normal places," she said.

He started laughing, uncontrollably.

"You're funny," he said.

"By the way, what's your first name again," she said.

"It's Zed," he said.

He stared into her eyes. There was an awkward silence, again.

Clearing her throat she broke eye contact.

"Pass me the sunshine yellow paper, please," she said.

"Sure … whatever you need," he said.

She placed each decoration on the wall, perfectly. He admired how precise she was. While decorating they laughed and talked, about the protest and discussed funny moments(about teaching). It was surprising since she met him, recently. It felt good to relate to an educator that could relate to her experiences.

"Oh … no, what time is it," she said.

"About 8:00 … why," he said.

"I need to go, my husband is waiting for me," she said. Quickly she gathered her belongings and rushed to the staircase.

"Slow down, you don't want to trip," he said.

"Walking in heels is second nature," she said.

"Wow a woman with many talents," he said.

"Well, thanks for your help, the room looks gorgeous," he said.

"I agree," she said.

"Let me walk you to your car," she said.

They walked downstairs and parted ways. Casey was grateful for his help. Immediately, questionable thoughts ran across her mind. She remembered her mother's advice. She had a wonderful husband. All she wanted was his support, regarding her passion and career. Nevertheless, it was no justification for entertaining thoughts for Satan. She was petrified to have another argument with her husband. She made it home, safe and sound. Slowly, she turned the front door handle, unprepared for the unknown.

"Where were you," he said.

"Where I was," she said.

"Play with me not," he said.

"Oh my gosh, record yourself and press play, it's the same question—all the time," she said.

"I don't feel like arguing," he said.

"I don't know, how much longer your career gets to take the passenger seat, while I ride in the back," he said.

"Wow, let's not do this," she said.

"How about a vacation to decompress," he said.

"A vacation that's your great suggestion," she said.

"Salaries, security policies, and the lives of students are in limbo and you want to take a vacation," she said.

"Paradise will have to wait, you know why," she said.

"Wow oh wow, I'm going to bed," he said.

"I'll be joining you soon," she said.

"Let me guess, you need to spend time with your second husband, the almighty laptop," he said. She ignored the comment and watched her husband walk, upstairs. She whipped out her computer and opened her email.

Mr. Wu replied.

Good afternoon,

Sorry for the late response, my first day went well. The office staff threw a welcome breakfast for me. Some of these fourth graders are big. I played your explanation video, about the switch and why you had to do it. One of the students went to the restroom and started to cry. She is attached to you. Elementary teachers sure put in work. We had a meeting, during planning, today. It was about testing and how to handle disciplinary issues; the administration provided a behavioral matrix. I guess many students are being sent to the principal's office. Some of your former fourth graders need their reality show. I am so sorry to read about the fight. Are you okay? Unfortunately, traumatizing events are the norm, at The Best High. I pray the fights decrease. Your positivity is admirable. Let's continue emailing each other with updates.

Sincerely,

Lyde Wu

Powerful Educator

We Will Thrive, Elementary School

Untold Truth brings a Tragic End-Lyde Wu

She was sad to read her students missed her, so much but she refused to back out of The Teacher Switch. Ms. Zebedee and the administrators were right. The best option for information, the students were not in a person, it would be emotional. She was so happy Mr. Wu was changing his outlook on educators, who teach elementary school.

Ding! Ding!

Hey, girly,

It's your old friend. What's up with you? I hope everything is fine. It's been a while. Text me, when you can. Love Ava.

Casey ignored the text. She did not need anyone in her circle, who would not support the Teacher Switch. She would reply, eventually. She closed her computer, went upstairs, and hopped into bed. She was so grateful for her husband, They had ups and downs but ultimately, she knew his intentions were good.

She slowly caressed his face.

"I still and always will love you," he said.

"I still and always will love you, too," she said.

Four
Two for Five

"Yo! I got two for five from Favors, yestaday," said Lanson.

"For real, where," said Sanrell."

"Everything went down, in da bathroom," he said.

"For real, man Favors talented," said Sanrell.

"Them two for five deals, be priceless," he said.

"I always be missin da good stuff," he said.

"That's yo skip-pin school behind," he said.

"If yo lazy, lanky behind would slither out da bed, you could get some too," he said.

Students who use their pidgin always threw Casey off. Certain educators were happy to make it to the next period, without a fight. She was not one of them. She wondered what the students were talking about, hopefully, it wasn't drugs. Their words caused her thought indigestion. She searched for answers but came up short.

"Don't forget to complete your test prep. packets, by the end of the week," she said.

"You know the drill, don't even try, turning them in, without a name and date," she said.

"Yes, Mrs. C.," said the class.

"You're dismissed, have a great day," she said.

"Da'Zay," she said.

"Yes," she said.

"Do you know, who the boys were talking about," she said.

She took a long breath and looked over her shoulder, in paranoia.

"Yes, but please don't say I told you," she said.

"Please tell me, I won't say anything," she said.

"Well, this girl a freshman, she be doin nasty thangs wit boys for money," she said.

As she continued, the shock of the news caused her pupils to dilate. How in the world, was this reality? She could not face the horror of a fifteen-year-old girl, diminishing her self-worth to five dollars.

"Who's this girl, what's her name," she said.

"I ain't no snitch," she said.

"No one will know you told me," she said.

"If this get out my rep. gonna be trash," she said.

"That's why I'm committed to protecting you," she said.

"For real dough, they gonna say I'm the snitch witch," she said.

"I changed the second word, cuz I respect you," she said.

"Don't you have little sisters," she said.

"Yes," she said.

"What if one of them offered sexual favors for money," she said.

"Nah, it ain't gonna happen," she said.

"Why would it be impossible for them—because, they too good," she interjected.

"Anyone has the potential to make good or bad choices," she said.

"Um… I don't know, about that," she said.

"This girl is confused and needs help. No one is better than anyone else," she said.

"But what she did"—Quickly, she cut her off.

"Everyone deserves the chance to be saved," she said.

"I'm going to ask one last time," who is this girl," she said.

"Aight, her name Lyric," she said.

"Do you know, how often this happens," she said.

"I heard she was supposed to be doin three guys, after school, today," she said.

"What," she said.

"You know what doin, mean," she said.

"I'm not that out of the loop," she said.

"Aight," she said.

"I appreciate your honesty," she said.

"Let me write you a pass to your next class," she said.

"Thanks," she said.

"Remember, people, can't find out, who told you," she said.

"I would never betray your trust, one last thing," she said.

"Yes," she said.

"Thanks for your help," she said.

"Anytime, well, maybe not anytime," she said.

As she shut the door, tears mounted in her eyes, forming a sea of sorrow on her desk. She demanded to get answers. What detrimental occurrence/s caused this student's self-worth to equal a negative number? First, how is self-worth diminished to performing sexual acts for five dollars? Next, how do certain fast-food meals, value more than a person's perception of their body, mind, and soul? Where was the staff, while this occurred? Lastly, how could she help raise this girl's self-worth? Her thoughts made her head pulsate. She looked up, at the clock, dismissal was in three hours. She had to do something.

"Ms. Tooks, I need to leave, early," she said. Two teachers looked at her, in astonishment.

"Why did you come bursting in here, everything okay," she said.

"I'll be fine. I just need the rest of the afternoon to get myself together," she said.

"Alrighty, just sign out," she said.

After she signed out, she raced to her car. Her hands shook, as she put her belongings in the trunk. She wondered what Lyric looked like. She braced herself for the worst and headed toward building ten. The bell just rang and the hallway was flooded with freshmen.

"Excuse me, my name is Mrs. Coper," she said.

"Mrs. Fine that's what you mean," said student one.

They were brazen. What happened to shy freshmen, who were petrified to speak, she thought. Locating this young impressionable girl was her priority. She ignored the comment.

"I teach juniors, in the upper school building," she said.

"Wish you was my teacher," said student two.

"Do you know, a student named Lyric," she said. They turned to each other, smirked, and laughed.

"Yeah we know her real good," said student three.

Their reaction made her insides twist. She tried hard, not to show emotion. These students did not view Lyric, as a person. It was a harsh but sad reality.

"She talented know all the tricks," said student four.

"Where can I find her," she said.

"This time, she be outside," said student five.

"Mrs. Cooper," said student five.

"It's Coper," she said.

"My fault, my name Lo, imma help you find her," he said.

"Thanks so much," she said.

She noticed he knew, Lyric's pattern of behavior. He expressed she would need a prep. talk before she met Casey. She was apprehensive to speak with adults(especially teachers).

"I just want to make sure, she ain't doin some-thin crazy," he said.

"I appreciate you caring so much," she said.

"Aight she gotta be in here, let me keep lookin and find her, so I could let her know, she ain't gonna be in trouble," he said.

"Sure, I'll wait, here," she said.

The second bell rang, and students started heading to their classes. She noticed the time was going and Lo still had not returned. She suspected something strange was going on. Casey decided to search the annex herself. She checked the outside field, cafeteria, restroom, band room, and any other place, students would go to skip class. Casey was running out of options. She was not familiar with the freshman building. As Casey returned to where the search started, she heard noises, coming from inside the restroom. Slowly, she opened the door to find a girl with her skirt up on the bathroom sink and the "so-called" helpful student(Lo), engaging in intercourse.

"What in the world, are you doing," she exclaimed.

The girl's face turned pale and she darted into the restroom stall.

"Miss … miss … Please don't say nothin, I play ball," he said.

"You lied," she exclaimed.

"Sorry … she my girl, dough," he said.

"No, she's not, you need help," she said.

"She is Miss, for real," he said.

"Lo, you hit an all-time low," she said.

"Don't say nothin, I play ball," he said.

"How could you, get out," she said.

She did not want Lyric's first impression of her to be scary. Unfortunately, the action of the "helpful student" caught her off guard. She wanted to believe Lo had Lyric's best interest in mind. She felt betrayed and sickened, at the thought of how many other times, this occurred.

"Lyric," she said. She locked herself in the bathroom stall and stood on the toilet seat.

There was no response. She noticed Lyric gasping for air.

"My name's Casey … um … Mrs. Coper," she said.

"Shhh," she kept taking deep breaths.

"I'm new here, I teach English to juniors," she said.

The heavy breathing persisted.

"Could you come out and speak with me, this is a no-judgment zone" she said.

"Miss," she said.

"Yes," she said.

"I can't breathe, I got asthma," she said.

"Do you have an inhaler," she said.

"Yes, it fell out my purse," she said.

She fell to her knees scrambling to find it, in front of the rust-stained wall, below the sink, next to a battered notebook. Quickly, she rolled it, under the stall. She was relieved to hear her breath in deeply, as she used the inhaler.

"I'll be right back," she said.

"Could you come out of the stall? I have some water for you," she said.

"You goin get me in trouble," she said.

"Never, please come out of the stall," she said.

"I don't trust watchu sayin," she said.

"It's important for you to drink water, after using an inhaler," she said.

Lyric was not buying a word she said. She realized being candid was the only way to get through her reluctance.

"I'm asthmatic, trust me …your health is more important than what I saw," she said.

Slowly, she pulled the door latch back and came out of the stall. Lyric was 5'9' with smooth cocoa skin and auburn ringlet curls that fell just beneath her shoulder; she had a striking appearance. She could not understand, how such a beautiful girl saw herself in a negative light.

"Ain't nobody care-in bout me dying," she said.

"Real teachers like me care," she said.

"Why you lookin for me, anyway," she said.

"I'm thinking about launching a freshman-middle school peer writing program for students and teachers," she said.

She never thought of what to say, in case Lyric asked why she was looking for her. On such short notice that was the best excuse.

"I can help with your homework and understanding school policies," she said.

The program was fabricated, but her motives were authentic.

"None of my teachers ain't never cared, don't nobody care," she said.

"I can't speak for other teachers but I care," she said.

"Teachers ain't no angels, stop tryin to act like you give a damn," she said.

"I give more than that," she said.

"Could you pick your head up, and look at me," she said.

"You don't need to look at me," she said.

"Why wouldn't I want to look at such a beautiful girl," she said.

"Ain't nothin to look at," she said.

"If you don't feel worth looking at, how about looking at me," she said.

"What," she said.

"I didn't put lipstick on, but I don't think my face looks that bad," she said.

Lyric smirked and slowly lifted her head. She saw beauty, in her brokenness.

"That wasn't bad, was it," she said.

"Naw, guess not," she said.

"Okay, let's grab a bite to eat and talk, at the coffee shop, around the corner," she said.

"I just want to go home," she said.

"It'll be fun," she said.

"Aight, if it'll stop yo nagg-in," she said.

"Great, let's get your stuff, off the floor," she said.

They left the restroom and headed to the coffee shop. Thus, her mission to find who Lyric was, amongst the hurt and pain, began.

Coffee with Tiers

Although the coffee shop was less than two minutes away, the walk seemed endless.

"Are you okay," she said.

"Yeah," she said.

Her taunting silence was louder than the unaddressed awkwardness, in the restroom. She decided to save her questions for later. She pondered how to approach her. Finally, the two arrived.

Upon entrance, Casey glanced at the clock. It was 3:30; school just got dismissed. She was determined to keep Lyric from sexually exploiting herself. Lyric kept tugging at her short skirt. Although it resembled a strapless bra, she needed support, not another critic.

"Welcome to Cough up the Coffee, what can I get you," said the high-spirited waitress.

"Order whatever you want," she said.

"You ain't gotta buy me nothin," she said.

No one offered anything to her without an open-leg contribution.

"Well, I guess we'll make the customers behind us upset," she said.

"People can't stand wait-in," she said.

Lyric gave her a confused look.

"Could you hurry it up," said a nasty customer.

"Yeah," said another customer.

"These people look like they need coffee, hurry up and order," she said.

"Aight, I'll get a blueberry muffin," she said.

"Sounds delicious; I'll have the same with a small coffee," she said.

"Two blueberry muffins and one small coffee coming right up," said the waitress.

"Please have a seat; I'll bring your order, once it's ready," she said.

"Awesome," she said.

"You don't need to pull down your skirt, I'm not judging you," she said.

"Yeah right, why we here," she said.

Casey noticed she had two extra-large wrist bands. She wondered when those came back in style.

"I want to know, your story, " she said.

"Why ... I would say some-thin, I don't know if you real," she said.

"Because I'm telling you, I'm for real," she said.

"Last time I told my story, I got put in the foster house, where three men had they way wit me," she said.

She took a deep breath and braced herself for the worst.

"I don't have all the answers, but I would never do anything to betray your trust," she said.

"You don't know, me," she said.

"I want to," she said.

"Why you care, so much," she said.

"I'm sorry to interrupt, enjoy," said the waitress.

"Thank you," she said.

"We went over this, in the restroom. I care because you are worth it," she said.

"If I'm so worth it, why you keep lookin at the clock," said Lyric.

"It's something personal; I apologize," she said.

Lyric had no clue, her time fixation revolved around her.

"I ain't worth nothin," she said.

"Eventually you'll understand, self-worth is priceless, " she said.

"Nope, everything got a price," she said.

"We need to talk, about what I saw," she said.

She hung her head down, avoiding eye contact.

"If any other teacher walked into that restroom, the ending would've been different," she said.

"I know," she said.

"Please, open up to me," she said.

"Aight Mrs. Nosey, here go my story," she said. Casey braced herself for what she would hear.

"My step-daddy was my first man," she said.

The first man she thought. Was she referring to an intimate partner? Quickly, she refocussed.

"When I was real little, he always pulled me on his lap and made me play with his zipper," she said.

Casey's skin started to crawl.

"Eventually playing went to bang-in," she said.

The words rolled off her tongue like they made the situation easier to digest. She could not believe this was the reality of the beautiful yet broken young woman who was sitting in front of her. She continued to listen, as Lyric poured her heart out.

"My step daddy taught me, ain't nothin free and took care of me and my mama since I was two," she said.

"How's that taking" —she caught herself. Lyric didn't need a judge or jury. She needed to feel free.

"I apologize ... please continue," she said.

"When I was seven, bet I knew more about bang-in, than you know now, no disrespect," she said.

Her heart pounded so hard, she thought the pressure would cause a heart attack.

"I still love him, more than all my other step-daddies," she said.

"It's what we did ... now ... it's what I do," she said.

This was no useful trade. The behavior turned into a sick form of currency. She was seeking validation, at an early age. Her actions make sense.

"When my mama would work late, he came in my room and would touch on me. At first, it was just touch-in but then we started bang-in," she said.

Bang-in she thought it had to be a sexual term. What if it was more than that? Was this a trafficking term? She did not want to ask a lot of questions but was puzzled.

"You know what bang-in mean, right," she said.

She tried to hold back tears, as Lyric asked the question. She was familiar with the term.

"I think so, it means sex ... right," she said.

"Yeah—seven-year-old girls ain't pose to worry about gettin banged.

"That's true," she said.

"I still love my stepdaddy," she said.

She recalled reading several books about victims turning perpetrators into gods. Why did this happen? It seems strange to merge abuse with happiness. Sometimes the mind doesn't provide detailed explanations of our feelings. Without a whole self-image, the concept of abuse is distorted. Hurting turns into a way to help a victim. Casey would hear about these scenarios and not fathom anyone feeling so low they could no longer tell the difference between good and bad intentions. Sadly, the reality we experience is what matters. If people took the time to understand the perspective of others experiencing pain, coming up with realistic solutions would be more of a reality.

"I would let him bang me, and he would leave," said Lyric.

"When we was together, it was like I left my body and would look at the both of us, from the other side of the room," she said.

Although she tried to mask it, Lyric noticed she looked uncomfortable.

"I ain't like talk-in about this cause don't nobody understand, my step daddy still love me.

How often did she repeat this lie to justify the actions of a pedophile, she thought.

"One night, my mama came home and saw us, in the room," she beat my behind and begged my stepdaddy to stay," she said.

Stay, she was screaming on the inside. Why should he stay but again, she needed to train her brain to empathize. Was this her upbringing? No! It did not mean this young woman deserved judgment. She kept telling herself it takes more effort to try and sympathize than judge.

"My stepdaddy said, he was leavin. I cried my eyes out when he did," she said.

"Did you blame yourself," she said.

"Yeah ... mama said, it was my fault I was a fast little fish. She said I was teas-in him, maybe I was," she said.

Or maybe your mother has no soul, she thought. What kind of mother subjects their child to such horrific circumstances? She made a promise to herself not to judge Lyric but should she grant her mother the same allowance? Maybe the same things happened to her? How often do we judge the parent/s of victims, without thinking this could be a twisted cycle that leads back—generations?

She came close to her face with sympathy in her eyes.

"No, a child can't tease an adult," she said.

She wanted her to believe the words but breaches in her mentality would not allow it. Several horrific circumstances brought her to this point, it would take more than a few phrases and consoling looks to change her mind.

"You were only seven. Don't you dare, blame yourself," she said.

"Missus, you know that's the last day, I cried.

"It's healthy to cry, I understand what you went through was painful," she said.

"After he left, my mama got me a new step-daddy," she said.

"He wasn't so nice when he first got wit, my mama," she said.

Wasn't so nice were not words she would use, she thought. She made light of the abuse to cope that was the only way to survive. Several children run to their parent/s for protection and are told to stop being dramatic, it is unfortunate.

"You still listening," she said.

"Yes, I apologize, I'm taking everything, in," she said.

"One night, he got drunk and came in my room," she said.

What type of cycle was this? Once was not enough. How did she survive and function?

"After he was done bang-in me, he beat me, until I ain't know where I was," she said.

Lyric paused and took a deep breath. As Casey listened to her story, she felt sick. It was difficult to allow her to proceed, but she had no choice, she was all in.

"I have to ask, in the middle of everything, how did you not lose your mind," she said.

"My first-grade teacher taught me to go to a vacation spot, in my head, when life get hard," she said.

The suggestion made sense. She knew her teacher had no clue, she was referring to how to escape molestation/abuse. The suggestion became a defense strategy that saved her from having a nervous breakdown.

"When he started punch-in me, I went to the beach or sometimes Paris, in my head, until I blacked out," she said.

The room was becoming dim. This made no sense. Why couldn't she bring another life into existence with her husband? Why was Lyric's mom granted such a blessing, while she experienced fertility treatment side effects and major depressive states? She was numb.

"I still blackout, some days, sometimes just sit-in and stare-in, look at the clock and hours go by," she said.

She related to the feeling. During fertility treatments, she would do the same thing. Rye would try to stop her from disengaging from society, as a result of depression but there were days, he gave in and watched movies for hours while holding her. One month, that was the only activity they did, each week. Although their pain came from different sources, it was a strong connection that strengthened as the depth of Lyric's story increased.

"The next day, I went to school, and the teacher saw marks on me, she asked me if something was wrong," she said.

"Oh," she said.

"I said, no," she said.

"Mama always told me bad things happen to little girls, who run they mouth," she said.

Why do we protect toxic people? She defended a woman whose title should be demolished. How could she be blessed with such a great daughter and stomp her self-esteem to the floor? She was subjected to a cycle of hatred. Situations like this made her irate. If Lyric was her daughter, she would protect and love her. She would know what love was. True love is not about feelings that fluctuate or using others for self-gain. Love is constant. She needed assurance of commitment and security. Understanding no matter how much she messed up, she would have a mother, who would support every attempt for her to be a better person.

Although it was difficult, she continued to listen.

"Next thing I know, I'm in some lady office tryin to tell me, I'm goin to some safe place wit. ops," she said.

"Please don't be upset at your teacher. She was doing what anyone would do, protect her student," she said.

"Oh ... for real how ... they took me to a foster home, the same night," three strange men was bang-in me," she said.

She was quick to comment, not realizing the story may cause her to sink into a depressive abyss. I need to shut up and listen—she thought to herself.

"How the system care and take me from my mama and stepdaddy to let three men have they way wit me. Ain't the foster house pose to be safe," she said.

She held her head down and looked the other way. Lyric was right. The system failed her by making a promise, it could not uphold. This goes back to people meaning well but doing the opposite. She tried to stop the tears from falling, but they streamed down her cheek, leaving traces of sadness and despair. She had to tell her, everything.

"I'm so sorry, the system let you down but I won't," she said.

Rolling her eyes she was reluctant to believe her words. She pulled out the tattered journal, she saw earlier, in the restroom.

"Anyways you wanted to know, so I told you, now what," she said.

"Well, ... what about the writing club," she said.

"What about it," she said.

"Is that something you would be interested in," she said.

"Well,... I love to write. My whole life is in my outlet," she said.

"You mean your journal," she said.

"I say outlet. My first-grade teacher gave it to me," she said.

She looked down and noticed it had several tears and stains on the outside.

"I know what you think-in," she said.

"What am I thinking," she said.

"My outlet old worn out but I won't ever trash it," she said.

"No, I get it, the sentimental value outweighs the way it looks," she said.

"You right ... it was under my pillow when my stepdaddies would come in my room; it saved me," she said.

She noticed Lyric had a strange blank stare and was completely disengaged, during parts of the conversation, and then she would connect, again.

"Lyric," she said.

"I'm here," she replied.

"Were you having sex with Lo for money, earlier," she said.

"I do, what I got to do. The funny thing is, I don't be feel-in like bang-in, most of the time, I just do it. The bigger I got I figure use-in what my stepdaddy taught me would be my job," she said.

Of course not. Due to her experiences, she had a misguided mentality about her worth. Physically, she was a mule for her mother to get/keep horrible partners. Lyric needed to dismantle and replace her negative self-concept and understand there is no price tag for her body. Casey had a hard decision to make, she could refer Lyric to the guidance counselor/social worker or maintain the vow to keep everything she disclosed, private.

"You're an inspiration, the things you survived are incredible. Don't put a price tag on your greatness," she said.

"What I should do, when I need money," she said.

"You could come by my room to help me out," she said.

"Help wit what," she said.

"I'll allow you to earn fifty to one hundred dollars, every week," she said.

"You gonna give me that much to help you," she said.

"I'm a woman of my word. Besides, I could help you, start the peer writing program," she said.

"What's it about," she said.

"There are so many students, who share the same story, but feel they have no outlet," she said.

"I could help them," she said.

"I agree. They need someone, who can relate to help with writing and mentorship," she said.

"That ain't nothin," she said.

"There's only one condition," she said.

"Ah ... I knew it, what," she said.

"No, wait ... listen, you can no longer exchange sexual favors for money," she said.

The uneven exchange of demeaning sexual occurrences, she was addicted to needed to stop. She lightly rested her hand on top of Lyric's hand. How could she convey true feelings, regarding the worth of such a unique flower?

"Do you promise," she said.

She looked long and hard, at the half-eaten muffin, on the table, before making her commitment. She never thought, being used would eventually become useless. There was nothing to lose but the gut-wrenching void, present after every sexual encounter. She knew how to perform sexual acts, but was unsure, why she did not expect more, of herself.

"Aight, but why teachers be make-in us write to punish us," she said.

"I don't know, that's a great question," she said.

"That's so stupid," she said.

"It would be bad if teachers think make-in me write is cuz I did some-thin bad, lol" she said.

"I agree 100 percent," she said.

"I ain't never read nothin, from my outlet to nobody, but I like you," she said.

"I feel honored," she said.

"You want to hear a poem," she said.

"Of course," she said.

"Okay, this poem is called Present but Not Here," she said.

Present but Not Here

**Lyric ... here, Josie ... here
Does my teacher notice, the deep thoughts in my mind,
or is she blind?
I'm present but not here,
My soul is full of despair.
My body is the shell,
I wish I didn't know, so well.
Last night my stepdaddy came in,
I begged him not to commit an unlawful sin.
My mind wants to focus on math,
but bruises on my arm lead me down a different path.
I'm present but not here,
Every day I want to disappear.
My teacher keeps telling me,
To display respect and responsibility.
She says, I never do my homework,**

her words often cause a tear-jerk.
If she only knew, how my will and pain collide,
Maybe she could help my pain subside.
In the end, I could only count on me, to end this horrific tragedy.
Does she notice how sad my expressions look? Or am I just another character, from a textbook? Hopefully, the day will come,
When anger + anguish no longer equals my emotional sum.
Until that day finally appears,
I remain present but not here.
by Lyric Casanova—Royal Authoress

She could not believe, what she heard. Lyric's English was far from proper; however, her written expression was superb.

"That was such a beautiful poem, " she said.

"Naw for real," she said.

"Royal Authoress that's fancy," she said. She looked down and smiled.

"Would you like to be president of the freshman writing club," she said.

"Missus, I know ... I be missing class, sometimes but dis school don't got that," she said.

"You're right, but that doesn't mean we can't start one," she said.

"I ain't never started nothin, in my life but trouble," she said.

"Perfect now's a great time to start an innovative trend," she said.

She stared at her for a while.

"Aight, if you think I can," she said.

"You can do anything, you set your mind to," she said.

"Missus you aight," she said.

"Just aight," she said.

She started to chuckle.

"Mrs. C. don't talk, like that," she said.

"Sorry, I got caught up, in the moment," she said.

"You funny, I like yo rings," she said.

Lyric traced her engagement ring and wedding band. She was mesmerized by them. The concept of people committing to each other intrigued her.

"I hate when kids be call-in teachers, Miss, when they married. You know the history of the word, Missus," she said.

"I'm not sure," she said.

"You lying, but it's all good," she said.

"In one of my books I learned the difference, between Miss and Missus, she said.

"Okay ... go on," she said.

"You introduced yourself, as Mrs. Coper, so you should be called Mrs. C.," she said.

"That's true, I did," she said.

"Since the seventeenth century the word was split, why would I say miss, when you married," she said.

She was not dealing with an average student. Normally, high school students do not want to know about etymology, they go along with norms. They continued to talk and laugh. Casey was enjoying every second they spoke.

"Mrs. C., it's five o'clock," she said.

"Really," she said.

"You been watch-in the clock, the whole time," she said.

"No, I'm thrilled, aside from the time, I reached another level," she said.

"Instead of Missus, I'm Mrs. C., yup I'm moving up, in the world," she said.

"I like you, but you out there," she said.

"As opposed to being in there," she said.

"Oh my gosh, you goofy," she said.

"Thanks for the muffin and everything," she said.

"It was my pleasure," she said.

"Do you have a ride home," she said.

"Yeah, I'm good," she said.

"Okay, please don't forget, our deal, I'll see you, after school, tomorrow," she said.

"Aight," she said.

Casey left the coffee shop full of a new perspective and a major sense of accomplishment. On her way home, she received a text. I miss you. Rye was making a funny expression, holding a taco. Immediately, she started to laugh. He always had a way of indirectly cheering her up. After a long day, she arrived home.

"What in the world is going on," she said.

"You're what's going on, ADORATION," he said.

"Never say that, again, lovesicle," she said.

"Don't ruin things, I'm in my zone," he said.

"Your zone," she said. She couldn't help but smile. He was trying so hard to make this dinner perfect.

"That's my girl," he said.

"Here's your dinner, sit and let's talk," he said.

"I will but I only have fifteen minutes," she said.

"Trying is a new pastime for me," he said. This dinner took a while and it is very special," he said.

"Here we go," she said.

"Don't you remember what today is," he said.

"Yes, it's Thursday, December 18," she said.

"Exactly, the day we went on our first date," he said.

"That's so sweet," she said.

"Yes, I guess it is. Happy first date anniversary," he said.

"Happy first-date anniversary to you too," she said.

"Out of all the girls, I dated, you melted my heart," he said.

"Those other cupcakes never stood a chance," she said.

"I still love you and always will, love you," he said.

"I still love you and always will, love you," she said.

"Okay, I need to work on these lesson plans and pop open my abundance of emails," she said.

I'm practicing being understanding," he said.

"You'll be happy to know, my other husband[the laptop] will be in the other room, tonight," she said.

"Oh boy, the whole night," he said.

"Listen before you go upstairs, I met a special girl today," she said.

"Great, is she a new girl in your class," he said.

"No, she's a freshman," she said.

"They're involving freshman in the challenge, now," he said.

"No, this is independent of The Teacher Switch," she said.

"Okay, cool," he said.

"Tell her your husband[a cool insurance banking agent], says hello," he said.

"You okay," he said.

Casey stared out in space, processing information, from earlier. How could someone hurt their daughter, like that? She was in disbelief. She needed to be the role model, Lyric never had.

"Yes," she said.

"You can go on upstairs, now," she said.

"Should I fetch my toy and roll over, too," he said.

"Go please, I need to get work done," she said.

"Okay, don't forget to eat," he said.

Mr. Wu's Rewind

Mr. Wu could not believe the day, he had. The students were amazing. Although they were a tough little bunch, he enjoyed interacting with them. His favorite time of day was during Q. & A. The students were so engaged. Other than a few snags, appeared to comprehend the strategies and skills, he taught. After a great morning lesson, he sat down to run an update of the student progress report, based on the school's academic monitoring program. He took a sip of coffee and logged in. When the scores popped up, Mr. Wu spit his coffee, all over the desk. How in the world, did the scores only increase two percent? Just then, he remembered Mrs. Batet's words, "It's one thing to be good at a subject, it's another thing to help students get on your level." He needed to try new strategies to help these students. Teaching fourth grade was a lot more intricate than he gave Casey credit for. It was pity party time. While in a low state, he decided to write her an email. It read as follows:

Good afternoon,

I just received disturbing news, about my students' scores. This is so depressing. How in the world did this happen to me? I feel like a failure. This pity party is no fun. Teaching fourth grade is a humbling experience. Aside from thinking about the scores of my high school students, I am having a great time. I'm giving these fourth graders everything. Their personalities keep me engaged and the excitement on their faces is my motivation to keep pushing. How are things going with you? Are the students okay?

Regards,

Lyde Wu

Powerful Educator

We Will Thrive Elementary School

Untold Truth Brings a Tragic End-Lyde Wu

Good evening,

I just saw your email. Sorry for the late response, don't come down too hard on yourself, midyear scores can be challenging. A lot of times, the content the students are assessed on, has not been covered. You still have time, before the Bigwig Test. You are correct, pity parties are no fun, so get up, dust yourself off and keep teaching.:-) You have a great group of kids. Try using all the academic computer programs, during independent learning time. Also, use my chart to target specific learning goals, accordingly. Here is the update on your former students, they are amazing. I am so thankful for this opportunity. Although they have moments of laziness, overall their performance is increasing. Keep up the Motiv'Plication; stay in touch.

Sincerely,

Casey Coper

Phenomenal Teacher

The Best High School

-Loveless learning is lifeless learning.-Casey Coper

After replying to his email, she thought about how the new information would sway the votes of many teachers, who felt intermediate teachers did not have many challenges. The outcome of the meeting would be interesting. As she worked on her lesson plans, she thought about Lyric and wondered if she was okay that night. She was such a special girl. She didn't have a child of her own. Lyric could help take her mind off of trying to conceive. Finally, the lesson plans were done. She went upstairs, put the laptop in the guest room, took a shower, and headed to bed.

"Where's hubby number two," he said.

"I left him, in the other room," she said.

"Oh, you were serious, about getting sleep," he said.

"Yes, I wouldn't lie," she said.

As she made herself comfortable, he brushed a tendril of hair, from her face and rested his hand, behind her neck.

"I still and always will love you," he said.

"I still and always will love you," she said.

As she fell drifted off, visions of the conversation with Lyric engulfed her mind. She wondered how they would impact each other.

Five
Attention

The next morning, Casey overflowed with excitement and curiosity.

As positivity rushed through her veins, she burst into the principal's office. Ignoring the two bystanders, giving her funny looks.

"Is Principal Waggenport available," she said.

"Whoa, that coffee must be good," said the onlookers.

"Um ... sure, let me just wave my magic wand and make the three district officials who came in unannounced disappear," she said.

"I love you too," she said.

"In all seriousness, he just went into the meeting," she said.

"When do you think he'll be finished," she said.

"Never mind, I'll just come back, during planning," she said.

"I have no clue," she said.

"Okay, you do that," she said.

"Ms. Tooks," she said.

"Yes," she said.

"I dropped my pen, could you get it for me," she said.

"Why not," she said.

Rolling her eyes she bent down to find it.

"I don't see anything," she said.

"Never mind, I'm off to class," she said.

As she left the office, Ms. Tooks noticed a gift card to her favorite coffee shop. Attached was a note that read—I am so grateful for you. No one ever showed appreciation for what she did. This gesture was one of the kindest things, anyone did for her. Quickly, she realized, how nasty she acted; she started to tear up. Ms. Tooks knew she needed to work on being less sarcastic. She vowed never to be cruel to anyone, again. Well … at least for a while.

Casey had one more stop to make, before heading to her first class.

"Excuse me," I don't mean to interrupt but could I speak with Lyric," she said.

"Sure," said Mrs. Homes(Lyric's Language Arts Teacher).

"Thanks," she said.

"Good mornin Mrs. C., you stalk-in me, now," she said.

"Not exactly," she said. The duo smiled.

"I just wanted to make sure, we're still on for later," she said.

"Yes, Mrs. C.," she said.

"Okay, sorry to bother you," she said.

"It ain't no bother," she said.

"Thanks for checkin up on me," she said.

"Please come by later," she said.

"You tried to play it off, your stalk-ish ways that's cute," she said.

"Back to class," she said.

"Later," she said.

Casey rushed to her class.

"Good morning," she said.

"Good morning, Mrs. C.," said the students.

Quickly, she wrote the outline of the lesson on the whiteboard.

Lesson: Compare and Contrast__students' choices.

State Standard: HELP.ME.COMPARE&CONTRAST.1.1.

Golden Question: How can I compare and contrast_____, by brainstorming, while working in groups.

Objective: I can compare and contrast subject/s, by activating prior knowledge about_____.

Model: Read the golden question—out loud. Model how to complete a compare/contrast diagram. Explain how to complete the assignment and what is expected, during completion.

Engage: Review the compare/contrast skill, by completing the student-teacher contrast activity/discussion.

Evaluate: Students will demonstrate knowledge of the lesson by_____.

"Today we're going to review what it means to compare and contrast. The golden question is how can I compare/contrast_____, by brainstorming, while working in groups? If you notice there is a blank. I would like you to pick topics to contrast—today," she said.

"Mr. Wu taught you guys how to contrast details. Do you remember," she said.

"Yup," said the class.

"Do the beat," said Lancell.

"Um ... the beat ... what is that," she said.

"Mr. Wu taught us a song to help us remember how to do it," said Garnell.

"Sing y'all," he exclaimed.

"Compare means the same, compare means the same, contrast means different, contrast means different," they were in perfect harmony.

She was impressed with the way Mr. Wu appealed to the individual interests of the students. Several were musically inclined. This method of engagement worked well.

"Very cute, so you guys remember," she said.

"Yes," said the class.

"Great, here is an example, just in case," she said.

"Let's contrast detail/s — - between Smithna and me," she said.

Casey drew a line, down the board on one side stood Smithna and she stood on the other.

"Please draw a line down your paper," she said. As each student followed directions, she monitored their level of interest — through observing.

"Now, by using nice adjectives please contrast, go," she said.

The students had so much to write. After eight minutes she instructed them to put their pencils down.

"Garnell read me a sentence/words that provide a contrast, between Smithna and me," she said.

"Y'all better not try me," she said.

"Don't worry about that," she said.

"You're tall Smithna is short," said Garnell.

"Great job," she said.

"Biren could you provide a contrast, next," she said.

"You wearin Barbie Heels, Smithna wearin sneakers," he said.

"Okay, one more, Rimez," she said.

"Smitha ave blue weave you a natural lady," he said.

"I got my natural hair, dis a protective style," she said.

"A lie she a tell," he said. Everyone laughed.

"Okay that's enough, thanks Smithna, you may take a seat," she said.

"I want you guys to choose what we can compare/contrast and we can work, from there. Each group will need to come up with one topic," she said.

"No dummies better be in my group," said Smithna.

"Excuse me, you know the group rules," she said.

"Sorry," she said.

"Please turn to your groups and talk about it, you have five minutes," she said.

"Flip your We're Done Cups Up when you finish," she said.

"Bang! Bang!

"Mrs. C. Imma get it," said Greater.

"Wait, who is it," she said.

"Mr. Zee you want me to open it," he said.

"Sure," she said.

"Hey, just checkin on you, I had coverage for a little bit," he said.

"Really, who subs are a far memory, since the protest," she said.

"It's Veftel," he said.

"Security is covering your class and you came here," she said.

"Sound like love to me," said Da'Zay.

"Okay, not appropriate and get busy," she said.

"Yeah, you said it best," he said.

"So whatchu up too," he said.

"Teaching," she said.

"Sorry, I meant the class," he said. Some students overheard his comment and started laughing.

"They're working on a compare/contrast assignment," she said.

"Well, I'm headed back," he said.

"That would be wise," she said.

"Hopefully, I'll see you, later," he said.

"Maybe," she said.

"Bye Mr. Zee," said the students.

"That man like my teacher, y'all," said Smithna.

"Yeah, he be lurk-in, outside," said Lakes.

"He goin catch hands, she married," said Greater.

"Everyone, this is the second time I'm saying please focus and stick to appropriate topics," she said.

"We just say-in what we see," said Greater.

"Please keep your comments to yourself if it has nothing to do with the assignment," she said.

"Our fault," they said.

She walked around to make sure the students were discussing what she requested. They wrote down possible topics to compare and contrast.

"Excuse me, please make sure whatever you would like to compare and contrast is appropriate," she made eye contact with the whole group and then focused on Sanrell immediately, he erased the inappropriate topics he wrote down.

"Time in," she said.

This was a method she used with her fourth graders to make sure the entire class grasped a concept.

The students continued writing down topics—they were interested in. Finally, all cups were flipped up.

"That was pretty, fast," she said.

"Okay, all groups did well but there was one group who followed directions, perfectly," she said.

"It's us," said Da'Zay.

"Congratulations to the group who finished first, correctly, The Sparkle Group. They earned fifty points, toward the prize.

She collected the papers, from each group. After looking at the options, she projected the topics.

The Sparkle Group will present and everyone else will use their topic.

"Man is yo fault, we ain't finish," said Da'Zay.

"Man ... whatever," said her group members.

"Da'Zay could I see you for a second, Is there an issue," she said.

"No, Mrs. C.," she said.

"I decided to speak with you—in private," she said.

"I'm good," she said.

"If you're upset it's okay," she said.

"I want a different group," she said.

"It's important to work with people, even if you don't always win," she said.

"You right," she said.

"The process to get to the prize is very important too," she said.

"Aight, I'm good," she said.

"The spokesperson for The Sparkle Group, today, is ... Denny," she said.

She smiled, as they cheered for him.

"My group wanted to contrast schools with teachers vs. schools without teachers," he said.

"Okay, you guys have the topic, would all groups get to work," she said.

The groups started working, hard on the topic. They all put forth an intense effort and she gave them points for it.

"Mrs. C., how many points, I got," said Miken.

"Don't worry about your points, just work hard in your group," she said.

"Aight," he said.

"Okay, time up, who would like to share," she said.

"Us first," said Denny.

"Denny could you come to the front of the class and explain what your group came up with," she said.

"Okay, our group made a chart," he said.

"This chart looks amazing," she said.

"We did that," he said.

"How many of you have something to add to the chart," she said.

"Da'Zay do you have something to add," she said.

"Yes, a school with no teachers, would be bad," she said.

"I agree, teachers help create an environment of order that's why we need rules," she said.

"Ms.," said Vit(another student).

"Yes," she said.

"If we have no teachers we couldn't be by ourselves that's illegal," he said.

"That's a very good point, since you guys are under eighteen, you cannot be left, by yourselves, according to the law," she said.

"See —- now teachers won't catch a case," he said. She couldn't help but laugh with the students.

"Thanks for sharing such a great point," she said.

The bell is going to ring, in a few minutes, you guys did excellent, today," she said.

"This was fun," said Smithna.

"I'm giving everyone thirty points for trying and not losing their temper with anyone in the group," she said.

"Yeah, yelled," the class.

"Okay, settle down. Please write your homework," she said.

Before leaving, she reminded the students how much their participation meant to her. She also told them it is a privilege to be their teacher. They could not believe what they were hearing. Her feelings were reciprocated.

Casey barely made it, through the first period, without daydreaming about the peer writing club proposition and Lyric's Cumulative Information. She could not wait to ask Principal Waggenport, about her book. The time to address the issues she wrote about, was now. Her planning period arrived, finally. She darted toward the principal's office.

"Thanks so much for the gift card," said Ms. Tooks.

"You are most welcome," she said.

"How ... why ... Did you get me this," she said.

"Sometimes we need a little reminder, what we do matters," she said.

"It's true, sorry for snapping at you," she said.

"It's fine," she said.

"Please don't think I'm harassing you but I do need something," she said.

"What's up," she said.

"Before I see Big P.(a.k.a. Principal Waggenport) I was wondering if a certain cumulative folder for a very special student was available," she said.

"What's the student's name," she said.

"Do names matter," she said.

"You know what ... I'm trying to be patient, stop with the games, you ain't the P.E. coach," she said.

"It's just ..." she said.

"I need to know, who the student is," she said.

"Well, she's not exactly my student," she said.

"What in the world are you asking," she said.

"You want cumulative information on a student, who isn't yours," she said.

"Um ... yeah," she said.

"You're sweet, but keep dreaming," she said.

"This is life or death, I need to get a better understanding of this student," she said.

"My integrity is more important to me," she said.

"We're supposed to be starting several projects to help this school," she said.

"As much as I love your adorable smile and my gift card, you know I can't provide that information," she said.

"Duly Noted," she said.

"On that note, I'm leaving for lunch. Thanks again for the card," she said.

Every professional will face hard decisions. Anyone who loses sight of morals—will lose focus and watch their integrity derail. Casey admired the commitment she had to following protocol.

Ms. Tooks grabbed her lunchbox and darted toward the lounge. She forgot one pertinent detail. The Cumulative Folder Draw was unlocked. Since the other two girls were busy talking(about men they would never stop playing games with and social media posts), she took the opportunity to sneak into the cumulative folder draw. Casey understood this could get her in big trouble but the reprimand would be worth it. She headed straight for the A-D section. Immediately, she flipped to the C section.

"Perfect, Lyric Casanova," she whispered.

The records confirmed Lyric's placement in different foster homes, her severe asthma, and test results from second grade. Casey was right, according to her scores, she was gifted, academically. She also read she experienced severe mood swings, as a child. Quickly, she took pictures of the information and shoved the folder back in the draw. Since Casey was in chance mode, she decided to approach Principal Waggenport's office, he had a semi-open-door policy. Certain leaders were a ball of confusion, he was one of them. His claims were a mirage and his statements were fallible; nevertheless, she needed to speak with him.

"Come on in," he said.

"Hello," she said. His intimidating presence created a thick layer of anxiety.

"Um ... yeah ... I," she mumbled.

"I don't have a lot of time," he said.

"Well, I don't mean to bother you," she said.

"Stop, why do people say that, it's a waste of time," he said.

"Time ... um," she said.

"You don't know if what you're about to share will bother me," he said.

"Well," said Casey.

"I'll be candid, I hate trying to guess, what people are thinking," he said.

"I thought it would be a good idea to start a writing and emotional support mentorship club," she said.

"Sounds interesting ... what would it entail," he said.

"At least eight middle school students, struggling with writing and social skills could get help from myself and another student," she said.

"Is this student well-versed in writing and socialization," he said.

"Absolutely," she said.

"Does Gwen ... I mean Principal Morter know about this," he said.

She was stagnant to answer. If she replied yes, it would mean she went behind his back to propose a program, he did not know of; however, if she replied no, it points out the missing link in her proposition.

"Does the principal at Get Down Middle School know or not," he said.

"Not exactly," she said.

"Not exactly, or no," he said.

"No," she said.

"Well ... I think it's a great idea. I have a couple of questions," he said.

"Sure, what are they," she said.

"How long will the club run," he said.

"From next week to May, we will meet monthly/semi-monthly for an hour," she said.

"Next week, seems soon to start," he said.

"We'll be prepared," she said.

"How will the middle schoolers get here," he said.

"Could you request a bus/van for them," she said.

"Sure, anything to help, if I agree," he said.

"Great," she said.

"No problem, I'm here to support you," he said.

"Hopefully, if it's a hit, you could meet more frequently, next year," he said.

"Yeah and the club could expand to other grade levels," she said.

"Possibly, for now, let's take baby steps. I'll propose it to her, later," he said.

"That sounds great," she said.

"We're meeting to discuss the visit, we had from our district officials," he said.

"This will show the cohesiveness our cadre directors want," he said.

"One more thing, would it be possible to have a meeting with the staff, in March based on my book, Student Genres," she said.

"You wrote a book, that's an amazing accomplishment," he said.

"Yes, It's only ten chapters but the content packs a mean punch," she said.

Why did she always sabotage acknowledgments? Rye told her to stop doing that.

"If you agree to let me lead the training, you will have more than enough time to permit the book orders," she said.

"Yes, guess I have many talents," she said.

"You do, it's not surprising, considering you're participating in The Teacher Switch," he said.

"It's not just for me—the cause is greater," she said.

"I know, I hope you're not under immense pressure," he said.

"I'm fine," she said.

"Volunteering to take on high school students for the remainder of the year, writing books and who knows what else," he said.

"Yes, all that and more," she said.

"By the way have you spoken to Mr. Wu," he said.

"No, but we correspond, via email," she said.

"Okay, it would be nice if he would email me, back," he said.

"Back to the training and objective of my book," she said.

"Go on," he said.

"Addressing student genres is not a commonality, several gifted students remain undetected, based on our demographic," she said.

"That's true," he said.

"After reviewing the cumulative information of one of our students, I know this is a fact," she said.

He had a serious demeanor. It seemed like he could stare into a person's soul. Hopefully, he would be on board with the idea. Casey realized how much of a gaping hole, lack of differentiation created. She knew one of Lyric's largest issues was not being challenged. Her capabilities were diminished this triggered discontentment and boredom. She needed to deliver the information, the way any gifted individual would. She had a great idea.

"Gifted students are one of the genres, I elaborate on, in my book," she said.

"I would need to read the book, first, " he said.

"We don't want any of our teachers, reading curse words," he said.

She acknowledged he was trying to tell a joke and forced the corners of her mouth to elevate.

"I'll send you an electronic copy," she said.

She pulled out her phone and forwarded a copy of her book 'Student Genres' to him.

"Okay, as long as you do all the work, we can make it happen, in March," he said.

"Since the protest, we hold meetings, every three months with heavyweights, in attendance, you gotta love Ms. Zebedee," he said.

"She's the best," she said.

"Our next collaboration meeting is in March, make sure you are prepared," he said.

"Okay, one more question, could I deliver the information, my way," she said.

"Sure, it doesn't matter to me, deliver it standing on your head if you want," he said,

He kept trying to be funny ... well, at least he put in the effort.

"Great job, by the way," he said.

"The jump from elementary to high school is no easy task," he said.

You keep tackling several hard situations," he said.

"Thanks, champions live for challenges," she said.

"Correct, you're a champion," he said.

"Thanks," she said.

"Ms. Zebedee is right, unification is necessary for change," she said.

"I know, hopefully, the book is interesting," he said.

"It's a guarantee," she said.

"If it is, I'll order a copy for the entire staff and present it to the board, during our next leadership meeting," he said.

"That would be great, thanks so much," she said.

"Greatness should not be hoarded," he said.

"Agreed," she said.

"I'll email you, later," he said.

"Thanks," she said.

Principal Waggenport meant the next morning, he loved to send emails, at three o'clock a.m. Casey left the school. On the way home, she thought of unique ways to use members of Friendmanship to express the content of her book. Her synopsis slammed together, in delight. She received a text from her husband that read:

Where are you? This better be good. As she pulled into the driveway, she was greeted by the horrific sneer on her husband's face. What in the world, was his emotional malfunction? She could not deal with pressure at home and school. Although Casey knew her calling, she fought to achieve balance. She kept asking herself the same question, how in the world am I supposed to be an educator—when my wall of emotional support seems to be crumbling? Slowly, she opened the car door.

"You're late, I made pasta," he said.

"Yeah ... with a side of guilt," she said.

"You know ... your slick remarks don't help," he said.

"I'm sorry, it's just ... I had an amazing day and your facial expression, is draining me, already," she said.

"Wow, let me apologize—as if I'm the one who ignored you, after making dinner and nearly going out of your mind, my fault," he said.

"Keep your voice down, let's go inside," she said. Quickly, they rushed inside.

"You weren't always coming home late, during your internship it wasn't like this," he said.

"How in the world can you compare the two," she said.

"Are you seeing someone—be honest," he said.

"OFF LIMITS" she said. Those were safe words for when she felt overwhelmed.

"You can't use those, I'm not in the bad territory," he said.

"You are to me," she said.

"Somethings off with you, who's Mr. Zee," he said.

"A teacher at the school," she said.

"Why does he need your line," he said.

"He helped out with something major, my first day, thank God I had his number," she said.

"What happened," he said.

"I already can't stand his vibe," he said.

"Why—because he helped me and you couldn't," she said.

"Maybe," he said.

"Was I supposed to have you leave your job to come over a tiny argument the students had," she said. Her memory was intact but the initial reason she could not reveal the depth of what happened remained.

"What happened," he said.

"Just teen stuff," she said.

"Nobody got hurt, right," he said.

"Leave it in the past," she said.

"I don't like this whole thing," he said.

"So sad, it's not over," she said.

"We're part of something—Yeah ... I know ... something greater put yourself on a recorder," he interjected.

"We're trying to have a baby," he said.

"Last time I checked, I knew our agenda," she said.

"It's always the TEACHING SHOW ... starring Casey Peinst—aka Casey Coper and her husband when it's convenient," he said.

"You used to support me," she said.

"Used to as in past tense, I support you now," he said.

"I'm tired of infertility, this raise delay, and everything," she said.

"You're constantly working, it's gone to the extreme, that's why," he said.

"You don't think I notice but I do, you're on the computer, at three a.m., what teacher does that," he said.

"Lord help me," she said.

"Your contract says nothing about—Don't tell me about my contract," she interjected.

Her eyes burnt with disgust. He was morphing into some twisted unsupportive being, she did not recognize. Casey was nauseous. She ran to the restroom dropped to her knees and started to vomit.

Rye ran after her and held her hair.

"Hey, it's time to take it easy," he said.

She got up, flushed the toilet, and washed her hands.

"Whatever," she said.

"I don't want you passing out, from exhaustion, the switch is taking a toll on you," he said.

"Just stop, I don't want to hear this, now," she said.

"The hormone injections are so much for your body," he said.

"So what do you want me to do, roll over and fetch, at your command," she said.

"Don't be like that," he said.

"Like what, realistic," she said.

"I made such a special dinner for us and all I get lately are apology texts," he said.

"Someone sounds mighty SIMPY," she said.

"Wow ... SIMPY ...," he said.

"You keep playing the feel sorry for me roll, I'll take a pass on all guilt trips," she said.

"Look, you're not feeling well, let's talk about this, some other time," he said.

"Yes, let's do that," she said.

"Your dinner is in the microwave," he said.

"I'm not hungry, at this point, I have no appetite for guilt trips or pasta," she said.

"Fine, I'll be upstairs," he said.

It was time for her fertility injections, but she could not handle it, tonight. The last thing Casey should have thought about was her meeting, in March, but the thoughts could not stop. She decided to whip out her second husband(the laptop) and make an outline. Casey decided to make the student genre training, unlike any preparation event she attended in the past. She would get students and teachers to explain the minds of different student genres(including the gifted population), by analyzing her book. Since she constructed a guide on different types of students and how teachers should interact with them, it would be simple. She was so excited. A few hours went by and she lost track of time. Soon, she heard the sound of familiar footsteps.

"It's been hours, let me take you upstairs," he said.

"Fine," she said. Rye came downstairs and picked her up and gently placed her on a chair, in the restroom.

"You forgot your shots," he said.

"It can't happen, tonight, I need a break," she said.

"Okay," he said. Quickly, he left. As she took a shower he kept trying to understand, why she refused to set expanding their family, above everything else. After she finished, she entered the bedroom and eased into their bed.

"Goodnight ADORATION," he said.

"Night," she said.

"Sweet dreams, I still and always will love you," he said.

"I still and always will love you, too," she said.

Keep Going

The next morning, Casey went into work, extra early. She reviewed the lesson plans and noticed the skill of the week was sequencing. Based on recent activities, she decided to incorporate the school rules, during the lesson.

"Knock ... knock ... good morning, partner," said Mr. Zee.

"Good morning," she said.

"Did you get the lesson plans," he said.

"Yes, we have the freedom to teach the skill however we want, correct," she said.

"Sure, teach it dancing on your head, as long as the kids get it and you're following their I.E.P., Waggenport doesn't mind," said Mr. Zee.

"Great," I'm going to start setting, up," she said. He watched as she wrote the lesson's objective and academic standards on the board.

"I always feel so behind, around you. I have no idea why, since teaching high school is familiar for me," he said.

She started to smile. He was invaded by her personal space.

"What," she said.

Slowly, he leaned forward.

"Wait, I just want to remind you, I'm married," she whispered.

"Of course you are," he said.

"I know but you're such a special, pretty, and smart—married woman," she interjected.

"Well, see you later," he said.

"Yeah ... maybe," she said.

As she turned around and continued writing, he decided to leave.

Finally, the bell rang.

"Welcome," she said.

"Hey Ms. C.," said the class.

"How are you, this morning," she said.

"Good," said the class.

"Let's expand the conversation," she said.

"Huh," said Greater.

"When I ask how you are, reply by saying ... I'm fine, how are you," she said.

"All that," said Stilts.

"Yes," she said.

"Let's practice, how are you class," she said.

"I'm fine, how are you," they said.

"I'm fine thank you," she said.

"She such a lady," said DenJ.

"Alright, let's get started," she said.

Lesson: Rule Order
State Standard: HELP.ME.SEQUENCE.1.1.

Golden Question: How can I sequence(put things in order, from first to last), by making connections, while working in groups?

Objective: I can put events in order, from first to last, by making connections to school rules.

Model: Read the question. Model how to put things in order from least to greatest. Explain how to complete the assignment and what is expected, during completion.

Engage: Introduce sequencing, by engaging in a discussion about the school rules activity.

Evaluate: Complete the school rules activity.

"Today we're going to sequence rules," she said.

"Our golden question is, how can I sequence(put things in order, from first to last), by making connections, while working in groups?

Let's go over, each part of the question before we move on.

If I sequence, I am putting things in order. Here's an example:

Every morning I get ready for work. First, I wake up, next I brush my teeth, then I eat breakfast, last, I get dressed, finally, I drive to work," she said.

"Before we move on, does everyone understand, the directions," she said.

She did a quick check of their understanding by dividing the students into five categories: leading4, learning3, latent2, lagging1, and lost 0. These were the same categories, from her book, Student Genres. She asked them to put their heads down and hold up the number of fingers, based on their level of understanding. This was done so they would not be scared to reveal their level.

"Mrs. Coper, mi beg ya pardon, is dis for di rules," said Rimez.

"Yes, we're going to sequence rules," she said.

"You'll work in groups to put the school rules in order from first to final," she said.

"Man ... I hate groups," said Da'Zay.

"Let's work together, please," she said.

She gave her a stern look.

"Sorry Ms.," she said.

" No problem," she said,

"This will reflect which rules you view, as most/least important," she said.

"After you finish, we will discuss the reasons you think some rules are more important," than others.

"You each have a copy of the school rules on your desk," she said.

They looked down, at the rules.

The rules are:

1.) No form of disrespect toward anyone.

2.) No electronic usage, period!

3.) No fighting under any circumstances.

4.) No cheating or plagiarizing.

5.) No requesting makeup work, from peers during class, if you are tardy or absent. "Once you finish, please flip it over your We're Done Cup," she said.

"Okay, let's begin," said Casey.

The students started working hard. They were engaged. Casey observed the students and monitored the conversations of each group. She loved how engaged the students were. She alerted the groups of the five-minute warning.

"Y'all hurry up," said Da'Zay.

"You guys did a great job," she said.

"Thanks, Mrs. C.," they said.

"The Shine Group is up first, Today, your group representative Smithna, please explain how your group ranked the rules," she said.

She went to the front of the class and started speaking on behalf of her group.

"Hey errybody ... okay, for number one we chose no fighting cause someone could get hurt, arrested, and kicked out of school. Don't none of us want that. For number two we chose no cheating or plagiarizing under any circumstances. The group came up with this because kids who cheat get slow-acting. We work hard to stand out on social media but then we want to copy everybody else, in class. That don't make sense," she said.

"Very interesting," said Casey.

"For number three we chose no form of disrespect toward anyone. My group and I feel if you disrespect us, we will give you a chance but if you do it again, you will get disrespected, right back. For number four we picked no requesting makeup work from peers, during class if you were tardy or absent. "People in my group come to school on time, why should you stop our learning, cause you were up the night on the phone? We ain't have-in it," said Smithna.

Casey smiled. For number five, we chose no electronic usage, period! This was not at the top of our list, because we don't understand why listening to headphones if we working is bad," she said.

"Thanks for sharing, I appreciate the honesty and hard work, your group put in," she said.

"Next is the Sparkle Group, Garnell your group representative," said Casey.

"Please come to the front please explain how your group ranked the rules," she said.

"My name is Garnell and I'm group rep.," he said. He was proud of the title. Garnell's group started cheering him on.

"Go ahead," she said.

"First, is no fighting under any circumstances, because fighting is bad and as good students we need to be examples. Y'all never fight. Second is no cheating or plagiarizing under any circumstances, since cheating is very bad, especially on yo girl or yo man," he said.

"Oh ... true ... true," said the class. They started to laugh.

She called him, closer.

"Please stick to the topic and stop trying to tell jokes, she said.

"Sorry, my fault," he said.

He returned to the front of the class and kept going. The third is no form of disrespect when you—do you will not fight and it will help you do good. Number four is no electronic usage, period! Everyone in my group need they phone—more than water so we don't think not being able to have it on, all day is fair," he said.

"That's sad but true," she said.

"Last, we chose no requesting makeup work, from peers during class, if you're tardy. This was the last cuz sometimes you wake up late and you need to get your assignment ASAP," he said.

"That was a great presentation," she said.

"One more thang our group fire," he said.

The class started laughing and clapping.

She could not hold in her laughter.

"Great job Sparkle Group," she said.

"Now we have The Neon Group. Today's group representative is ... Spenez," she said.

"Oh ... here I go," he said.

"Please explain, how your group came up with the order of rules," she said.

"Yeah Mrs. C.," he said.

The Neon Group

"First, we picked no form of disrespect toward anyone, it makes rule number two automatic because if you have respect for a person, you won't fight them. Next, we picked, no fighting under any circumstances. Fighting hurts people. Then we chose no electronic usage, period! My group don't agree, cause in case of an emergency we need our phones. Fourth is no cheating or plagiarizing under any circumstance because sometimes you just can't study. Finally, we thought no requesting work from peers, during class, if you are tardy or absent, should be obvious so we replaced it with no skipping school or being tardy. Thank you.

Casey was blown away. She was impressed at the level of concentration The Neon Group had. It was amazing.

"I would like to say thanks to everyone for participating, in this assignment," said Casey.

"This was fun," said Money and Do.

"Achoo, achoo, all of a sudden, they started coughing.

"Are you guys sick," she said.

"We good," said the boys.

"You should drink a lot of water and some soup," she said.

"We love you, Mrs. C.," said Zaire.

"Awe ... you guys are sweet," she said.

"Don't forget to review your test prep sheet," tonight.

The bell rang and several students hugged her, before leaving. She felt a genuine sense of accomplishment. All aspects of the lesson were engaging and fun. Although she experienced a rocky start, her end goal was in clear view.

Eat N' Express

Today, was Eat N' Express, a trend for her students to relax and express themselves, during lunch. She figured it was a great reward for students, who earned enough points for positive behavior and academic performance. They placed orders and she honored their requests.

"Yeah, we get to eat wit da teacher," said DenJ.

"She everything man," said Swoon.

"Am I really," she said.

"He ain't lie-in," said Lakes.

"This man right here bout to die of thirst," said Greater.

"Shut up, we was playin ball," said Lanson.

"Yo … stop swallow-in like dat, man, dang," he said.

"Okay, relax guys, leave him alone, he's parched," said Casey.

"What's parched, it's bad," he said. The students chuckled.

"No, it just means you're really thirsty," she said.

"Yeah, all y'all be quiet like Mrs. C. said, I'm parched," he said.

"Man, be quiet," said Greater. They continued to laugh.

"No, let him use the word that's the best way to expand vocabulary or the words you know," she said.

"Mrs. Coper, them boys fickle," said Rat.

"What dis man say," said Money.

"You watch every strikin ting," he said.

"Um … okay, we're speaking nicely," she said.

"It don't matter, he stay complain-in," said Lakes.

"You a great teacher," said Garnell.

"Well, you guys are great students, don't great students deserve great teachers," she said.

"Yeah … I guess we do," he said,

"What do you guys want to talk about," she said.

"We got so much to know, how'd you start teach-in," said Zaire.

"When did this become an interview," she said.

"Please tell us," said Stilts.

"I wanted to teach, ever since I was a kid, I used to line my teddy bears up and put books in their laps, if they got questions, wrong they were put in the timeout corner," she said.

"Man … you did em dirty, lol," said Greater.

"Okay, this is my first year, teaching," she said.

"Mrs. C. You ain't telling the truth," said Greater.

"We had teachers before, they said they been teaching twenty years, they wasn't nothin like you," said Sanrell. "We know you care about us," said Greater.

"There's no doubt, about how I feel, toward all my students," she said.

"True," he said.

"The question is how do you guys feel toward yourselves and others," she said.

They looked at each other, confused.

"You do understand if you disrespect a female or anyone, it's a really bad thing," said Casey. She didn't want to directly refer to Lyric but the message needed to be put out there. "Taking advantage of anyone or anything takes away from your character," said Casey. "Mrs. C. What if a girl want you, real bad," said Lanson.

"My boys would clown me so bad if I walked away from a fine girl," said Greater.

"Okay, so they clown you, and they would keep clown-in me til I do somethin about it," said Greater

"Oh, so you answer to your friends, are they your parole officers," said Mrs. Coper.

The boys started laughing.

"No, don't laugh this is very serious.

"You shouldn't let anyone pressure you, into anything," she said.

"Taking advantage of confused girls or anyone, is not the thing to do," said Casey.

This was her opportunity to address future interactions with Lyric, indirectly.

"If I find out you boys are doing this, I'll be very disappointed, understand," she said.

"Yes," said the boys.

"Our minds, bodies, and soul deserve a high level of respect, once we respect ourselves, we will respect others," she said.

"What's wrong," said Money.

"Nothing," she said. Lying to students was not her preference. The truth was in that moment she thought of Lyric.

"We should never compromise our minds or bodies by taking part in risky behavior, she said.

"Yeah like Biren SIMP behind," said Nazaire.

"Let's not revisit that situation," she said.

"My fault," he said.

"If you compromise and make poor choices, it's disrespectful to yourself and others," she said.

"I ain't disrespecting myself," said Money.

"We not goin disrespect ourselves, no more, or other people," said Stilts.

"What do you think you boys would be doing if you dropped out of school," she said.

"Probably be in jail, like some of my homeboys," said Lakes.

"That's why I try so hard to do better," said Lakes.

"Sell-in guns," said Greater.

"Me too," said Nazaire.

"I would be sell-in eeeeeeiiiiillegal substances," said Stilts.

"Did you have to drag the word out like that, so extra," she said. The classroom permeated with joy and laughter.

"He extra," said Zaire.

"I can't say how, I just would," he said.

"Who would you get it from," said Casey.

"You for real, we could walk down the street and get a gun, easy," said Stilts.

"It ain't how to get a gun, it's when," said Greater.

"Some of us need protection in my neighborhood," said Zaire.

"Why don't you feel protected," she said.

"Mrs. C., You ain't just protected, we be protect-in you," said Stilts.

"What do you mean," she said. Casey tried to disguise her concern.

"You know how many people round here think you fine and would try you, we ain't have-in it," said Stilts.

"True," said Lanson.

Casey agreed. The school had one resource officer on call and one security guard(who was extra tired, from working an overnight shift on another job). When major issues, came up the cops would take a long time to respond. She did not feel protected but could not disclose the truth to anyone, especially Rye, he would not want her teaching at The Best High School.

"We ain't got no guns but we respected, at this school," said Zaire.

"If you guys know anyone, selling guns or anything illegal, you need to report it," she said. The students looked at each other, wondering if she understood the challenges that emerged, daily. She got a taste of it her first day.

"We know," said the students. They decided to humor her.

"Security need to tighten up," said Nazaire.

"I think we all agree that's the case," she said.

"Plus ni---- I mean I'm so sorry miss," said Stilts.

"I get it, just no more slip-ups, go ahead," she said.

"People be out they minds, they need help," he said.

"Mental health is a huge issue, I agree every decision starts with reasoning," she said.

"Yeah, my cousin kept sayin he was bout to kill his girl, ain't nobody listen, he did it, they was shook," said Do.

"It's sad how many warnings we ignore," she said.

"Yup," he said.

"I'm so sorry for your family's loss," she said.

"Boy ... we need to march, like the teachers ... like you," said Zaire.

"I'm all for peaceful protests," she said.

"How we stand up for what we believe in and not get arrested or shot," said Greater.

"Yeah, we get looked at sideways goin to the store," said Money.

"The first step to standing up for equality—is getting rid of an it's not my problem mentality," she said.

"Whachu mean Mrs. C.," said Swoon.

"Accountability opposes selfishness," she said.

"Aight Ms.Tubman, write a book about that," said Stilts. The students chuckled.

"Ms. Tubman ... wow ... anyway, I write a book but not about that, specifically," she said.

"I'm mess-in witchu, what's it about," he said.

"Just how every student is different and teachers need to relate to them," she said.

"Imma buy a billion copies from a billion stores so you could get a billion dollars," said Greater.

"That's your tagline," she said.

The students laughed.

"Seriously, thanks for the support," she said.

"Ain't nothin," he said.

"Oh ... me and my boy got a game, next week, you come-in," he said.

"Of course, gotta support the Number Ones," she said.

"You the best teacher," said Zaire.

"You guys are the best students," she said.

"Dang Mrs. C. you tatted up," said Stilts.

Quickly, she pulled her hair down. She never discussed the tattoo on the back of her neck or its meaning. Trying not to get emotional she pulled her hair in place to cover it.

"Let's not talk about that," she said.

"Aight, ain't nothin," said Stilts.

Before lunch was over, the students helped her clean up and get ready for their next class. She hoped the words stuck with them. She believed purposeful intervention changes minds.

Mr. Wu's Day

Mr. Wu was having a challenging day. His principal came by, during a test prep lesson. He was sitting behind the desk, which was considered taboo, during an observation. Principal Lazmun wrote him an email of suggestions. He was confused. Wasn't his teaching style flawless? The time to swallow prideful desires and change was here. After coming in from lunch he heard screaming.

"It's my pencil," exclaimed Kaz.

"Naw, that's mine, I got it, today," exclaimed Phaze.

"That ain't yours," he said.

Both students started rolling around on the floor and he had to break up the fight.

Mr. Wu asked the class who had the pencil first and the majority of them said it was Phaze.

He gave him the pencil and turned to sit at his desk. When he thought the drama was over, Kaz got up, snatched the pencil out of his hand, and attempted to stab him. Thankfully, he was swift and dodged the attempt. He ran over, picking him up with one hand in anger. He asked Mrs. Batet to watch the class and marched him down to the principal's office. He filled out a referral and left Kaz in the office and returned to his students. Then he had one of the weirdest parent-teacher conferences, in the history of his teaching career.

Parent Meeting

This afternoon was Mr. Wu's fourth parent meeting. The parents that showed up, were supportive of him. It was time to produce results. He prayed he would not get cursed out, since it happened, at his former school.

"Hello, could I come in," she said.

"I'm Miss Beauty-Built —Kaz's mom, nice to meet you," she said.

He was taken back, by this woman's beauty but he had to maintain the straight face of professionalism. She wore a short dress, low-cut blouse, and heels.

"It's nice to meet, you," he said.

"Oh … sweetness … it's my pleasure," she said.

"Please have a seat," he said.

"I called this meeting to let you know, your son's reading and math grades have gone down," he said.

"He always says how nice his new teacher is," she said.

He tried not to let her winking and attempts to change the subject, distract him.

"As I was saying, your son's grades have gone down, there are ways to bring them back up," he said.

"Yeah, back up … you right," she said.

"Also, there was an incident between Kaz and another student," he said.

"Who Phaze, they get into it, all the time, they stay around the corner from each other," she said.

"I can't speak about another student," he said.

"Just lettin you know, I know—who you talkin about," she said.

"Noted," he said.

"They be gettin into it, all the time," she said.

"This fight was very serious," he said.

"Kaz got upset and tried to drive a pencil through the other student's cheek," he said.

"They were just playin," she said.

"It was urgent, he ended up going to the office," he said.

"Yeah... I heard," she said.

"I had to write him up, he will be suspended for at least a day," he said.

"I know, he be on his game so that's okay," she said. He couldn't believe the words she expressed. Her son's reward for fighting was to play a video game. What in the name of We Will Thrive Elementary was going on?

"Well anyway … about his grades, we could change it," she said.

"What about them," he said,

"He likes you, so much," she said.

"I am fond of him also but grades are earned, in my class," he said.

"Oh … bet … aight," she said.

"Kaz needs to increase comprehension and he needs to practice story problems," he said.

"That stuff be so confusin," she said.

"Here's information on how he can improve, it also has test preparation material," he said.

"You so different from his other teacher," she said. He wanted to say yes … you didn't try to flirt with her. Instead, he vowed to remain professional.

Do you have any questions," he said.

"There's a new buffet they just opened, around the corner, we could go and talk about my baby there," she said.

"Unfortunately, that's not possible," he said.

After she noticed he was not influenced by her provocative clothing and flirtatious attempts were in vain, her expression changed.

"If you don't have any other questions, our conference is over," he said.

"Okay, you have my number," she said.

"I will contact you if it's necessary," he said.

" I don't know, how y'all do it, I could never be no teacher, bye," she said.

"Goodbye," he said.

This was not the time to hear that comment. He was already stressed out, from other challenges. Why would she make this statement, now? He maintained a professional demeanor.

"It was a pleasure meeting you," he said.

This meeting caused him to rethink his decision. He wondered if Casey was experiencing moments of regret. Was this the time to back down?

Six
Friendmanship

The next morning, Casey opened her email. There were two important emails, in her inbox.

Good morning,

I hope all is well. We are coming up to testing time. Your students miss you; I think they are getting used to me, lol. There were several incidences. One of your former students who always says, "I ain't doin nothing when asked to do an assignment, got mad and tried to drive a pencil, through his friend's cheek. Ten seconds later he hugged him. Also, the students are under so much pressure about taking the Bigwig Statewide Test. Several students are absent, constantly. I had no idea, elementary school teachers struggled with truancy issues. I guess ... I have a lot to learn. One more thing, a parent came in wearing provocative clothes to convince me her son's grade should be changed. She means well ... I'm sure. Unfortunately, a pushup bra and heels won't change it. At the end of our meeting, this parent dared to say, "I could never be no teacher." If she only knew what teaching entails, she would have swallowed her words.

I reached a whole new level of respect for you. How are things, at my school? I'm sure, you will let me know. Until then, have a fabulous and productive day. Sincerely,

Lyde Wu

Powerful Educator

We Will Thrive Elementary School

Untold Truth Brings a Tragic End-Lyde Wu

After reading Mr. Wu's email, she replied ...

Good morning,

I understand the challenges you are facing. Based on the quote, I know the student, you are referring to. Remind him of the anger management techniques, we practiced with the guidance counselor. If you want to help him calm down, make sure, his fists are not balled up. Children are not like certain adults, they tend to forgive, so his behavior is not odd. I usually provide the students with stress management techniques, during testing. It is not uncommon for the clinic referrals and absences to increase, before the Bigwig Test. The techniques are listed, in my folder. Frequent absences are handled by the social worker. Pushup bra convincing is a strategy I never encountered with any parent, lol. You did the right thing. Grades cannot be altered, based on flirtation. If this parent insists on persisting with this behavior, have an administrator or third party present, when she comes around. Grades are earned, bribes don't increase, percentage points. You are doing awesome. Here is an update on me. I asked a freshman to lead the club. She is such a special girl. Although she has issues, we are working through them, daily. I made a proposition to Principal Waggenport to start a peer writing/emotional support club. It is called Friendmanship. It will not only help high school students who need to focus on something positive, but it will help middle schoolers (from Get Down Middle), as well. If the results are positive, this may be widespread. Who knows? In repose to the "I could never be a teacher" comment, one of the parents of the students I worked with during my internship, made the same comment to the teacher who trained me. Below is an excerpt, from my book, Student Genres, addressing her perspective.

2
Reasoning

"I don't understand, how you taught my child with reading problems and he's gifted," said the student's parent.
"He worked hard and passed the end-of-year test, I'm proud of him," said Mrs. Coper.
"Proud of him, I'm proud of you, making no money and doing so much," she said.
"It's my passion," I said.
"Passion to work for pennies," she said.
 I tried not to get emotional.
"Dealing with nasty kids all day, not getting paid, and having to act phony," she said.
I told myself to stay calm. The conference was over and I encountered people like this, in the past.
"Thanks again but I could never be a teacher," she said.

'I Could Never Be A Teacher'

The raw reality of her words stirred a zeal inside of me that was the catalyst to strike a change. Usually, my poker face was good; however, this time the comment hit close to my heart. Her comment was igniting—due to the blood, sweat, and tears, invested to make sure her child, (as well as others) thrived, daily. The fire burned in me, stronger than ever before? Tears began to fill my eyes—since the comment was necessary to proceed with my hard work and dedication.
I wanted to reply by saying,
"Correct, you could never be a teacher. My God-ordained assignment holds the key that unlocks the future of tomorrow." You could never be a teacher, The Lord granted me strength, endurance, and patience not to succumb to light-weight comments, stemmed from individuals, who are blindsided to the reality of what we call INSTRUCTION. Sweat invested by educators is shed constantly. When your child seemed disengaged, I took initiative to implement innovative activities that would enhance the learning process, causing him to thrive. You could never be a teacher. It requires a certain level of innovation, technique, and sensitivity. You could never be a teacher that is my calling. I was created for the field of education. Each key I provide students with,

unlocks another level of their potential. In reality ... my professional response was, "Teaching your child, was a pleasure." Whenever someone says something out of ignorance, it is the listener's choice to let the person walk away in their clueless state or enlighten them. Don't take the comment to heart. A lot of people don't understand, details of what we do, every day. Remain in a positive state of mind. Keep up the motivation!

Please note: there is a flu of some sort going around. Educators can never afford to get sick. Make sure to take care of yourself. Keep up the Motiv'Plication.

Sincerely,

Casey Coper

Phenomenal Teacher

The Best High School

-Loveless learning is lifeless learning.-Casey Coper

Good morning,

Mrs. Coper I opened your book and could not stop reading it. The way you addressed the needs of each student and spoke about details, regarding the teachers, is amazing. You have a very special gift. I especially like the rubrics, we could use these, districtwide. The main aspect of the rubrics, I recognized was the consistency. It is a major issue, in several circumstances. I purchased books for all the teachers and recommended it as a top read for our Superintendent. The information is useful and relatable, regardless of what grade level the teacher using specializes in. Congratulations! You have the leverage to base the upcoming training on Student Genres. If you have any questions, please email me. Sincerely, Principal Waggenport—"Integrity Bound While Leading to Win!"

The Best High School

Casey knew he would email her, around 3 a.m. She was so happy, he enjoyed Student Genres. It meant a lot to have a leader—open to new ideas did not limit her, creativity. Positive leaders make a huge difference, in setting the school's climate.

Good morning,

Thanks for replying, so soon. I am really happy to hear, you enjoyed reading, Student Genres. It took me a while to complete. The purpose of the book was to help teachers, leaders, students, and parents gain understanding before the upcoming meeting. Students in Friendmanship will be involved, in a performance, after teachers analyze a couple of chapters, from the book. Thanks for supporting me. Keep up the Motiv'Plication.

Sincerely,

Mrs. Coper

Phenomenal Teacher

The Best High School

-Loveless learning is lifeless learning.-Casey Coper

As Casey closed her computer, the students started walking in. Once the bell rang, she went to the front of the class, held up five fingers, and started counting down.

"Good morning, I need it quiet, in 5,4,3,2,1," she said.

The class got quiet and did not resemble the students from Her first day, at The Best High School. Over the past months, she established a level of respect, between the students and herself. She was so proud to see how far the students, came.

"We have another test to take, today," she said.

"You serious," said Do.

"Yes, please remain quiet," she said.

The students followed directions and remained testing for the entire class period. The frequent testing was a familiar excessive regimen. She worked closely with Mr. Zee to monitor each student's progress. Although this was her first experience, teaching high school, she caught on, quickly.

"Knock knock ... Sleeping on the job," he said.

"Maybe, how's that your concern, testing was intense, I needed a nap," she said. Slowly, she stretched and yawned.

"I just don't want administration, walking in your room, asking if you mistook this for preschool," he said.

"It's after school, we had an intense day of testing, I needed a nap, before writing club starts," she said.

"Oh, that's right ...I heard you're starting it, today," he said.

"That's right," she said.

"You sure don't waste time," he said.

"Time is too precious to waste, once it's gone, it's gone," she said.

"True," he said.

"I have one of the best freshmen on campus, leading the club," she said.

"Which freshman is this," he said.

"Her name is Lyric," she said.

"Lyric Casanova," he said.

"Yes, how do you know her, she is a freshman and you teach juniors," she said.

"Oh, I've heard some things," he said.

"Anyway, she's a great girl, rumors are not important," she said.

He noticed Lyric's name changed Casey's countenance. He decided to cut the conversation, short.

"I know you guys will help the middle schoolers, a lot," he said.

"That's the plan," she said.

"I need to head out," he said.

"Thanks for stopping by," she said.

After he left, she set her alarm and put her head back down, she was exhausted.

"Mrs. C. ... wake up," said a familiar voice.

She picked her head up—in time to see one of the greatest transformations— she experienced.

"Why you lookin at me like you caught your husband, cheating," said Lyric.

"Sorry ... you look so professional," she said.

She wore a pencil skirt with a button-down lace front top and heels. Her hair was pulled back with beautiful auburn ringlet curls that grazed down her back. She looked so professional.

"Your sense of humor is out of this world," she said.

"Too extra," she said.

"It's just ... you look so elegant," she said.

"Yeah, yeah ... I look aight," she said. Her reaction was familiar. Casey also downplayed compliments. It was Rye's pet peeve.

"The middle school students will arrive in twenty minutes," she said.

"Aight," she said.

"We're going to meet, after school," she said.

"What's that," she said.

"It's a list of students participating, she said.

"Okay, where's the big white paper pad," she said.

"The chart paper and other materials are inside the cabinets," she said.

Lyric started getting everything ready. She started to create charts to enhance the writing of each student she planned to mentor.

"Were you tested for gifted," she said.

"I guess, I took this long test, when I was little," she said.

"It was probably that one," she said.

"I took so many tests, cause when I was a girl —I got sad sometimes and I still do," she said.

"Mrs. C.," she said.

"Yes," she said.

"I don't think I can do this," she said.

"Why," she said.

"Ain't nobody care-in what I have to say or teach," she said.

"I'm not concerned, about the perception of imperfections, you feel are there. The fact is, they're in your head. I'm focused on your future contributions to society and how you'll use the gift of writing to help students, express themselves," she said.

"That's a whole speech," she said.

"Seriously, I see the caring, smart and beautiful young lady, standing in front of me," she said.

"What if I can't do it," she said.

"I wish you could use your capabilities, as a mirror of your true reflection," she said.

"My reflection ... I try not to look at myself, in the mirror," she said.

Casey pulled out her mirror and asked her to sit down.

As she placed it, in front of Lyric, she turned her head away.

"Ain't nothin to see," she said. She refused to allow her to push the mirror away, again.

"I'll tell you what I see—a beautiful, smart, woman in training ready to take over the world," she said.

"I don't know about all that," she said.

"Well, I do know about all that," she said.

"There you go tryin hard, again," she said. They looked at each other and smiled.

"Seriously, the biggest mistake is to critique yourself through a skewed viewpoint," she said.

"I know I'm advanced and all because I understood what you just said, but you are pushing it," she said.

"You a fortune cookie communicator," she said.

The duo laughed and continued to prepare for the students to arrive.

"Before the students come, I want to let you know, they have major struggles," she said.

"You do understand, we all from the same neighborhood, right," she said.

"Plus I'm a freshman, I just left middle school, a lot of the kids have seen me around," she said.

"I get it, that's why you're the best person to help them, never underestimate the power of relativity," she said.

"There you go—another fortune cookie quote," she said.

"You love them," she said.

"You right," she said.

"A lot of us have it hard, you know my story, Imma help them, push through," she said.

"You're so courageous," she said.

"Awe, thanks, for real feeling sorry for yourself, pays no bills," she said.

Her statement was credible. She was a strong young woman. People feel entitled to give up for a fraction of what Lyric went through.

"Just a quick preview before you meet the students—- please don't tell me nothing, before I meet them," she interjected.

"Okay," she said.

"Do me a favor, could you ask, if they would be interested, in doing the skit, at a big meeting, we're having in March," she said.

"Yeah, what's it about," she said.

"It would give the students a chance to show how they feel, about school/teachers," she said.

"This could change things," said Casey.

"Oh, yeah ... they gonna love that," she said.

"You don't think they'll get shy," she said.

"Kids from my neighborhood, shy ... naw," she said.

Casey smiled and continued helping her prepare for their group meeting. Upon arrival, the adolescents were rowdy. The peer writing club had a total of ten members.

"Good afternoon," she said.

"Hi," said the students.

"She fine," said Irv.

She shook her head, in disapproval.

"Let's be respectful," said Casey.

"I am, I'm respectfully sayin you and my new teacher," said Irv.

"You're a student and we are teaching you, saying a teacher is fine is unacceptable," she said.

"My fault," he said.

"Let's start by introducing ourselves, in one sentence," she said.

"We can begin with the beautiful lady, in gold and white," she said.

"Hello, my name is Mrs. Coper, I teach juniors and love to write," she said.

"Hey Miss," said Irv.

"I'll be here, in case Miss Casanova needs me," she said.

"I am yo ... I mean ... your peer writing club leader," she said.

"Hey Lyric, we seen you at the store," said Rose.

"Yup she was at our school too," said Gesa.

"Hey guys, in here my name is Miss Casanova," she said.

"Like the song," said Rose.

"Yes, but what do you know, about that song," she said.

"My momma be listening to that granddaddy music," she said.

The group laughed, as she elaborated.

"I am so excited to lead this group," she said.

"Let's introduce ourselves, in one sentence," she said.

Casey noticed she corrected her grammar. She didn't realize she was a chameleon communicator. During the club meeting, she was somewhat slang-free.

"Here's an example, My name is _____, I'm a _____ grader who loves to talk and sing," she said.

"Let's start with this pretty girl, in the front," she said.

"My name is Polly, I'm in sixth-grader and a very good student," she said.

"My name is Sarah, I'm a seventh grader and I love to write and draw," she said.

"My name is Na'tess, I'm a sixth-grader who loves to act and dance," she said.

"My name is Loreel, I'm a sixth-grader, who loves to laugh and sing," he said.

"My name is Don, I'm a seventh-grader, who loves to make jokes and sleep," he said.

"My name is Nescai, I'm a sixth-grader who loves to write and do good," he said.

"My name is Irv, I'm a seventh-grader who loves to be nice and play basketball," he said.

"My name is Rose, I'm a sixth-grader who loves to do makeup and hair," she said.

"My name is Gesa, I'm a seventh-grader who loves to be funny and help my friends," she said.

"Hold on, what about the beautiful girl, in the back," said Casey.

"She didn't say her name," said Lyric.

"Introduce yourself, we're listening," she said.

"My name is Ivory and I'm in seventh grade, I moved here, from California," she said.

"Shortie a white ... as white can be," said Irv.

"Black girls ain't pose to have cream fill-in," said Gesa.

"Miss, tell da new girl stop talking white—ook, we are not having that, at all," Casey interjected.

Quickly, the students stopped jeering Ivory. She looked even more disengaged, than before. Lyric glanced over and noticed Casey was staring in space. The students' words reopened gaping wounds, which she thought were healed.

Every social experience triggers a positive or negative mental response. Growing up, hearing the words you a white girl and stop talking white was an unfortunate commonality for her. She reached back and lightly traced her fingers on the faint letters that formed a scar, in the back of her neck. It was the railroad to a very dismal past, she hid, under lock and key.

The student's comment caused her to revert to the eleven-year-old girl. Casey came from a family, who took pride in perfect articulation. She remembered her mother's words: "Sit up straight."

"Don't speak with your mouth full and never use slang," she said. All her mother's suggestions were well noted. Before her first day of fourth grade, she never thought anyone would make fun of her choice of expression, but it happened. Accentuating every syllable made Casey's teacher's eyes sparkle, adversely, it made her the target for envy. One day, one of her classmates blurted out the question, "Why you talk-in white?" This was extremely confusing since words have no racial connotation. Say any word, ask the word to identify its race, and wait for a response, it will never come. Her friend's comment would be the beginning of a very long trajectory of word profiling.

This act was inhumane and horrific. Her elementary grade crew consisted of the following races: Asian, Black, and Caucasian. They were each beautiful and held different means of expression. When her black friend(who expressed herself, through ebonics), called her a chocolate creamy pop and accused her of talking white, the allegations confused her for the following reasons: first, her mother never taught her about one uniform means of expression; however, she did teach Casey, about grammar and the proper way to convey thoughts. Next, she was not a type of food.

Why did she correlate articulation with a fruit? Then, her family was diverse, if black people all spoke the same way, how would she explain how black people from Paris expressed themselves?

Finally, who gave her complete autonomy to sign off on how black people should speak? This is a misfortune, since expecting everyone from the same race to speak uniformly, is stereotypical.

As she got older, the comments intensified. After hearing "you're a white girl, trapped in a black girl's body," she built up an emotional wall. She never viewed her teacher as having the authority to change the situation. This was and is dangerous for students being bullied, in the same manner. Her perspective of the teacher was skewed, based on how she handled situations. The bullying needed to stop! She decided to never submit to the pressure of speaking a certain way. Sixth grade was years ago but there was a particular day that triggered a change, in her life forever.

"Hey Case, you coming to practice," said Heather.

"Sure, l just need to get changed, first," she said.

"Cool," she said.

As she entered the girls' restroom to change for cheer practice she heard two familiar voices. Dasha and Lanell were bitter neglected bullies that thrived off of harassment. The two drug abusers wore the same dirty clothing to school, daily. They were held back in the same grade, twice. Many parents lodged complaints, against them; however, the issues went unaddressed. Casey shuttered at the sound of their voices. She figured somehow the restroom door was closer, but it was so far away. Both girls stood, staring at her, as she approached the sink, time froze. Quickly, she turned the faucet on.

"A white girl, why you talk like that," she said.

She proceeded to wash her hands. Ignoring was the best policy to deal with bullies, wasn't it?

"You ain't hear my homegirl, should I bust yo ear," she said.

Suddenly, the girl who was twice her height and weight slammed her, against the wall.

"Just leave me alone. I'm not talking like a white girl, this is who I am," she said.

"Girl real ni**az don't talk like that," she said.

"You can say whatever you want but my mother taught me to speak proper English," she said.

"Oh ... wow ... white girl," she said.

"Didn't your mother teach you the same," she said.

"Shut the hell up, white girl," she said.

"My mama ain't teach me noth-in," she said.

"Tell her Dash," she said.

"But Imma teach you to keep your honkey behind quiet," she said.

"No ... please, stop," she exclaimed.

In a split second Dasha spit out a razor, and carved the initials W.G.(that stood for a white girl) in the back of Casey's neck. The bullies disregarded her pain infiltrated bellows. Eventually, she passed out. The next morning she woke up with her neck wrapped, in a large bandage. Her mother was happy, they didn't kill Casey. The family pressed charges. While recuperating she vowed to never let the initials carved in her neck be in vain. Her family and Rye were the only people who knew the story. As a teenager, she got a tattoo of a butterfly to cover the scar. She wanted a symbol that would force her to transition the hatred she felt toward the bullies. When people asked the meaning of the tattoo, she refused to discuss it. The sick twisted cycle of critiquing needed to end.

"Mrs. C ... hello, you good," said Lyric.

"Yes, I zoned out for a second, my apologies," she said.

"Listen, we're all human beings who decide to express ourselves, uniquely," she said.

"Do you guys know, what that word means," said Casey.

"Yes," said Sarah.

"Good there's no such thing as talking white or black," she said.

"We are people who choose to speak anyway we want, based on freedom of choice," she said.

"Never make someone feel bad about the way they communicate," she said.

"There's no one way to express yourself," she said.

"I'm sorry," said Sarah.

"Thanks, but Ivory deserves the apology," she said.

"Sorry Ivory," said Sarah.

"No issue," she said.

"We want to know, the most important things you would like to learn, in this group," she said.

"We want teachers to listen to us," said Loreel.

"They be yelling and embarrass-in people," said Rose.

"It's like my teacher say stop and I don't be doing nothing," she said.

"I want y'all to think about emotions, we go through so many, every day," she said.

"Sometimes we talk to help our emotions but what happens when you feel no one is listening," she said.

"You could write," said Irv.

"Exactly, I love to write," she said.

"Writin be fun sometimes," said Gesa.

"Ever since I was a little girl, writing helped me, so much," she said.

"Whenever people was not listening to me, the writing was my way out," she said.

"Whatever problems you feel teachers or anyone else it giving you, write about it," said Lyric.

"Ooooh ... now we could tell our sides," said Rose.

"Yes, what should we name the club," she said

"Parties ... Everyday all day," she said. The students chuckled.

"Seriously... stop joke-in—remember what the club is about before you suggest a name," she said.

"How 'bout Always Friends," said Rose.

"That's a great name but what about the writing part," she said.

"Good Friends Write Together," said Loreel.

"Nah ... Friends Do Good Writing," said Sarah. "Y'all I want one name for the club," she said. "Me too," said Rose.

"Me one hundred," said Don.

"How about Friendmanship," said Casey.

"Oh ... that sound fancy," she said.

"What that mean," he said.

"It means —it's a combination of two words that explains what the club is about, friendship and writing a.k.a. penmanship. The teacher put the two words together," Ivory interjected.

"See ... she always trying to look smart," said Rose.

"Enough that's not true," she said.

"She's not trying, smartness is all over her, said Lyric. Ivory smiled.

"You're right, by the way," said Casey.

"Thanks, Mrs. C.," she said.

"Just because someone shares what they know, doesn't mean they're showing off," she said.

"I be trying to tell her, stop hat-in," he said.

"Boy quiet," she said.

"Stop you guys, I'm sure there are things you know the Ivory doesn't and vice versa," said Casey.

"The purpose of our group is to help each other, grow," she said.

"Raise your hand, if you like the name Friendmanship," she said.

Everyone raised their hands, they loved the name.

"Okay, that's the name of our club, thanks Mrs. C.," she said.

"It's no problem," she said.

"Friendmanship is a support group for you guys to vent," she said.

"It's official y'all ... we got a name," said Don. The students started to cheer.

"Okay ... okay ... let's go over some rules," she said.

"That's easy ... eat pizza, write and have fun," she said.

"Um ... there's more to it, what we speak about is private," she said.

"Whatchu mean," said Sarah.

"It means whatever we share in our club stays between us," she says.

"I'm happy but some of these kids got big mouths," said Sarah.

"You should know, you got the biggest mouth at school," said Don.

"Hush," she said.

"Our fault, go head," he said.

"If you have a bad day, this is a safe place to talk and write about it," said Lyric. "Like we could say whatever," said Gesa.

"Yeah ... and we're not going to hurt each other with words or actions," she said.

"I like that sometimes I feel like there's no one to talk to," said Ivory. "Friendmanship is about helping each other to get better, if don't you want me to cancel the club," everything shared in this room, is private," she said.

"True," said Sarah.

"This club is about you guys," she said.

"We ain't never had a club for us," said Sarah.

"That's why it's special," she said.

"Real special," said Gesa.

"I want you to write things you want us to talk about, then I can make it into writing topics for you guys," she said.

"This club is everything," said Don.

"I'll collect papers, in five minutes," she said.

The students wanted to write and discuss topics including bravery, drug use, alcoholism, why they should respect adults(when they don't feel respected, and more).

"Today, let's talk/write about fear, and why it's important to confront it," she said.

"What's important," she said.

"If you don't paralyze fear, it will paralyze you," she said.

"Y'all know what that means," she said.

"Yes, my uncle paralyzed, it means you can't use your legs," she said.

"I'm sorry, about your uncle and you are right," she said

"Basically to be paralyzed is not being able to move a part of your body," she said.

"So many people have hidden talents that stay in their capability closet, because of fear," she said

"Does everyone know, what capability means," she said.

"No," said the students.

"It means you can do something," she said.

"I think I heard that," she said.

"I want you to write down what you're scared of," said Lyric.

Casey could not believe, how in the world did she start the first Friendmanship Meeting with the same assignment she gave her classmates, at the end of her graduation speech? Lyric was a good influence on them.

"After you write about what you're scared of, I want you to write how you dealt with it," said Lyric.

"Irv you go first," she said.

"Aight Miss, I was scared when my stepdaddy told us, there wasn't no more food and he ain't know how we was gonna make it," he said.

"What did you do, about your fear," she said.

"I don't know," she said.

"That means you never faced it, you still walk around scared like it will happen again," said Lyric.

"I can't lie, sometimes I be think-in about that night, like wit my brother and two sisters," he said.

"I know ... I see the 'round were we stay, they so cute," she said.

"Yeah ... I be think-in maybe school ain't the best, I should be on the block," he said.

"Exactly, that's what you think to do about it, but selling drugs is not a solution," she said.

"What happens if you get locked up and your brother and sisters don't have you, around anymore," she said.

"Come up with a better plan," she said.

"Y'all can't tell me a thing, I know y'all neighborhood cause it's mine, too and you can't face fears until you have a plan for what to do about them," she said.

"Irv, tell me your new plan," she said. He hung his head, in deep thought. She approached him with a blazing fire, in her eyes.

"Look at me, what's your new plan," she said.

She was impressed with Lyric's passion and desire to make the students understand, their decisions could be life-threatening.

"Imma write it, miss," he said.

Lyric refused to play with the thought of some of the students, making poor choices, the way she did. She felt a new sense of purpose, helping them. Lyric understood the streets did not give them second chances. A bullet in the spine or permanent brain damage would not be their fate. Her self-worth increased when she provided the students with new ways of reasoning.

"Time's up Irv, share with the group, please," she said.

"I won't be scared, anymore, because I know if I need food for me or my family I can reach out to someone to let them know. I can also get a job that pays money not breaking the law. Selling drugs is not the only way to help. If I get caught, it could cause me to go to jail, get shot, or be dead.

"That was beautiful and real, thank you," she said.

"Ain't nothin," he said.

"Ms. C. we want to work in a group," she said.

Sarah, Na'Tess, Gesa, and Don all turned their desks, toward one another.

"Okay, but first write the fear you have and what you want to do about it," she said. Lyric gave them time to reflect. The group spoke about a tragic event. They witnessed a five-year-old girl get shot to death while playing in the park. This was nerve-racking for the students and it hurt them, deeply.

"We ready to share, Mrs. C., I want to speak for my group," said Gesa.

"Go ahead," she said.

"We all scared to play in the park, where that girl got shot," she said.

"We was talk-in about it, getting a gun is how you solve the problem," she said.

"Why do yo feel that is the only way to solve the problem," said Lyric.

"Cause when my uncle got shot, his friend shot the man who killed my uncle," she said.

"My family don't get down like that, it's a life for a life," she said.

"That little girl was so tiny, she ain't bother no-one," said Sarah.

Natalai and Sarah started to cry. Casey consoled them.

"We know what happened to the little girl was wrong," said Lyric.

"What happens if someone shoots at you and you shoot back when does it end," she said.

"No disputes," said Irv.

"I hear you, Mr. Vocab.," she said. They started laughing and it lightened the mood.

"Your deepest fear is getting shot for no reason," she said.

"How 'bout helping to spread what you know, in our community 'bout ways to handle fear and get rid of violence," she said.

"Oh, like we could start something like wit rules," said Gesa.

"Exactly," said Casey.

"Please hear me, if whoever you live wit said don't go to the park … don't but eventually everywhere will be off limits, if we don't do something," she said.

"That's right like just like this one time bad things happened at this game but I love ball," said Loreel.

"I'm witchu," said Irv. The group chuckled.

"You could get rid of fear by changing the way you see things and helping to keep the community safe, or you could move but getting a gun to kill someone is not the answer," she said.

"My mama say these streets ain't safe," said Natalai.

"So you stay as safe as you can but stopping life isn't smart, we need to keep fighting to live, no matter what happens," she said.

"Saying you'll never go to any park again, is not facing your fears," she said.

"You right Miss C.," she said. The group nodded their heads.

"What's your deepest fear, Loreel," she said.

"Me and Irv working together to write about it," he said.

"You have five minutes, we gotta talk about this," she said.

Although they looked reluctant, he jumped in and started to share.

"Our deepest fear is for our house to get burnt up," again.

"I'm sorry that happened to you guys, she said.

They were cousins, who lost their home, in a fire; they were staying in a shelter.

"You been through it and you gotta deal with it, don't run," she said.

"We can stop being afraid by not moving to another house, it could burn down, again," said Irv.

"Good try, that's not what I mean, how will you stop being afraid of fire," said Lyric.

"You already lost a home to it, now how will you deal with it," she said.

"That's a deep question," said Irv.

"You are letting the fear of fire cause you not to live, think about it," she said.

They thought about what Lyric said. She was right, they were always scared the place they were in would burn down, so they did not want another house.

"Deal with your fears, by helping move into another house, you and your mamas deserve another house, it will be even nicer than the one that burned down," she said.

"You need to understand, bad things happen to everyone," she said.

"How you bounce back from those bad things is what counts," she said.

"Saying you won't want to live in a house again, ain't how to face your fear," she said.

"You right Miss C.," they said.

"Okay," who's next Nescai.

"My fear can't go away," he said. He was writing the entire time, she was talking. He looked very hurt.

"Why not," she said.

"My momma she was killed, she ain't coming back, look," he said.

He pulled out a picture of a beautiful woman, he resembled.

"I don't want no more mommas," he said.

"My daddy ain't getting no-one," he said.

Everyone was quiet. They understood avoidance is used, as a tool to remain fearful. Nescai was scared another woman would take the place of his mother.

She walked over and looked him in the eyes.

"I can't tell you, I know what you feel that would make me a liar," she said.

"Don't try miss," he said.

"I can't stand when people try to say things to take away your moment to be sad," she said.

"It be hard," he said.

"It's okay to feel mad and sad, especially with the way you lost her," she said.

"Your mom was really special, right, is your dad special, too," she said.

"Yes, I love my daddy," he said.

Lyric liked to hear those words since it was common for students to feel nothing but hatred for their parents/guardians.

"If he met a nice lady who would never take the place of your mother but loved him and cared for you, would you let her to love you guys, she said.

"I don't know," he said.

"Okay, that's better than never," she said.

"I'll tell you something, my momma was around but she wasn't. Casey drew near to hear details.

"Can't nobody tell you how to feel, but you need to help yourself," by not walking around scared," she said.

"Fear is a bad emotion to answer to, you feel me," she said.

"Yeah," he said.

"If you blame everyone for how you feel, it's on you," she said.

"I wanna stay mad cuz she not here," he said.

"The only thing that will happen is you'll get bitter," she said.

"Bitter," he said.

"Yeah, you know, what bitter means," she said.

"Naw, miss.," she said.

"Bitterness is when you are so angry and hurt because you think something that happened to you, was unfair," she said.

"Yeah a belligerent state of mind is trash," said Lyric.

"Y'all real smart but my brain can't take so many big words," said Irv. As the class laughed they continued.

"Picture your mind at war, stuck between what people did to you and feeling deeper pain from it, every day," she said.

"That was one of the vocabulary words for the test, last year boy," said Polly.

"Qui—et here she go gnaw-in again," he said.

Casey cleared her throat and looked at them, sternly.

"Our fault, go, head miss," he said.

"You get to the point it's almost beyond cure and start taking out your anger on other people for no reason because you think someone could have stopped the situation but did nothing," she said.

"I don't want to be bitter," he said

"So make the choice, not too," she said.

"Okay, you know what to do to feel better, we all here for you," she said.

"You know we are," said Rose.

"It's that time," she said.

"We don't wanna go," said Nescai.

"We have another meeting, don't worry," she said.

"Oh ... one more thing," she said.

"Who wants to be part of a skit, about how kids feel, in class," she said.

They all raised their hands. She was happy.

"Okay, listen to Mrs. C.," she said.

"The big meeting is in March, it's about some scenarios from my book and other twists I want you guys to write about," she said.

"That ain't far, it's a little scary but we in," said Gesa.

"Girl you ain't my lawyer, don't speak for me—naw ... we all in, I'm playin," said Polly.

"You will get to explain how teachers make you feel and all kinds of good stuff," she said.

"Finally, our side of the story gets told," said Ivory.

"It'll be, in front of the adults from the district, they are really important people, so that means, it's really important for us to be ready, she said.

"You can't get scared, when the time, comes," she said.

"We ain't scared," said Loreel.

"We will practice, before then," she said.

"Okay, it's settled Friendmanship in the world, will let the powerful people going to the meeting know, how students truly feel," she said.

"I love that name," she said.

"Let's all huddle up," said Casey.

"Mrs. C., what that mean," said Rose

"It means to get together," she said.

"Aight," said Rose.

As the club members got together, in a circle, Lyric said, "repeat after me—I do not fear," said Lyric.

"I do not fear," said the students.

"Anyone or anything," she said.

"Anyone or anything," they said.

"I will try my best," she said.

"I will try my best," they said.

"At whatever I do," she said.

"At whatever I do," they said.

"Everyone did great," she said.

They walked the students downstairs. Before long, the bus was outside to pick up them up. She walked with Lyric, her car.

"Aight, see you tomorrow, I'm gone," said Lyric.

"Wait, you have a ride," she said.

"Yup, my chariot is on the way," she said.

"Seriously," she said.

"Naw, I could walk," she said.

"I prefer to give you a ride," she said.

"I'm good," she said. As she started to walk, she felt eyes peering at her.

"Why you lurk-in," she said.

"I would feel better if, you let me give you a ride, home," she said.

"Fine ... it's around the corner," she said.

As she drove, Lyric was staring in space. Casey noticed she would zone out, sometimes. It was strange.

"You know I don't sleep," she said.

"What do you mean," she said.

"Just what I said, I don't sleep," she said.

"Sometimes I feel so tired, but I can't sleep cause the thoughts in my head be on repeat," she said.

"That's a major concern," she said.

"I don't mind, it's when I write my best poems, sometimes the pen goes so fast, my head starts to spin," she said.

"That's a health issue and I don't doubt you write great poetry," she said.

"Try some hot vegan milk," she said.

"Mrs. C. I know you wanna help, but naw," she said.

"Vegan milk is great," she said.

"I tasted it before," she said.

"So you know how great it is," she said.

"Anyway, the kids worked hard, huh," she said.

"Subject change ... nice," she said smiling.

"I'm proud of how you handled the students," she said.

"Proud," she said. She looked shocked.

"What's with the look," she said.

"People don't say they proud of me, like that," she said.

"Well, the way you got in the hearts of the kids and helped them express their fears, is a gift," she said.

"It helps that me and the kids from the same neighborhood," she said.

"I mean ... human beings, can come from a place of fear, based on our experiences if they are not dealt with," she said.

"Slavery's over, fear can't tell me what to do," she said.

"You right Harriet," she said.

"What," she said.

"That's who you remind me of, you got your railroad and everything," she said.

"Why do you always make me smile," she said.

"The gifts keep popping out," she said.

"You know what I want ... it's what we want," were lyrics from a provocative song, coming from her phone.

"My fault, I thought I put my phone on silent," she said. Casey wondered who kept calling her. She was making progress and didn't want anyone pulling her back to a negative mindset.

"Wow, Ms. Popular, that's an interesting ringtone," she said.

"Yeah, yeah, it's a song and I know you aint talk-in, your man blows your phone up," she said.

"I guess, you have a point," she said.

Although she put her phone away, the bright light was blinking, constantly.

"Sure you don't want to get that," she said.

"Naw, I'm good," she said.

"Oh, I almost forgot, here's the money for the session," she said.

"Thanks, wait ... this almost a stack, why so much," she said.

"Some jobs give pay advances," she said.

"You ain't no loan company," she said.

"I thought you could use something extra," she said.

"I'm good," she said.

"But ... I—don't worry, I ain't doin nothin bad," she said.

"Okay, here's what we spoke about," she said. As Lyric triple-checked the amount, she wondered why she did not take the extra money.

"Thanks, I love teach-in the kids," she said.

Casey was so proud of her. After only one meeting, she was making better choices. She saw the dimness in Lyric's eyes, disappear. The group would do wonders for her self-worth.

"Mrs. C. ... you daydream, sometimes," she said.

"Sorry, sometimes I zone out," she said.

"Awe man ... you not on some-thin," she said.

"Of course not," she said. She smirked and shook her head.

"I have a question, what's your biggest fear," she said.

"Do you want to know," she said.

"Um ... yeah, that's why I asked you," she said.

"Not having the child, I always wanted," she said.

She lowered her head, as tears streamed down her cheek.

"You goin be aight," she said.

"Alright doesn't seem to be enough for me," she said.

"I got a plan, the lady down the street get real mad, at her kids, she say she need a vacation, from them," she said.

"Wait ... what," she said.

"Maybe your house could be the vacation spot," she said.

"Lyric, what in the world," she said.

"But ... hold up, you tried me," she said.

"How," she said.

"I'm your daughter, you don't want to say it, but I am," she said.

"Oh wow," she said.

"We too alike, you gotta claim me, I'm your child, well ... grown child," she said.

"Every time I feel sad you cheer me up," she said. They smiled as Casey wiped her tears.

"For real, I know you'll have a baby, I need a little brother," she said.

She knew this girl was special but times like these reaffirmed it.

"You know, after me my mama can't have no more kids," she said.

She looked at her, astonished.

"Yup, it's good for her, she would mess them up, we don't need no more messed up mistakes, walk-in around," said Lyric. She grabbed her chin, quickly.

"You're not a mistake, don't believe those lies. You touched so many lives, including mine," she said.

Lyric started to rub the large bands around her wrists.

"I see you look-in, first in the coffee shop, you wanna know, what these about," she said.

"Yes," she said.

"People who supposed to be grown too funny—if you wanna know some-thin—ask," she said.

"That's true, I apologize, I should've just asked," she said.

"It's all good, I'll tell you," she said.

"You know, some months back, I figured I would do everyone a favor and just leave," she said. Slowly, she started to remove the wristbands. She had several cuts on her inner wrists, from suicide attempts. Casey's eyes started to fill with tears. She also saw two tattoos covering the scars. She was emotional for several reasons but the hurt manifested due to Lyric feeling invisible. How many students experience their feelings being swept under the rug and hidden? This was a lot for a fifteen-year-old to go through.

"I'm so sorry, go on," she said.

"I never had control over noth-in so I figured my life would be a good start, no one took it yet, so I could," she said.

"That makes sense," she said. Casey never verbalized it but whenever they couldn't conceive, she felt less human. There were times she contemplated taking her life due to her inability to reproduce. Should she share it, she thought. No! I refuse to take anything else from her. It's her time to vent, she thought. She continued to listen, attentively.

"I ain't never had no control over my mama or my stepdaddies, this part I would control. I got tats to represent the pain I was feeling, at the time," said Lyric.

"These are two hearts with barbwire, you know why I got these," she said.

"No," she said, solemnly.

"This wire represents choking, and these hearts are my feelings. The wire was tattooed on the top of the words **WHY LOVE ME?** split between both wrists. Casey started to console her. She attended trainings regarding how to relate to students while maintaining professionalism. She crossed so many lines but at this point, their bond mattered more. She leaned closer to Lyric and held her hand.

"Crazy part is my mama found me on the floor bleeding, she came to my auntie's house and when I woke up she told me the only reason she called the cops was for the check," she said. This was another inhuman act. As time went on, Lyric felt comfortable exposing another layer of venerability.

"Whenever I want to take my life I look down and the tats remind me my heart is still beating for a reason," she said.

"You don't need tattoos to remind you, you have me and a bunch of others to live for but most importantly, you have yourself," she said.

"Now is different, I got the writing club with you and different things to look forward to, it ain't like things used to be," she said.

"Yes, and we're all counting on you," she said.

"Wow, no pressure or anything, lol. Their laughter lightened the mood.

Lyric started coughing heavily.

"Are you okay," she said.

"Yeah," she said.

"There must be a flu going around, make sure to wash your hands, drink lots of fluids and keep personal space, personal," she said.

"Yes, Dr. Coper, lol," she said.

"You sound like the PSA person keep personal space, personal," said Lyric, in a jeering voice. The duo started to laugh.

"Here we go at the palace, my aunty house," she said.

"Bye, thanks for the ride," she said.

"See you tomorrow," she said.

"I'll see you, tomorrow," she said.

"Okay, Mrs. C., thank you," she said.

As she pulled off, she heard her name.

"Yo, Mrs. C. Whatchu doin here," said a familiar voice.

"Just dropping my writing club leader home," she said.

"Teachers give-in rides now," said Do.

"Anyway, don't forget your homework, guys," she said.

"We won't, it's please go home, you too pretty to be round here, late," said Money.

"Anyway, I'll see you guys, tomorrow," she said.

"Later," they said.

Casey looked in her rare view mirror to ensure Lyric didn't come outside. At this point, she may have crossed lines but helping her was crucial, she refused to allow any setbacks.

Hurtful Repetition

"Welcome home ADORATION, you got here on time," he said.

"What's the special occasion," she said.

"Life," he said.

"Oh really, that's ironic, I want to take another pregnancy test," she said.

"Are you sure," he said.

"Positive," she said.

"I want you to know whatever the results are, my love is constant, it's not contingent on our pregnancy," he said.

"I know, give me a sec.," she said.

Casey was sure, she was pregnant for the past month she was showing signs, no period, nausea, and tiredness.

"I'm going to take a shower and then we'll celebrate," she said.

He loved her commitment and determination to remain in a good state of mind.

"Hey, wait out here, the next time you see me I want my expression to be unforgettable," she said.

"Um ... okay," he said.

She ran inside the restroom, a few minutes later, he heard loud noises, coming from upstairs. Bang! Bang! Bang!

He tried opening the door but it was locked.

"Please let me in," he said.

"Why ... no," she cried.

Slowly, the door handle turned, he entered the bathroom and was greeted by a used pregnancy test, next to his sobbing wife on the floor. He was devastated.

"Let's go sit on the bed," he said.

"I don't have the energy," she said.

"Okay," he said.

He picked her up and laid her down and rubbed her back. She continued to cry, staring out in space, wondering why they could not conceive. Pregnancy was a dream that had to become a reality. She did more than one round of fertility treatments and could not take being pricked or poked, anymore.

"I can't ... I mean I won't ... take any more shots," she said.

"Hush, relax," he said.

He rubbed her feet. She understood moments like these had to happen. She needed a strong testimony of how they overcame the impossible. How would she go to work, tomorrow operating on two percent? Maybe she should share her struggle. Would it make a difference? As she contemplated possibilities, hopelessness took over. She was unsure teaching was the best idea. Every time she looked at Lyric or other students she would pair their features to a child they could not conceive. The pain was excruciating. Maybe it was time to give up.

Seven
Tracking Priorities

The next morning, Casey popped open her email, trying not to think about what happened less than 24 hours prior, she started to read.

Goodnight,

How did the peer writing club meeting go?

I can't believe we are months into the switch. The students' scores are increasing. You were right. I was so upset, about their original scores but I chose to stay positive. All challenging students are improving on behavior. It took consistency and your charts were helpful. How are my students? I'm looking forward to the big meeting, in March. See you then.

Sincerely,

Lyde Wu

Powerful Educator

We Will Thrive Elementary School

Untold Truth Brings a Tragic End-Lyde Wu

Good morning,

I'm so happy to read how well the students are doing. Improvement is a state of mind. Once we set goals, they can be achieved, if we are persistent and don't give in to negative feelings. The writing club(Friendmanship), is a real hit. We have our next meeting, today. Members of the club will be performing, at our next district meeting. The Best will be hosting it and yours truly will be the coordinator. Principal Waggenport agreed to all terms. My students are doing great. They are so funny and sweet. Speaking of their awesomeness, the scores are in and the students have all shown improvement. Remember, we have no limitations, regarding growth. Have a fabulous day. Keep up the Motiv'Plication!

Sincerely,

Casey Coper

Phenomenal Teacher

The Best High School

-Loveless learning is lifeless learning.-Casey Coper

The bell rang and the students entered her class.

"Today I'm going to give you an update on your points and help you, get ready for the Big Wig Test," she said.

"Awe," said Da'Zay.

"Calm down," she said.

"We're also going to talk about the way tests make us feel and issues with them," she said.

"Mrs. C.," said Anfel.

"Yes," she said.

"We have to take that junk, I mean the test," he said.

"Yes, you need to take the test," she said.

"Why we need tests," he said.

"Yeah ... why," said Stilts.

"I hate tests," said DenJ.

"Okay, before we start going in on how bad testing is, let me give you your scores," she said. Casey called each student up and showed them, how much they improved. They were shocked. She also showed them their behavioral points and provided prizes for students who earned them.

"Okay, now that we got that out of the way, let's talk," she said.

"Bout what," said Swoon.

"You'll see, turn our desks, in a circle and share how testing makes us feel," she said.

"Man ... Miss... I don't feel like feel-in today," he said.

"Could you do me a favor and participate," she said.

"Aight ... just cuz you nice," he said.

"Thank you," she said.

"Before you share, please be respectful toward one another—We know Mrs. C." The students interjected.

"Okay let's start with Miken," she said.

"Okay ... it's yo boy ... Money —you know ... you know ...," he said

The class cheered.

"Miken ... please—settle down everyone—we don't need a hype man, back to the topic," she said.

"My fault—I don't like tests," he said.

"Care to explain why," she said.

"They make me itch and it ain't no point, I'm allergic," he said.

She raised her sign to disagree.

"Okay, may I respond," she said.

"Yeah ... go head," he said.

"There's a point to taking tests, we need to measure how/if you're learning," she said.

"In life, we need tests, like Drivers License Tests," she said.

"True ... and I'm bout to get my auntie car," he said.

"Would you trust a driver, without a license," she said.

"My brother don't got no license and he drive," said Da'Zay.

"Could you please spare me those types of details," she said.

The class started laughing.

"The point is, I wouldn't want someone to drive me around," without a license, she said.

"You got a point, Mrs. C.," said Nazaire.

"We don't need so many tests, though," said Money.

"We gotta take a test to use the restroom, a test to do a fire drill, a test to go to dismissal, and a test to raise our hands," said Greater.

Casey tried to hold in her laughter.

"We need a test for everything," said Do.

"I agree, you take a lot of tests but did you know, there was such a thing as an exception," she said.

"What's that," said Swoon.

"Exemption means if you have an A or B in a subject, you don't need to take a final exam," she said.

"For real," said Money.

"That's one less exam for you to think about if you have the right grades," she said.

"Oh, guess what that means some of us will need to come to school, every day to learn," she said.

"Oh ... she tried you," she said.

"Quiet girl," he said.

"It's hard to get an A in something, you know nothing about unless you cheat and when you cheat it will always catch up to you," she said.

"I told you, I was Greater for a reason—I only got two Cs," said Greater.

"You ain't better den me," said Smithna.

Casey held up her sign and the whole class got quiet. The sign method was so much help. It reminded students, not to argue or speak over each other or their teacher.

"None of us like them tests," said Do.

"Sometimes we need to do things in life that may not be at the top of our list," she said.

"I guess," said Greater.

"Would anyone else like to share," she said.

"Yeah me and Smithna hate tests," she said.

"Is it because they make you nervous," she said.

"Yeah, us both," she said.

"Our guidance counselor could give you exercises to help with it," she said.

"He mean," she said.

"I'm sure that wasn't his intention," she said.

Test anxiety was a topic several schools overlooked. She recalled one of the students, during her internship earned a twenty percent on her midpoint practice Big Wig. No one could figure out what the issue was, she earned straight A's. Casey suggested she use strategies from the No **ANX Test Prep Series**—she created. After the student practiced the techniques, she increased her score to ninety-five percent. She tried to explain—the program would be beneficial for the district but she never received a response. Several students don't realize their battle with pre-test anxiety. It is often misdiagnosed as laziness or indifference.

"Don't none of us like tests," said Stilts.

"Yeah ... I be biting my nails wit tips doin a test," said Treasure(another student).

"I can't change the way you feel but I can make sure you're ready for The Big Wig," she said.

"We goin pass," said Swoon.

"Keep up the positivity," she said.

"The bell is about to ring, please make sure you have your homework written down and use the test prep. sheets, I sent home to get ready for your test," she said.

"We will," they said.

"As always, you guys did great, today," she said.

"You did great, too," said Greater.

"I think you did great too," said Swoon.

They patted each other on the back. She could not help but smile. These students were so funny. The bell rang and they were dismissed.

As Lyric approached Casey's class, she saw Greater and Stilts. Quickly, she looked down and kept walking.

"Oh ... you don't know us," no more," they said. Greater pressed his lips, together, in a kissing motion. She dismissed the comment and gesture, while entering the classroom, quickly.

"Hey ... Friendmanship Superstar .... everything alright," she said.

"Yeah, 100 percent non-GMO," she said.

"You're too creative," she said. She noticed her face was flushed and she looked dazed.

"I just want to start getting ready for the meeting," she said.

"Okay, you know where the supplies are," she said.

She started writing the topic of the meeting on the board. Today, the members would write about how to model the example they expect others to set.

"I like the way you help the students understand the topics, they picked," she said.

"It's how we relate," she said.

"Buzz .... Buzz ...

"Wow, there goes the buzz," said Casey.

We can't stop think-in bout you, what's up witchu, it's been a minute.

"Is everything okay," she said.

"What ... yeah ..., just some random text," she said.

"I hate those," she said.

"For real," she said.

"Anyway, how do you come up with such great ways to explain them," she said.

"A lot of times adults would tell me to set an example but a lot of times they never did, so it confused me," she said.

"That's confusing, we need to do better," she said.

"Nah ... you good—- it's them others with the phoniness," she said.

"You can't ask someone to always do something, you don't always do, yourself," she said.

"That's real," she said. Lyric smiled.

"There's that smile," she said.

"You been round us and the slang is contagious," she said.

"So true," she said.

"It's not about being perfect, it's about being real, kids don't like that," she said.

"That makes sense," she said.

"I know, I mean thanks," she said.

The students entered the classroom and couldn't wait for their meeting to start.

"Whoa ... don't knock me over, just kidding love hugs," said Casey.

"You been good," Lyric said.

"Yes," said the students.

"Okay ... Friendmanship--time to start," said Lyric.

"Everyone has their journals, good," she said.

"Today, we're writing about how to be the example we expect others to set," she said.

"Oh ... Miss ... I could say somethin," said Gesa.

"Yeah ... quick please," she said.

"So it's like one of the teachers at my school—he say no phones but always texting," she said.

"Yeah and Mr.—hold on no names please"—said Casey.

"Sorry ... like this other teacher be saying don't eat or drink in class—she got all the food places in her purse," said Nescai.

"She do for real, she got Yum Chicken Yum, Veggies Don't Taste Like Veggies & Slap Me Steak, all the good food places," said Polly.

The group started laughing, uncontrollably.

"I cannot with this lol," she watched as Casey held her stomach and tried not to fall over, laughing.

"This we relate to, we know teachers and people in authority expect us to set examples, regardless," she said.

"It don't be fair," said Don.

"I'm with everyone on that but instead of playing I'll Do It If You Do It, set the example, regardless," she said.

"I love that game," said Loreel.

"I know ... you understand what I'm talking about," she said.

"That's crazy though," said Rose.

"Think about it—how many of you have little brothers or sisters," she said.

Everyone raised their hands—except or student.

"Like it or not they look up to you, set the example for them," she said.

"Miss you smart," said Na'tess.

"You're smarter," she said.

"Remember ... when you set the example you earn respect, be leaders," she said.

"Please complete the sentences on the board," she said.

Setting an example is hard for me—when adults don't set because_____.

"Who wants to share, you don't have to read the whole thing, follow the numbers," she said.

"We know how it go," said Polly.

"Go head," she said.

"Setting an example is hard for me because my science teacher don't always set an example, she wants me to work when she disrespects me," she said.

"Are you disrespectful to her," she said.

"Sometimes," she said.

"Okay, that's the first problem," she said.

"I guess," she said.

"You can't expect to get the respect you refuse to give," she said.

Lyric knew she was preaching to herself when she spoke to the group. It was therapeutic for her and the students.

"No matter what, you need to set an example, even if your teacher is not trying to keep it one hundred, you need to try to," she said.

"The teacher don't like us," they said.

"Why do you think that," she said.

"Cause when we do someth-in he look at us, not the other kids," said Loreel.

"So we don't even try, in class," said Natalai.

"He forever embarrassing somebody," she said.

"Try to be respectful, anyway," she said.

"Challenge yourself... it's easy to talk back and just be disrespectful," she said.

"I do bad on my tests cuz he trash," she said.

"Me too," he said.

"If you feel you about to go crazy, just go to the corner and breathe, don't do bad on your tests that's hurting y'all not him," she said.

"That's true, it be hard sometimes," they said.

"My choice hurt how my friends and teachers see me," said Don.

"Share ... go head," she said.

"One time, I tried to fight a teacher," he said.

"I know it's hard to hold things in that's why this group matters," she said.

"True, he been looking at me sideways, ever since," he said.

"So you paranoid, now," she said.

"Para what," he said. The class chuckled.

"You paranoid, no matter how the teacher acts with you, you think he'll never like you, cause of what you did," she said.

"Yeah ... I'm that," he said.

"Change the way you think your teacher is looking at you," she said.

"So Imma think he ain't pick-in on me," he said.

"Think about it, if someone tried to fight you, wouldn't you think twice to see if they would try you, again," she said.

"Ima answer ... he would," said Gesa.

"Respect please," she said.

"Naw ... you right and she right," he said.

"Respect him and do what you go to school for—learn and get ready for next year," she said.

"Imma do it, miss," he said.

"The skit is coming up—in the meantime, you need to set an example for yourself, if for nobody else and family," said Casey.

"I remember when it was Thanksgiving, I told my reading teacher I don't like holidays, it was cuz my mom was sick but she ain't need to know, all that," said Nescai.

"She made me write bout the plan was for Thanksgiving. I couldn't take her, after that," he said.

"You feel she didn't care," she said.

"She don't—I ain't sett-in no example or do nothin for her," she said.

"Where you think that's going to get you," she said.

"Why you want to give up on yourself, I won't let you," she said.

She was thinking deeply.

"People don't know our story, sometimes you have to remember that," she said.

"Imma try and work hard, anyway," he said.

"That's all I want to hear," she said calmly. It was that moment that caused the students to respect her, more.

"I don't think it's hard to set an example for me but for my teachers it's hard," said Irv.

"Our teachers think we set an example, some of the time but sometimes we do bad things," said Rose.

She was speaking on behalf of Gesa.

"Our teachers know we steal," said Rose.

"We just take what we want, if we can't buy it, we tryin to stop," she said.

"Look, either you stop stealing or the cops are going to stop you," from doing it," she said.

"When you can, try to apply to get a job, at least it is upright money and you don't need to worry about what happens if you take something," she said.

"I babysit," you could do that," she said.

"Teachers don't leave nothin out when we come round," she said.

"You blame them," she said.

"You need to stop making excuses for yourselves and do the right thing, it's way easier to take advice than to learn in handcuffs," she said.

"You right, Miss C.," they said.

"I don't have any issues with my teachers, other than them always using me as an example," said Ivory.

It's great in class but horrible for my social life," she said.

Casey's heart melted, Ivory was her back in middle school. She only had a few friends due to jealousy and misunderstandings.

"If you don't feel comfortable with your teacher using you, as an example, why not share it," said Casey.

"I always try but she won't listen," she said.

"Just keep trying," said Casey.

"My teacher be call-in me NIGHT TIME NESC. And BLACKONY," said Nescai.

The students started to laugh.

"They be sayin it, miss," she said.

"And they be call-in me LIGHTS ON," he said.

"In class they say, we gotta keep the lights on or I'll get lost," he said.

Casey's facial expression changed. Immediately, the students stopped laughing. Why in the world were these kids using the color of their beautiful skin, negatively?

"Do you know what ignorance means," she said.

"No," said the students.

"One definition of ignorance is a lack of knowledge," she said.

"We're going to throw those names in the trash with other ignorant statements," she said.

"You know we play like that," said Rose.

"I'm with her," said Lyric.

Black people have different shades, all of them are beautiful," she said.

"Why do you think lighter skin is better," she said.

"Cause it be in songs," he said.

"Entertainers are there to entertain, don't take everything they say to heart," she said.

"Melanin(what makes our skin dark) is over five hundred dollars per gram," she said.

"We walk around worth millions—because of our beautiful black and brown complexion," she said.

"Everyone is beautiful and one of a kind—all races, colors, and tones," said Ivory.

"True—it's a sad fact—lighter versus darker skin is something slaveowners tried to push on black people," she said.

"That's true, my auntie said a man said that on the radio," said Polly.

"They used to have people with light skin, in the house and people with dark skin, in the field," she said.

"It was put in place to set another level of division, between us," she said.

"Wow miss ... that's sad," she said.

"Years later, it leads to comments like you're too black," she said.

"Every time you open your mouth and to cut down someone because they're darker, we do a U-turn back to a slavery mindset," she said.

"It's aight, we know you serious," said Lyric.

"I get emotional because we came too far to take steps back," she said.

"Miss you just told me more than my history teacher, all year," said Irv.

"She be preach-in," said Rose.

"That's real talk," he said.

"We won't say it, no more," she said.

"One more thing, if a teacher did call you that, you need to let them know, it's not okay," she said.

"What if they don't listen," she said.

"Then tell me," she said.

"She don't play," said Polly.

"We're going to have a really good skit," she said.

"True," said Lyric.

"Wait, everyone didn't finish their fill-in work," said Ivory.

"It happens, the discussion got carried away," said Casey.

"Before everyone goes let's talk about which characters you would like to play and what to add for the skit," she said. The students had great responses. They worked intensely, making sure each part was relatable.

"You got us workin, Mrs. C.," said Rose.

"Hard work pays off but our time is up, Miss C., it's time to dismiss our beautiful club," she said.

"Let's huddle up, it's time to go," said Casey.

"She say that, every time," said Sarah. The group started to laugh, as they placed one arm toward the middle of their dismissal circle.

"I will set an example," said Lyric.

"I will set an example," they said.

"Regardless of what anyone thinks," she said.

"Regardless of what anyone thinks," they said.

"I am worth more than silver and gold," she said.

"I am worth more than silver and gold," they said.

Friendmanship was a dream come true. They had Lyric who was smart and relatable and believed anything was possible. The situation created an impact of positive circulation.

Mr. Wu's Realization

That afternoon Mr. Wu was reviewing preparation material for The Big Wig Test. The students were trying so hard to master everything. They were playing a comprehension game. He figured it would trigger a couple of students, struggling with that skill. Regardless, he thought the competition would be healthy.

"I can't do this junk," said Kaz. He chose not to react and waited for him to calm down and return to the lesson. He used the techniques, Casey recommended and he felt better.

"My fault," he said.

"This test junk is hard, sometimes, huh," he said. The students started to chuckle. He never used slang.

"Thanks for apologizing," he said.

"Just know, we don't have any time to waste," he said.

"My fault," he said.

"Every minute is dedicated to the test, I can't stop a lesson, because you have a meltdown," he said.

"I know," said Kaz.

His attitude changed, tremendously as opposed to when Mr. Wu first started. As the students worked in groups, he said a prayer and pulled a new report. Mr. Wu was so happy, the scores increased, over fifty percent.

"Since everyone's scores went up, I'm giving you special rewards," he said. The class started cheering. They were so proud of their hard work.

"This proves, when you work hard, you can achieve anything," he said.

"I'll be letting Mrs. Coper know," he said.

He realized although the students' scores increased, getting them to understand the content was no easy task. He would never underestimate the role of an elementary teacher again.

Gotta Pass That Test

"Restroom breaks are permitted, only at the discretion of the test proctor," said Mr. Hez. This was the second time, Casey had to listen to the same speech, from him.

"If for any reason you're caught cheating, you'll never be able to retake this test, again," he said.

As he continued to read the test protocol, her heart started to beat, uncontrollably. She was petrified. Between trying to be Lyric's anchor, participating in The Teacher Switch, married life, and other obligations? she did not feel prepared.

Casey remembered the words of Monica. "Casey, you still have that test to take," she said. She was worried but felt some way she would pass, even though the situation seemed contrary. "Once you enter the test room and are seated, you may begin," he said.

Slowly, she took her seat. She was scared to crick her neck. The sample questions were easy. The first portion was writing. She felt confident, regarding this part. The topic was: gaining confidence in a world of shame. Casey typed with agility. Next, was the reading segment of the exam. She read through the paragraphs and answered all the questions. It was easy. Finally, part three reared its ugly head—Math. She had a hard time remembering formulas. Oh no ... slopes she thought... my worst enemy and Calculus made her cringe. The first three questions were fine, then, she had no idea, what she was reading. The entire math portion seemed like an uninterpretable code no one could debunk. Suddenly, she started to feel clammy. The room seemed hot and she started to sweat. In nervous haste, she went through and guessed on the majority of the questions. The notification read: You are now finished. Please raise your hand and the test proctor will assist you. Slowly, She raised her hand. Mr. Hez entered the room and escorted her out. She entered her passcode to view the results on a screen—in the lobby. She passed her reading and writing portion; however, she missed the math segment by three points. Three points. How in this world did I miss the math by three points? An additional point of failure, made Casey feel horrific. Her efforts to change the method of approach for educators would be for nothing—if she did not pass this test. Would people ridicule her? This was hurtful. She was nominated for influential roles; failing the certification exam was not part of the plan. She could not deal with her score; denial set in. Although she had a short time to pass this exam, she could not focus on it. Eventually, she would pass and everything would be fine. She left the building and started to drive home. She was petrified to see Rye.

"Hey beautiful, how did everything go," he said.

"Everything went well," she said.

"Time to celebrate, again," he said.

"I mean ... I have one more part to take, again," she said.

She was nervous, would he see right through her lies?

"I thought this was the last part," he said.

Her lips uttered words, contrary to her facial expression.

"Well, I was wrong," she said.

"Oh ...," he said.

"The policies keep changing," she said.

"Sounds foreign," he said.

"Can they keep doing that," he said.

"They can," she said.

"Stop with the question drills," she said.

"Okay, topic dropped—your dinner is on the table," he said.

He was an amazing husband. How could she betray his trust? They always told each other the truth.

"Could you leave me alone for a while," she said.

"Sure, I need to pick some stuff up, at the store," he said.

"Okay," she said.

"See you in a little bit," he said.

He kissed her and headed out.

Ding! Hey! It's been a while. Could you call me? Did I do something wrong? It was Ava. Casey did not understand this aspect of her personality. She cut people off, without an explanation, sometimes. It was wrong.

Casey wrote:

How are you? I know it's been a while. Honestly, I think we should stop contacting each other. I don't feel you're supportive. She knew, providing her with closure was the right thing to do but pressing send was next to impossible.

After twenty minutes, Ava replied:

I don't know, what happened but I'm sorry. I respect your decision. If you ever need me, I'm here.—Ava

She resented her response. There were many times, she needed her and she was nowhere to be found. This was an excuse to control her decision to continue with the switch. She would not fall for it. She did not reply. Casey was engulfed with the sick twisted feeling of defeat. Her test results took precedence over this foolishness. She felt uncertain and lost. Exhaustion from the thought of not being able to get her certification, due to a three-point inadequacy wore her out.

What's Up Witcha Girl

The days were flying. Although her new school had drawbacks, she enjoyed the change of environment. The students were progressing and Friendmanship was getting stronger. Eat N'

Express was a hit. Principal Waggenport loved the idea. However, certain coworkers were not thrilled. They disliked Casey because the students adhered to her requests and ignore them. She tried to create a plan with them but Mr. Zee was the only person to run with the idea. After school students would meet up to relax, talk and watch the football players, practice. The picnic benches by the field were packed and students were having fun.

"Y'all heard from Favor's," said Sanrell(Stilts).

"Naw, nothin," said Money.

"What's up wicha girl," said Do.

"She been missin, a while," said Money.

"Favors fine too bad she bang-in eeeerybody," said DenJ.

"Text her Anfel," said Money.

"Naw, I got a girl now," he said.

"Man dis man here, swear he in love," he said.

"Imma be good fa her, no stepp-in out," he said.

"No steppin out," he said, mockingly. The group chuckled.

"You gotta phone, handle that," he said.

"Man … I ain't tryinna come off thirsty," he said.

"Here he go," said Sanrell.

"Unno too tersty mon," said Rat.

"Yo, ain't nobody tryin to hear you, rude booyyyyyy," he said.

"You hit that, too," said Money.

"He ain't neva lie," said Zaire.

"So what … not again, my frien," said Rat.

"Yeah right," said Money.

"We all hit that," said (Greater).

"You could be thirsty, just not parched," said Lakes. The group laughed, loudly.

"This man got a new teacher, he learn-in new words, now he Mr. Dictionary," said Swoon.

"I love her," he said.

"We do too," said the group.

"She so pretty and real smart," said DenJ.

"We know," said Do & Money.

"Dang man … I can't start after drills, I left my ball, real practice 'bout to start, " he said.

"Go get it, before coach kill you," said Stilts.

"It don't matter to y'all plastic coach, no way," said Lakes.

"Anyway, y'all help me out," said Money.

"This girl got him soudin crazy," said Swoon.

"I gotchu," said Greater.

"Sanrell & Garnell get out here," exclaimed the coach.

"Coach, I forgot someth-in," said Greater.

"What is it," exclaimed the coach.

"Man … an excuse is a misuse of your time and mine," he said.

"Louder, I can't hear you," exclaimed the coach.

"An excuse is a misuse of your time and mine," he said.

"Coach, I ain't forget my ball," said Stilts.

"Watchu want a pat on the back for do-in what's expected, start drills," he said.

"Yes coach," he said.

"Greater, I catch you leav-in your ball again, bring a blanket to keep that bench nice and warm for the next game, you smell me," he exclaimed.

"My fault, sorry coach," he said.

The group laughed, as he was chastised.

"See what I'm sayin, y'all swear I'm good off that man," said Lakes.

"This man lyin, why you try out den," said Zaire.

"I ain't speak-in on that right now," he said.

"Yeah … I bet," he said.

"Now we ain't goin know when she text back, cuz Anfel wanna act funny," said Money.

"Take yo scary behind and go ask Greater," he said.

"So you want the coach to die, " he said.

"Watchu mean," he said.

"You know you can't go on the field before his heart bust," he said. They started to laugh.

"Y'all swear I'm playin, he talk to me like he out his mind, he goin ball up," he said.

"Yu ago bust im ead," said Rat.

"You already know," he said.

"Naw, don't try it," said Swoon.

Meanwhile …

"Where you want these,"

"Those book bins need to go back, in the corner," said Casey. Lyric was setting up for their next Friendmanship Meeting.

"Aight," she said.

"I can't wait to hear what the next topic is Mrs. Casanova," she said.

"Don't get all formal on me," she said.

"You're funny," she said.

Buzz! Buzz!

What's up wichu, ghost. As she read the text, she prayed Casey would not notice the change in her disposition.

Buzz! Buzz!

"Everything okay," she said.

"Yeah, it's good," she said.

"Yo Mrs. C., I forgot my … oh … what's up," said Greater.

As Casey jumped in front of her, she wanted to disappear.

"You good Mrs. C.," he said.

"Yes, we're good, forgot what," she said.

"Oh, my basketball, from the lunch party," he said.

"Great, please get it and I'll see you, tomorrow," she said.

"She be help-in you, now," he said.

"Yes, we're really busy," she said.

Lyric gripped her shirt, cringing.

"Aight then, tomorrow," he said.

After he left, she hugged Casey, tightly and was shaking.

"Where you goin," she said.

"I'm locking the door, so we have no other interruptions," she said.

"Hey, no judgment remember," she said.

"I know," she said.

"I … I was with him and some other—don't explain," she said.

"Please understand, he is my student but I will protect you, no matter what," she said.

"You the only mama I know," she said.

At that point, there were no words to express the wounds that reopened, as a result of seeing him.

"Are you okay to run the group," she said.

"No but it don't matter, I gotta help them," she said.

"Whenever you're ready, we can talk about it or not," she said.

"Naw, let's leave the past, where it's at," she said.

"The only problem is, the past remains present when you relive it," she said.

"There go another billion-dollar meme," she said. They filled the room with laughter.

"I want a fresh start, no more doin boys for money," she said.

"You have no idea how happy it makes me that this is what you want," she said.

"It is and I want you to know, how much you matter," she said. Casey looked at her as tears filled her eyes.

"Don't go cryin," she said.

"You know, I'm emotional," she said.

"Let's keep setting up," she said.

As they got ready for members of Friendmanship, they spoke about several topics. Casey forgot she was only fifteen. Their bond was an unstoppable force.

Update

"Sweeyouuu," yelled Greater. That was the group's call for an emergency.

"Y'all guess who up in the teacher room," said Greater.

"Mr. Zee huh, he stay trynna get some, he can't pull that," said Lakes.

"Naw, I forgot my ball at lunch in the class and saw Favors in there," he said.

"You lyin, but she a Freshman, why she in her class," said Do.

"I dunno," he said.

"Favors in a whole 'nother building," said Lakes.

"Yeah and she was actin different," he said.

"Who, Favors or Mrs. C.," said Ziare.

"Both," he said.

The group was quiet.

"You don't think … she said some-thin," said Lakes.

"Garnell get out here, now," exclaimed the coach.

"You better go," said Lakes.

"Ten laps for every minute you were late," he exclaimed.

"It. Could. Not. Be. Me.," said Lakes.

"I know she best not say nothin to teach," said Do.

"Man forget it, imma text her," said Do.

Conventional Responses

"Hello everyone, welcome back," said Casey.

"Hey teachers," said the group.

"Everybody sit down, please," said Casey.

"What's up, Friendmanship," said Lyric.

"Hey miss," said the students.

"We ready to get smarter and write," said Gesa.

"I'm excited," said Ivory.

"Us too," said Rose.

"What we writin bout," said Irv.

"Well … let's read the board," she said.

"How do you feel for real," they said.

"That's the question," she said.

"Watchu mean, for real," said Polly.

"I know, like how we doin," said Sarah.

"Write on the piece of paper on your desk, how many times do you ask people how they feel," she said.

"Now, hold your paper up," she said.

"I always ask people how they doin, even at the store," said Gesa.

"That's good, I see high numbers, okay, now let's be real, how many times do you want them to tell the truth," she said.

The group members looked at each other, confused. They didn't know, how to respond.

"It's like this, the checkout lady at the store, she don't know you and ask everybody the same thing, how are you, she don't care," she said.

"That be so true, " said Gesa.

"It ain't cuz be bad people, she don't know us enough to care," she said.

"Sad part is, sometimes we don't know us, enough to care so why should anyone else," she said.

"That's real," said Casey.

"True, we gotta be genuine," she said.

"What's that," said Nescai.

"It means we gotta be real, no plastic," she said.

"We so focused on us, listening to other people is hard but we gotta focus," she said.

"It be like when I been talk-in for long on FT and ask-in a question some people keep sayin that's crazy," said Na'Tess.

"Right, they too wrapped up to care how you feel-in," she said.

"It's real sad, we all don't be listen-in," said Polly.

"Thanks for being real and sayin that, like we know it's a lie if you say you listen, to everybody, all the time," she said.

"Imma ask my mama how she feel, later," said Rose.

"That's a great start," she said.

"So fill in the blank, I will make sure to listen when someone is talking by_____," she said.

She gave the group time to work, it was time to share.

"Do everyone gotta share," said Gesa.

"No," she said.

"I'll make sure to listen when someone is talking by saying what they say when I start to not pay attention," said Polly.

"Yup, that's good, if you repeat what the person says to make sure, it will keep your attention," she said.

"No one wants to share," she said.

"Aight just write, I guess, and I'll come around to check your papers," she said.

"Hold up miss, it's cuz I feel bad like you got me think-in, I don't be listen-in," said Irv.

"We feel bad," said Don.

"Look, we can't go back and change the past, sitting think-in about how you didn't listen and feeling guilty isn't helping, now we know what to do, let's do it," she said.

"Aight that's true, Imma go," said Loreel.

"Okay," she said.

"I'll make sure to listen when someone is talking by not scroll-in in," he said.

"Y'all know we scroll when people tryin to talk and only get twenty percent of what they sayin," she said. The group laughed.

"That's true, miss," said Don.

"It be happen-in with my auntie, she say why y'all young people always scroll, then she do it," she said.

"Too much," said Lyric.

"Oh … now y'all all wanna go," she said. She looked up and several students raise their hands.

"It's a great thing," said Casey.

"That's right ma—I mean Mrs. C.," she said. Casey looked her in the eyes and yearned to correct her but the situation was already awkward.

"Y'all good, cuz I'm ready fa my turn," said Gesa.

"Yeah, go head," she said.

"Okay, I will make sure to listen when someone is talking by taking notes," she said. The entire group burst into laughter.

"Be respectful please," said Casey.

"Miss, how you goin take notes," said Irv.

"On my phone, dummy," she said.

"Remember no names, that ain't a bad idea," said Lyric.

"I know it ain't," said.

"He always be tryin somebody," she said.

"Relax, explain what you mean," she said.

"Like you could take notes on your notepad or some-thin like we be doin for class," she said.

"Takin notes does help, people remember important details," said Casey.

"Thank you … see I told y'all, don't laugh," she said.

"They won't no more," said Lyric.

"Plus the principal be takin notes, when my mama come in complain-in and she say, I know that lady care cuz she write what I say," she said. The class got quiet. It was a great tactic, several leaders utilized to help irate parents calm down.

"She a smart lady, that's why I said that's a good idea, you gotta wait to hear people out, Irv," she said.

"My fault," he said.

"Go head Na'Tess," she said.

"What about like doin videos," she said.

"Um, well you could but how would you give advice, and make sure to listen, in the moment," she said.

"Oh … okay I got it, say I heard you and mean it," she said. Casey and Lyric started to giggle.

"I ain't laughing at you it's just—what you said ain't plastic, thanks for that," she said.

"Welcome," she said.

"A lot of time we in our world, not car-in just sayin, yeah but not listen-in," she said.

"Tess that's true," said Ivory.

"Right," said Rose.

"Sometimes I feel real bad and all my girls wanna do is make videos, "said Polly.

"Like I wanna hear real words for my real problems," she said.

"Right, that's it whatever you need, me and Mrs. C. gotchu," she said.

"We love y'all," said Sarah.

"We love this club," said Lyric.

"Make sure to listen when someone is talking by being in the moment for real," she said.

"That's a great plan," said Casey.

"Okay, Ivory, your turn," she said.

"I think people who aren't deep just don't think outside of themselves," she said.

"First we was hat-in but you smart, for real," said Polly.

"You got us think-in," said Irv. The group giggled and provided her with positive affirmations.

"See this is what the club is about, making others feel good," she said

"I ain't goin lie, I was hatin hard on you, at first, my bad," said Gesa.

"It's cool, guys, I'm not from around here and it's normal to give the new girl a hard time," she said.

"All this love got me feeling woozy," said Loreel.

"Boy, be quiet," said Rose as the group laughed.

"Goin back to what Ivory said, thinking outside of yourself, is important," she said.

"Yeah, we are so preoccupied with what's in our world it's not on purpose but there's no room for anyone else's problems," she said.

"Beautiful explanation," said Casey.

"That's true, so selfishness is a huge issue of why it's hard for us to focus," said Lyric.

"Yeah and some people give the lame excuse they have a low attention span, really and you can sit on someone's page for hours, I don't buy that," she said.

"This girl preaching," said Irv.

"Everyone made some great points, Nescai you're next, then it's time to close out after we talk about our answers in groups," she said.

"The time be goin fast," said Polly.

"Very true," said Casey.

"Well, I think … or I know when people I talk to brink up things I said to help some-thin new I talk about it makes me feel good," he said.

"Why," she said.

"Cuz so many people be forget-in or they don't listen so you gotta start all over," he said.

"So true, how many times you gotta repeat yourself, hold up a number," she said. They wrote double-digit numbers.

"It's sad the numbers are so high but we all do it," she said.

"Aight' Don. You could go," she said.

"Mine was the same as Ivory's but I will make sure to listen by snapp-in my band when I start think-in 'bout someth-in else," he said.

"Your band," said Casey.

"Yeah, I be use-in it when my mind wanna run away," he said.

"In class, when he almost sleep, he snap it," said Loreel. The group started to laugh and inquire about this method.

"It's not a crazy idea but it don't hurt," she said.

"Naw, it helps me, not stray," he said.

"Wow, that's different," said Casey.

"Aye whatever works," she said.

"Thanks so much for giving great answers, now turn to someone who shared a point you could relate to and add details to the topic," she said.

"I love this part," said Gesa.

"Everyone has twenty minutes," she said. As the students elaborated on their experiences, she monitored them.

"Hey, quick question, what was with the slip-up," said Casey.

"It's my fault, how I felt took over, my bad," she said.

"No judgment, it was a little awkward, but you know I care for you," she said.

"I know, there's a game tonight, here," she said.

"A football game," she said. She thought of the occurrence earlier and knew Lyric didn't feel comfortable going to the game, alone.

"Are you going," she said.

"I kinda want to, I asked the friends I don't have but they don't exist," she said.

"Please stop, I'll stay if you need me to," she said.

"Naw, you got a platinum husband to make dinner for," she said.

"I don't want you here after dark, besides he knows I work late, sometimes, she said.

"Aight," she said.

"Plus you'll need a ride, home," she said.

"Okay everyone, times going, it's time to wrap up," she said.

"Let's huddle up," said Casey.

"That still sound funny," said Polly. Laughing she redirected the students to the front of her classroom.

"Everybody say … I will listen," said Lyric.

"I will listen," they said.

"I won't be selfish," she said.

"I won't be selfish," she said.

"Alright Friendmanship, that's it," said Casey.

They walked the students downstairs ensuring they loaded on the bus, safely.

"My Ms. C's," said the group.

"Bye everyone, great job," she said.

"Bye, see ya'll soon," said Lyric.

Hey sweetheart, I need to work late, I won't be home until later, eat dinner. I still and always will love you, Casey.

"You gonna call your husband," she said.

"I just texted him, the game starts at what time," she said.

"Like an hour," she said.

"Hungry," she said.

"A little," she said.

"That means a lot," she said.

"I have a supermarket, in the class or I can order something," she said.

"Mrs. C., y'all don't make money," she said.

"You're right but thank God my husband does, we have the whole protest going on, he's a lifesaver," she said.

"I wanna marry rich," she said.

"I wouldn't describe us that way but if that's what you want, go for it," she said.

"Man, if I live that long," she said.

"Don't you ever say that, " she said.

"Okay … don't get so mad," she said.

"I'm not, Lyric you're very special to me and so young, " she said.

"You ain't know when it's time to get married I'll be nursing home age in my neighborhood," she said.

"Are you okay," she said. As they climbed the stairs to get back to the classroom, Lyric was out of breath.

"Yeah, I'm good, see I'm gettin old already," she said.

"You're funny," she said.

They continued to engage in discourse. She wanted to ask Lyric if she texted or called home but the question was rhetorical.

Beep! "I hate the intercom," said Lyric.

"Yes," she said.

"Um … Mrs. Coper, someone is looking for you," said Ms. Tooks.

"What is the front office still doing open," she said.

"I'm here still because there is a game and a parent meeting, tonight, " she said.

"Oh, who is looking for me,"

"Someone you know, should I let him up," she said.

"It gotta be Mr. Zee," said Lyric.

"Hush," she said.

"Sure, let him up," she said.

"Maybe it's the delivery guy, why would you say it was Mr. Zee," she said.

"Imma Freshman and I know bout it what you think people sayin," she said.

"There's nothing to say, I'm married," she said.

"You married and fine he still like you," she said.

"Thanks for the"——Boom! Boom! Boom!

"Did you let the police up or the delivery man," she said.

"Wait here, as she approached the door, she noticed a familiar silhouette.

" My ADORATION," he said.

"What are you doing here," she said.

"I got your text and figured you'd be hungry," he said.

"Dang, that's yo husband, "said Lyric.

"I'm Mr. Coper," he said.

"Call him Rye, she said.

"I'm Lyric, nice to meet you," she said.

"I have to stay for the game," she said

"Really, yeah it's a" —Boom! Boom! Boom!

"Who in the world is that," he said.

She opened the door, reluctantly.

"Rye meet Mr. Zee," she said.

"This is my husband, Rye," she said.

"Great meeting you, he said.

"Your wife is an amazing teacher," he said.

"I know," he said. Rye looked at him, scowling. As Lyric watched the interaction, she tried not to laugh.

"Hey, you stay-in for the game," he said.

"Yeah, I'll be around," she said.

"Awesome, well it was nice meeting you Rye, I'm headed to the field to help set up," he said.

"Likewise," he said. Quickly he pulled Casey and place his arm around her shoulder. The tension was thick and awkwardness overflowed from all ends.

"Mrs. C. Imma go downstairs to get the food," she said.

"Not alone, I'll walk with you," she said.

"I'm good, no diaper needed, I got it," she said.

"But—She can handle grabbing some food, Case," he interjected.

"Please don't," she said. As they bickered, she left the classroom.

"Look, I brought all your favorites, some vegan chili, and cornbread, you have snapper and—

"Great thanks," she said.

"Well, I need to go, she said.

"Why do you look frazzled," she said.

"I'm not," she said.

"I'm in my work element and we keep our professions separate for a reason," she said.

"All of a sudden that's what we do, all I hear about is the switch and everything else," he said.

"Please don't start," she said.

"I wish I could stay for the game but I have a ton of paperwork," he said.

"That's sweet, but you don't have to," she said.

"I could bring it here and wait for you," he said.

"That's so extra," she said.

"Well, I wanted to make sure you were fine, please reply to my texts," he said.

"Sure thing boss," she said.

"You want me to give you the shots," he said.

"I got it," she said.

"I still and always will love you," he said. Grabbing the back of her neck, he kissed her, gently.

"I still and always will love you too," she said.

Boom! Boom! Quickly, she ran to the door.

"Here go the food," said Lyric.

"Thanks," she said.

"We got us a whole picnic," she said.

"Very true, you're funny," said Rye.

That she is," she said.

"I got your rat with a side of tofu, " she said.

"Cool girl," he said.

"Well I'm gone, it was great meeting you, Lyric," he said.

"Me too Mr. Coper," she said.

As he left she felt torn. When would she feel comfortable telling him about Lyric? The reason she wanted him to leave had everything to do with feeling unjustified. She did not know how to explain giving a student a ride home, she did not teach. This was above her head but she made a commitment and emotional waves clouded her judgment.

"Aight it's time," she said.

"I'll bring our bags downstairs, that way we won't need to make two trips, she said.

"Cool, I got a mini purse anyway," she said.

"I was meaning to ask, that seems to be trending," she said.

"No, it is trending," she said.

As they walked downstairs she felt the strings to their bond tighten. Lyric needed someone to protect her. The field was packed and it was evident not all people were there to watch the game. There were girls in revealing clothing making hand gestures Casey didn't understand and men wearing long coats that had serious demeanors. There were no security guards and one officer was at the snack stand.

"Yo ... Mrs. C. Whatchu doin here," said Money.

"Well I said I would come to a game, right," she said.

"What's good, Lyric," he said. She looked at him surprised considering he never referred to her by that name.

"Hey," she said.

"Where y'all sit-in," he said.

"At the top, let's go," she said. She ensured Lyric walked ahead of her, as he watched them walk away.

"Man, y'all seen Mrs. C. wit Favors, he said.

"Naw for real," said Lakes.

"They sit-in up there," said Money.

"Crazy," said Lakes.

"Whatever Greater out here showin his behind again," said Do.

"You crazy … yo … this man slapped da back of my helmet, hard why I gotta ride da bench," he said.

"Who cares, now the kid's missing a tooth," said the coach.

"I told him keep the helmet on cuz he goin get knocked out, if he take it off, he ain't listen," he said.

"No that's not Number One behavior, you're nuts if you think I'm putting my job on the line you can't punch another player," he said.

"He slapped it hard, he ain't on my team, can't get too comfortable," he said.

"People do it, all the time," he said.

"You're out the rest of the game," he said.

"Naw, we got scouts here, man … I'm good," he said.

"Where you goin," said the coach.

"This man out here slapp-in people you suppose to be da coach, be on my side," he said.

"What else can I do, thanks to you, he's missing a tooth," he said.

"Man I'm out," he said.

"Get back here or don't come back period," said the coach,

"Look this team need me, I'm receiver, don't try me," he said.

"Yeah … receiver not quarterback," he said.

"Man he throw it, I catch it … now ain't nobody good catch-in," he said.

"Jose's the backup, he's good," he said.

"He trash just like that man miss-in a tooth, fake behind, don't touch people you don't know, moral of the game," he said.

"What's good G.," said Money.

"We gotta handle some-thin for you after the game," he said.

"Naw I got it," he said.

This man wanna catch himself slap-pin my helmet then jump in my face, I told him take the helmet off, don't back down,

You had some-thin for him," said Do laughing.

"Yup, now he over there crying, oh well, don't touch me, if you dunno me," he said.

"Blood all over the field, the benches all that," said DenJ.

"I'll be right back," said Casey to Lyric.

"Okay," she said.

She watched the incident and started walking down the bleachers.

"Greater could I speak with you," she said.

"Mrs. C. I'm hot dis man put hands on me," he said.

"Let's take a little walk," she said.

"I need you to understand that wasn't a good decision, there are scouts here, I see a bunch of them recording," she said.

"Watchu know 'bout my world," he said.

"A lot, football is a big deal … well my husband and I have been preoccupied but we were really into it, in college," she said

"More I know you is the more we get each other," he said.

"That didn't need to get physical," she said.

"You look like the bad guy the video shows you hitting him not the other way around, practice self-control," she said.

"I think I'm off the team," he said.

"Is that what the coach said," she said.

"Naw, I just walked away, he said I gotta ride the bench probably for the season, everything blown," he said.

"No, it's not, go back and sit out the game, every action triggers a consequence," she said.
"What," he said.

"You opened this door by hitting him now you need to show you're sorry, walking away from your team will hurt them but it will hurt you, more," she said

"You right Mrs. C. imma go back As they headed toward the field, Lyric watched from the bleachers.

"I'm back, sorry coach," he said.

"Is this the influence you have over my players," he said.

"I only made suggestions, he decided to listen that's what matters," she said.

"You're sitting out the rest of the game and I dunno about the rest of the season," he said.

"I know, my bad," he said.

Quickly, she remembered Lyric was alone and darted toward her.

"Let's go," said Lyric, Money, and DenJ followed as she walked down the bleachers.

"Everything okay," she said.

"We all good, right Lyric," said DenJ.

"Yeah, I'm just ready to go," she said. She followed her as they headed to the parking lot.

"See you in class, Mrs. C.," exclaimed Money. Casey waved and continued walking.

"What's going on did they bother you, she said.

"You pick them over me, why you left," she said.

"Greater was in trouble you could've gotten suspended, it was for a second, she said.

"Whoa! What's wrong," she said. Lyric held her stomach and keeled over vomiting.

"He ain't great he trash—they all trash you can't recycle," she said

She held her hair rubbing her back.

"You don't get it," she said.

"I do that's why I would never let you come here by yourself, "she said.

"Naw, they trash," she said. She gazed into her eyes, deeply.

"Is there something you want to tell me," she said.

"I ain't been with none of them I ain't text them nothin see, she said. Quickly she showed her the text that she received, earlier.

"I'm tryin hard but you can't pick them, I need you, she said.

She held her tightly

"I know, I'm sorry," she said.

"I wanna go home," she said.

The ride to her aunt's house was awkward. Lyric stared out the window, as she drove.

"Okay here we go," she said.

"Thanks for the ride," she said.

"See you tomorrow," she said.

"Yeah, bye," she said.

As she shut the car door, Casey regretted rushing to Greater. What message did that send? She was at the bottom her entire life. How could she be so insensitive? Thoughts overwhelmed her, as she pulled into the driveway.

"Hey love, I thought you were inside, why are the lights on," she said.

"What are you doing with this girl," he said.

"What do you mean, " she said.

"I never left," he said.

"Wow your stalker tactics just shot through the roof," she said.

"It's not about that, I asked you to respond to my texts," he said.

She was so distracted by both situations(at the game) she never checked her phone. There were several texts and calls from Rye.

"I followed you from the game to her house, that poor girl's neighborhood—spare me the phony political relation," she interjected.

"Now I'm phony," he said.

"Yeah, it's none of your business where she lives or how I'm helping her," she said.

"Helping her, why does everything and everyone else get catapulted to your priority list, while I and the baby suffer," he said.

"What baby," she exclaimed.

"Exactly, when will you prioritize," he said.

"I'm going upstairs," she said.

"No, you're not running away," he said.

"I need to pee, do you want me to go here," she said.

"What's up with you and that girl," he said.

"She has issues, I need to help with," she said.

"No, you don't," he exclaimed.

"She's a Freshman, who I mentor," she said.

"Now you're her mentor," he said.

"Yes, we started a writing club and she basically runs it, " she said.

"I bet it was your idea," he said.

"Yeah, you're right but it's helping her and a lot of the students," she said.

"How about helping your husband not worry," he said.

"What are you saying," she said.

"Give me your phone, I called and texted you so many times," he said.

"No,"she said.

"Keep this up and I'm— you're what, he interjected.

They vowed to never tread in the low-blow territory.

"Look, we can't keep going back and forth," she said.

"No, we can't say the words we can't," he said.

"Quitting on communicating, having a family or love, aren't options, they never were and never will be," he said. "Wow, is this a gang, maybe we should've gotten initiation tattoos and jumped each other in, after the wedding," she said.

Her acerbic comment reflected her perception of what was necessary.

"Guess what, she needs me," she said.

"You have wounded bird syndrome," he said.

"What," she said.

"Every time someone appears to need help, you flip into Casey the Superhero," he said.

"Who are you calling," she said.

"I knew it, your phone was on silent, a football game isn't a meeting, " he said.

"I'm getting in the shower," she said.

"No, we're getting in the shower," he said.

"Stop, she said. As she ran upstairs, he followed her. She entered the restroom and tried to close the door but he intervened and broke the doorknob. Slowly, she placed her back against the bathroom wall, as they sunk to the floor.

"I just want you to be honest," he said.

"It's too much and I gave her my word she would not be let down again," she said.

"Making promises like that automatically disqualifies our commitment to make a family," he said.

"Not true," she said.

"Those are gigantic words to fulfill and you know it," he said. Gently, he placed her face in the palm of his hand.

"You have a lot going on, adoration," he said.

"We won't have these issues, please don't take on any more projects," he said.

"She needs me," she said.

"We need you, the baby, and me, we will get pregnant," he said.

Turning she buried her head, in his shoulder and started to cry.

"That's what it is and that's okay, I know you and you know me that's why we're a team," he said.

"You're afraid of failing but there's no need to hide your fears," he said.

"I was petrified, after the last time and can't do it," she said.

"We were petrified and we can do it," he said.

"You in deep with this girl, I can tell, it was just like the puppy project," he said.

"Rye stop, she's not a dog," she said.

"I know but your heart is wrapped up in helping her, just like the puppy," he said.

"I guess you're a little right," she said.

"You gotta keep it professional with these kids," he said.

"They're not kids, you mean teens," she said.

"Whatever, look don't get too involved, a lot of them have sad stories and you can't be their savior," he said.

"I signed up to teach," she said.

"Exactly, keep it at that just like I keep it professional at the bank," he said.

"Two different professions," she said.

"I won't try to understand your world, it would insult your professionalism but I'm sure, you crossed certain boundaries," he said.

She was quiet. He was correct. She violated several segments of her contract but backing away(from Lyric) was not an option.

"I know you will still be involved just take it down a couple of notches, okay," he said.

"Okay," she said.

"We still and always will know and adore each other," he said.

"It's getting late, I love you ADORATION," he said.

"I love you so much," she said. Gently, he helped her off the floor and they prepared for bed. As they settled down holding each other, she thought of how distraught Lyric was, in the parking lot. Eventually, they drifted to sleep.

Nauseous Updates

Good morning, How are you feeling? I'm sorry we didn't get to talk, at the game, I'll see you, soon. Mr. Zee had a hard time understanding, Casey was involved. What was he thinking? What if her husband saw the message? She was exhausted and the first person she thought of after waking up was Lyric. Was her stomach feeling better? Did helping Greater put a strain on their relationship? Why did she make such a mistake? The drive to school was short but attempting to get out of the car, took a while. Thankfully, she did not have another argument with Rye.

"Hey it was great meeting the hubby, yesterday," said Mr. Zee.

"The or mine, she said," she said.

"Great catch, I meant your hubby," he said.

The feeling was mutual," she said.

"He seems like a sweet guy," he said.

This was a sad attempt to make a pointless conversation, considering she was exhausted, was ruminating about Lyric's wellbeing, and had to set up for class.

Anything I can help with, he said.

"Not really, I did want to ask what the text at 4:30 a.m. was about," she said.

"Oh, just checkin on you," he said.

"Look, I don't want to be rude but my husband does not appreciate that," she said.

"My apologies, guess I'll go to my room," he said.

"Yeah, sounds like a great plan," she said.

"See you later," he said.

"Maybe … or maybe not," she said.

She inherited her mother's cold shoulder gene. She was great at making people feel uncomfortable when she determined their interaction was pointless. Finally, he left. She wanted to change her number but his heroic actions(in the past) made her feel conflicted. The warning bell rang and she could not believe how fast the time went.

"Oh shoot, Lyric," she said.

"What's good, Mrs. C.," said Money.

Hey everyone, turn to page 103 in your workbooks and re-read the passage, I'll be right back," she said.

"You good," said DenJ.

"Of course," she said.

"Quick favor, could you watch my class," she said. She burst into Mr. Zee's room as if their strange interaction was years ago.

"Sure, I'll leave the emergency sign for my class and they'll join us, in your sanctuary," he said. This guy told the weirdest jokes, she thought.

"Thanks," she said.

Second Bell

"Good morning everyone," said the teacher.

"I hope you read the chapter on—

"Excuse me, is Lyric Casanova, here," she said.

"Yes, do you need something, Mrs. Coper, said the teacher.

"Could I speak with her," she said.

"Go ahead," Lyric

"Thank you and sorry for interrupting," she said.

"Hey, how's your stomach," she said.

"You ova here, bout that," she said

"Of course, your health matters," she said.

"My stomach a lil sick but I'm good," she said.

"Want anything a soda … I mean not soda it's morning … well ginger ale would be—stop, I'm in your eye, you see me, I said I'm good," she interjected. Lyric looked at her without blinking once.

"Okay, great," she said.

"You wanna say … is we good and yeah, we good," she said.

"I know you care you crazy care halfway cross the campus when you gotta she said. They smiled, as she emitted a long breath.

"Now, imma go back and act like I'm listen-in," she said.

"No, you need to listen," she said.

"It's the same bor-in junk, ain't her fault but now it's all bout you and the club," she said. Friendmanship was a form of Enrichment Work. She was happy to provide Lyric with a challenge.

"I get it," she said.

"Aight, later," she said.

"Sorry, again," she said.

As she re-entered the class, her teacher gave Casey a strange look. She darted back to her room.

"Phew just in time, I was about to text you but never mind," said Mr. Zee. A few boys chuckled.

The class had a large number of students, her former principal would not mind but high school is different.

"Thanks again, sorry," she said.

"Everything okay," he said.

"Yeah," she said.

"Anything else I can do is a text away," he said.

"I appreciate it," she said.

"Great, she's in a settled, my clan let's go," he said.

"Awe man, I like this class," said one of his students.

"I do too, trust me, oh well, back to our class," he said. He stared at her as they left. Usually, the class was talkative but the room was silent.

"Alright everyone, ——Ohhhh, Mr. Zee be lik-in you miss," Da'Zay interjected.

"Okay, inappropriate," she said.

"I'm trynna help y'all," she said.

"No need to and who's y'all," she said.

"You and that big, ice pack on yo finger," she said.

"That man know what he got," said Money.

"Alright, anyway, you should have read the paragraph—what did you think," she said.

"First whatchu think of the game, we won," said Stilts.

"For the small part I saw, you guys did great," she said.

"This man lost it, miss," said Stilts.

"Y'all know what happened though, don't touch me when you don't know me," said Greater.

"Miss I ain't know who to throw to cuz I ain't throw to Over Here," said Stilts.

"I know this man was rid-in the bench but I wanted to throw it to him, regardless," he said. The class agreed, laughing.

"Wait … who's Over Hear," she said.

"Oh … that's the backup receiver," said Greater.

"Why's that his nickname," she said.

"Cuz like in the beginning, at practice in the summer that's all this man, would be sayin," he said.

"Wow, really," she said.

"I never throw nothin to him," said Stilts.

"It's true miss," he said.

"Coach was on me all da time," he said.

"Alright, back to the paragraph," she said.

"Yes Rimez," she said.

"It speak 'bout morals, what good and bad," he said.

"Correct, you just earned ten points," she said.

"This man here," said Do.

"Da hatas crazy … because them so lazy," he started to sing, as the class cheered him on.

"Enough, please," she said.

"Remember, when anyone gets points, we celebrate," she said.

"My fault, good job Rat," he said.

"Tanks," he said.

"Much better, yes—it was about morals," she said.

"What are they," she said. As she wrote on the board, the class took notes. They were engaged.

"Morals hold people in society to a certain standard," she said.

"What's that," said Lakes.

"A breakdown would be what we expect from ourselves versus what society expects from us," she said.

"Standards are rules or expectations how we should act," she said.

"Oh, like how Da'Zay should take that wig off, lean-in to da side," said Lakes.

"Boy you try roast-in one more time, I swear," she said.

"Enough everyone, especially Lakes, no more interruptions," she said.

"My fault miss," he said.

"Let's speak about what happens in a society with no morals," she said.

"I gotta question," said Anfel.

"Go ahead," she said.

"IT be like over there in Anderstamp," he said.

"I don't understand … where," she said.

"Where the people be that wear the shoes wit wood," he said.

"Oh, Amsterdam," she said. The class burst out in laughter.

"Y'all shut up," he said. She started to get emotional, Casey vowed never to embarrass a student, especially one who was receptive to the learning process.

Everyone laughing lost a point, I'm serious, at least he's paying attention, this needs to stop, don't make fun of anyone," she said.

"We sorry miss," said Money.

"Sorry means it won't happen again, I don't mind us having fun but disrespect is something different," she said. Quickly, she approached Anfel.

"I am so sorry, next time I'll correct you, in private," she said.

"It's aight you good," he said.

"I love the point you made, about Amsterdam but there are certain lines, over there you can't cross," she said.

"Where that is," said Smithna.

"It's in a place called Holland, far away from America, in Europe another continent," she said.

"Dis man smart, he be talk-in bout stuff far in the world," said DenJ. Casey looked at him, affirming his action. He could provide peer positive reinforcement, she loved it.

"Thank you, DenJ," she said.

"I be read-in that's why," he said.

"Yeah and Mr. Wu told us bout the continents," said Da'Zay.

"That's a great thing," she said.

"Back to the topic, why does society need standards," she said.

"Yes, Swoon," she said.

"Society need standards to make sure we ain't break-in no laws and to keep things goin," he said.

"Exactly, please write this down—order is important," she said.

"Oh … miss in trouble, as she wrote the last letter on the board, a familiar face came in and sat at her desk.

"Let's keep going, all eyes should be on me and all thoughts on morals," she said.

"We make decisions and follow through with answers," she said.

"Like what's right and wrong," said Da'Zay.

"Yeah, like tell-in the truth," said Anfel.

"Right, we need to hold ourselves to a high standard, being honest helps to maintain a positive reputation and is a form of morality," she said.

"Any more examples," she said.

"Yes," she said.

"Like not cheat-in on your girl," said Stilts.

"Correct, trust is crucial for any relationship to survive," she said.

"Right boyfriends and girlfriends need that," said Da'Zay.

All relationships do and cheating is morally wrong, in a lot of places," she said.

"Need to be everywhere," said Smithna.

"Yes but that's not the case, all over the world, different places have different standards," she said.

"As we wrap up, turn your teammates and talk about morals that are important to you," she said.

"I love this part," said Greater.

"Flip you I'm Done Cups Over if you finish before the timer goes off," she said.

"We know, Mrs. C.," said Swoon.

"That man left," said Da'Zay.

"That's fine, focus," she said.

"We know you wasn't in trouble," said Swoon.

"He would be in here, all da time wit Mr. Wu, not you dough," said Greater.

"Focus please," she said.

"We have time for two group leaders to share," she said.

Let's use the random choose button to see who will speak, there we go, Da'Zay and Sanrell, again," she said.

"They stay talking," said Smithna.

"Go ahead Da'Zay," she said.

"Aight we said cheat-in, stealing, and ly-in," she said.

"Why is it important not to show those actions," she said.

"It's important cuz if you lie no-one could trust you, steal-in is too much pressure, watch-in for --ops ain't fun," she said.

"--Ops, I don't understand," she said.

"That's cops miss," she said.

"Oh, -ops ... I understand, sorry," she said.

"Oh and cheat-in will get you stabbed," she said.

The class laughed and Casey tried to stifle her smile.

Okay, not being morally correct could put you in danger, great job," she said.

"Go ahead Stilts," she said.

"We said ly-in cuz your words lead to actions, people can't trust what you say they can't trust you to do nothin," he said.

"That's a strong point," she said.

"Oh and we wasn't be-in funny but no punch-in people in games, that's not show-in morals," he said.

"Here this man go," said Greater.

"Maybe this is the way your Q.B. is letting you know— how much it matters for you to play," she said.

"That's true I still can't stand this man, sometime," he said. The class laughed and started clapping.

The students continued to give great answers on the topic of morality. As the period culminated, she felt excited about the lesson.

"Alright, you all shared great examples," she said.

"Yeah, we ain't lyin, steal-in or cheat-in," said Do.

"Sounds like a great plan," she said.

"You a great teacher," said Greater.

"Thank you, so you're not greater than me at that," she said.

"Oh, checkmate," they said.

Ring! Ding! Ring!

The observation notification ignited an emotional response of nausea. All observations were informal(due to The Teacher Switch). This was the first time Principal Waggenport provided feedback on her lesson. Quickly, she logged into her account.

Mrs. Coper,

I want to commend you on the fabulous job you are doing, here. The students were engaged, your objective/goals were listed on the board, you provided an opportunity for peer interaction— relative to the content and feedback that was not demeaning. Each I.E.P. was in the correct order and organized(in your playbook). You adhered to several accommodations, visibly.

I give you a 10/10.

Principal Waggenport—"Integrity Bound While Leading to Win!"

She was amazed at his positive feedback and wanted to express her happiness, but was silenced. There was no one she trusted to share it with.

"You good," said Lakes.

"Yes, I'm amazing," she said.

As the bell rang, the students continued to provide positive feedback on the lesson. These are moments that help educators thrive.

"Don't forget to read for at least twenty minutes, tonight and continue working on your packets," she said.

"We won't," said several students.

"Greater, Miken, Lakes & Do, could I speak with you," she said.

"Yeah, what we do, we good Mrs. C.," they said.

"Yes, I just wanted to let you know, I'm working hard with Lyric, we started something amazing," she said.

"That's good what that gotta do with us," said Money.

"It's just she can't have distractions," she said.

"We ain't doin that," said Do.

"I just wanted to make sure," she said.

"I ain't talk to her in a minute," said Greater.

"Great, she's a Freshman, I'm mentoring," she said.

"Oh, that's why she be in here," said Money.

"Yes," she said.

"We mentor the little ballplayers," he said.

"I had no idea, that's, amazing," she said.

"We takin donations, you could support us, it's good for morals," said Lakes.

"I guess ... sure," she said," smiling.

"Man don't ask that lady fa nothin you know they was shout-in on t.v. 'bout money," said Greater.

"It's not an issue, what's the Donation Jab on our school page," she said

"Help Number 1's Stay Number Ones—all one word," he said.

"Done," she said.

"Thanks miss," he said.

"Of course, generosity is an important character trait," she said.

"What's that," said Lakes.

"Something that helps shape good character, what makes a person who they are," she said.

"You deep," said Money.

"So are you," she said.

"Not like you miss," said Greater.

"Examples of character traits are kindness and generosity what makes us gives," she said.

"That donation was one token of my generosity," she said.

"Thanks miss, for real, you ain't have to do that," said Do.

"Sure, so … we do have an understanding about my mentee, right," she said.

"These big words," said Lakes.

"That's who she mentor-in, coach said it before, " said Greater.

"Oh … Fav. I mean Lyric, yeah," said Lakes.

"Great, here are some passes to you next class," she said.

"It's Pink Day we got weight lift-in," said Do.

"See you during next class," she said.

"Oh, one more thing, Greater could you stay a couple more minutes," she said.

"Yeah," he said.

"What's going on with the rest of your games," she said.

"Well, I gotta write the apology to the boy, plus the school pay-in to fix his tooth," he said.

"Where'd the money come from, never mind," she said.

"I gotta sit out the year, I ain't off the team, just suspended," he said.

"Wow, that's amazing, things did go your way," she said.

"I guess, it's better to ride the bench than be off the team," he said.

"I'm happy everything worked out, please remember what we talked about," she said.

"I will, thanks miss," they said.

"No problem," she said.

   As they left she felt a sense of control. It was amazing. She could not stand Lyric going through any more pain. This was the exclamation point to her statement. Over the next few weeks, Friendmanship continued to thrive causing Lyric's self-esteem to establish. She raised the writing and communication tone of each group member. Each time Lyric was successful it reaffirmed her decision to participate in The Teacher Switch.

<u>Eight</u>
<u>An Unconventional Approach</u>

During the next meeting, members of Friendmanship worked to perfect their lines for the upcoming skit. The performance was coming up.

"I keep forgettin my one part when I go to the principal's office," said Natalai.

"Don't think about it, too hard," said Lyric.

"Be natural, remember these are all things, you went through," said Casey.

"I'm scared, what the teachers goin say, what if we forget everything," said Gesa.

"Forget what they have to say, you have somthin to say," said Lyric.

"I know ... we have so much to say," said Polly.

"So say it ... everybody feels ready, right," said Lyric.

"Kind of," said the students.

She noticed how nervous they were. The skit would reveal true controversial experiences, certain educators may not be ready to face.

"Keep practicing your lines, at home, the skit will be fabulous," said Casey.

"We believe in you," she said.

"Imma practice hard, tonight," said Natalai.

"Everybody so brave, we'll be there with you," she said.

"We love y'all," said the students.

"We love you guys too," they said.

"Now, let's focus on the topic," she said.

"Oh ... I'm excited y'all," said Polly.

"What it is," said Gesa.

"Shhhh ... let miss talk," said Don.

"Okay ... let's talk about whose influence you're under," she said.

"Yes, I wanna write about this," said Loreel.

"Everyone please write the topic, down," she said.

"Okay, how many of y'all used to get blazed or know somebody who did," she said.

"Let's talk about the past, not what y'all do, now, but you better not be doin none of it," she

said.

The entire group raised their hands.

"Oh ...everyone's being so real," said Casey.

"Mrs. C., you doin too much, lol," she said. She laughed.

"We taught her that," said Don.

"Trust me—I know, lol," she said.

"Back to it ... how many of you used to get wrecked or blazed," she said.

"That's gettin drunk," she said.

"Oh ... right ... let me start grading some papers, continue to run the group," she said.

She made sure to ask the question, in past tense that way Casey wouldn't get in trouble. As a teacher, it's a mandate to report underage drug use or drinking.

The students looked at each other. Reluctantly, everyone raised their hands.

"You fight so hard when teachers tell you what to do but you let drugs and lique. control you, why," she said.

"No, they don't control me," said Rose.

"If they don't, why did you take them," she said.

"I don't know, my friends used to be taking them," she said.

"Imma tell you a secret, I used to drink, a lot," said Gesa.

"Why used too," she said.

"One night I got too wrecked, they called the ambulance, my momma beat me so bad," said Gesa.

"Whoa," she said.

"I had to get pumped," she said.

"Girl all yo business out there," said Rose.

"That's the point, It's good she opened up, I'm proud of you," she said.

"Thanks miss," she said.

"I started gettin lit and wrecked, in elementary," she said. Casey was not alarmed. The life Lyric had would not make it difficult to acquire alcohol or drugs, so young. It was sad.

"That little," she said.

"Yes," she said.

Lyric was not proud of drinking at such a young age. The choice was taken from her the minute her stepfather shoved alcohol down her throat. As she got older, liquor was the sorry excuse for a coping mechanism to ease the pain of what men expected her to do. She yearned to reveal all her secrets to the students. She fought to spare the group of details. It hurt to tell fifty percent of the story when she expected the students to be one hundred percent real. The paradox felt unnatural.

"It's like when we be at parties," said Gesa.

"You hear the music better when you gone," said Rose.

"Lies you tell—Irv drop that beat," she said.

She started dancing and the students were cracking up. She knew how to keep them, engaged. It was a talent—certain educators lack. Casey loved how natural she made it look.

"I ain't take pills, drink or nothing," she said.

"True miss—you could Gloss," said Nescai.

"Yeah ... and I did it on nothin," she said.

"You could dance," said Gesa.

"I'm decent," she said.

"Focus though—on the topic," she said.

"Before I never liked none of that like pills or nothin—these girls said you have more fun wit on somethin," said Sarah.

"Where we stay gettin zooted be everything," said Nescai.

"Just because it's everything to other people, doesn't mean it should be everything to you," she said.

"Take us to church, again ... please," said Don. This was the classroom climate she loved.

They all spoke, sometimes out of turn but they were listening, actively.

"I used to think people wouldn't like me, in reality," said Ivory.

"Telling yourself lies like people won't like you if you ain't them, is dangerous, you know why," she said.

"Naw," he said.

"Lie long enough and you believe what's real is fake and what's fake is real," she said.

"That's —-we know ... real," the students finished Casey's comment and everyone laughed.

"So serious though—don't let your fake friends pressure you," she said.

"You right Miss," said Irv.

"If you don't want to do something, don't do it, your knockoff friends will drop you, anyway," she said.

"That's right ... those phony girls match my momma's Fucci purse," she said.

Casey relished in their creativity and could not believe how much fun the group was.

"If you end up doing something, you don't want to, it gets to the point where you hate your reflection," she said.

Her words yanked at Casey's heart.

"Could we make a pact not to do no more drugs or drink or repeat the past," she said.

"Miss ... I'll be real, I don't know bout ever," said Irv.

"Oh, I want you to tell the cops that, if they catch you," said Loreel.

"All of you, don't do it," she said.

"Man ... aight miss," said the students.

"Now, why it's not good to be "under the influence," she said.

"Cause it could hurt you and you don't know, what will happen," said Don.

"Exactly, when you take drugs or drink, you make bad choices," she said.

"We passed the time," she said.

"Everyone huddle together and repeat me," she said.

"Oh ... I hate when time's up," said Rose.

"Us too," said the other group members.

"Come on ... you don't want to be late for the bus," she said.

"Repeat after me—drugs and liquor are not for me," she said.

"Drugs and liquor are not for me," said the group.

"Okay everybody, the next time we meet, it'll be in the cafeteria for the big meeting," said Casey.

"They all ready," said Lyric.

"We ready," said Nescai.

"We already, ready," said the group.

"Great talk, meeting over —," she said.

They walked the students to the bus. Each student looked so happy.

"Bye Mrs. C.'s," they said.

"Do they ever listen, sometimes," she said.

"Please get into the car,"

"So ... you not gonna ask, what if I have a ride," she said.

"You don't, inside please," she said.

"Achoo, achoo, ahem!" As she closed the car door, she coughed and sneezed, continually.

"You okay," said Casey.

"Yes, mama," she said.

"Oh, Lyric," she said.

She felt her forehead and neck. She had a crackling cough and kept sneezing.

"You're a little warm, and a little skinnier," she said.

"Don't even say that, I'm tryin to get Rump Roast Thick," she said

"Too funny," she said,

"You did a fabulous job, again," she said.

"Oh ... that's me the fabulous Lyric, those kids have my heart," she said.

"This club is helping them, so much," she said.

"I can't wait for the meeting, tomorrow," said Casey.

"Yup, we're doing something fresh and new," she said.

"That's true, escaping monotony feels so good," she said.

"And you can't stop feeling ... what I'm feeling .... Lyric turned the radio button up and started singing, her voice was soothing.

"I had no idea, you could sing," she said.

"With a name like Lyric, would be a shame, if I couldn't," she said.

"You have so many covert talents," she said.

"They pop up at random times," she said.

"Well, here we are," she said.

"Yup, home sweet havoc," she said.

Casey paused and looked at her. She reminded her of a bird yearning to fly away.

"Oh ... how do I respond to that," she said.

"Don't, some comments should be left alone," she said.

"Well, see you tomorrow, thanks for the ride," she said.

"See you," she said.

As she left the car Casey was tempted to walk her, inside. Every time they were together, another emotional wall tumbled down. Lyric took her away from the fertility injections, rejection, and every challenge she faced. She cherished her creativity. Every word of wisdom she spoke cracked open another crevice in her perception.

Training Time

The room was packed with educators. It was time for the training, Friendmanship prepared for. She wasn't sure how the educators would react to her book or the skit.

"Thanks for coming to our training, Mrs. Coper made such an impact, at The Best High School, during The Teacher Switch," he said.

As he continued, his voice seemed far away. Nerves infiltrated her eardrums, making it hard to focus.

Casey prayed he would not start the training off with all the things she did right. Sometimes, educators cork their ears, during excessive acknowledgment.

"I need all claps on deck for our fellow educator, Mrs. Coper," he said.

As the crowd clapped, her heart started to race.

"Welcome to your first counterclockwise training, please turn your attention to the screen, this is our agenda for today," she said.

The Best High School's Teacher Training

Thursday, April 28, 20_ _

3:30-5:00 P.M.

Agenda

I.Introduction-Principal Waggenport

II.Counterclockwise Expectations-Mrs. Coper

III.Student Genre Breakdown-All Educators

IV. We Have Something to Say Skit Friendmanship

V. Refreshments

"Um ... excuse me, what's a counterclockwise training," said one of the teachers.

"I'm so happy, you asked. If something is counterclockwise it moves in the opposite direction of how the clock rotates. Let's take a detour, from traditional and redundant delivery. We know the drill, I'm supposed to hand you chart paper and you're supposed to act interested, in the same tired instant replay material with a so-called "different twist," she said.

"I want everyone to understand, how student genres impact the learning process," she said. Everyone looked shocked. They could not believe she was so candid.

There were reports of several students, fighting, not doing their work, and disrespecting teachers, currently. This behavior may partially be attributed to us not meeting the needs of certain students," she said.

She seemed confident but inside she was petrified. Although she was concerned about the reception of her book. She was nervous about the teacher's response to the skit. Certain educators don't like "kids" treading on their territory. What constitutes as a teacher's territory? The teacher's lounge, training, and any place students do not have autonomy. It was time for a change.

"Thanks to Principal Waggenport's large purchase, you all get copies of my book. This year, I came into contact with a special student, who was tested but never received gifted accommodations. This should never happen. This is one example of a student genre, the district overlooked. When students feel neglected it can cause f issues.

"I also had the privilege of helping to lead a peer writing club, called Friendmanship. The iconic group is made up of ten middle school students, led by a special freshman named Lyric and overseen by myself," she said.

"After you read chapters one and two of the book, you will see an amazing skit, the students, Lyric and I put together. They are going to show how the characters felt, based on past experiences. I suggest all sensitive people put their feelings to the side and pay attention to the message of the skit. The teachers gasped, as their pupils dilated with envy. Casey knew they were wondering when she had time to write a book. Dodging the teacher's lounge(at times) and staying up late, does pay off.

"Your time begins, now," she said.

Student Genres

Although the term "modified instruction" seems self-explanatory, it's complex. It should begin with educators changing their outlook on how to approach students. They are the primary focus of daily intent. Placing your personal life to the side to educate students, is a mandate. Ill will toward coworkers, petty competition and negativity, all take a back seat to how we deliver content. Every student is unique. Academic lessons should reflect their differences. There are several methods of delivery we utilize to educate. Field trips, academic/communication differentiation, and understanding your audience contribute to learning outcomes.

Field Trips

As a child, the term "field trip" always intrigued me. I was excited when my teacher announced we were going on one. Years later, who would think students would take field trips with no correlation to academic standards or personality traits? Who came up with the idea to drag students to a less than enriching learning environment? During my internship, we took students to a kiddie waterpark. I wanted to scream, "Please take these students to a place they can make a meaningful connection." The words came rushing to my mouth but hit the back of my teeth and were swallowed up by apprehension and fear. Who was I to make suggestions, I was only an intern.

Unfortunately, students who felt their intelligence was insulted, would act out, during each boring field trip. The countless eye-rolls, nail picking, and outright rage proved they wished the principal would stop the madness. Eventually, I decided to voice their opinion. I wrote a proposal on the importance of field trips and how aspects of curriculum relation should be the premise for each one. After the principal read the proposal, she agreed students should go on academically enriched field trips with a follow-up assignment. This made a major difference. It decreased poor behavior and reinforced reading, writing, and reflective skills, we taught.

Differentiation

A large population of students I worked with was considered gifted. Sadly, many of them were neglected due to financial insufficiency. Giftedness does not discriminate, based on race, socioeconomic status, or gender. There are many children in low-income areas, considered gifted. Although we have programs that lightly address this injustice, we need assertive individuals to shed more light on the matter. Selective districts do not feel implementing gifted programs is necessary since high achieving students and gifted students are the same. This is incorrect. There is a clear difference.

Classification

High achieving vs. gifted student classification can be a perplexing concept. The High Achieving Student, displays the following characteristics: easy memorization, is interested and engaged in the lesson, works on assignment completion, understands concepts without difficulty, is fully engaged, works to full potential, has great ideas and listening skills, and follows the grain without question.

The gifted student has exceptionalities that include:

Formulating new concepts/ideas, arguing against or for a particular aspect of the lesson, extreme sensitivity, asking questions within questions, feeling intense passion, is very observant, and interacts with older individuals, without additional mental effort.

Each gifted child needs activities, conducive to their thought process, personalities, and efficacy. Below is a snippet of one activity, I did—during my internship with this population. The activity kept the students engaged and challenged.

Lesson: Certain Parts of the Brain's Anatomy to classroom connection

Learning Goal

Identify and correlate parts of the brain and their function to your class. Compare your work with a partner and discuss different parts of the brain. Use the "think harder chart" to challenge yourself.

Golden Question

How can you identify, aspects of the brain and relate them to our class? Cerebrum

The cerebrum is the biggest part of our brains. It has tools to help the brain operate the right way.

Wernicke's Area to Class Correlation

It is correlated to practicing reading passages. They help us practice the right way to pronounce words.

Hypothalamus

The hypothalamus controls the way we feel, how hungry we get, how thirsty we get, and body temperature.

Hypothalamus to Class Connection

This portion of the brain represents the positive reinforcement/feedback, we receive from our teacher. It ignites our hunger and thirst for new content and learning skills.

Getting to Know Our Students

Understanding our audience is crucial when addressing gifted students. They need to believe you are modifying assignments, based on who they are and their aspirations. Busy work will only trigger discontent, in a gifted child. Certain teachers prefer not to teach this population because it increases their workload. Before constructing assignments for this student genre, you must answer the following: How can I slay the beast of boredom, during this activity? How do I modify instruction on a personal level to ensure they are enriched and pushed to grow? I instructed several gifted students. This chapter explores my experiences and how to deal with them.

1.) The Gifted Constructor (Dream)

"Do it the way I say," said Dream.

"I hate this, can I work by myself," he said.

"I need to see you work alone and in groups."

"But Mrs. Coper, I don't understand," he said.

"Understand what," she said.

"They won't listen, I'm trying to help them, but they want to do it wrong," he said.

"I don't want to fail, because of them," he said.

Dream began to sob, intensely. I inclined to comfort him. He meant well; however, he could not communicate the reason he wanted to work, alone. The start and endpoint of completing assignments was his ability to control group members.

Autonomous gifted students can be a challenge. I recommend activities that help them, feel a sense of control. Assigning specific roles(within groups) will maximize the behavioral, academic, and emotional well-being of group interactions. This will help eliminate the need for constant superiority to be displayed.

Instructional/Behavioral Implementation Goal/s

Teachers should use unique strategies that will help students like Dream, feel a sense of control. He will be challenged and encouraged to maximize positive academic and behavioral achievement.

2.) The Mathematically Inclined Gifted Student (Max)

"Mrs. Coper, I want a new partner," said Al.

"I can't work with Max! He keeps doing his own thing," he said.

"What do you mean," she said.

"You said to create a story, using sequencing; he keeps trying to build a house, out of paper," he said.

She glanced at the group table and noticed his claim was correct.

"I care about my grade, and don't want to fail," he said.

"Okay, calm down," she said.

"I tried to tell him to stop, he says building the house to tell what happened in the story, is better than writing it," he said.

"It's more fun this way," said Max.

"You're an amazing student, help your group understand, why you want them to explain the story this way," she said.

"Okay, thank you, my favorite teacher," he said.

"It's no problem," she said.

Instructional/Behavioral Implementation Goal/s

The teacher will model how to work in groups and provide opportunities for engagement that require in-depth thought. Before my arrival, Max was disrespectful, insubordinate, and had a short attention span. His behavior improved when the visible behavior plan was utilized. It was a star chart. He ended up succeeding. He was rewarded for each positive cooperative behavior, demonstrated.

3.) The Obnoxious Gifted Student (Axell)

"Mrs. Coper, why's my name in a group of imbeciles," she said.

"Excuse me," she said.

"I'm in the pink group with imbeciles not on my level," she said.

"Please don't use that word to describe anyone," she said,

"Sorry, I'll try not to use it, the keyword is try," she said.

"If I hear you use the word again, I'll **try** not to write you a referral," she said.

Axell's mentality was detrimental. She believed the actions of others should begin and end with her affirmation. This led to feeling ostracized and unpopular. No matter how many times I tried to warn her, she insisted on proving her point. One of her goals was to minimize sarcastic and rude comments and strengthen her leadership skills.

Instructional/Behavioral Implementation Goal/s

The teacher will model how to express feelings, and formulate activities that will help the student feel valued. During each activity, I encouraged her peers to help her achieve the goal, by not responding to every snide remark. Thankfully, the class obliged. She earned incentives while exhibiting healthy communication skills. This created a sense of leadership and autonomy. In turn, her facetious comments decreased.

4.) The Politically Inclined Gifted Student (Polly)

"Mrs. C. my little brothers always say we too little to change the world, but I say they can," said Polly.

"Not everyone believes one person can do that," she said.

"I need to help them, get on my level, they can do whatever they try to do," she said.

"You're right," she said.

"One day, I'll be the president," she said.

"I have no doubt you'll be the best president," she said.

"I believe in changing the world to be better," she said.

"Exactly, that's why your assignments explain how to do it," she said.

"The first step is flushing the word CAN'T," she said. She laughed at her comment.

"I know, it's a curse word, in this class," she said.

"That word swallows attempts to carry out positive actions," she said.

"You're right," she said.

Polly was an amazing student, who had an uncanny way of exerting positivity. Her endless idealistic expectations would offer hope to students, who felt useless. My goal was to ensure she utilized strategic intervention to enhance her skills.

Instructional/Behavioral Implementation Goal/s

The Teacher will formulate activities that will reinforce Polly's communication skills by keeping her challenged. Activities include mediation within class groups and offering assistance to students who were not as vocal. Implementing the strategies above, helped her performance. She viewed our class as The White House and was a great diplomat.

5.) The Gifted Peacemaker Student (Shalom)

"What could we do to make this school, better," said Shalom.

"Why not create an action plan on what you feel, our school needs," she said.

"You're so right," he said.

Students like Shalom need challenges based on an unselfish premise. To academically and emotionally stimulate them, educators need to formulate academic activities that will speak volumes for the greater good. The Save the Animals Project helped him. He formulated one of the best projects, in the class and was able to reach out and help the community. This increased his self-esteem and strengthened his gift.

Instructional/Behavioral Implementation Goal/s

The teacher will assign academic activities that are challenging and encourage interaction between the student and their peers. Each activity will pinpoint the specific strategy the student uses to complete it. Students will be given opportunities to share details about their assignments with the class and teacher.

6.) The Practical Gifted Student (Prissy)

"Mrs. Coper you said we could work in groups for this assignment but yesterday we worked by ourselves," said Prissy.

"Why do we need to work in groups, if the assignment is the same," she said.

"I don't understand," she said.

"Sometimes things change," she said.

"I think we should take information from yesterday and keep working by ourselves to prove our points," she said.

"I understand yesterday you worked alone, but today is a new day," she said.

"The reason we're working together in groups is ... I'm completing observations," she said.

"Oh," she said.

"Would you like to help," she said.

"Sure, why not," she said.

Prissy had a smirk on her face. She was aware the term was over her head but would not back down.

Students categorized as "practical" constantly question opinions/changes. These students need factual explanations of the motives of their teachers/classmates. In their world, if evidence does not support your claim, there is no concrete ground to stand on.

Instructional/Behavioral Implementation Goal/s

The teacher will provide feedback to encourage ways to verbalize concerns, respectfully. Encourage these students to share thoughts, either via The Classroom Communication Mailbox(a way to communicate that avoided constant interruptions) They were able to write notes and place them in the mailbox. I would respond by the next day. Nonverbal cues to prevent outbursts were another helpful method. Both actions were a lifesaver for students, who struggled with expressing themselves, at an appropriate time. Gifted students in this category, tend to undermine authority if answers provided are not what they consider "up-to-par."

7.) The Overly Concerned Gifted Student (Dinero)

"I want to help the world," said Dinero.

"That's amazing," said Mrs. Coper.

"I want to be a big part of the community, killing animals for fun is wrong," he said.

"I agree," she said.

"What a great idea," she exclaimed.

"If you're concerned about human and animal cruelty, start a campaign," she said.

"You'll need to come up with an action plan and express your concerns to others," she said.

"After providing details of your concerns, you'll need to get signatures and implement your plan," she said.

Dinero was an intelligent, sensitive, and inquisitive soul. Students in this category would like to know, you understand them and will not disregard their creativity.

Instructional/Behavioral Implementation Goal/s

The teacher will exhibit sensitivity toward the student's needs by providing them with opportunities to help peers. He/she will create exciting ways for students to express themselves that will increase academic achievement.

8.) The Legally Inclined Student (Lawson)

"Mrs. C., we have a problem," he said.

"Yes," she said.

"Do you know, we're not allowed to dress out of uniform," he said.

"Yes, let's talk about this, later," she said.

"I object," he said.

"This isn't a courtroom," she said.

"Everywhere is my courtroom," he said. The class chuckled.

"Let's not discuss this, now," she said.

"When can we," he said. She knew where his comment would cause either another complaint from a student or the third indentation(in the side of her jaw), from her trying not to lash out.

"This school lets us have No Uniform Day," he said.

"Also correct," she said.

"Technically that's wrong," he said.

"Again, let's not discuss this now," she said.

"Why did my parents and I waste time, reading and signing the handbook, if this school doesn't stick by it," he said.

"I mean ... if they knew we would have these days, why not include it, in the handbook," he said.

"Okay, since you insist on interrupting the class, page 72 of the handbook states the principal reserves the right to add/take away special days/events," she said.

The class started to laugh and speak down to him.

Immediately, Mrs. Coper put a stop to it.

"Please come to my desk," she said.

"Why did you put me out there, in front of everyone," he said.

"Oh ... I put you out there ... really," she said.

"Please understand if you address concerns, in front of the class, you run the risk of being wrong," she said.

"I'm never wrong," he said.

"Oh really," she said.

She gave him a stern look of disapproval.

"Sorry," he said.

"Okay, I tried to address your question, without getting the class involved but if you want to talk about issues, in the middle of class, you may not always get responses you like," she said.

"Do you understand," she said.

"Yes," he said.

"How about you leave the logistics to me," she said.

"Okay," he said.

If policies had friends, these students would be so popular. They memorize school policies and procedures and can be disrespectful.

Instructional/Behavioral Implementation Goal/s

The Teacher will model ways to communicate and provide academic activities that will strengthen the ability to disagree with others. These students love to debate. Create assignments that will help them voice concerns, positively. Designate a communication tool that would avoid disrupting the class. Every student has a voice and wants to be heard; however, legally inclined students need to address concerns, at appropriate times.

9.) The Mini-Administrative Gifted Student-(Jacob)

"Mrs. Coper, could I be teacher helper," said Jacob.

"After you finish, the assignment," she said.

"I'm done," he said.

"May I see it," she said.

"Well, I'm kind of finished," he said.

"Kind of finished doesn't count," she said.

"Please bring me your work," she said.

"Why do we need to finish, could I be the teacher," he said.

"What do you mean," she said.

"Make sure, everyone is doing their work and be the boss of them," he said.

"Every good worker needs a great boss; I'm perfect," he said.

"Jacob there's one person in charge, you're speaking with her," she said.

"Sorry," he said.

"Please sit down," she said.

These students tend to make snide remarks, during a lesson. They believe classroom management revolves around them and rules hold little to no weight. You will hear students in this category, suggest other activities, aside from the original academic activities, you planned. They are always on the list of students you leave in your substitute plans, as the "go-to" people, in the class.

They can help maintain a state of consistency, in the classroom; however, they can harm the perception of other students by undermining authority/rules set in place.

Have you ever met the types of students, you feel could run the classroom, in your absence?

Instructional/Behavioral Implementation Goal/s

The teacher should provide students with opportunities to feel autonomous, during academic activities.

Helping with center stations/small groups and organizing papers are a few actions I utilized with Jacob. These students have the potential to be lethal with their mouths. It is important to monitor/reward them for using positive words/not undermining their teacher/classmates.

10.) The Gifted Prodigy-(Gustavo)

"I don't think being in the same group, all the time is helpful to me or my friends," said Gustavo.

"I wrote an essay to prove my point," he said.

"If you read it, could I help other groups?"

"Absolutely," she said.

"Don't forget to provide evidence to support your claim," she said.

"I already did, no disrespect," he said.

All the students left an impression on me however, Gustavo holds a special place, in my heart. He never interrupted my lessons and gave one-hundred percent of himself, during every activity. He had displayed several positive character traits.

The Gifted Prodigy may seem disengaged but they are not. He was an auditory learner, primarily. Students like Gustavo are aware of the issues, in their environment and think about how to fix them, constantly.

Instructional/Behavioral Implementation Goal/s

The Teacher will provide students with challenging academic activities, focused on unique capabilities. No objective can be left to chance. Identify their strengths and seek an attainable end goal to increase their potential. Students in this category, are motivated when their engineering abilities are utilized. For educators to appeal to students like him, they need to create incentives, based on performance. For example, an educator could reward these students by allowing them to complete a fifteen-minute segment, during morning announcements to display craftsmanship.

11.) The Gifted Thrill Seeker-(Molena)

"Molena, should you be drawing, now," said Mrs. Coper.

"I'm sorry, I love to draw, it helps me," she said.

"I'm not against you drawing, just not on your test," she said.

"It's so hard, all I see are the pictures, in my head," she said.

Students in this category, tend to maintain the balance between the learning process and suggesting fun ways to approach new topics. They're the heartbeat of any classroom. Molena was an amazing artist, who could appeal to all five senses with a picture. Her issue was focusing on the subject matter and not daydreaming about drawing/other subjects she loved.

Instructional/Behavioral Implementation Goal/s

Students like Molena need time for artistic expression. The Teacher will offer art completion as an incentive, daily. A time slot to share and show will be given to the student, once academic activities are complete. These students need immediate gratification to engage, in the learning process. After implementing this strategy, I noticed an improvement, in her academic progress.

12.) The Gifted Tycoon In Training-(Israel)

"Israel could I speak with you," said Mrs. Coper.

"Yes," he said.

"I heard students are paying you, not to share secrets(you know) about them, is that true," she said.

"Yes," he said.

"You can't blackmail students, you could get in big trouble for this," she said.

"Celebrities pay people to keep quiet, why can't I make money for the same thing," he said.

"Sorry," he said.

"Okay, you're going to return every dime and apologize to everyone you took money from," she said.

"But that's like three hundred dollars," he said.

"Sorry, you need to do it," she said.

"I'm telling your parents," she said.

"Oh, no ... okay ... fine," he said.

"I thought it was a good idea to practice," he said.

"For what," said Mrs. Coper.

"I want to own a business when I grow up(all the way)," he said. She smiled. He had exceptional articulation.

"Well, when you grow up(all the way), you will have a great business, I believe in you," she said.

"Really," he said.

These moments are crucial for students. Hearing the words "I believe in you," can change their vantage point.

"Will you help me, learn how," he said.

"Do you know the project, we're getting ready to do requires you to research on business/careers," she said.

"I want to build my news station," he said.

"Understanding how a business is run means you'll need great math skills," she said.

"I don't like doing budgets," he said.

"You'll learn to appreciate, business plans," she said.

"I hate those," he said.

"If they'll help me with my business, I'll do them," he said.

"Sounds good," she said.

The partial definition of a tycoon is a powerful person. These students grow up to become business professionals/moguls. Students in this category are observant and will push boundaries. Academic assignments must be relatable. Our job is to ensure students like Israel are given opportunities to innovate. We need to enter their world, to breakthrough, academically.

Instructional/Behavioral Implementation Goal/s

The Teacher will provide students in this category with opportunities to explain aspects of their business plan. They are allowed to share results with classmates.

13.) The Gifted Three Ring Circus Leader-(Trinx)

"Miss, Why girls wear tight clothes with no booty," said Trinx.

The class started to giggle.

"May I speak with you for a moment," said Mrs. Coper.

"Could you save the jokes for comedy hour," she said.

"When we got a comedy hour, at this school," she said.

"We just started one," she said.

"Really," she said.

"I'll make a deal with you, if you don't make any more jokes, during class," said Mrs. Coper.

"You'll be the host of comedy hour, once a week," she said.

"Okay, deal," he said.

"One more thing," she said.

"What," she said.

"All jokes must be appropriate," she said.

"Okay," he said.

If you have the Three Ring Circus leader, in your class, deal with them, strategically.

Instructional/Behavioral Implementation Goal/s

The Teacher will encourage students in this category to diminish outbursts, by engaging in learning activities that enhance unique abilities. Since class clowns thrive off of making others laugh, I suggest granting these students opportunities to learn, through drama, song, or poetic means. I had a comedy hour related to academic content. It will force class clowns to create and divert their attention to skills they are learning.

14.) The Gifted Read My Mind Student (Kel)

"Good morning, Mrs. Coper!" "I have a note for you, from my mom," he said.

"Okay," she said.

The letter from his mother read:

Dear Mrs. Coper,

I have several concerns, regarding Kel. For the past few weeks, another student has been bullying him. Accompanied by this occurrence, is another issue, he feels his friends have turned against him. I am outraged that my child feels so uncomfortable. Could you please handle these problems?

Thanks!

My response:

"If you were having issues with the other students, why didn't you tell me," she said.

"I don't know," he said.

"If someone bothers you, how can I do something, if you don't tell me," she said.

"I don't know," he said.

"Please don't keep quiet, about things like this, in the future," she said.

Instructional/Behavioral Implementation Goal/s

The Teacher will utilize an incentive chart to encourage these students to communicate, effectively.

Students in this category, tend to experience several issues, unfortunately, the teacher is usually the last to know. As a result, the educator suffers from unwarranted negativity. Kel was scared to tell me things that made him uncomfortable. I had to implement a note system. He felt comfortable writing over verbalizing his problems. The mailbox technique worked, perfectly. He wrote down, issues and place the notes in our class's communication mailbox. This did not work for urgent situations that occurred outside of my presence. I explained Kel's struggle to his other instructors and ensured they understood my plan. We implemented a behavior chart, he could travel with. Every time he was vocal, he earned a star. When the star chart was full, he received an incentive.

General Education Students

During my internship, encounters with general ed. students were vast. They faced many triumphs and tragedies. I implemented strategies to enhance their learning process. The experiences below will help you understand them.

1.) The Insecure Student (Monet)

"Why do gifted kids, always think they are so special, said Monet."

"Why do you mean," said Mrs. Coper.

"My mother says, I can do everything they can, they, not the only special kids," she said.

"We're all special but certain students may need extra support or learn differently," she said.

"My grades are good, mommy says I'm getting tested for gifted," she said.

"If she feels you should be tested, ask her to give me a call," she said.

Students in this category, tend to struggle with measuring up to gifted students. The driving force that fuels insecurities[for these students] are internal and external. Internal based on the daily occurrences, they envision themselves completing and external based on parental input. Parents of these students struggle with inferiority. They believe their child should be labeled gifted when test results reveal otherwise.

Instructional/Behavioral Implementation Goal/s

The Teacher will acknowledge small steps toward progression, by providing positive reinforcement. This will help, students in this category recognize positive traits they may overlook. Students like Monet should be monitored to ensure they are not demeaning to others.

2.) The Verbally Aggressive Student(Nell)

"Yo, why do you even come to school, you slow," she said.

"May I speak with you, immediately," she said.

"Okay," she said.

"Please control yourself by not calling people names," she said.

"But he acts dumb," she said.

"No, he doesn't and I will give you a referral if you don't calm down," she said.

"Fine ... sorry," she said.

"I would never embarrass you, in front of the class," she said.

"I know," she said.

"Have I ever embarrassed you," she said.

"No," she said.

"Please, use kind words in this classroom," she said.

"Okay," she said.

Instructional/Behavioral Implementation Goal/s

Students like Nell tend to demean their peers. As educators, we must acknowledge why these outbursts, occur. Her life was not up to par. She lived in a single-parent household. Her mother worked two jobs and her eldest sister was fifteen years old, pregnant, and aggressive. Demeaning her peers was the only autonomy she had.

Teachers will help these students, acknowledge their positive characteristics, weekly.

Meetings to provide one on one attention to students in this category are necessary to help them feel a deeper connection with their teacher. Ultimately students like her will need to work toward staying positive and tackling bouts of verbal aggression. They get highly offended when the weakest points are exposed.

3.) The High Achieving Student(Tellen)

"Mrs. Coper, do you know where I came from, in Europe, I memorized the entire L part of the Dictionary," she said.

"Really," said Tellan.

"Yes, I finished, one of the top three students, in my class," she said.

"Wow, that's interesting," she said.

 Tellan and I would have conversations, regularly. She expressed how well her academic performance was, in London, constantly. Her peers were tired of her interrupting their lesson for self-gratification. Students in this category, tend to follow the rules and not question the basic aspects of the lesson. They are great at memorization; however, high achieving students can put high levels of pressure on themselves. This self-induced pressure can be the result of several factors: competition, entitlement/fear. Healthy competition is encouraged but desperation can cause them to resort to unethical choices.

Instructional/Behavioral Implementation Goal/s

The teacher will diminish outbursts by utilizing an incentive chart to focus on the student's accomplishments.

4.) Speech Challenged Student (Daisy)

"Ms. Cop., could I -ork myself," said Daisy.

"Working by yourself would be fine if you need to work in a group for this assignment," she said.

"No," she said.

"You're working, so hard to earn points," she said.

"Do you want to spoil it," she said.

"No, Daisy do better," she said.

"Yes, Daisy will do much better," she said.

Students in this category, are introverted. They may have a language delay or speech impediment. What does the term introverted mean? Introverts tend to be interested, in self-awareness and perception, predominantly. She would respond to one on one personalized feedback/positive reinforcement.

Instructional/Behavioral Implementation Goal/s

 During small group instruction, I worked with her on individualized speech short and long-term goals. She had to understand how to function, with others and independently. At the end of the year, I was grateful and proud of the strides she made, regarding communication and working well with others.

5.) The Tattletale (Holden)

"I need a snack, I want her cookies," said Holden.

"You have a snack, the cookies are for students who don't have anything to eat," said Mrs. Coper.

 "But I want it; I'm telling my mommy," he said.

Holden was compliant until things did not go his way, then, he would switch to his alter-ego. He fell on the floor screaming, often. Students in this category try to intimidate teachers, while threatening to inform their parent/s/guardian/s, about incidences, constantly. Once you give in, the demands will increase.

Instructional/Behavioral Implementation Goal/s

Never let students in this category intimidate you. Make sure the student knows tantrums will not alter your decisions. Although it may be difficult, avoiding the word no will prevent long tantrums, during instruction. If the student is not disruptive, celebrate the moment by acknowledging their behavior. I may not extinguish the pattern, completely but there will be some progress.

6.) The Songbird Student(Harmony)

"I'm hot, hot, hot ... and blazing," sang Harmony.

The class laughed, as she sang songs, randomly.

"May I speak to you a second," she said.

"Didn't we agree singing, during class, is wrong," she said.

"Yes," she said.

"You know, I'll give you opportunities to make up songs to go along with our lesson," she said.

"Sorry, Mrs. Coper," she said.

Instructional/Behavioral Implementation Goal/s

Music is a great way for students to express themselves. Harmony[and students like her], would be allowed to make up songs, related to academic content. Once I allowed her to incorporate it, in the lesson, singing out of turn diminished.

7.) The Competitive Class Act Student

Three students would crack jokes, at the beginning of class. They were seeking gratification, from peers. Students in this category are entertaining. Establishing a ground set of rules, was the first step to understand, joke-telling during class, was inappropriate.

Instructional/Behavioral Implementation Goal/s

I implemented a behavioral plan that would work from the outside in. We had positive reinforcement goals, within the classroom. I decided to reward students, who did not entertain inappropriate behavior. Although this can be challenging, it may be worth, the extra effort. This plan worked by extinguishing the behavior. Eventually, their comments stopped and the class was rewarded.

8.) The Special Needs Student(Cainey)

"Mrs. Coper, my friend keeps trying to help me, but I don't need help," said Cainey.

"There's nothing wrong with accepting help," she said.

"When we help each other, it makes us better people," she said.

"For real," she said.

"Yes," she said.

"I didn't know that, I love you," she said.

Cainey had a disability. She was a charismatic student. She would want to play, complete activities, and interact as if she did not need help. Part of her Individualized Educational Plan was to ask for assistance and increase socialization.

Instructional/Behavioral Implementation Goal/s

I made sure, she identified positive aspects about herself, frequently. Teachers need to ensure these students feel comfortable receiving assistance, without feeling inadequate. This helped her, gain a positive perspective, about who she was and her capabilities.

9.) The Daydreamer (Tripp)

"The first part of the assignment should show your understanding of at least four characters, from the story," said Mrs. Coper.

"Tripp, Tripp, Tripp," said Mrs. Coper." She had to elevate her voice to get his attention. He was daydreaming.

"Yes, he said."

"What did I say," she said.

"To read the story, I think," he said.

"May I speak to you, a moment," she said.

"You're doing great, but I need you to pay attention, while I give directions," she said.
"Sorry," he said.

Students in this category, tend to drift off. They have a motto "there are no dreams, like daydreams." Attaining a deep appreciation of their creativity is crucial. They envision themselves, in another world, story or play, constantly. Although this is amazing for creative thought, it is detrimental, while educators are trying to explain important aspects of a lesson.

Instructional/Behavioral Implementation Goal/s

A behavioral plan was implemented for Tripp. He was given star tickets for restating all parts of directions. Once he earned enough tickets, I gave him a treat. The plan worked, well.

10.) The Tardy Student (Rex)

"Why were you late," said Mrs. Coper.

"I was up late, playing video games, my mom always tells me to go to sleep but the game is fun," he said.

"That's interesting, you choose to be tardy," she said.

"Yeah … I need the work that I miss, every day," he said.

"I'll call your mother on my break to explain what happens when students are late," she said.

"My mom said, if I am late, you need to review, the assignments you gave," he said.

"I can't review the assignments if you do not enter the class with a pass," she said.

Students in this category, are late, habitually. Their tardiness is not the result of emergencies. They believe the world owes them a special level of understanding. We need to help reset their misconception. Since Rex chose to be late, he needed to figure out directions for our morning assignment, independently. Eventually, his tardiness decreased.

Instructional/Behavioral Implementation Goal/s

Every day, Rex was on time, he received a gold star. Once his star chart was filled, he earned a special treat. Tardy incentives do not work in every situation. It irritates me when adults hold students accountable for circumstances, beyond their control. The elementary and middle school students, I know, do not drive. There are laws/policies in place to hold parents[of students] accountable for frequent tardies/absences, not students. I hear adults make snide remarks to students, regarding the issue. That is unacceptable. It is embarrassing for them to take the verbal lashing from an adult because he/she is scared to address the issue with the student's parent. Let's strive not to do this.

11.) The "I'm Sick" Student(Illy)

"Mrs. Coper I'm sick," she said.

"What's wrong," she said.

"This weekend my family took me to the hospital," she said.

"Why," she said.

"My heart and lungs just stopped working," she said. This was the same excuse that would come up, during reading, daily. Ironically, her organs worked during recess.

"Can I go play," she said.

"I thought you were sick," she said.

"I'm all better now, my heart works," she said.

Students in this category may have ailments but most of the time, they make the illness up for attention.

After considerable complaints, I contacted Illy's mother, who informed me, she was pregnant with her little sister and would say anything for attention.

Instructional/Behavioral Implementation Goal/s

The goal of this plan would be to encourage students to tell the truth by helping them feel valued. I constructed special jobs for her, during class. This helped her get the attention she was seeking. Eventually, she did not fabricate anymore.

12.) The Rebellious Student (Rueben)

"I noticed you're not completing your home/classwork," she said.

"So," said Rueben.

"Do you understand, if you don't pass this class, you'll fail," she said.

"And," he said.

"Tonight, your homework is to write reasons you believe school is helpful," she said.

"Oh … man … why," he said.

"I'm going to do the same; we can discuss it, tomorrow," she said.

While shrugging his shoulders, he responded, "Okay, whatever."

These students have fragmented self-esteem.

Instructional/Behavioral Implementation Goal/s

Unfortunately, Rueben's home life was out of control. He felt no one cared, except his older brother. As part of his academic incentive plan, they would eat together, weekly. I modified the content of my lessons to entice the learning process for him. The results were positive.

13.) The Struggling Student (Zet)

"If this little boy don't stop telling me how to read, I know what to do," said Zet.

"He said yesterday, wrong, I was helping him," said one of his peers.

"Okay, come here," she said.

"I appreciate how hard you're trying, would you like me to read along with you, until you feel comfortable, again," she said.

"Yes, please," he said.

"Okay," she said.

Students like Zet do not understand the academic content that is delivered. As a defense mechanism, they resort to the "I Already Know" default. These students are placed in the below level, reading category. They need extra attention and differentiated instruction that will improve their capabilities.

Instructional/Behavioral Implementation Goal/s

Zet's family was not very sympathetic to his reading deficiency. Although he did not say it, the positive reinforcement expressed by me, meant the world to him. He was a great student, given a raw deal. Unfortunately, I refused to highlight his weaknesses. Instead, I focused on his strengths. He already acknowledged, what could not be done. Why reiterate it? He struggled with word identification and fluency. He earned a ticket, every time he mastered a skill. Ultimately, he would earn a large reward of choice. This encouraged him, during the reading process. He showed improvement, throughout the year.

14.) The "No Homework" Student (Pat)

"Pat where's your homework," she said.

"I did it but, I left it," she said.

"What happened," she said

"My mom ain't come home till late," she said.

"Okay, so you don't have your homework, again," she said.

"No," she said.

Instructional/Behavioral Implementation Goal/s

These students always have an excuse for why their homework is incomplete. She came from a family with a single mom of five kids. Unfortunately, there was no one available to help her with concepts she struggled to understand. Circumstances can make completing assignments(at home) challenging. This is a hard subject since we do not want to make excuses for why homework is incomplete. Students in these tricky circumstances, increase responsibility by earning a reward if they complete a section of homework. I assisted by pinpointing the problems that were difficult and addressed them, during the remedial time.

Realistic expectations are the starting point for educators, dealing with similar situations. If she completed two out of five pages, she earned a reward. Over time, I noticed she started to complete most of the homework packet.

Input

The rubrics below have categories for key elements of success. They address diverse student genres. For content to be effective, frequency is important. Although educators play a crucial role, in the learning process, parents help lay the foundation that sets the tone for student achievement. After careful thought and observation, I formulated rubrics to serve as a blueprint for parents[of students], in different categories, based on fundamental components.

	Self Evaluation Rubric, Grades K-12 Gifted Educators (Score points within each domain include most of the characteristics below.)		
Score	**Gifted Student Differentiation (4 Point Rubric)**	**Gifted Evidence and Elaboration (4 Point Rubric)**	**Academic Personalized Connections (4 Point Rubric)**
4 LEADING	The gifted educator sustains and focuses on the individualized needs, of **every** gifted student. The gifted educator explains **the goal** of each lesson and allows all gifted student/s to notate various ways, problems could be solved on **an operational and individualized basis.** The gifted educator takes into account **all characteristics.** correlated to the subject matter that will enhance **every** academic activity. The gifted educator **always** ensures **all** students can **connect the underlined learning basis**, across the board.	The gifted educator **always provides the gifted child with a myriad of expressive options**, before, during and after academic activities. The gifted educator **always encourages** individualized self expression that directly correlates to logical, creative, and critical enhancement. The gifted educator **always** develop personalized rubrics/lesson plans/ **evaluation tools**, directly correlated to each gifted student. The gifted educator **encourages all** students to develop new methods, regarding content-based inquisition.	The educator develops **all** lessons, conducive to the **gifted state standards.** If the state does not posses these standards, the educator will meet with administration/well-versed gifted expert to **ensure academic standards are always up to par.** The gifted educator **always** provides the opportunity to respond to questions with multiple answers/ viewpoints. The educator **always encourages each gifted child** to **think divergently**, regarding each topic. The gifted educator **always provides opportunities for verbal expansion**, during all academic activities.

	Lesson Differentiated Objective & Goal	Gifted Evidence and Elaboration	My Basic Needs Are Met
3 L E A R N I N G	The gifted educator sustains and focuses on the individualized needs, of **most** gifted students. The gifted educator explains **the goal** of **most aspects of the** lesson and allows **selective** gifted student/s to notate various ways, problems could be solved on a **operational and individualized basis.** The gifted educator takes into account **most characteristics.** correlated to the subject matter that will enhance **selective** academic activities. The gifted educator **ensures a large number** students can **connect the underlined learning basis**, across the board.	The gifted educator **provides the gifted child with a myriad of expressive options**, before, during and after academic activities. The gifted educator **always encourages individualized self expression** that directly correlates to logical, creative, and critical enhancement. The gifted educator **selectively develops** personalized rubrics/lesson plans/ **evaluation tools**, directly **correlated to most** gifted students. The gifted educator **encourages most** students to develop new methods, regarding content-based inquisition.	The educator develops lessons, **semi-conducive** to the **gifted state standards.** If the state does not posses these standards, the educator will meet with administration/well-versed gifted expert to **ensure academic standards are up to par, most of the time.** The gifted educator provides the opportunity to respond to questions with multiple answers/viewpoints. The educator **encourages certain gifted children** to **think divergently**, regarding **selective topics**. The gifted educator **provides opportunities for verbal expansion**, during **most** academic activities.

Self Evaluation Rubric, Grades K-12 Gifted Educators
(Score points within each domain include most of the characteristics below.)

Score	Lesson Differentiated Objective & Goal Orientation (Rubric) This Lesson relates to me.	Gifted Evidence and Elaboration to Remain Engaged. (Rubric)	My Basic Needs Are Met, During Each Lesson to Enhance the Learning Process.
2 L A T E N T	The gifted educator focuses on the individualized needs, of **certain** gifted students. The gifted educator is vague **the overall goal** of **certain aspects of the** lesson and allows **selective** gifted student/s to notate various ways, problems could be solved. The gifted educator takes into account **certain characteristics.** correlated to the subject matter that will enhance **selective** academic activities. The gifted educator ensures **certain** students can **connect the underlined learning basis**, across the board. The educator somewhat sustains the gifted student/s, regarding the lesson.	The gifted educator **provides the gifted child with a limited number of expressive opportunities**, before and after academic activities. The gifted educator **places little to no emphasis on** logical, creative, and critical enhancement. The gifted educator **develops generalized** rubrics/lesson plans/ **evaluation tools**. The gifted educator **encourages certain** students to develop new methods, regarding content-based inquisition.	The educator develops lessons, **loosely based on gifted state standards.** The gifted educator provides **a low number of opportunities** for students respond to challenging questions. The educator **encourages certain gifted children** to **think deeply**, about **selective topics**. The gifted educator **provides opportunities for verbal expansion**, during **selective** academic activities.

1 **L** **A** **G** **G** **I** **N** **G**	The gifted educator provides **little to no** differentiated sustenance to keep gifted students, engaged. . The gifted educator **obscurely** explains **the overall goal** of **certain aspects of the** lesson and allows **selective** gifted student/s to notate various ways, problems could be solved on a **collectively operational and individualized basis.** The gifted educator takes into account **certain characteristics.** correlated to the subject matter that will enhance **selective** academic activities. The gifted educator ensures **certain** students can **connect the underlined learning basis**, across the board. The educator somewhat sustains the gifted student/s, regarding the lesson.	The gifted educator **provides the gifted child with rare options**, before, during and after academic activities. The gifted educator **provides little to no individualized self expression,** correlated to logical, creative, and critical enhancement. The gifted educator **develops generalized** rubrics/lesson plans/ **evaluation tools**, directly correlated to each gifted student. The gifted educator **does not encourage students** to develop new methods, regarding content-based inquisition.	The educator develops lessons, **conducive** to the **gifted state standards.** If the state does not posses these standards, the educator addresses the matter **rarely.** The gifted educator provides little to no opportunities for students to respond to questions with **certain** answers/viewpoints. The educator **encourages certain gifted children** to **think divergently**, regarding **selective topics**. The gifted educator **provides opportunities for verbal expansion**, during **selective** academic activities.
0 **L** **O** **S** **T**	The gifted educator provides **no** differentiated sustenance to keep gifted students, engaged. . The gifted educator **Does not** explain **the overall goal** of the lesson and **discourages** gifted student/s from notating various ways, problems could be solved on a **collectively operational and individualized basis.** The gifted educator **never** takes relatively, into account regarding academic content dissemination. The gifted educator **discourages** students from **connecting the underlined learning basis**, across the board.	The gifted educator **discourages each gifted from conveying the lesson's content/comprehensive material.** The gifted educator **never encourages individualized self expression** that correlates to logical, creative, and critical enhancement. The educator **does not develop** personalized rubrics/lesson plans/ **evaluation tools**, correlated to each gifted student. The gifted educator **discourages** students to develop new methods, regarding content-based inquisition.	The educator **does not align** the lesson's content to the gifted state standards. The gifted educator **Never** provides students with opportunities to respond to questions, based on **their** answer/viewpoints. The educator **discourages certain gifted children** to **think divergently**, regarding **any topic**. The gifted educator **never provides opportunities for verbal expansion**, during academic activities.

Gifted Educator Reading/Writing Individualized Rubric, Grades K-12 (Rate the content of each individualized lesson, based on the following)		
S **c** **o** **r** **e**	**Lesson Differentiated Objective & Goal Orientation** **(4-point Rubric)**	**Gifted Evidence and Elaboration** **(4-point Rubric)**	**Gifted Academic Personalized Connections** **(4-point Rubric)**

	Lesson Differentiated Objective & Goal Orientation	Gifted Evidence and Elaboration	READING/WRITING Academic Personalized Connections
4 **L E A D I N G**	The gifted educator differentiates **all** literally assignments, according to various perspectives/insight/ characterization of **each** student, in the class. The gifted educator's literary assignments strikes a **high** level of curiosity, that triggers **each** student to go above and beyond their present academic capability. The gifted educator assigns literary tasks that help **each** student gather information, based on distinct complexity. The gifted educator **always** personalizes assignments, based on a student's individualized humor, intensity/curiosity.	The gifted educator provides **each** student with vast opportunities to pose unforeseen questions, during **all** literary activities. The gifted educator allows **all** students to formulated evaluations that will **cause** academic synchronization and diversification. The gifted educator **always** utilizes original student feedback by carrying out **in-depth** conversations, during/after each literary lesson. The gifted educator provides opportunities **for all** students to generate literary evidence that will support **all** written claims/ activities.	The gifted educator proposes constant ways **each** student can make correlations between new literary concepts and how these concepts are applicable to their hopes, dreams and purpose. The gifted educator encourages **most** students to research/discuss **all** literary concepts with their peers. The gifted educator encourages development of **personalized** literary connections, **throughout** the **year**.
3 **L E A R N I N G**	The gifted educator differentiate-sassignments, according to various perspectives/insight/characterization of each student, in the class, **the greater part of each assignment**. The gifted educator's literary assignments strikes a level of curiosity, that triggers **each** student to go above and beyond their present academic capability for **most** of the class. The gifted educator assigns literary tasks that help **the majority of the class,** gather information, based on distinct complexity. The gifted educator **personalizes most** assignments, based on a student's individualized humor, **intensity/curiosity.**	The gifted educator provides **most** student with vast opportunities to pose unforeseen questions, during **most** literary activities. The gifted educator's allowance for students to formulate evaluations that **trigger** academic synchronization and diversification, is **habitual**. The gifted educator utilizes **modified** student feedback by carrying out conversations, during/after each **a large number of** lessons. The gifted educator provides **frequent** opportunities **for most** students to generate literary evidence that will support written claims/activities.	The gifted educator proposes ways **each** student can make correlations between new literary concepts and how these concepts are applicable to their hopes, dreams and purpose. The gifted educator encourages **the majority of** students to research/discuss all literary concepts with their peers. The gifted educator encourages **recurring** development of **semi-personalized** literary connections, **throughout** the **semester.**

Gifted Reading/Writing Individualized Rubric, Grades K-12 **(Rate the content of each individualized lesson, based on the following)**		

S c o r e	**Lesson Differentiated Objective & Goal Orientation** **(4-Point Rubric)**	**Gifted Evidence and Elaboration** **(4-point Rubric)**	**READING/WRITING Academic Personalized Connections** **(4-Point Rubric)**

2 **L** **A** **T** **E** **N** **T**	The gifted educator differentiates **selective** literally assignments, according to various perspectives/insight/characterization of each student, in the class. The gifted educator's literary assignments **that may** strike a level of curiosity that may trigger **certain** students to go above and beyond, **at least half of the time.** The gifted educator assigns literary tasks that helps **certain** students gather information, based on distinct complexity. The gifted educator **personalizes** assignments, based on a student's individualized humor, **intensity/curiosity, most of the time**	The gifted educator provides students with vast opportunities to pose unforeseen questions, during **selective** literary activities. The gifted educator's allowance for students to formulated evaluations that **trigger** academic synchronization and diversification, is **inconsistent**. The gifted educator utilizes student feedback by carrying out **vague** conversations, during/after each literary lesson. The gifted educator provides opportunities **for selective** students to generate literary evidence that will support **most** written claims/activities.	The gifted educator proposes ways **certain** student can make correlations between new literary concepts and how these concepts are applicable to their hopes, dreams and purpose. The gifted educator encourages **a small amount of** students to research/discuss all literary concepts with their peers. The gifted educator encourages development of literary connections, **occasionally.**
1 **L** **A** **G** **G** **I** **N** **G**	The gifted educator differentiates **constructs** literal assignments, according to various perspectives/insight/characterization of each student, **occasionally.** The gifted educator's literary assignments promote a **narrow** level of curiosity, regarding the literary content. The gifted educator assigns literary tasks that are **vague** . The gifted educator **encourages personalized** assignments, accompanied by directives that are **inexplicit**.	The gifted educator provides students with **rare** opportunities to pose unforeseen questions, during literary activities. The gifted educator's allowance for students to formulate evaluations that **trigger** academic synchronization and diversification, is **inconsistent**. The gifted educator utilizes **censored** student feedback by carrying out **vague** conversations, during/after each literary lesson. The gifted educator provides **unreliable** opportunities **for a small number** students to generate literary evidence that will support **certain** written claims/activities.	The gifted educator **places little to no effort on** proposes ways students can make correlations between new literary concepts and how these concepts are applicable to their hopes, dreams and purpose. The gifted educator encourages **selective** students to research/discuss all literary concepts with their peers, **occasionally.** The gifted educator **does not elaborate** on why the literary connections, are important and useful, throughout the **month/week**.

0 L O S T	The gifted educator **does not** **foster** literally assignments, according to various perspectives/insight/characterization of each student, in the class. The gifted educator's literary assignments promotion of curiosity, regarding the literary content, is **nonexistent**. The gifted educator **does not modify** literary tasks, tailored to **each** student that **will ignite** curiosity and a rigorous mindset. The gifted educator **does not personalize** assignments, accompanied by directives that are **explicit**.	**In no way**, does the gifted educator provide students with opportunities to pose unforeseen questions, during literary activities. The gifted educator **does not** allocate time for students to formulate evaluations that **trigger** academic synchronization and diversification. **At no time** does the gifted educator utilize student feedback/conversations, during/after each literary lesson. The gifted educator **never** provides opportunities for **students** to generate literary evidence that will support written claims/activities.	The gifted educator **does not** propose ways students make correlations between new literary concepts, and how these concepts are applicable to their hopes, dreams and purpose. The gifted educator **never addresses** relational research or promote conversations, related to literary concepts with their peers. The gifted educator **ignores student elaboration** on why literary connections are important and useful.

Gifted Math Individualized Rubric, Grades K-12
(Rate the content of each individualized lesson, based on the following)

S c o r e	**Lesson Differentiated Objective & Goal Orientation (4-point Rubric)**	**Gifted Evidence and Elaboration (4-point Rubric)**	**Gifted Academic Personalized Connections (4-point Rubric)**
4 L E A D I N G	The gifted educator affords **all** students, the opportunity to identify and utilize their outstanding capabilities to **enhance** the mathematical knowledge of their peers and others. The gifted educator **always** encourages students to analyze each portion of the affiliated standard and make the necessary accommodations, accordingly. The gifted educator **motivates all** students to formulated ideas, activities and goals that trigger outlandish yet achievable mathematical activities. The gifted educator promotes complex tasks, critical thinking and individualized project completion, **consistently.**	The gifted educator **Encourages all** students to discuss mathematical content, in their lingo, **consistently.** The gifted educator **makes** personalized feedback to modify aspects of future activities/lessons, relative **to each student.** The gifted educator **always** entices mathematical content by referring elements of various subject areas. **Every time** a gifted student brings a complex mathematical aspect to light, the educator encourages elaboration.	The gifted educator **provides opportunities for mathematical verbal expansion**, during **all** academic activities. The gifted educator **Provides all** students with opportunities to create a multi-dimensional mathematical activities that bridge the gap, between academic content and personal experiences. The gifted educator **encourages** development of **personalized** mathematical connections, **throughout** the **year**.

3 **L** **E** **A** **R** **N** **I** **N** **G**	The gifted educator **encourages most stu**dents, the opportunity to identify and utilize their outstanding capabilities to **enhance** the mathematical knowledge of their peers and others, **most of the time**. The gifted educator encourages **most** students to analyze each portion of the affiliated standard and make the necessary accommodations. The gifted educator **motivates** students to formulated ideas, activities and goals that trigger **outlandish** yet achievable, mathematical activities, often. The gifted educator promotes complex tasks, critical thinking and individualized project completion, **most of the time.**	The gifted educator **encourages** students to discuss mathematical content, in their lingo, **most of the time.** The gifted educator **uses** personalized feedback to modify aspects of future activities/ lessons, relative **to most students.** The gifted educator entices mathematical content by referring elements of **most** subject areas. When gifted students brings a complex mathematical aspect to light, the educator encourages elaboration, **often.**	The gifted educator **always provides opportunities for** **mathematical verbal expansion**, **during several** academic activities. The gifted educator **Allots the majority of** students with opportunities to create a multi-dimensional mathematical activities that bridge the gap, between academic content and personal experiences. The gifted educator encourages development of **personalized** mathematical connections, **throughout** the **semester**.
2 **L** **A** **T** **E** **N** **T**	The gifted educator provides students with, **minimal opportunities** to identify their outstanding capabilities in order to **enhance** the mathematical knowledge of their peers, **minimally.** The gifted educator places little emphasis on students to partially analyze portions of the affiliated standard and make necessary accommodations, **some of the time.** The gifted educator **encourages a small number of students** to formulated ideas, activities and goals that trigger **outlandish** yet achievable mathematical activities. The gifted educator **motivates students to attempt** complex tasks, critical thinking and individualized project completion, **some of the time**.	The gifted educator's actions, regarding in-depth mathematical student-led discussions, are **unreliable**. The gifted educator **places little emphasis on** personalized feedback to modify various aspects of future activities/lessons, relative to each student. The gifted educator addresses mathematical content by referring to elements of subject areas, **a low amount of times.** When a gifted student brings a complex mathematical aspect to light, the educator **disregards times of** elaboration.	The gifted educator **provides opportunities for** **mathematical verbal expansion**, during **a low percentage of** academic activities. The gifted educator **prompts** students opportunities to create a multi-dimensional mathematical activities that bridge the gap, between academic content and personal experiences, **infrequently.** The gifted educator **shows little interest in** development of **personalized** mathematical connections, **throughout** the **month.**

1 **L** **A** **G** **G** **I** **N** **G**	The gifted educator takes into account the individuality of **certain students,** regarding mathematical practice and effectiveness. The gifted educator overlooks portions of the lesson that each student is allowed to analyze, **based on a biased viewpoint.** **Individuality is not the primary goal** of each mathematical lesson, thus, academic differentiation is ignored, causing each students' unique characteristics to **become opaque.** The gifted educator makes comments that **discourage** students, from sharing their **creative** and **outlandish** mathematical ideas.	The gifted educator **does not** allow students to identify uneven, mathematical evidence/support pertaining to the lesson's content; mathematical concepts **are not discussed.** Students **are not given the opportunity** to cross-pollinate relative content, related to the subject matter. Gifted students **are not given the right** to voice their **content-based opinion/s** to their teacher and classmates. The gifted educator's promotion of mathematically complex evidence-based elaboration, is **uncommon**.	The gifted educator encourages students to generate mathematical mental surges, **occasionally.** The gifted educator **discourages construction** of mathematical activities based on a one-dimensional train of thought. The gifted educator **does not promote** academically relative activities that will enhance a dynamic train of thought on occasion. The gifted educator **reprimands students who reject** the **default mentality**, regarding new mathematical concepts, relative information and future strategic usage.
0 **L** **O** **S** **T**	The gifted educator **never** takes into account the individuality of each student, regarding mathematical practice and effectiveness. The gifted educator **does not** explains portions of the lesson that each student is allowed to analyze, based on a biased viewpoint. **At no time, is the primary goal** of each mathematical lesson, thus, academic differentiation is ignored, causing each students' unique characteristics to **become opaque.** The gifted educator makes comments that **discourage** students, from developing individual characteristics that are directly pertinent to their outstanding mathematical capabilities.	The gifted educator **discourages** gifted students from identifying mathematical evidence/support pertaining to the lesson's content; mathematical concepts **are not elaborated on.** Students **are discouraged from** cross-pollinating relative content, related to the subject matter. Gifted students **are not given the right** to voice their **content-based opinion/s** to their teacher and classmates. The gifted educator's promotion of mathematically complex evidence-based elaboration, is **nonexistent**.	The gifted educator **does not** encourages students to produce mathematical mental surges. The gifted educator ignores the capabilities of each student to **construct mathematical activities, based on a multidimensional train of thought.** Dynamic personalized content-relative activities, **are not identified/enhanced.** Gifted students are **discouraged** from utilizing their eccentricities to formulate innovative mathematical concepts/ideas.

	Gifted Science/Social Studies Individualized Rubric, Grades K-12 **(Rate the content of each individualized lesson, based on the following)**		
S **c** **o** **r** **e**	**Lesson Differentiated Objective & Goal Orientation** **(4-point Rubric)**	**Gifted Evidence and Elaboration** **(4-point Rubric)**	**Historical/Social Studies' Connections in the REAL WORLD** **(4-point Rubric)**

4 **L** **E** **A** **D** **I** **N** **G**	The gifted educator **always inspires** students to analyze the science/S.S. Essential Question/standards/lesson content. The educator **displays open satisfaction**, when students innovate new possibilities, instead of simply adhering to the guidelines of **each** standard. The educator views individualization as an **integral** part of how each student's will approach the lesson's elements e.g., the setting, chronological timing and experimentation necessary for assignment, completion. The educator allows all students to tweak various scientific/historical concepts/ideas.	The gifted educator **encourages all** students to elaborate on various means of feedback. The gifted educator **encourages** original ideas in their raw form. The gifted educator **always encourages** conversations that will deepen scientific/historical vocabulary knowledge. **Every time** a gifted student is allowed several avenues of expression, regarding different components of the subject matter.	The gifted educator always **fosters every student** who are driven by curiosity to make connections between the subject's content and personal experiences. The gifted educator **promotes the S.S./Scientific Content is relative to each student,** if for some reason the student is having trouble, correlating the two, the educator assists in the process. The gifted educator **always** promotes original academic expressiveness, in order to **eliminate** conceptual redundancy. The educator **encourages** development of **personalized** scientific/historical connections are made, **throughout** the **year.**
3 **L** **E** **A** **R** **N** **I** **N** **G**	Advancement through **most** science/S.S. Standards, is the priority of the gifted educator, **most of the time**; students are **encouraged** to dissect the essential question and assignment, through peer and individual interaction. The educator **affirms**, students innovate new possibilities, instead of simply adhering to the guidelines of most aspect of **every** standard. The educator promotes individualization, during **most** assignments. Making the association between the lesson's elements, is necessary for assignment, completion. The educator allows **most students** to tweak various scientific/historical concepts/ideas.	The gifted educator **encourages most** students to elaborate on various means of feedback. The gifted educator **encourages a large number** to generate original ideas in their raw form. The gifted educator **stimulates** conversations that deepen scientific/historical vocabulary knowledge. Gifted students are given **several avenues of expression**, regarding different components of the subject matter.	The gifted educator **ignites each** student, driven by curiosity to make connections between the subject's content and personal experiences. The gifted educator **ensures most S.S./Scientific Content is relative to each student,** if for some reason the student is having trouble, correlating the two, the educator assists in the process. The gifted educator **almost always** promotes original academic expressiveness, in order to **eliminate** conceptual redundancy. The educator **promotes** the development of **personalized** scientific/historical connections are made, **throughout** the **semester/quarter.**

2 **L** **A** **T** **E** **N** **T**	Advancement through **selective** science/S.S. Standards, is the priority of the gifted educator, most times; students are **discouraged** from dissecting the essential question and assignment, through peer and individual interaction. The educator **affirms**, students innovate new possibilities, instead of simply adhering to the guidelines of most aspect of **selective** standards. The educator promotes individualization, during **some** assignments. Making the association between the lesson's elements, is necessary for assignment, completion. The educator allows students to tweak various scientific/historical concepts/ideas, **irregularly**	The gifted educator **values** student elaboration and feedback, **occasionally.** The gifted educator **does not encourage** students to generate original ideas in their raw form. The gifted educator **shows indifference toward** conversations that will deepen scientific/historical vocabulary knowledge, **rarely.** Allowance for several avenues of expression, regarding different components of subject matter, is **infrequent.**	The gifted educator **shows little appreciation for** students, driven by curiosity to make connections between the subject's content and personal experiences. The gifted educator **generalizes the S.S./Scientific Content.** The gifted educator **places little to no emphasis on** original academic expressiveness, in order to **eliminate** conceptual redundancy. The gifted educator **encourages** the development of **personalized** scientific/historical connections, **throughout** the **month.**
1 **L** **A** **G** **G** **I** **N** **G**	Dissection of the content within the S.S./Science Standards, **is rare.** The educator **overlooks each** students' ability to innovate new possibilities, instead of simply adhering to the guidelines of most aspect of **every** standard. The **promotion** of uniqueness per the capability of each gifted student, is undermined, **regularly.** The educator **encourages** students to analyze standards by relational measures, **infrequently.**	The gifted educator **provides preferential input,** **regarding** student elaboration and feedback. The gifted educator **prompts students,** in the process of generating new scientific/historical ideas, thus stunting individualistic growth. The gifted educator **takes over certain aspects of** scientific/historical vocabulary-based dialogue, **frequently** The gifted educator's allowance for several avenues of expression, regarding different components of subject matter, **fluctuates.**	The gifted educator **does not acknowledge** students, driven by curiosity to make connections between the subject's content and personal experiences. The gifted educator **does not encourage** organic personalized relations. The gifted educator promotes original academic expressiveness, **rarely** . The educator **encourages** the development of **personalized** scientific/historical connections , **throughout** the **month.**

0 L O S T	Dissection of the content within the S.S./Science Standards, **never** occurs. **Under no circumstances,** does the gifted educator **notice each** students' ability to innovate new possibilities. The **promotion** of uniqueness per the capability of each gifted student, is undermined, **regularly.** The educator **does not encourage** students to analyze standards by relational measures.	The gifted educator **provides preferential input, regarding** student elaboration and feedback. The gifted educator's **ability to encourage,** creative ways to express new ideas, is **absent**. The gifted educator **does not address** scientific/historical vocabulary-based dialogue. The gifted educator's allowance for several avenues of expression, regarding different components of subject matter, **is nonexistent**.	The gifted educator **does not acknowledge** students, driven by curiosity to make connections between the subject's content and personal experiences. The gifted educator **never** organic personalized relations. The gifted educator **never** promotes original academic expressiveness, in order to **eliminate** conceptual redundancy. The educator **discourages** the development of **personalized** connections,

Gifted Parent Self Evaluation **(Score points based on individualized gifted characteristics.)**			
S c o r e	**School to Home Implementation** **(Rubric)**	**My Child's Individualized Relation** **Gifted** **(Rubric)**	**Conventions of a Gifted Parent-Frequent** **Reminders are Crucial** **(Rubric)**
4 L E A D I N G	The parent always fosters a **challenging** environment, based on the **individualized** needs of their child. The parent always makes every effort to communicate with the gifted student's teacher/teachers, in order to stay abreast, regarding **all** activities. Personalized home academic goals/objectives are **always established**, after input is provided by both the child's teacher/teachers and the gifted child.	I provided my child with **various** opportunities for self-expression, based on their personalized academic goals. My child is given **frequent** opportunities to explain personal relation to all subject/project content. My child is afforded **continual** opportunities to indulge in activities, based on their individualized needs.	My child is given **perpetual** opportunities to express content learned, in **several** ways. The parent encourages frequent inquisition, regarding **all** daily homework assignments, school experiences and extra-curricular activities. After careful research and personalized experiences, I **always allow** my child to express how they will use their gifts, in the future.

3 L E A R N I N G	The parent fosters a **challenging** environment, based on the **individualized** needs of their child, **most of the time**. The parent **makes numerous efforts** to communicate with the gifted student's teacher/teachers, in order to stay abreast, regarding all activities. Personalized home academic goals/objectives are established, after input is provided by both the child's teacher/teachers and the gifted child, **almost all of the time.**	I provided my child with **several** opportunities for self-expression, based on their personalized academic goals. My child is given **droves of** opportunities to explain personal relation to all subject/project content. My child is afforded **respective** opportunities to indulge in activities, based on their individualized needs.	My child is given **many** opportunities to express content learned, in **several** ways. The parent encourages frequent inquisition, regarding **nearly all** daily homework assignments, school experiences and extra-curricular activities. After careful research and personalized experiences, I **allow** my child to express how they will use their gifts, in the future, **frequently.**
2 L A T E N T	The student's home environment, **lacks focus; the student's parent/guardian encourages** opportunities for individualistic expression. The parent's efforts to communicate with the gifted student's teacher/teachers, in order to stay abreast, regarding all activities, are **few and far between.** Personalized home academic goals/objectives are **unclear,** in spite of the input of the child's gifted educator and the student.	I provided my child with **particular** opportunities for self-expression, based on their personalized academic goals. My child is given **a small amount of** opportunities to explain personal relation to all subject/project content. My child is afforded **rare** opportunities to indulge in activities, based on their individualized needs.	My child is given **rare** opportunities to express content learned, in **a handful of ways.** The parent encourages frequent inquisition, regarding **selective** daily homework assignments, school experiences and extra-curricular activities. After careful research and personalized experiences, I **allow** my child to express how they will use their gifts, in the future, **occasionally.**
1 L A G G I N G	The student's home environment, **appeals to a small percentage** of individualistic expression. The parent **takes minimal opportunities** to contact the gifted student's educator/s regarding classroom activities. Personalized home academic goals/objectives **are not viewed by the parent, as significant.**	I provide my child with opportunities for self-expression, based on their personalized academic goals, **once in a while.** My child is given opportunities to explain personal relation to all subject/project content **on an infrequently.** My child is afforded **scarce** opportunities to indulge in activities, based on their individualized needs.	My child **is allowed rare** opportunities to express content learned. The parent **addresses** daily homework assignments, school experiences and extra-curricular activities, **occasionally.** The times I provided my gifted child to express their giftedness **infrequently.**

| 0 L O S T | The student's home environment, **never** promotes individualistic expression.

The parent **makes no attempt** to contact the gifted student's educator/s regarding classroom activities.

Personalized home academic goals/ objectives **are not addressed by the parent/guardian.** | **I evade opportunities** for my child with opportunities for self-expression, based on their personalized academic goals.

My child **is not given** opportunities to explain personal relation to all subject/project content.

My child is afforded **no** opportunities to indulge in activities, based on their individualized needs. | My child **is not given** opportunities to express content learned.

The parent **avoids** frequent inquisition, regarding daily homework assignments, school experiences and extra-curricular activities.

I do not provide my gifted child to express their giftedness. |

Self Evaluation Rubric, Grades K-12 Educators
(Score points within each domain include most of the characteristics below.)

S c o r e	Student Genre-General Ed. Differentiation (4 Point Rubric)	Student Genre-General Ed. Evidence & Elaboration (4 Point Rubric)	Student Genre-General Ed. Personalized Connections (4 Point Rubric)

4 L E A D I N G	The educator sustains and focuses on the individualized needs, of each student, both separately and in groups, **carefully**.
	
	The individualized lesson **always** consists of the following:
	  The educator **unfailingly provides** students with an introduction of the lesson, peer insight on the essential question and overall objective was expressed pre, and post lesson.
	
	  The educator **always ensures** the content based material, does not create a frustration level that causes the student to become disengaged.
	
	As a result of differentiation, all students are afforded **consistent** academic assignment opportunities, in several formats. These opportunities include but are not limited to: **sensory, concrete information, use of detailed responses, as a result of the educator's unique appeal and enhancing the vivid images for every student.**
		The educator researches and **modifies all** content, according to the assessed data, accumulated, through **observations, teacher-student interviews, informal/formal assessments and evaluations.**
		
		The educator holds **each** student to a unique standard, allowing **each** student to convey details, about lesson improvements.
		
		The educator **asks each student** to express constructive feedback, regarding which aspects of the lesson should be changed for.
			An educator allows **all students** to elaborate on aspects of the **lesson's standards, objectives and essential questions,** accordingly.
			
			The educator **always** utilizes personalized rubrics/lesson plans/evaluation tools, **correlated to each student's personalized insight/experiences.**
			
			The educator **provides numerous** motivational circumstances that encourage students to make personalized content connections, **at all times.**
			
			The educator **always** provides content that **peaks curiosity**, during every lesson.

| 3 L E A R N I N G | The educator sustains and consistently focuses on the individualized needs, **of each student, both separately and in groups.** The individualized lesson consists of the following:

The educator **provides most** students with an introduction of the lesson, peer insight on the essential question and overall objective was expressed pre, and post lesson.

The educator **ensures** the content based material, does not create a frustration level that causes the student to become disengaged, **frequently.**

As a result of differentiation, most students are afforded **an array of** academic assignment opportunities, in several formats. These opportunities include but are not limited to: **sensory, concrete information, use of detailed responses, as a result of the educator's unique appeal and enhancing the vivid images for most students.** | The educator researches and **modifies** content, according to the assessed data, accumulated, through **observations, teacher-student interviews, informal/ formal assessments and evaluations.**

The educator holds **each** student to a unique standard, allowing **each** student to convey details, about lesson improvements, **most of the time.**

The educator holds **several** data chats, regarding the student's personalized academic goals/objectives.

The educator **asks almost all students** to express constructive feedback, regarding which aspects of the lesson should be changed for. | The educator allows **the majority** of students to elaborate on aspects of the **lesson's standards, objectives and essential questions.**

The educator utilizes personalized rubrics/lesson plans/evaluation tools, **correlated to selective student's personalized insight/experiences.**

The educator provides motivational circumstances that **normally** encourages students to make **personalized content connections.**

The educator provides content that **typically peaks curiosity**, during **certain** lessons. |

	The educator sustains and consistently focuses on the individualized needs, **of each student, both separately and in groups.** The individualized lesson consists of the following: The educator **provides most** students with an introduction of the lesson, peer insight on the essential question and overall objective was expressed pre, and post lesson. The educator **ensures** the content based material, does not create a frustration level that causes the student to become disengaged, **frequently.** **As a result of differentiation, most students** are afforded **an array of** academic assignment opportunities, in several formats. These opportunities include but are not limited to: **sensory, concrete information, use of detailed responses, as a result of the educator's unique appeal and enhancing the vivid images for most students.**		
Self Evaluation Rubric, Grades K-12 Educators			
(Score points within each domain include most of the characteristics below.)			
S c o r e	**Student Genre-General Ed. Differentiation (4 Point Rubric)**	**Student Genre-General Ed. Evidence & Elaboration (4 Point Rubric)**	**Student Genre-General Ed. Personalized Connections (4 Point Rubric)**

2 **L** **A** **T** **E** **N** **T**	The educator focuses on the individualized needs, of **a small number students.** The individualized lesson consists of the following: The educator **provides** students with an introduction of the lesson, peer insight on the essential question and overall objective was expressed pre, and post lesson. The educator **provides** the content based material that does not create a frustration level causing the student to become disengaged. **As a result of differentiation**, students are afforded academic assignment opportunities, in **at least two of the following** formats: **sensory, concrete information, use of responses, as a result of the educator's unique appeal and enhancing the vivid images for most students.**	The educator **modifies** content, according to **certain aspects of** assessed data, observations, teacher-student interviews, informal/formal assessments and evaluations, **some of the time.** The educator holds students to a unique standard, allowing them student to convey details, about lesson improvements. The educator holds data chats, regarding the student's academic goals/ objectives, **infrequently.** The educator **encourages** students to provide constructive feedback, regarding which aspects of the lesson should be changed, **intermittently.**	The educator asks **selective** students to elaborate on aspects of the **lesson's standards, objectives and essential questions.** The educator utilizes rubrics/lesson plans/evaluation tools, **somewhat correlated to selective student's personalized insight/experiences.** The educator provides students with opportunities to make personalized content connections, **once in a while.** The educator provides content that **may peak curiosity, occasionally.**
1 **L** **A** **G** **G** **I** **N** **G**	The educator **lacks the ability to focus** on the individualized needs, of each student, **both separately and in groups.** The individualized lesson **lacks** the following: The educator **provides** students with one of the following: an introduction of the lesson, peer insight on the essential question and overall objective was expressed pre, and post lesson. The educator the content based material that does not create a frustration level causing the student to become disengaged, **infrequently.** **As a result of differentiation**, students are afforded academic assignment opportunities, in **at least one of the following** formats: **sensory, concrete information, use of responses, as a result of the educator's unique appeal and enhancing the vivid images for most students.**	The educator **does not focus on** content, according to the assessed data, accumulated, through **observations, teacher-student interviews, informal/formal assessments and evaluations.** The educator holds **a low percentage of** students to a unique standard, allowing **them** student to convey details, about lesson improvements. The educator **encourages** data chats, regarding the student's academic goals/objectives, **some of the time.** **The educator discounts** constructive feedback, regarding which aspects of the lesson should be changed.	The educator **prompts a low percentage of students** to elaborate on aspects of the lesson's standards, objectives and essential questions. The educator utilizes rubrics/lesson plans/evaluation tools, correlated to selective student's personalized insight/experiences, **inconsistently.** The educator provides students with opportunities to make personalized content connections, **rarely.** The educator provides content that **has a low chance of enhancing curiosity.**

| 0 L O S T | The educator **never addresses** on the individualized needs, of each student.

The individualized lesson **does not address any of the following:**
    The educator **does not provide** students with one of the following: an introduction of the lesson, peer insight on the essential question and overall objective was expressed pre, and post lesson.

    The educator **never provides** content based material that does not create a frustration level causing the student to become disengaged.

    The educator **does not appeal to various learning** formats: **sensory, concrete information, use of responses, as a result of the educator's unique appeal and enhancing the vivid images for most students.** | The educator **does not modify** content, according to the assessed data, accumulated, through **observations.**

    The educator **does not address** unique standard and lesson relativity.
    The educator **never holds** data chats, regarding the student's academic goals/objectives.

The educator ignores constructive feedback, regarding which aspects of the lesson should be changed. | The educator **never prompts** students to elaborate on aspects of the lesson's standards, objectives and essential questions.

The educator utilizes rubrics/lesson plans/evaluation tools, **does not correlated to selective student's personalized insight/experiences.**

The educator **overlooks** students who make personalized content connections.

The educator gives no thought to how content relativity **peaks curiosity**. |

| Educator Reading/Writing Individualized Rubric, Grades K-12 |||
| (Rate the content of each individualized lesson, based on the following) |||

S c o r e	**Lesson Objective & Goals (4-point Rubric)**	**Evidence and Elaboration (4-point Rubric)**	**Realistic Usage (2-point Rubric)**

4 **L** **E** **A** **D** **I** **N** **G**	The educator explains the content-to-personal primary goal of the lesson, **clearly.** The educator **uses a combination of tools** to sustain the student population. The educator **gained a deep understanding** of SCHEMA, based on the lesson's content/subject matter. The educator **uses phrases** to identify and connect with during all sequencing, comprehension, fluency, and phonetic during **all aspects** of the lesson.	The educator provides students with insight on all material, taught. **All students** are afforded the right to construct an argument based on how subject content is useful, using various methods. For example, the story Student Genres could be used in a debate. The students will have a chance to construct a mini speech on the relevant/irrelevant details. The class could be split in two parts one part for and one part opposed. **All students are able to identify specific details** from the prelude that will aide in the pro vs. opposed argument. Based on the strength of each claim, the teacher decides which argument was the strongest and why. The educator ensures the outcome encompasses supporting details, aspects aligned with the genre and several other pertinent aspects, necessary to win the argument.	The educator **provides ample usage** of why the students are learning specific content by doing all of the following: 1.)Providing visual proof that the standard covered, will be retaught **in-depth** in later grades. 2.) Making content-to-personal connections, regarding the academic content. 3.) Encouraging all students to participate in skits/song construction/ etc. related to the academic content. 4.) Assigning aspects of the skill to each student. After each aspect is assigned, the student will do a detailed project that explains how the skill is used, in the career of at least two people, they admire. 5.) The educator provides <u>all student/s</u> with an adequate amount of insight, regarding how the lesson's content will be applicable, in real world situations.
3 **L** **E** **A** **R** **N** **I** **N** **G**	The educator explains the content-to-personal primary goal of the lesson to <u>all students.</u> The educators utilizes **a combination of tools** to sustain the student population. The educator **gained a deep understanding** of SCHEMA, based on the lesson's content/subject matter. The educator uses commonality phrases to identify and connect with during <u>most</u> sequencing, comprehension, fluency, and phonetic aspects of the lesson.	The educator provides students with insight on **most** material, taught. **Most students** are afforded the right to construct an argument on how content is useful, by applying methods. For example, the story Student Genres could be used in a debate. The gifted students will have a chance to construct a mini speech on the relevant/irrelevant details. The class could be split in two parts one part for and one part opposed. The students could use specific details, from the prelude that will aide in the pro vs. opposed argument. Based on the strength of each claim, the teacher decides which argument is the strongest and why. The educator **ensures** the outcome encompasses supporting details, aspects aligned with the genre and several other pertinent aspects, necessary to win the argument.	The educator provides **a detailed explanation** of why students are learning specific content by doing at least **four** of the following: 1.)Providing visual proof that the standard covered, will be retaught in-depth in later grades. 2.) Making content-to-personal connections, regarding the academic content. 3.) Encouraging students to participate in skits/song construction/etc. related to the academic content. 4.) Assigning various aspects of the skill to each student. After each aspect is assigned, the student will do a detailed project that explains how the skill is used, in the career of at least two people, they admire. 5.) The educator provides the student/s with an adequate about of insight regarding how the lesson's content will be applicable, in real world situations.

2 **L** **A** **T** **E** **N** **T**	The educator **is vague** content-to-personal primary goal of the lesson. The educators utilizes **unreliable of tools** to sustain the student population. The educator **is perplexed regarding** the lesson's content/subject matter. The educator uses commonality phrases to identify and connect with during all sequencing, comprehension, fluency, and phonetic aspects of the lesson, in**frequently.**	The educator provides students with insight on **a small percentage of** material, taught. Students are afforded the right to construct an argument on how content is useful, by applying 1/4 methods: For example, the story Student Genres could be used in a debate. The gifted students will have a chance to construct a mini speech on the relevant/irrelevant details. The class could be split in two parts one part for and one part opposed. The students could use specific details, from the prelude that will aide in the pro vs. opposed argument. Based on the strength of each claim, the teacher decides which argument is the strongest and why. The educator **is not positive** the lesson's outcome encompasses supporting details, aspects aligned with the genre and several other pertinent aspects, necessary to win the argument.	The educator provides **an ambiguous explanation** of why students are learning specific content by doing at least **three** of the following: 1.)Providing visual proof that the standard covered, will be retaught in-depth in later grades. 2.) Making content-to-personal connections, regarding the academic content. 3.) Encouraging students to participate in skits/song construction/etc. related to the academic content. 4.) Assigning various aspects of the skill to each student. After each aspect is assigned, the student will do a detailed project that explains how the skill is used, in the career of at least two people, they admire. 5.) The educator provides the student/s with an adequate about of insight regarding how the lesson's content will be applicable, in real world situations.
1 **L** **A** **G** **G** **I** **N** **G**	The educator explains the content-to-personal primary goal of the lesson, **some of the time.** The educators does not use **a combination of tools** to sustain the student population. The educator **did not gain a deep understanding** of SCHEMA, based on the lesson's content/subject matter. The educator **never** uses commonality phrases to identify and connect with during all sequencing, comprehension, fluency, and phonetic aspects of the lesson.	The educator provides students with insight on **a small amount** material, taught. **Selective students** are afforded the right to construct an argument on how content is useful, by applying methods. For example, the story Student Genres could be used in a debate. The gifted students will have a chance to construct a mini speech on the relevant/irrelevant details. The class could be split in two parts one part for and one part opposed. The students could use **vague** details, from the prelude that will aide in the pro vs. opposed argument. The educator **does not ensure** the outcome encompasses supporting details, aspects aligned with the genre and several other pertinent aspects, necessary to win the argument.	The educator provides **a detailed explanation** of why students are learning specific content by doing at least **two** of the following: 1.)Providing visual proof that the standard covered, will be retaught in-depth in later grades. 2.) Making content-to-personal connections, regarding the academic content. 3.) Encouraging students to participate in skits/song construction/etc. related to the academic content. 4.) Assigning various aspects of the skill to each student. After each aspect is assigned, the student will do a detailed project that explains how the skill is used, in the career of at least two people, they admire. 5.) The educator provides the student/s with an adequate about of insight regarding how the lesson's content will be applicable, in real world situations.

| O L O S T | The educator **does not** explain the content-to-personal primary goal of the lesson.

The educators uses **one/no** to sustain the student population.

The educator **did not have an understanding** of SCHEMA, based on the lesson's content/subject matter.

The educator does not commonality phrases to identify and connect with during all sequencing, comprehension, fluency, and phonetic aspects of the lesson. | The educator **does not provide** students with insight on material, taught.

Students are not given the right to construct an argument on how content is useful.

For example, the story Student Genres could be used in a debate. The gifted students will have a chance to construct a mini speech on the relevant/irrelevant details. The class could be split in two parts one part for and one part opposed.

The students cannot use specific details, from the prelude that will aide in the pro vs. opposed argument.

. | The educator **does not provide a detailed explanation** of why students are learning specific content by doing at least **one/none** of the following:

1.)Providing visual proof that the standard covered, will be retaught in-depth in later grades.

2.) Making content-to-personal connections, regarding the academic content.

3.) Encouraging students to participate in skits/song construction/etc. related to the academic content.

4.) Assigning various aspects of the skill to each student. After each aspect is assigned, the student will do a detailed project that explains how the skill is used, in the career of at least two people, they admire.
5.) The educator provides the student/s with an adequate about of insight regarding how the lesson's content will be applicable, in real world situations. |

General Education Math Individualized Rubric, Grades K-12			
(Rate the content of each individualized lesson, based on the following)			
S c o r e	**Lesson Objective & Goals** **(4-point Rubric)**	**Evidence and Elaboration** **(4-point Rubric)**	**Mathematical Connections in the REAL WORLD**

4 **L E A D I N G**	The educator provides **an adequate introductory [to the lesson]**, before beginning the lesson. The students **have a clear understanding** of the lesson's content and relevance. The student is given **ample opportunities** to express their mathematical knowledge, in various environments/ways. The students **are given several opportunities** to tweak the lesson's content, according to the overall goal, per the District Pacing Guide, skill-based gifted activities, etc. The students **are given several opportunities** to express knowledge of mathematical content to their teacher and peers. The student **incorporates extensive information**, regarding the subject matter to their peers, teacher and guardian/s.	The educator provides **thorough and convincing support/evidence** for the lesson's content. Students **are given extensive time t**o discuss the subject matter an innovated various activities, accordingly. Students **are afforded frequent rights** to construct individualized evaluation tools, relative to the academic standards. Students are given the right to voice their opinion/s to the teacher and classmates. Through extensive research, **students are encouraged** to share their perspective on all subject matter.	The educator **encourages** peer interviews, group interaction and group innovation, **all the time.** Through the sharpening of kills , **every student** is allowed to document their findings, relative to the subject matter. After the research portion is complete, students are allowed to share the relativity of the lesson's content and how they plan to utilize **all** skills/strategies, taught.
3 **L E A R N I N G**	The educator provides a **semi-adequate** introductory, before beginning the lesson. The students had a **ninety percent** understanding of the lesson's content and relevance. The students are **persuaded** to express their mathematical knowledge, in various environments/ways. The students are given **extensive input**, regarding the overall goal, per the District Pacing Guide, skill-based gifted activities, etc. The students are given **opportunities** to express knowledge of mathematical content to their teacher and peers.	The response provides **thorough and convincing** support/evidence for the lesson's content. **Students are given extensive time** to discuss the subject matter an innovated various activities, accordingly. They **are afforded the right** to construct individualized evaluation tools, relative to the academic standards. Students **are given several opportunities** to voice their opinion/s to the teacher and classmates. Through extensive research, students **are encouraged** to share their perspective on all subject matter.	The teacher **encourages most** peer interviews, group interaction and group innovation. Through the sharpening of skills, students are **urged** to document their findings, relative to the subject matter, at hand. After the research portion was completed, students are **prompted** too **allowed** to share the relativity of the lesson's content and how they plan to utilize all skills/strategies, taught.

2 LATENT	The educator provides **an inadequate introduction**, before beginning the lesson. Students **have an unclear understanding** of the lesson's content and relevance. The student is given **sparse opportunities** to express their mathematical knowledge, in various environments/ways. The students **are given the opportunity** to tweak the lesson's content, according to the overall goal, per the District Pacing Guide, skill-based gifted activities, etc. The student is given the opportunity to express knowledge of mathematical content to their teacher and peers. The student incorporates extensive information, regarding the subject matter to their peers, teacher and guardian/s.	The educator **provides scarce opportunities** for students to identify uneven, mathematical evidence/support pertaining to the lesson's content. Mathematical concepts are **rarely allowed** to extend upon the subject matter with contextual support. Students **are not afforded the right** to construct individualized evaluation tools, relative to the academic standards. Students are **rarely** given the right to voice their opinion/s to the teacher and classmates. Through extensive research, students are rarely encouraged to share their perspective on all subject matter.	The teacher encourages peer interviews, group interaction and group innovation, **infrequently.** Through **constant sharpening of the skills above,** students are allowed to document their findings, relative to the subject matter, at hand. After the research portion was completed, students **were allowed** to share the relativity of the lesson's content and how they plan to utilize all skills/strategies, taught. The educator utilizes **motivational** words, before, during and after the mathematical lesson, **rarely.** The educator encourages students to make references to other subject matter, pertinent to the skills/strategies, taught, **rarely.**
1 LAGGING	The mathematical content explanation(given by the educator), **expresses little to no information** that could be utilized by the targeted population. The educator provides students with **scarce** opportunities to modify the lessons content, utilize the strategies of the lesson independently and encourage their gifted peers, accordingly.	The educator **allows** the students to identify uneven, mathematical evidence/support pertaining to the lesson's content, **rarely.** Mathematical concepts are not elaborated on. Students **are not given** the opportunity to cross-pollinate relative content, related to the subject matter. Students **are not given the right to voice their opinion**/s to the teacher and classmates.	The educator has elaborates on the basic mathematical mechanics of the lesson; but **does not provide** students with the opportunity of assertion, according to their gifted modified needs. Students are given **selective** opportunities to express their mathematical to self connection,
0 LOST	The mathematical content explanation(given by the educator), expresses **no information** that could be utilized by the targeted population. The educator **provides** students with **no opportunities** to modify the lessons content, utilize the strategies of the lesson independently and encourage their gifted peers, accordingly.	Students *are not given opportunities* to correlate the mathematical content, on various levels. They **are not encouraged** to express their ideas independently and in groups. Students **are never allowed** to demonstrate their knowledge of the mathematical mechanics, accordingly. They are not encouraged to reflect back no content learned, during prior lessons.	The educator **does not modify** the instructional content, according to his/her gifted students. The educator **does not elaborate** on the basic mathematical mechanics of the lesson or provided students with the opportunity of assertion, according to their gifted modified needs. Students **are not given** opportunities to express their mathematical to self connection.

General Ed. Social Studies/Science Individualized Rubric

Grades K-12

(Rate the content of each individualized lesson, based on the following)

Score	Lesson Objective & Goals (4-point Rubric)	Evidence and Elaboration (4-point Rubric)	Historical/Social Studies' Connections in the REAL WORLD
4 **LEADING**	The lesson's goals are **explained** to **all gifted students** understand the different between the goal and objective. The lesson provides relevant information that is **one hundred percent** pertinent to the core of Social Studies/Historical Content. The educator uses a **variety** of innovative techniques to convey **relevant** information, based on socially relevant information. The educator **always** takes a survey, prior to disseminating all historical content to **gain a deeper understanding** of prior knowledge.	The educator **provides** gifted students with tools to research the content based material. The educator **provides a clear paradigm** of evidence-based information to gifted students on **all levels.** The educator encourages innovative usage of vocabulary, during **every aspect** of the lesson. The educator **encourages-frequent** elaboration on all historical/social content. The understanding of the content, is displayed through various aspects.	The educator provides **several** opportunities for gifted students to express their personal experiences, related to the subject matter. The educator provides **several** opportunities for all students to recall various circumstances of how the lesson's vocabulary is utilized, in real-life circumstances. The educator provides **several** opportunities for students to collaborate and share various problems, in which the strategy could solve. The educator encourages **all** students to choose the academic strategic approach, utilized to solve the historical/social issues.
3 **LEARNING**	The educator **focuses on relevant** material, **most of the time.** The educator provides a **sufficient** amount of explanatory time for students to convey their personal relational value between the lesson's content and their personal goals/objectives. The educator **provides insight of lesson's objective** and end goal to **all** students. The educator provides students with **adequate time** to formulate hypothetical questions for the historians/relevant individuals, in their community.	The educator provides an **adequate** progressive model of historical/social **paradigm** of ideas to most gifted students. The educator provides **a large number of** accommodations, regarding the subject matter. The educator provides a **vast** amount of time for reflection, regarding the subject's content. The educator provides examples of evaluation tools that correlate to **eighty-percent** of the the academic content.	The educator provides **several** opportunities for gifted students to express their personal experiences, related to the subject matter. The educator provides **opportunities for most stu**dents to recall various circumstances of how the lesson's vocabulary is utilized, in real-life circumstances. The educator provides **most** opportunities for students to collaborate and share various problems, in which the strategy could solve. The educator encourages **most** students to choose the academic strategic approach, utilized to **explain/solve** the historical/social issues.

2 **L** **A** **T** **E** **N** **T**	The educator **provides** sufficient focus on all relevant material, **a low number of times.** The educator provides a **scarce** amount of explanatory time for students to convey their personal relational value between the lesson's content and their personal goals/objectives. The educator **places low emphasis on** overall lesson's objective and end goal. The educator **does not provide** students with an **adequate time** to formulate hypothetical questions for the historians/relevant individuals, in their community.	The educator **does not provide** an **adequate** progressive model of historical/social paradigm of ideas to most gifted students. The educator provides **marginalized** accommodations, regarding the subject matter. The educator provides a **small** amount of time for reflection, regarding the subject's content. The educator provides examples of evaluation tools that correlate to **sixty-seventy percent** of the academic content.	The educator provides **selective** opportunities for gifted students to express their personal experiences, related to the subject matter. The educator provides **narrow** opportunities for students to recall various circumstances of how the lesson's vocabulary is utilized, in real-life circumstances. The educator **provides rare** opportunities for students to collaborate and share various problems, in which the strategy could solve. The educator encourages **selective** gifted students to choose the academic strategic approach, utilized to **solve** the historical/social issues.
1 **L** **A** **G** **G** **I** **N** **G**	The educator **does not** focus on all relevant material. The educator provides an **insufficient** amount of explanatory time for students to convey their personal relational value between the lesson's content and their personal goals/objectives. The educator **does not clarify** insight of overall lesson's objective and end goal. The educator **does not take into account** the significance for students to formulate hypothetical questions for the historians/relevant individuals, in their community.	The educator is indifferent toward a progressive model of a historical/social paradigm of ideas to **a small percentage of students.** The educator **provides** accommodations, regarding the subject matter, **rarely.** The educator provides an **almost no** amount of time for reflection, regarding the subject's content. The educator provides examples of evaluation tools that correlate to **less than 50 percent** of the academic content.	The educator provides **little to no** opportunities for students to express their personal experiences, related to the subject matter. The educator provides **little to no** opportunities for students to recall various circumstances of how the lesson's vocabulary is utilized, in real-life circumstances. The educator provides **selective** opportunities for students to collaborate and share various problems, in which the strategy could solve. The educator **does not address** the academic strategic approach, utilized to **explain/solve** the historical/social issues.

| O L O S T | **In no way** does the educator focus on all relevant material.

Under no circumstance does the educator allot explanatory time for students to convey their personal relational value between the lesson's content and their personal goals/objectives.

The educator **never clarifies** insight of overall lesson's objective and end goal.

The educator **does not address** significance for students to formulate hypothetical questions for the historians/relevant individuals, in their community. | The educator **is indifferent** toward a progressive model of a historical/social paradigm of ideas to most students.

The educator **never provides** accommodations, regarding the subject matter.

The educator provides **no amount of time** for reflection, regarding the subject's content.

•

The educator provides examples of evaluation tools that correlate to **less than 10 percent** of the academic content. | The educator provides **no** opportunities for students to express their personal experiences, related to the subject matter.

The educator provides **no** opportunities for students to recall various circumstances of how the lesson's vocabulary is utilized, in real-life circumstances.

The educator **does not provide** opportunities for students to collaborate and share various problems, in which the strategy could solve.

The educator **does not address** academic strategic approach, utilized to **explain/solve** the historical/social issues. |

Varied Student Genre Self Evaluation **(Score points based on individualized gifted characteristics.)**			
S c o r e	**School to Home Implementation** **(Rubric)**	**My Child's Individualized Relation** **Gifted** **(Rubric)**	**Conventions of a General Ed. Student's** **Parent** **(Rubric)**
4 L E A D I N G	**I/we always** support the individualized needs of my child/student by engaging in in-depth conversation on a regular basis. **I/we frequently stay abreast** of all district/county academic standard replacement, usage and at home implementation. **At all times** my child's individualized needs are analyzed through several avenues, **daily.** My child's teacher and I/we communicate effectively, meaning … **I/we always** classify the conversation's purpose, prior to reaching out.	Even if my child does not identify what makes him/her unique, I will make it my duty to highlight/pinpoint **at least four** academic/social characteristics that make them one of a kind. **My/our** child's unique gifts **are at the forefront of my mind**, while completing homework, supporting their extracurricular interests and during **all** conversations. **I/we constantly ensue** to help my child create engaging projects that directly appeal to my child's specified needs. **I/we make certain to acknowledge** special days that specifically commemorate my child's academic attempts.	**I/we constantly** keep in mind the individualized interests of my child, while planning vacations/family events. **In no way** does my words cause my child to regress, academically/socially. **In several instances, I/we** reinforce positive motives, through various avenues, **daily.** **I/we always** appeal to all subject areas, in need of mastery, daily.

| 3 LEARNING | **I/we provide several avenues** of support the individualized needs of my child/student by engaging in in-depth conversation on a regular basis.

TypicallyI/we stay abreast of all district/county academic standard replacement, usage and at home implementation.

Often times my child's individualized needs are analyzed through several avenues, **weekly.**

My child's teacher and I/we communicate effectively, meaning … **I/we** classify the conversation's purpose, prior to reaching out, **most of the time.** | Even if my child does not identify what makes him/her unique, I will make it my duty to highlight/pinpoint **at least three** academic/social characteristics that make them one of a kind.

My/our child's unique gifts **are generally at the forefront of my mind**, while completing homework, supporting their extracurricular interests and during **all** conversations.

I/we ordinarily ensue to help my child create engaging projects that directly appeal to my child's specified needs.

Most of the time, I/we acknowledge special days that specifically commemorate my child's academic attempts. | **I/we usually** keep in mind the individualized interests of my child, while planning vacations/ family events.

In no way does my words cause my child to regress, academically/ socially.

In several instances, I/we reinforce positive motives, through various avenues, **weekly.**

Almost always I/we appeal to all subject areas, in need of mastery, **weekly** |
| 2 LATENT | **I/we provide selective avenues** of support the individualized needs of my child/student by engaging in in-depth conversation on a regular basis.

Sometimes I/we stay abreast of all district/county academic standard replacement, usage and at home implementation.

At times my child's individualized needs are analyzed through several avenues, **monthly.**

My child's teacher and I/we communicate effectively, meaning … **I/we sometimes** classify the conversation's purpose, prior to reaching out. | Even if my child does not identify what makes him/her unique, I will try to highlight/pinpoint **at least two** academic/social characteristics that make them one of a kind.

My/our child's unique gifts **are sometimes at the forefront of my mind**, while completing homework, supporting their extracurricular interests and during **certain** conversations.

I/we selectively ensue to help my child create engaging projects that directly appeal to my child's specified needs.

I/we make certain to acknowledge special days that specifically commemorate my child's academic attempts. | **At times, I/we** keep in mind the individualized interests of my child, while planning vacations/ family events.

My words cause my child to regress, academically/socially, **intermittently.**

In several instances, I/we reinforce positive motives, through various avenues, **monthly.**

At times, I/we appeal to all subject areas, in need of mastery, **monthly.** |

1 **L** **A** **G** **G** **I** **N** **G**	**I/we little to no selective avenues** of support the individualized needs of my child/student by engaging in in-depth conversation on a regular basis. **I/we stay abreast** of all district/county academic standard replacement, usage and at home implementation, **occasionally,** My child's individualized needs are analyzed through **narrow** avenues. My child's teacher and I/we communicate effectively, meaning … **I/we** classify the conversation's purpose, prior to reaching out, **at times.**	Even if my child does not identify what makes him/her unique, I try to highlight/pinpoint **at least one** academic/social characteristic that make them one of a kind. **My/our** child's unique gifts **are nearly ever at the forefront of my mind**, while completing homework, supporting their extracurricular interests and during conversations. **I/we try** to help my child create engaging projects that directly appeal to my child's specified needs, **some of the time.** **I/we make certain to acknowledge** special days that specifically commemorate my child's academic attempts.	**I/we** keep in mind the individualized interests of my child, while planning vacations/family events, **minimally.** My/our words cause my child to regress, academically/socially, **rarely.** **I/we** reinforce positive motives, through various avenues, **some of the time.** **I/we** appeal to all subject areas, in need of mastery, **occasionally.**
O **L** **O** **S** **T**	**I/we provide no avenues** of support the individualized needs of my child/student by engaging in in-depth conversation on a regular basis. **I/we never stay abreast** of all district/county academic standard replacement, usage and at home implementation. My child's individualized needs **are not analyzed** through **any** avenue. My child's teacher and I communicate effectively, meaning … **I/we do not-classify** the conversation's purpose, prior to reaching out.	Even if my child does not identify what makes him/her unique, **I do not try to highlight/pinpoint** academic/social characteristic that make them one of a kind. **My/our** child's unique gifts **are not at the forefront of my mind**, while completing homework, supporting their extracurricular interests and during conversations. **I/we do not ensue** to help my child create engaging projects that directly appeal to my child's specified needs. **I/we am indifferent regarding** special days that specifically commemorate my child's academic attempts.	**I/we never** keep in mind the individualized interests of my child, while planning vacations/family events. My/our words **always** cause my child to regress, academically/socially. **I/we never** reinforce positive motives, through various avenues/ **I/we barely ever** appeal to all subject areas, in need of mastery.

Capability Reflective Log **Through the Eyes of Various Student Genres**		
Articulation	**Math**	**Science**

Day 1	Dear Reading, Today, we had a really hard job to do. My teacher asked if the directions were confusing. Since I did not want to look like a complete idiot, I said, "No." Okay … great! Most of the class is gifted! What was I supposed to say? "I don't get it." The look my teacher and classmates gave me the last time I admitted to not understanding something, was ruthless. The assignment for our group, was too rewrite an interpretation, based on our strong Figurative Language Skills. Our teacher did not base our assignment on observation. She claimed the groups were made, using our school's great academic computer program. Was this a bad time to tell her my older brother(who is in high school), does my comprehension reading assignments? How could I admit that? Oh well … it was sink or swim time; I was bound to sink. The situation made me feel LESS THAN. I always get this feeling, at home, as the middle child my mother constantly compares me to my older brother. You would think … school would be my comparison getaway. Oh … no! Now my reading skills are compared to genius. Is the playing field ever fair?	Dear Math, You are my favorite subject. The gifted students are usually thinking on another level but burned out by the end of the day. I decided to use the anger from reading time to run circles around them. This was my time to shine. A lot of gifted kids hate multiplication. They can't stand basic memorization. According to my teacher, they detest learning them. She says detest, a lot. Because of her, I detest the word, detest. Unlike my teacher, the evident detest of my classmates, impact their ability to learn. This was my time to shine. The spotlight was off of all the gifted kids and on me. Math was the only time, I felt worthy of raising my hand. The teacher loves my participation and always says, "Great Job," in front of the class. I am one of five non gifted students, in the whole class. The other four students, just can't be bothered to memorize their time tables. Since this is the one subject that lets my light shine bright, I study them day and night. Today we played Multiplication Mash. The game lets me slam-dunk on my classmates. As usual, the winner was me.	Dear Science, We are rarely ever in our class, during science time. My teacher normally takes us outside to change our environment. Today, we learned about OUTER SPACE. This is such an amazing subject! I don't raise my hand, a lot. My teacher's face always lights up, when one of the gifted kids raises their hand. When I raise my hand, the excitement drains, from my teacher's face. This week, I'm going to try my hardest to create a project explaining the planets. Hopefully, my project will be on display. Today, my brain neurons were working, extra hard. Food was always on my mind. I decided to make my planet project, our of food items and tie in what we are learning, about shapes. This would be great! At recess my idea was breaking news on the playground. My friend Shelly, really loved my planet project idea. Shelly is gifted. Tomorrow, we will turn in our project ideas. My teacher is going to love it. Maybe the newspaper will want to cover my project. My project thesis is_____ _____ _____ _____.

Day 2	Dear Reading, Okay … although the problem is not solved, I was determined to put on a show. You know, like the show my teacher puts on when she thinks we don't know, her nervous level, when her ten bosses come to visit. I don't get it. Why do these people come to visit, twice a year, expecting to understand what we do, everyday? It always makes my teacher put on a show. We do things that are outside of the box, all the time. Hopefully, they will come back and visit, more often. Today, the show's stage was set … my teacher introduced, Figurative Language. What in the world is up with that? Why are there so many categories? Simile? Idioms? I can think of a word that will take care of me learning all these categories that rhymes with Alliteration … how about obliteration. The reaction from people in my group was more important than understanding you're silly meanings … reading. Honestly, who came up with this stuff?	Dear Math, Today, I hit the ball out of the park. As usual, math is my favorite part of the day. My quiz score was a perfect one-hundred. I wish my parents would tell me how great my math skills are, when they lecture me, about poor reading etiquette. If my parents understood what getting great grades in math does for me, maybe they would give me more encouragement? It's just a thought … anyway my teacher asked us to identify different types of shapes, today. It was a part of the lesson. The way my teacher explained how people should see shapes, was amazing. She explained, shapes exist in tiny crevices. The main though of the day was_____ _____ _____ _____ _____. Right now … I am looking at the ceiling fan, my bike wheels and the circles on the stove, in a whole new light. Going to school should leave thought trails, everyday.	Dear Science, How could I make myself stronger? At recess, I was tried to create a short explanation of my planet project. This would be important for my teacher and parents. The project overview explained how I would make planets, using food. It was such a great plan! Finally, this idea was going to make my teacher excited to call on me. While we are in groups, the gifted students and myself would actually share common ground. When our class came in from recess, my teacher looked so tired. I ignored her glum face and handed in my project idea. "Well, this seems like it will be fun." You have my permission to create your own food Solar System. The words leaped out of her mouth and landed in my heart. You and I are going to make a great team, Science. In the past, everything my teacher asked me to do was hard. Now, this project will make science fun!

| Day 3 | Dear Reading,
My teacher was not impressed with my wisecrack, yesterday. At least she knows I exist, during reading time. Maybe jokes are a way to get her attention. Dealing with understanding all of this stuff, is too much. My parents say, tutoring is my only option and the gateway to get to the next grade level. Reading, why do you have to be so hard? Even though math is my strength, story problems are impossible, without you. It is safe to say, we have a **give** and **take** relationship. You give me hard assignments, and it takes me forever to understand them. Why can't we just get along? The Figurative Language Lesson was even harder, today. My teacher's bright idea was to make "ask" who is struggling with this concept, put me visual headlock and wait for me to raise my hand. After she waited … the students who were struggling, i.e., three of us, were led to the computer, while the gifted students did fun activities. There has got to be a better way of helping me that does not include embarrassment. The sad part was, my teacher had no clue. | Dear Math,
If you were a real person, our friendship would be solid. Get it? Solid! Anyway my teacher took us outside on a shape walk. We were getting in shape, while identifying shapes. This was one of the greatest ideas, my teacher had. This time of day, we are usually "antsy." Our teacher encourages us to get up and stretch but it usually isn't enough. Math you are so friendly and kind. I love spending time, learning about all the cool parts of the world, you are in. After school, my parents took me to a really cool restaurant. My parents kept talking about the decorations. The shapes my teacher taught me to identify, were everywhere. While my parents were talking about the food's consistency, I wondered how many circles, squares, quadrilaterals, octagons, hexagons and ovals, were around us. We are learning, all experiences relate back to school. This is really great lesson, since our learning should be practiced. Friday's test will be a breeze. Math you sure are fun. If all other subjects disappeared, it would be fine. I see you in everything! You are always there to help my self-esteem, grow. How in the world do people hate you? | Dear Science,
This project is so exciting. My parents took me to buy all project materials, last night. I needed to make sure the project was refrigerated, since it had so much candy. The Solar System is so cool. The sun was made out of lemon drops, Venus was made out of Red Hots, Earth was made out of blue gummy worms, Mars was made out of Fire balls, Jupiter made out of Skittles, was extra yummy! Saturn was made out of caramel and a thin layer of white cotton candy(to represent the ring), Uranus was made out of blue Air Heads and Neptune was made out of blue gum balls. The project was huge and the background was black licorice with white rock candy to represent the stars. My teacher said the project needed to address the following:
1.)Descriptive words related to the Solar System
2.) Address the ways the materials you use represent the Solar System
3.) Identify the contrast between the real Solar System and the one you create. |

Day 4	Dear Reading, The background of this Figurative Language stuff, is useless. Why can't people just say what they mean? All the world is a stage. Really Shakespeare? Why are they teaching these examples, when we don't even read Shakespeare. Anyway, I guess all the world is a stage, I am acting everyday. Since my teacher can never know, about my struggles, the classroom is my stage. Maybe my understanding of Figurative Language will get better, if my teacher used real life examples, instead of just asking us to copy down these crazy quotes. When our teacher walked around to monitor us, she asked me if everything was okay. If the neurons in my brain could communicate on their own the response would be … "okay?" "This is torture! "Could we change the game plan, please?" Yet again, the nod beat my response and yes was the only answer, given.	Dear Math, My teacher actually let me work, buy myself … today. Division is my new best friend! The math helpmeets, from our upper school monitored me, during centers. This made me feel really special. The helpmeets were amazing! They were not just there to pass time. We used all types of materials to show how division is used, in the real world. We use division, all the time. My helpmeets reminded me of times my division was handy. Their lunch example was the best. I always divide my cookie, into two parts. Recognizing math on so many levels makes me feel great! My teacher is the master of teaching math. The three best parts of the math lesson were_____ _____ _____ _____ _____ _____ _____.	Dear Science, Today was extremely exciting! The presentation of my candy Solar System Project went well. Everyone wanted to taste it. My teacher was really impressed with my writing. Everything started heading downhill, when my teacher asked me to read, in front of the gifted kids. My reading is getting better but not good enough to read out loud, in front of the entire class. My teacher assumed since my project was complete, reading the explanation part, was easy. She was wrong! Again, reading ruined everything! My teacher is always saying, "You better master reading and comprehending information, if you plan to make it to the next grade level. Does she really think that comment is motivating? It makes me even more nervous. We have a science test, tomorrow. Thank God, the test will not require me to read out loud. Hopefully, a someone will pull the fire alarm the next time, I present.
Day 5	Dear Reading, Instead of throwing myself another let me feel sorry for myself party, I wrote down every part of the reading lesson, after our test and shared it with my teacher. My sadness made her upset. My teacher could not believe how horrible, I felt. From now on she will know about all my problems. It is not fair to expect my teacher to read minds. Otherwise, my reading score as a C+, Maybe failing is not an option, after all. Telling myself the same problem, this week did not work out. The solution came, after my teacher knew, what was going on. In the future, my teacher will always know, what problems are by_____.	Dear Math, Today's pop quiz was the best. Overtime as my grades keep climbing, I want to train as an Engineer. The parents and professionals should plan Field Trips, based on what we would like to be, in the future. Math you are always so great to me. I realized, how helpful you are, everyday. The best part of my week was_____. My teacher let me color, outside the lines by_____ _____ _____ _____ _____ _____ __.	Dear Science, This week made me think of the first steps we learned about, regarding the Scientific Method. If I told my teacher about my problems, she could have helped me. Next time, I will use the Scientific Method, as an outline of my concern letters. The problem I have is_____an educated guess about how my problem could be solved is _____ _____ observations and facts will help my teacher_____ ___if I do not tell my teacher about the problem, she will not be able to experiment, in order to draw a conclusion.

Self Evaluation Rubric, Grades K-12 Educators
(Score points within each domain include most of the characteristics below.)

Score	English Language Learners Differentiation (4 Point Rubric)	English Language Learner Evidence & Elaboration (4 Point Rubric)	English Language Learner Basic Needs of Influence (4 Point Rubric)
4 LEADING	The E.S.O.L. Educator sustains and focuses on the **all** individualized needs, of each E.S.O.L. Student. The E.S.O.L. Educator differentiates each assignment to **both conserve and challenge** each E.S.O.L. Student. The E.S.O.L. Educator attempts to increase **the** knowledge of each E.S.O.L. by using culturally competent information, **during each activity.** Each modified lesson sets **high stakes** of relativity, in order for each E.S.O.L. Student to **relate** to the content, **one hundred percent** of the time.	The E.S.O.L. Educator **always** researches and modifies methods of instruction on with socialization in mind. The E.S.O.L. Educator utilizes rubrics modified to the capabilities and idealistic levels of each student, **during** all activities. The E.S.O.L. Educator **always** keeps phonology, syntax, semantics and spacial concepts in mind, when prompting students to converse about academic material. The E.S.O.L. Teacher **ensures all** elaborative activities, are built on a strong basis.	The E.S.O.L. Educator develops **all** lessons, conducive to state and E.S.O.L. Standards. The E.S.O.L. Educator carefully adheres to **all** state E.S.O.L. guidelines, while formulating relatable activities. The E.S.O.L. Educator modifies **all** subject content, based on the E.S.O.L. Student's level of proficiency to trigger **both language** and **academic** personalization. Each student is given the opportunity to **modify/ construct** subject relativity, **in various ways.**
3 LEARNING	The E.S.O.L. Educator sustains and focuses on the individualized needs, of each E.S.O.L. Student, **most of the time.** The E.S.O.L. Educator attempts to increase the knowledge of each E.S.O.L. by using culturally competent information, **during each activity.** Each modified lesson sets **high stakes** of relativity, in order for each E.S.O.L. Student to **relate** to the content, **eighty-percent** of the time. The educator **often** affirms individualization, during all activities, thus, modifying **all** expectancy levels.	The E.S.O.L. Educator researches and modifies methods of instruction on with socialization in mind, **repeatedly.** The E.S.O.L. Educator utilizes rubrics modified to the capabilities and idealistic levels of each student, during **most** activities. The E.S.O.L. Educator keeps phonology, syntax, semantics and spacial concepts in mind, when prompting students to converse about academic material, **regularly.** The E.S.O.L. Teacher **ensures all** elaborative activities, are built on a strong basis.	The E.S.O.L. Educator develops **most** lessons, conducive to state and E.S.O.L. Standards. The E.S.O.L. Educator carefully adheres to **the majority of** state E.S.O.L. guidelines, while formulating relatable activities. The E.S.O.L. Educator modifies **most** subject content, based on the E.S.O.L. Student's level of proficiency to trigger **both language** and **academic** personalization. Each student is given the opportunity to **modify/ construct** subject relativity, **in various ways.**

2 L A T E N T	The educator provides **partial insight** on the lesson's objectives/goals. The lesson's objective and goals, are a **distant referent.** The lesson's personalized goals/objectives, **are utilized on occasion.** The subject's content is built on **uneven progression.** The educator's **paradigm is inconsistent** with the subject matter.	The educator **expresses content based evaluation** material without verbal expansion. The educator **interjects,** when content based material has a weak premise, **inconsistently.** The educator provides a **superficial feedback.** The educator does not elaborate on the concerns of the gifted students, after gaining feedback.	The educator **provides an oversimplified** version of personal-to-content based examples. The educator **explains** how the content learned, is useful in the real world, **rarely.** The educator **provides rare opportunities** for creativity, related to the academic content. The educator **does not express** the difference between social subjective versus objective content.
1 L A T E N T	The educator provides **little to no in-depth** goal/objective referents. The educator **rejects** students who give insight on the subject matter to standard correlation. The educator **never** permit insight on various parts of the content, covered. The educator **solely** instructs and does not facilitate students, during the learning process.	The educator provides **little to no** opportunities for valuable feedback. The educator provides **little to no** options for evaluation formulation, based on personal beliefs. The educator **does not** correct fallacies and explicitly avoids example provisions. The educator **penalizes students** for self-expression, regarding the evaluation process.	The educator refers to complex issues with a **simplistic viewpoint.** The educator provides **little to no** fact-based relational evidence for students who are formulating social/historical responses, during the learning process. The educator provides **little to no** opportunities for group collaboration and expression, regarding personal experiences/subject integration.
0 L O S T	The educator's support for the population, regarding the subject matter, is **insufficient.** Students were given **little to no time** to reflect on the subject matter. The educator **does not take into account**, personalization audience and provides no personalized objective content.	The educator **discourages valuable feedback.** The educator **grants no time** for reflection, regarding the lesson's content. The educator **discourages** collaboration to formulate feedback tools, related to all aspects of the lesson.	The educator **rejects** factual information that is related to the academic content. The educator **demotes** individuality expressiveness, correlated to the subject's content. The educator **discourages group interaction**, related to realistic experiences that correlate to the subject at hand.

	Self Evaluation Rubric, Grades K-12 Educators		
S c o r e	English Language Learners Differentiation (4 Point Rubric)	**English Language Learner Evidence & Elaboration (4 Point Rubric)**	**English Language Learner Basic Needs of Influence (4 Point Rubric)**

2 LATENT	The E.S.O.L. Educator realigns the objective of each lesson to match the response of each learner, **some of the time.** The E.S.O.L. Educator attempts to increase the knowledge of each E.S.O.L. by using culturally competent information, **during some activities.** Each modified lesson content with a low level of relativity, in order for **some E.S.O.L. Student to relate.** The educator affirms individualization, during **certain activities.**	The E.S.O.L. Educator **does not regard** researches and modifies methods of instruction on with socialization in mind. The E.S.O.L. Educator utilizes rubrics modified to the capabilities and idealistic levels of each student, during **selective** activities. The E.S.O.L. Educator keeps phonology, syntax, semantics and spacial concepts in mind, when prompting students to converse about academic material, **irregularly.** The E.S.O.L. Teacher does not try to create elaborative activities, built on a **strong** basis.	The E.S.O.L. Educator develops lessons **semi-conducive** to state standards and does not take into account, how the information will be utilized, personally. The E.S.O.L. Educator carefully adheres to **selective** state E.S.O.L. guidelines, while formulating relatable activities. The E.S.O.L. Educator modifies **most** subject content, based on the E.S.O.L. Student's level of proficiency to trigger **either language** or **academic** personalization. The E.S.O.L. Educator **possesses a narrow viewpoint**, regarding subject modification.
1 LATENT	The E.S.O.L. Educator sustains and focuses on the individualized needs, of each E.S.O.L. Student, **less than ten percent of the the time**. The E.S.O.L. Educator has a **narrow viewpoint**, regarding how each student's knowledge of cultural competency, is increased. Each lesson has **little to no content-based relativity.** Affirmation of individualization, during academic activities and expectancy levels, **occurs on an occasional basis.**	The E.S.O.L. Educator researches and modifies methods of instruction on with socialization in mind, **infrequently.** The E.S.O.L. Educator utilizes rubrics modified to the capabilities and idealistic levels of each student, **scarcely.** The E.S.O.L. Educator **does not address** phonology, syntax, semantics and spacial concepts in mind, when prompting students to converse about academic material on occasion. The E.S.O.L. Teacher address how elaborative activities, are built on a strong basis, **some of the time.**	The E.S.O.L. Educator develops lessons **aligned** to no state standards and does not take into account, how the information will be utilized, personally. The E.S.O.L. Educator carefully adheres to **a small portion of the** state E.S.O.L. guidelines, while formulating relatable activities. The E.S.O.L. Educator modifies subject content, based on the E.S.O.L. Student's level of proficiency to trigger **either language** and **academic** personalization, **sometimes.** **A low number of** students is given the opportunity to **modify/construct** subject relativity.

O L O S T			
	The E.S.O.L. Educator **does not** sustain and focuses on the individualized needs, of each E.S.O.L. Student. The E.S.O.L. Educator **disregards** how each student's knowledge of cultural competency, is increased. Each lesson has **no content-based relativity.** Affirmation of individualization, during academic activities and expectancy levels, **does not take place.**	**In no way**, does the E.S.O.L. Educator research/modify methods of instruction on with socialization in mind. **At no point**, does the E.S.O.L. Educator utilize rubrics modified to the capabilities and idealistic levels of each student. The E.S.O.L. Educator **Does not consider** phonology, syntax, semantics and spacial concepts in mind, when prompting students to converse about academic material. The E.S.O.L. Teacher **does not address** how elaborative activities, are built on a strong basis.	The E.S.O.L. Educator **does not** develop lessons aligned to state standards. The E.S.O.L. Educator takes into account, the state E.S.O.L. guidelines, while formulating relatable activities, **rarely.** The E.S.O.L. Educator **makes no allowance** for each student's level of proficiency that triggers **language/academic** personalization. No students are given opportunities to **modify/construct** subject relativity.

ESOL Educator Reading/Writing Individualized Rubric, Grades K-12
(Rate the content of each individualized lesson, based on the following)

S c o r e	Lesson Objective & Goals (4-point Rubric)	Evidence and Elaboration (4-point Rubric)	Realistic Usage (2-point Rubric)
4 L E A D I N G	The E.S.O.L. Educator promotes literary attainment f**or all students.** The E.S.O.L. Educator modifies **all** literary activities, based on SCHEMA, self-efficacy and mentally stimulating activities. **At all times**, the E.S.O.L. Educator assimilates all literary activities, according to all standards, goals and cultural relevance. The E.S.O.L. Educator **ceaselessly** invigorates the learning process by reassessing personalized short and longterm goals.	The E.S.O.L. Educator determines future academic activities based on student feedback/elaboration, **all the time.** The E.S.O.L. Educator's encourages all students to evaluate communicative techniques, **continuously.** The E.S.O.L. Educator **makes attempts** to monitor all class discussions, via several avenues. The E.S.O.L. Educator encourages students to possess an empathetic mentality(regarding feedback), during **all** literary activities.	The E.S.O.L. Educator **encourages** students to make **clear connections** between the literary subject content and goals. The E.S.O.L. Educator motivates students to utilize literary strategies, across **all** subject areas, is **evident.** The E.S.O.L. Educator engages all students, during relatable literary activities, daily. The E.S.O.L. Educator **makes certain**, relatable resources are at bay for all students.

Score			
3 LEARNING	The E.S.O.L. Educator promotes literary attainment, through individualized means **most of the time.** The E.S.O.L. Educator modifies literary activities, based on SCHEMA, self-efficacy and mentally stimulating activities, **consistently.** **Most times**, the E.S.O.L. Educator assimilates all literary activities, according to all standards, goals and cultural relevance. The E.S.O.L. Educator **almost always** invigorates the learning process by reassessing personalized short and longterm goals.	The E.S.O.L. Educator determines future academic activities based on student feedback/elaboration, **most of the time**. The E.S.O.L. Educator's **generally** encourages all students to evaluate communicative techniques. The E.S.O.L. Educator **makes several attempts** to monitor most class discussions, via several avenues. The E.S.O.L. Educator encourages students to possess an empathetic mentality(regarding feedback), during **The majority of** literary activities.	The E.S.O.L. Educator **motivates most** students to make **clear literary connections,** between the literary subject content and goals. The E.S.O.L. Educator motivates students to utilize literary strategies, across all subject areas, is **evident most of the time.** The E.S.O.L. Educator engages **most** students, during relatable literary activities, daily. The E.S.O.L. Educator, **makes attempts** to make relatable resources available for **most students**

E.S.O.L. Reading/Writing Individualized Rubric, Grades K-12
(Rate the content of each individualized lesson, based on the following)

Score	Lesson Objective & Goals (4-Point Rubric)	Evidence and Elaboration (4-point Rubric)	READING/WRITING PERSONALIZED CONNECTIONS (4-Point Rubric)
2 LATENT	The E.S.O.L. Educator promotes literary attainment, through individualized means, **sparingly.** The E.S.O.L. Educator modifies literary activities, based on SCHEMA, self-efficacy and mentally stimulating activities, **irregularly.** **Sometimes**, the E.S.O.L. Educator assimilates all literary activities, according to all standards, goals and cultural relevance. The E.S.O.L. Educator's propensity to invigorate the learning process, is **unreliable.**	The E.S.O.L. Educator determines future academic activities based on student feedback/elaboration, **invariably.** The E.S.O.L. Educator has an **attitude of indifference,** toward evaluate communicative techniques. The E.S.O.L. Educator monitors or encourages class Discussions, **barely.** The E.S.O.L. Educator **loses interest**, during the literary evaluation process.	The E.S.O.L. Educator **creates a state of confusion,** between literary subject content and goals. The E.S.O.L. Educator addresses literary strategies, across all subject areas, **inconsistently .** The E.S.O.L. Educator **rarely** provides students with opportunities for engaging content relativity. The E.S.O.L. Educator, **makes considerable attempts** to make relatable resources available for all students.

1 L A G G I N G	The E.S.O.L. Educator has **a non-chalant attitude**, toward individualization. Opposition between The E.S.O.L. Educator's lesson content and the academic standard, is evident. The E.S.O.L. Educator assimilates **almost no**, literary activities, according to standards, goals and cultural relevance. The E.S.O.L. Educator's propensity to invigorate the learning process, is **obscure.**	The E.S.O.L. Educator's ability to construct future academic activities based on student feedback/elaboration, is **unclear**. The E.S.O.L. Educator **does not** provide support, during certain aspects of the communicative technique evaluation. The E.S.O.L. Educator **provides little to no explicit feedback**, while encouraging class discussions. The E.S.O.L. Educator **loses interest easily**, during the literary evaluation process.	The E.S.O.L. Educator correlates literary subject content and goals, **during selective activities.** The E.S.O.L. Educator addresses literary strategies, **regarding a low number of subject areas.** The E.S.O.L. Educator **does not address** how students should identify, engaging content relativity. The E.S.O.L. Educator, **makes infrequent attempts** to make relatable resources available for all students.
O L O S T	The E.S.O.L. Educator **does not** personalize aspects of the academic standards for students. The E.S.O.L. Educator's lesson content and the academic standard, is **unclear.** The E.S.O.L. Educator assimilates **selective** literary activities, according to standards, goals and cultural relevance. The E.S.O.L. Educator's propensity to invigorate the learning process, is **obscure**.	The E.S.O.L. Educator constructs future academic activities based on student feedback/elaboration, is **nonexistent**. The E.S.O.L. Educator **does not** provide support, during certain aspects of the communicative technique evaluation. The E.S.O.L. Educator **provides no explicit feedback**, while encouraging class discussions. The E.S.O.L. Educator **causes student disengagement**, during the literary evaluation process.	The E.S.O.L. Educator **does not** correlate literary subject content and goals. The E.S.O.L. Educator **does not** address literary strategies, across all subject areas. **At no time** does the E.S.O.L. Educator address how students should identify, engaging content relativity. The E.S.O.L. Educator, **makes no attempt** to construct relatable resources, available for all students.

ESOL Math Individualized Rubric, Grades K-12
(Rate the content of each individualized lesson, based on the following)

S c o r e	**Lesson Objective & Goals** **(4-point Rubric)**	**Evidence and Elaboration** **(4-point Rubric)**	**Mathematical Connections in** **the REAL WORLD**

4 **L** **E** **A** **D** **I** **N** **G**	**All elements** of each math lesson, encompasses several segments that reinforce all mathematical concepts, correlated to each standard. The E.S.O.L. Educator formulates math activities that peak the interest of each student, **consistently.** Mathematical cultural relevancy aligned to each standard, is evident pre-current and post **every** mathematical lesson. The E.S.O.L. Educator promotes standard analysis, aligned to cultural awareness, **all the time.**	The E.S.O.L. Educator **makes certain,** all feedback is **precise and definitive.** The E.S.O.L. Educator sets **challenging** standards for all students, regarding group interaction and collaboration. The E.S.O.L. Educator's shares insight on how evaluation tools are constructed, during **all** math lessons. The E.S.O.L. Educator encourages critical thinking segments, while mathematical vocabulary is explored, **consistently.**	The E.S.O.L. Educator incorporates activities that lesson cultural misconceptions, **all the time.** The E.S.O.L. Educator **guarantees** each student is challenged on a mathematically universal level. The E.S.O.L. Educator **creates several** personally mathematically relative moments. The E.S.O.L. Educator **utilizes several avenues** of relativity, during all math lessons.
3 **L** **E** **A** **R** **N** **I** **N** **G**	Most **elements** of each math lesson, encompasses several segments that reinforce all mathematical concepts, correlated to each standard. The E.S.O.L. Educator formulates math activities that peak the interest of each student, **most of the time.** Mathematical cultural relevancy aligned to each standard, is evident **during most mathematical lessons.** The E.S.O.L. Educator promotes standard analysis, aligned to cultural awareness, **often,**	The E.S.O.L. Educator **ensures, most** feedback is **precise and definitive.** The E.S.O.L. Educator sets **challenging** standards for students, regarding group interaction and collaboration. The E.S.O.L. Educator's shares insight, regarding the construction of evaluation tools, **generally.** The E.S.O.L. Educator uses **several** opportunities for students to express mathematical knowledge.	The E.S.O.L. Educator **promotes** activities that lesson cultural misconceptions, across most subject areas. The E.S.O.L. Educator **makes sure** most students are challenged, **mathematically.** The E.S.O.L. Educator identifies **several** relative moments. The E.S.O.L. Educator **utilizes several avenues** of relativity, during all math lessons.

2 L A T E N T	The educator explains elements of the math lesson, correlated to each standard to **selective students.** The E.S.O.L. Educator formulates math activities that peak the interest of **certain** students. Mathematical cultural relevancy aligned to each standard, _evident_ during **selective mathematical lessons.** The E.S.O.L. Educator promotes standard analysis, aligned to **certain aspects of** cultural awareness. The E.S.O.L. Educator formulates math activities that **do not peak** interest of students.	The E.S.O.L. Educator **ensures**, **some** feedback is **precise and definitive.** The E.S.O.L. Educator sets **challenging** standards for students, regarding group interaction and collaboration for **a low percentage** of students. The E.S.O.L. Educator's shares insight, regarding the construction of evaluation tools, **some of the time.** The E.S.O.L. Educator uses **certain** opportunities for students to express mathematical knowledge.	The E.S.O.L. Educator **formulates** activities that lesson cultural misconceptions, regarding selective subjects. The E.S.O.L. Educator allots **scarce** opportunities for students to express themselves, from a universal level, regarding academic content. The E.S.O.L. Educator **makes few efforts** to identify mathematically relative moments. The E.S.O.L. Educator **provides avenues** of relativity, during **a small number of** math lessons.
1 L A T E N T	The educator explains elements of the math lesson, correlated to each standard **occasionally.** The E.S.O.L. Educator formulates math activities that peak the interest **for a low percentage of students.** Mathematical cultural relevancy aligned to **each standard**, is _evident_ mathematical lessons, **occasionally.** The E.S.O.L. Educator **sees no urgency in promoting** standard analysis, aligned to cultural awareness. The E.S.O.L. Educator formulates math activities that peak the interest of each student, **a low percentage of the time.**	The E.S.O.L. Educator **places low emphasis** on precise and definitive feedback. The E.S.O.L. Educator sets **a low bar**, regarding group interaction and collaboration. The E.S.O.L. Educator **does not** share insight, regarding the construction of evaluation tools. The E.S.O.L. Educator **does not pinpoint** opportunities for students to express mathematical knowledge.	The E.S.O.L. Educator **formulates a low percentage of** activities that lesson cultural misconceptions, across various subject areas. The opportunities for student expression, relative to academic content, is **few and far between.** The E.S.O.L. Educator **makes** identifying mathematically relative moments, **difficult**. The E.S.O.L. Educator makes mathematical **content relativity, a tedious task.**

O L O S T			
	The educator **does not address** elements of the math lesson, correlated to each standard. The E.S.O.L. Educator **does not formulate** math activities that peak the interest of **any** students. Mathematical cultural relevancy aligned to each **standard, is not blatant.** The E.S.O.L. Educator **does not promote** standard analysis, aligned to cultural awareness. The E.S.O.L. Educator formulates math activities that peak the interest of each student.	The E.S.O.L. Educator does not **ensure**, feedback is **precise and definitive.** The E.S.O.L. Educator sets **minimally challenging** standards formats students, regarding group interaction and collaboration. The E.S.O.L. Educator's **does not share** insight, regarding the construction of evaluation tools. The E.S.O.L. Educator uses **particular** opportunities for students to express mathematical knowledge.	The E.S.O.L. Educator **puts no extra effort,** into activities that lesson cultural misconceptions, across various subject areas. Opportunities for students to express themselves, from a universal standpoint, is **nonexistent.** The E.S.O.L. Educator **makes few efforts** to identify mathematically relative moments. The E.S.O.L. Educator **provides minimal avenues** of relativity, during all math lessons.

ESOL Social Studies/Science Individualized Rubric

Grades K-12
(Rate the content of each individualized lesson, based on the following)

S c o r e	Lesson Objective & Goals (4-point Rubric)	Evidence and Elaboration (4-point Rubric)	Historical/Social Studies' Connections in the REAL WORLD

4 **L** **E** **A** **D** **I** **N** **G**	The E.S.O.L. Educator **always** uses academic themes that integrate multicultural concepts, aligned to the state standards. The E.S.O.L. Educator **provides numerous opportunities** for students to discuss the weekly S.S./science objectives/goals **for an extended period of time.** The E.S.O.L. Educator **ensures all** students can express details from the lesson, correlated to the standard, fluently. The E.S.O.L. Educator **ensures** all students are able to produce a valid tangible product, that displays academic affirmation.	The E.S.O.L. Educator **guarantees each student** has several opportunities to express their levels of understanding, correlated to personalized rubrics. The E.S.O.L. Educator **ensures each student can express each academic concept, in an appropriate manner.** The E.S.O.L. Educator **affirms all** students having personalized and collective collaboration opportunities. The E.S.O.L. Educator **facilitates, all** academically related content-based correspondence.	The E.S.O.L. Educator **always** helps students makes personalized cultural, national, and ethnic relations to subject matter. The E.S.O.L. Educator expresses details from the subject content, **efficiently.** The E.S.O.L. Educator **makes sure** all students are able to construct academic content that incorporates relatable vocabulary and detailed phrases. The E.S.O.L. Educator **empowers every** student to correlate aspects of life to scientific knowledge and social awareness.
3 **L** **E** **A** **R** **N** **I** **N** **G**	The E.S.O.L. Educator uses academic themes that integrate multicultural concepts, aligned to **certain** state standards. The E.S.O.L. Educator **provides several opportunities** for students to discuss the weekly S.S./science objectives/goals. The E.S.O.L. Educator makes expressing details from the lesson, correlated to the standard, fluently **a priority.** The E.S.O.L. Educator **provides extensive opportunities for** students to produce a valid tangible product, that displays academic affirmation.	The E.S.O.L. Educator **places importance on most** students expressing levels of understanding, correlated to personalized rubrics. The E.S.O.L. Educator **makes certain each student can express each academic concept on a large-scale.** The E.S.O.L. Educator **focuses on** all students having personalized and collective collaboration opportunities. The E.S.O.L. Educator **provides in-depth feedback** on all academically related content-based correspondence.	The E.S.O.L. Educator demonstrates how to make cultural/national/ethnic relations to subject matter, **most of the time.** The E.S.O.L. Educator **places high emphasis on** subject content efficiency. The E.S.O.L. Educator **provides detailed explanations** on how students are able to construct academic content that incorporates relative vocabulary and detailed phrases, **most of the time.** The E.S.O.L. Educator **empowers** most students to correlate aspects of life to scientific knowledge and social awareness.

ESOL Social Studies/Science Individualized Rubric Grades K-12 (Rate the content of each individualized lesson, based on the following)		
Lesson Objective & Goals **(4-point Rubric)**	**Evidence and Elaboration** **(4-point Rubric)**	**Connections in the REAL WORLD**

S c o r e

4 **L** **E** **A** **D** **I** **N** **G**	**All elements** of each lesson, en-compasses several segments that reinforce all S.S./Science concepts, correlated to each standard. Before formulating assignments, the E.S.O.L. Educator **provides clear and condensed directives, explaining** how cultural relevance, is exemplified through the lesson's objectives/goals. The E.S.O.L. Educator reiterates aspects of **each** standard, objective or goal that is not clearly aligned with daily assignments. The E.S.O.L. Educator **always** promotes usages of culture relativity two aspects of each objective/standard/goal.	The E.S.O.L. Educator **always** holds themselves and students accountable by verifying each student is able to restate all aspects of the lesson. The E.S.O.L. Educator **always** provides an inquisitive segment, before and after each lesson is completed. The E.S.O.L. Educator's re-structures evaluation tools, conducive to the individualized needs of **every** student. The E.S.O.L. Educator conveys content knowledge by using several strategies, aligned with the English Language Learner Standards, **all the time**.	The E.S.O.L. Educator focuses on Tier Interpretation, as students present a clear correlation between academic content and the real world, **all the time.** The E.S.O.L. Educator **guarantees** every student understands how to express to personalized information, in several ways. The E.S.O.L. Educator **always** focuses on meaningful conversation, regarding content relativity and skill focus. The E.S.O.L. Educator **supports cultural diversity by clearly addressing cultural relativity and personalized knowledge.**
3 **L** **E** **A** **R** **N** **I** **N** **G**	The E.S.O.L. Educator documents what peaks the interest of **most** students, while explaining each objective/standard/goal. Each desire and goal of **most** students is compared to aspects of the lesson's goals/objectives/standard. The E.S.O.L. Educator reiterates aspects of each standard, objective or goal that is not clearly aligned with daily assignments, **frequently.** The E.S.O.L. Educator promotes S.S./Science discussions based on culture relativity of each objective/standard/goal, **often.**	The E.S.O.L. Educator assesses skill mastery, in **various** ways. The E.S.O.L. Educator provides an inquisitive segment, before and after each lesson is completed, **most of the time**. The E.S.O.L. Educator's re-structures evaluation tools, conducive to the individualized needs of **most** students. The E.S.O.L. Educator conveys content knowledge by using several strategies, aligned with the English Language Learner Standards, **80-90 percent of the time.**	The E.S.O.L. Educator focuses on Tier Interpretation, regarding academic relativity, S.S./Science Differentiated Instruction and projects, **frequently.** The E.S.O.L. Educator ensures **most students** understand academic content, based on personal experiences and relativity. The E.S.O.L. Educator provides students with **several opportunities** to convey cultural information, by focusing on segmentation. The E.S.O.L. Educator supports cultural diversity by clearly addressing cultural relativity and personalized knowledge, **most of the time.**

2 LATENT	The E.S.O.L. Educator documents what peaks the interest of **particular** students, while explaining each objective/standard/goal. Each desire and goal of **certain** students are compared to aspects of the lesson's goals/objectives/standard. The E.S.O.L. Educator reiterates aspects of each standard, objective or goal that is not clearly aligned with daily assignments, **inconsistently**. The E.S.O.L. Educator promotes S.S./Science discussions based on culture relativity of each objective/standard/goal, **sometimes.**	The E.S.O.L. Educator **makes few efforts** to asses skill mastery, in various ways. The E.S.O.L. Educator provides an inquisitive segment, before and after each lesson is completed, **some of the time**. The E.S.O.L. Educator's restructures evaluation tools, conducive to the individualized needs of **selective** students. The E.S.O.L. Educator conveys content knowledge by using several strategies, aligned with the English Language Learner Standards, **at least 60-70 percent of the time**.	The E.S.O.L. Educator focuses on Tier Interpretation, regarding academic relativity, S.S./Science Differentiated Instruction and projects, **inconsistently.** The E.S.O.L. Educator ensures **some students** understand academic content, based on personal experiences and relativity. The E.S.O.L. Educator provides students with **selective opportunities** to convey cultural information, by focusing on segmentation. The E.S.O.L. Educator supports cultural diversity by clearly addressing cultural relativity and personalized knowledge, **sometimes.**
1 LATENT	The E.S.O.L. Educator documents what peaks the interest of **particular** students, while explaining each objective/standard/goal, **occasionally.** Each desire and goal of **a low percentage of** students, are compared to aspects of the lesson's goals/objectives/standard. The E.S.O.L. Educator emphasis on aspects of each standard, objective or goal clearly aligned with daily assignments, is **rare**. The E.S.O.L. Educator places **little to no emphasis** on S.S./Science cultural discussions related to academic objective/standard/goal.	The E.S.O.L. Educator **sets a low bar** for students to display skill mastery. The E.S.O.L. Educator provides an inquisitive segment, before and after each lesson, **occasionally**. The E.S.O.L. Educator's restructures evaluation tools, conducive to the individualized needs students, **occasionally.** The E.S.O.L. Educator conveys content knowledge by using several strategies, aligned with the English Language Learner Standards, **less than 10 percent of the time**.	The E.S.O.L. Educator **takes into account** Tier Interpretation, regarding academic relativity, S.S./Science Differentiated Instruction and projects on an inconsistent basis. The E.S.O.L. Educator ensures **a low percentage of students** understand academic content, based on personal experiences and relativity. The E.S.O.L. Educator provides students with **rare opportunities** to convey cultural information, by focusing on segmentation. The E.S.O.L. Educator supports cultural diversity by clearly addressing cultural relativity and personalized knowledge, **occasionally.**

O L O S T	The E.S.O.L. Educator emphasis on aspects of each standard, objective or goal aligned with daily assignments, is **inexplicit**. The E.S.O.L. Educator places **no emphasis** on S.S./Science cultural discussions related to academic objective/standard/goal. The E.S.O.L. Educator **does not** address standard analysis, aligned to cultural awareness. The E.S.O.L. Educator **never** formulates math activities that peak the interest of each student.	The E.S.O.L. Educator **sets no expectations** for students to display skill mastery. The E.S.O.L. Educator **does not** encourage an inquisitive segment, before and after each lesson, **occasionally**. The E.S.O.L. Educator's **restricts** evaluation tools, formulation conducive to the individualized needs students. The E.S.O.L. Educator conveys content knowledge by using several strategies, aligned with the English Language Learner Standards, **0 percent of the time**.	The E.S.O.L. Educator **does not consider the importance of** Tier Interpretation, regarding academic relativity, S.S./Science Differentiated Instruction and projects. The E.S.O.L. Educator **deters students** from understand academic content, based on personal experiences and relativity. The E.S.O.L. Educator provides students with **no opportunities** to convey cultural information, by focusing on segmentation. The E.S.O.L. Educator **does not** supports cultural diversity by addressing cultural relativity and personalized knowledge.

	E.S.O.L. Parent Evaluation (Score points based on individualized characteristics.)		
S c o r e	**School to Home Implementation (Rubric)**	**My Child's Individualized Gifts (Rubric)**	**Conventions of an E.S.O.L. Parent (Rubric)**

4 **L** **E** **A** **D** **I** **N** **G**	The E.S.O.L. Parent **always** fosters a **supportive** environment, based on the **individualized** needs of their child. The E.S.O.L. Parent **places high emphasis** on communicating with every teacher, their child is learning from. The E.S.O.L. Parent **uses various methods** to monitor their student's progress, aside from progress reports & report cards. The E.S.O.L. Parent uses **concrete and vivid** strategic interventions to assist their child's teacher with academic understanding, **constantly.**	The parent **makes a conscious effort** to understand each unique gift their E.S.O.L. Child attends trainings to enhance their capabilities. **Effective use** of semantics, intonation and vocabulary, is addressed at home to increase the progress of the E.S.O.L. Student. The E.S.O.L. Parent **creates** an emotionally healthy environment and provides the child with positive reinforcement, **before, during and after all at-home academic activities.** The E.S.O.L. Parent **always encourages** the student to convey information, in several ways, thus, enhancing creativity and extensive responses.	The E.S.O.L. Parent **encourages** the formulation of support groups and collaborates with parents who have students who exited or nearly exited the E.S.O.L. Program. The E.S.O.L. Parent **engages in several** Title III events, hosted and carried out, through collaboration. The E.S.O.L. Parent **attains detailed feedback**, regarding academic enhancement, thriving socialization/other topics that could enhance or hinder aspects of the program. The E.S.O.L. Parent **questions/ addresses all activities** that would stunt academic/social growth, both in the school and home environment.
3 **L** **E** **A** **R** **N** **I** **N** **G**	The E.S.O.L. Parent **almost always** fosters a **supportive** environment, based on the **individualized** needs of their child. The E.S.O.L. Parent **places moderate emphasis** on communicating with every teacher, their child is learning from. The E.S.O.L. Parent **uses methods** to monitor their student's progress, aside from progress reports & report cards, **at least 90 percent of the time.** The E.S.O.L. Parent uses **concrete and vivid** strategic interventions to assist their child's teacher with academic understanding, **nearly all of the time.**	The parent **attempts** to understand each unique gift their E.S.O.L. Child has, and attends trainings to enhance their capabilities, **moderately.** **Effective use** of semantics, intonation and vocabulary, is addressed at home to increase the progress of the E.S.O.L. Student, **a reasonable amount of the time.** The E.S.O.L. Parent **creates** an emotionally healthy environment and provides the child with positive reinforcement, **before and during most** at-home academic activities. The E.S.O.L. Parent **almost always encourages** the student to convey information, in several ways, thus, enhancing creativity and extensive responses.	The E.S.O.L. Parent **encourages** formulation of support groups and collaborates with parents who have students who exited or nearly exited the E.S.O.L. Program, **often.** The E.S.O.L. Parent **engages in most** Title III events, hosted and carried out, through collaboration. The E.S.O.L. Parent **attains all detailed feedback**, regarding academic enhancement, thriving socialization/other topics that could enhance or hinder aspects of the program. The E.S.O.L. Parent **question/ addresses all activities** that would stunt academic/social growth, both in the school and home environment, **often.**

2 LATENT	The E.S.O.L. Parent supports environment, based on the **individualized** needs of their child, **some of the time.** The E.S.O.L. Parent **barely acknowledges the importance of** communicating with every teacher, their child is learning from. The E.S.O.L. Parent **has a narrow perspective, regarding** progress monitoring, aside from progress reports & report cards. The E.S.O.L. Parent uses **inappropriate** strategic interventions to assist their child's teacher with academic understanding.	The parent **makes minimal effort** to understand each unique gift their E.S.O.L. Child has, and attends trainings to enhance their capabilities. **Effective use** of semantics, intonation and vocabulary, is addressed at home to increase the progress of the E.S.O.L. Student, **sometimes.** The E.S.O.L. Parent **creates** an emotionally healthy environment and provides the child with positive reinforcement, **before/during certain** at-home academic activities. The E.S.O.L. Parent **encourages** the student to convey information, **in a confusing way.**	The E.S.O.L. Parent **encourages** formulation of support groups and collaborates with parents who have students who exited the E.S.O.L. Program. The E.S.O.L. Parent **engages in most** Title III events, hosted and carried out, through collaboration. The E.S.O.L. Parent **attains vague feedback**, regarding academic enhancement, thriving socialization/other topics that could enhance or hinder aspects of the program **on an inconsistent basis.** The E.S.O.L. Parent **question/ addresses all activities** that would stunt academic/social growth, both in the school and home environment, **sometimes.**
1 LATENT	The E.S.O.L. Parent **has an indifferent attitude toward acknowledging** environmental factors, based on **individualized** needs of their child. The E.S.O.L. Parent **has a narrow perspective** regarding communicating with every teacher, their child is learning from. The E.S.O.L. Parent **has a narrow perspective, regarding** progress monitoring, aside from progress reports & report cards. The E.S.O.L. Parent uses strategic interventions to assist their child's teacher with academic understanding, **incorrectly.**	The parent **does not try** to understand each unique gift their E.S.O.L. Child has, and attends trainings to enhance their capabilities. **The E.S.O.L. Parent considers** semantics, intonation and vocabulary, is addressed at home to increase the progress of the E.S.O.L. Student, **occasionally.** The E.S.O.L. Parent **creates** an emotionally healthy environment and provides the child with positive reinforcement, **before/during selective** at-home academic activities. The E.S.O.L. Parent **rarely encourages** the student to convey information, in several ways, thus, enhancing creativity and extensive responses.	The E.S.O.L. Parent **discourages** formulation of support groups and collaborates with parents who have students who exited or nearly exited the E.S.O.L. Program. The E.S.O.L. Parent **engages in most** Title III events, hosted and carried out, through collaboration. The E.S.O.L. Parent **attains useless feedback**, regarding academic enhancement, thriving socialization/other topics that could enhance or hinder aspects of the program **on an inconsistent basis.** The E.S.O.L. Parent **question/ addresses all activities** that would stunt academic/social growth, both in the school and home environment, **sometimes.**

O L O S T	The E.S.O.L. Parent **does not address** environmental factors, based on **individualized** needs of their child. The E.S.O.L. Parent **has no regard for** keeping the line of communication, between their child's teacher and themselves.. The E.S.O.L. Parent **does not** complete progress monitoring, aside from progress reports & report cards. The E.S.O.L. Parent **does not** use strategic interventions to assist their child's teacher with academic understanding.	The parent **never tries** to understand each unique gift their E.S.O.L. Child has, and attends trainings to enhance their capabilities. **The ESOL Parent does not consider** semantics, intonation and vocabulary, is unacknowledged at home, **causing regression** of the E.S.O.L. Student. The E.S.O.L. Parent **discounts** the impact of an emotionally healthy environment and positive reinforcement. The E.S.O.L. Parent **never encourages** the student to convey information, in several ways.	The E.S.O.L. Parent **dissuades** formulation of support groups and collaboration with parents who have students who exited or nearly exited the E.S.O.L. Program. The E.S.O.L. Parent **discourages** Title III events, hosted and carried out, through collaboration. The E.S.O.L. Parent **attains no feedback**, regarding academic enhancement, thriving socialization/other topics that could enhance or hinder aspects of the program. The E.S.O.L. Parent **does not question/addresses activities** that would stunt academic/social growth, both in the school and home environment.

My Capability Reflective Log
Through the Eyes of an E.S.O.L. Student

	Reading Articulation	Math	Science
Day 1	Today, we learned about characters, setting and events. We read a really boring story. My teacher says, to express myself, in different ways. Today, I did what she said. The ways were: _____.I wonder if we will go outside, tomorrow? There are so many questions, in my head. My teacher looks so tired and sometimes she screams, I cannot ask her to answer my questions. Even though my understanding of today's activity. It really hurts that I don't understand.	Today's lesson in math was about addition. We took a test, last week. My score was perfect! Since it was so easy for me(compared to other subjects), I wanted to show the whole class, my A+! After the teacher handed out my paper, I got up and walked across the room to show MY HELPING BUDDY. Immediately, my teacher started screaming, "You know better, sit down!" In my country, we always show how well we did on tests. The rest of the year, is going to be hard be- cause_____ _____.	My teacher is the best! She recorded herself, reading our science book chapter, slowly. I was able to understand, better. We are learning about the three-forms of matter. My teacher says, we are going to learn how states of matter are connected to digestion. This makes so much sense. The reason we burp, after drinking carbonated foods, is due to the gas matter component. My teacher wants we to write about different foods that cause matter conversion, in the body. I am so excited! We did challenging projects, like this … in my country.

Day 2	Today was really hard. I wish my teacher would stop screaming, during small group. Answering questions would be a lot easier, if she did not yell, at me. In my country, teachers do not yell. Why does she hate me? The ways I would have answered questions, about our reading book would be_____. Today I thought my teacher was mean to me. The reason I feel this way, is_____ ___. This is not a good thing to think, about my teacher. I will will help resolve this issue by_____	Yesterday, turned me off of talking about math. I used to get excited, now … I don't care. My teacher did not care about my good grade. She always tells daddy about the percent of my reading test. Daddy puts her on speaker phone. "Unfortunately, your child is considered an English Language Learner. She is struggling with new concepts of the English Language. Your child is fully capable." I got perfect grades, in my country. Fully capable meant failing to my dad. If only my teacher understood and provided a good solution. She does not get it.	A lot of my classmates, explained which foods cause matter transformation, in our bodies.Before it was my turn, my teacher asked me, if sharing was okay. I replied, "Sure." I chose to talk about how digestion works. I spoke about how when my dad makes my favorite dish, from my country, it causes my mouth to water. Once the food is ready, I eat it and it is broken down into water like molecules. My classmates started to laugh, when I explained, beans cause gas.
Day 3	Today was a better day. I asked my friend(who is my American but knows about my country), why the teacher always screams at me. My buddy said, sometimes the teacher cannot control her emotions. She told me, the teacher does not hate me but really wants me to learn English and different things. In the future, I will try to explain my feelings to my teacher by_____ _____ _____this will help my learning experience because_____.	Today, my teacher decided to take us outside. She asked us how many trees we saw. Next, my teacher wanted us to make up addition problems, using tree traits. I love learning, outside. It reminds me of my country. My teacher really cares. How did she know, learning outside would help me forgive her for screaming, Monday? I wrote over twenty problems, just to show her how much learning outside means to me. The best part of my day was_____ _____.	My teacher encouraged me to keep a science journal. In the journal, she interpreted and taped all vocabulary words, in my home language and English. My teacher is really helping me. I know she works really hard to teach our class. After lunch, we were placed in groups. Each person had a special job, about our weekly science topic. Our group wrote a story, about the digestive process and what would happen, if our body did not covert solids and liquids, during the process.
Day 4	Today was amazing! The main character of our story, was from my country. As our teacher read, I could almost taste the food, smell the flowers, see the colors, hear the music and feel my mom's soft hair, from my country. My teacher does not hate me, she loves me! I am going to try, really hard, from now on.	Today was really good! I have been using visual cues to communicate certain words. My accent sounds kind of funny but today, was different. My teacher made me feel so comfortable, I spoke to her. She was very happy and gave me a treat for using new words. I told her about my tree problems and asked if I could color a picture that looked like outside, yesterday. My teacher said, yes. My picture had all twenty addition problems with leaves of different colors. I counted the leaves, during the activity. Math is fun, again!	I love Thursdays! We get to take a test, about what we learned in science, so far. My teacher allows me to give my answers by using a special chart. Sometimes I do not need it but other times, it is so helpful. In the beginning of the year, my science grade was really bad. This made me feel really sad. My father would not let me have fun, because of my grades. Now, they are getting better. My father does not understand what E.S.O.L. is. He just knows I used to get great grades, in my country. Now, my grades are better.

| Day 5 | My teacher let us work in groups, today. I really like talking to my HELPING BUDDY. She helps to explain words and is really nice. Our class is really big, compared to my country. We spoke about the story, from yesterday. Although my buddy knew about my country, she never lived there. I wanted to explain how it was, but it was really hard. She understood, eventually. Thankfully, I did not give up. I kept trying to explain details, about my country. This made me really proud of myself. We should read this story, everyday! This week, we learned about characters, setting, and events. It was easy for me to understand, once my teacher read the story, about my country. | Math was great, this week! Even though my teacher yelled, at me … she planned such a great addition activity. I will never forget how hard she tried to teach our class addition. This proves she is the best teacher, in the whole world. I asked my teacher, if my addition picture was good. She said, it was excellent. Hurray! The way I will communicate better, next week is_____ _____ _____ If my teacher did not _____ _____ _____ this week, it would have changed my learning experience because_____ _____ _____. | This week was so much fun! The highlight of my week was_____ _____. If I could choose one thing to reteach it would be _____ _____ _____. As an E.S.O.L. Student, the special things my teacher did to help me understand matter and the digestive process were_____ _____. This week was awesome in science. My teacher helped me by teaching new vocabulary, helping me to talk about my project and telling me I did a great job. Next week, will be great, too. |

Self Evaluation Rubric, Grades K-12 Educators
(Score points within each domain include most of the characteristics below.)

S c o r e	Individualized Educational Differentiation/Evidence and Elaboration (4 Point Rubric)	Differentiation for Individuals with Education Plans Evidence & Elaboration (4 Point Rubric)	Basic Needs of Influence for Individuals with Education Plans (4 Point Rubric)

4 **L** **E** **A** **D** **I** **N** **G**	The special educator provides differentiated activities, related to the student's Individualized Education Plan, **regularly.** **Every** lesson has an individualized purpose that assists the student, during task completion. The special educator **always** encourages students to pinpoint aspects of the personalized goals/objectives. All student information is at the forefront of **all** individualized lesson activities, including specified skill focus, content variation and academic output stimulation.	The special educator allows an **adequate** amount of time to transition between various topics, hence off setting emotional breakdowns. The special educator formulates evaluation tools, geared toward benchmark measurements and individualized academic peaks, **all the time.** The special educator **ensures** the academic environment fosters cooperative learning styles that adhere to the specified needs of each student. The special educator **always utilizes** personalized rubrics/lesson plans/evaluation tools, directly correlated to each Individualized Education Plan.	An special educator develops **all** lessons, conducive to state standards. The special educator provides a Least Restrictive Environment, **directly** correlated to the needs outlined, in the student's Individualized Education Plan. The special educator provides **countless** motivational circumstances that adhere to the needs of each student. **All** students are provided with opportunities to correlate text-based material to real circumstances.
3 **L** **E** **A** **R** **N** **I** **N** **G**	The special educator provides differentiated activities, related to the student's Individualized Education Plan, **routinely.** **Most** lessons have an individualized purpose that assists the student, during task completion. The special educator encourages students to pinpoint aspects of the personalized goals/objectives, **usually.** All student information is at the forefront of **most** individualized lesson activities, including specified skill focus, content variation and academic output stimulation.	The special educator allows an **adequate** amount of time to transition between various topics, hence off setting emotional breakdowns. The special educator formulates evaluation tools, geared toward **most** benchmark measurements and individualized academic peaks. The special educator **almost always ensures** the academic environment fosters cooperative learning styles that adhere to the specified needs of each student. The special educator **utilizes** personalized rubrics/lesson plans/evaluation tools, directly correlated to each Individualized Education Plan, **consistently.**	An special educator develops **most** lessons, conducive to state standards. The special educator provides a Least Restrictive Environment, **mainly** correlated to the needs outlined, in the student's Individualized Education Plan. The special educator provides **several** motivational circumstances that adhere to the needs of each student. **The majority of** students are provided with opportunities to correlate text-based material to real circumstances.

Self Evaluation Rubric, Grades K-12 Educators
(Score points within each domain include most of the characteristics below.)

Score	Differentiation for Individuals with Education Plans (Rubric)	Evidence and Elaboration for Individuals with Education Plans (Rubric)	Basic Needs of for Individuals with Education Plans
2 LATENT	The special educator provides differentiated activities, related to the student's Individualized Education Plan, **inconsistently.** **Certain** lessons have an individualized purpose that assists the student, during task completion. The special educator encourages students to pinpoint aspects of the personalized goals/objectives, **a short amount of time.** All student information is at the forefront of **some** individualized lesson activities, including specified skill focus, content variation and academic output stimulation.	The special educator **allows an inadequate amount** of time to transition between various topics, hence off setting emotional breakdowns. The special educator formulates evaluation tools, geared toward benchmark measurements and individualized academic peaks, **inconsistently.** The special educator **rarely acknowledges the importance of** a healthy academic environment for **all** students. The special educator **utilizes** personalized rubrics/lesson plans/evaluation tools, **not correlated** to each Individualized Education Plan.	The special educator develops **a low number of** lessons, conducive to state standards. The special educator provides a Least Restrictive Environment, correlated to needs outlined, in the student's Individualized Education Plan, **a small amount of times.** The special educator provides **selective** motivational circumstances that adhere to the needs of each student. **The minority of** students are provided with opportunities to correlate text-based material to real circumstances.
1 LATENT	The special educator **will not take into account** the importance of differentiated activities, related to the student's Individualized Education Plan. **While planning, the** lessons had **little to no** individualized purpose to assist students, during task completion. The special educator **encourages** students to pinpoint aspects of the personalized goals/objectives, **some of the time.** Student information **is insignificant and barely addresses** lesson activities, including specified skill focus, content variation and academic output stimulation.	The special educator **barely** allows for an adequate amount of time to transition between various topics, hence off setting emotional breakdowns. The special educator formulates evaluation tools, geared toward benchmark measurements and individualized academic peaks **for selective students.** The special educator **acknowledges the importance of** a healthy academic environment for **selective** students.	The special educator develops **selective** lessons, conducive to state standards. The special educator addresses a Least Restrictive Environment, correlated to the needs outlined, in the student's Individualized Education Plan, **some of the time.** The special educator **nearly ever** provides motivational circumstances that adhere to the needs of each student. **Minimal emphasis is place on** providing students with opportunities to correlate text-based material to real circumstances.

| O L O S T | The special educator **ignores** the importance of differentiated activities, related to the student's Individualized Education Plan.

While planning, the lessons have **no** individualized purpose to assist students, during task completion.

The special educator **does not encourag**students to pinpoint aspects of the personalized goals/objectives.

Student information **is insignificant and never addresses** lesson activities, including specified skill focus, content variation and academic output stimulation. | The special educator **does not** allow for an adequate amount of time to transition between various topics, hence off setting emotional breakdowns.

The special educator **never** formulates evaluation tools, geared toward benchmark measurements and individualized academic peaks.

The special educator **does not acknowledge the importance of** a healthy academic environment for students.
The special educator **does not utilize** personalized rubrics/lesson plans/evaluation tools, directly correlated to each Individualized Education Plan. | The special educator **does not develop** lessons, conducive to state standards.

The special educator **does not provide** a Least Restrictive Environment, correlated to the needs outlined, in the student's Individualized Education Plan.

The special educator **does not** provide motivational circumstances that adhere to the needs of each student.

No emphasis is place on providing students with opportunities to correlate text-based material to real circumstances. |

Individualized Educational Reading/Writing Rubric, Grades K-12
(Rate the content of each individualized lesson, based on the following)

S c o r e	**Lesson Objective & Goals Provision** **(4-point Rubric)**	**Evidence and Elaboration** **(4-point Rubric)**	**Realistic Usage** **(2-point Rubric)**
4 L E A D I N G	The educator chunks **all** lesson's objectives, goals and standards, in mental bite-sized bits to help students complete reading/writing assignments. The educator **provides several** opportunities of text-based relation, according to each student's I.E.P. The educator **constantly** takes into account **all** aspects of both long and short term goals, while planning all academic activities. The educator **provides all** students with repetitional phrases, artistic integration and adaptable alternative learning environments, conducive to each special need.	**Within reason,** students/parents/ advocates are **strongly encouraged** to provide the teacher with constructive feedback. According to the provisional feedback, the teacher will **always ensure** students are able to read and reread, chunk information, sequence and complete all reading/writing assignments, aligned to their goals. **All** learning styles, environments and assignments will be formulated, based on the unique needs of each student. Evaluation surveys should be disseminated, **all of the time** in order to gain insight on reading portfolios, formal/informal assessments and goals.	The educator will provide **an unlimited amount** of time for emotional release, transition and literary expression. The educator will engage **all students** in horizontal planning with colleagues, specifying the individualized goals for reading, writing and language arts. The educator **explains** how to make content-to-personal connections, regarding the academic content, **clearly.** The educator **explains all literary content,** in great detail, without avoiding pertinent questions/comments from the student. The educator provides **an extended amount** of time for emotional release, transition and literary expression.

3 L E A R N I N G	The educator chunks **most** lesson's objectives, goals and standards, in mental bite-sized bits to help students complete reading/writing assignments. The educator **provides** opportunities for **most** text-based relation, according to each student's I.E.P. The educator **tends to** take into account **most** aspects of both long and short term goals, while planning all academic activities. The educator **provides most** students with repetitional phrases, artistic integration and adaptable alternative learning environments, conducive to each special need.	Students/parents/advocates are strongly encouraged to provide the teacher with constructive feedback, **on a regular basis.** According to the provisional feedback, the teacher will ensure students are able to read and reread, chunk information, sequence and complete all reading/writing assignments, aligned to their goals, **most of the time.** **Several** learning styles, environments and assignments will be formulated, based on the unique needs of each student. Evaluation surveys provide insight on reading portfolios, formal/inform assessments/goals, **most of the time.**	The educator engages in horizontal planning with colleagues, specifying the individualized goals for reading, writing and language arts, **often.** **The educator addresses** how to make content-to-personal connections, regarding the academic content, **most of the time.** The educator **explains most literary content,** in great detail, without avoiding pertinent questions/comments from the student. The educator provides **an adequate amount** of time for emotional release, transition and literary expression.

General/ESOL/S.P.E.D. Reading/Writing Individualized Rubric, Grades K-12
(Rate the content of each individualized lesson, based on the following)

S c o r e	**Lesson Objective & Goals** **(4-Point Rubric)**	**Evidence and Elaboration** **(4-point Rubric)**	**READING/WRITING** **PERSONALIZED** **CONNECTIONS** **(4-Point Rubric)**
2 L A T E N T	The educator chunks **some of** the lesson's objectives, goals and standards, in mental bite-sized bits to help students complete reading/writing assignments. The educator provides opportunities for text-based relation, according to each student's I.E.P, **occasionally.** The educator takes into account aspects of both long and short term goals, while planning all academic activities, **scarcely.** The educator **provides** students with repetitional phrases, artistic integration and adaptable alternative learning environments, conducive to each special need, **hardly.**	The topic of students/parents/advocates providing constructive feedback to improve the overall academic experience, is **rarely explored.** According to the provisional feedback, the teacher will ensure students are able to read and reread, chunk information, sequence and complete all reading/writing assignments, aligned to their goals, **some of the time**. **Selective** learning styles, environments and assignments will be formulated, based on the unique needs of each student. Evaluation surveys are disseminated to gain insight on reading portfolios, formal/informal assessment, **infrequently.**	The educator engages **a small number of students** in horizontal planning with colleagues, specifying the individualized goals for reading, writing and language arts. The educator **is not clear on** how to make content-to-personal connections, regarding the academic content. The educator **explains selective literary content,** without avoiding pertinent questions/comments from the student. The educator provides **a concise amount** of time for emotional release, transition and literary expression.

1 LATENT	The educator chunks lesson's objectives, goals and standards, in mental bite-sized bits to help students complete reading/writing assignments, **less than ten percent of the time.** The educator provides opportunities for text-based relation, according to each student's I.E.P, **once in a while.** The educator takes into account aspects of both long and short term goals, while planning all academic activities, **scarcely** The educator **provides a small number of** students with repetitional phrases, artistic integration and adaptable alternative learning environments, conducive to each special need.	The topic of students/parents/advocates providing constructive feedback to improve the overall academic experience, is **viewed as insignificant.** The teacher addresses students are able to read and reread, chunk information, sequence and complete all reading/writing assignments, aligned to their goals, **inconsistently.** **Selective** learning styles, environments and assignments will be formulated, based on the unique needs of each student. Evaluation surveys are disseminated ,to gain insight on reading portfolios, formal/informal assessment, **rarely.**	The educator **barely** engages in horizontal planning with colleagues, specifying the individualized goals for reading, writing and language arts. The educator **addresses** how to make content-to-personal connections, regarding the academic content, **occasionally.** The educator **explains at least one element literary content,** without avoiding pertinent questions/comments from the student. The educator **does not** allot time for emotional release, transition and literary expression.
0 LOST	The educator **never** chunks lesson's objectives, goals and standards, in mental bite-sized bits to help students complete reading/writing assignments. The educator **does not** provide opportunities for text-based relation, according to each student's I.E.P. The educator **does not** take into account aspects of both long and short term goals, while planning all academic activities. The educator **never provides** students with repetitional phrases, artistic integration and adaptable alternative learning environments, conducive to each special need.	The topic of students/parents/advocates providing constructive feedback to improve the overall academic experience, is **not addressed.** The teacher **does not address** students are able to read and reread, chunk information, sequence and complete reading/writing assignments, aligned to their goals. Learning styles, environments and assignments will be formulated, **are not based on prior knowledge.** Evaluation surveys are **not formulated** ,to gain insight on reading portfolios, formal/informal assessment.	The educator **does not take part** in horizontal planning with colleagues, specifying the individualized goals for reading, writing and language arts. The educator **does not addresses** how to make content-to-personal connections, regarding the academic content. The educator **does not explain literary content,** without avoiding pertinent questions/comments from the student. The educator **does not** allot time for emotional release, transition and literary expression.

Individualized Education Math Individualized Rubric, Grades K-12
(Rate the content of each individualized lesson, based on the following)

	Lesson Objective & Goals (4-point Rubric)	Evidence and Elaboration (4-point Rubric)	Mathematical Connections in the REAL WORLD
Score			

4 **L** **E** **A** **D** **I** **N** **G**	Students are given **detailed break-down** of each portion of the state standards, **before and after all** mathematical activities. Students are given **several** materials, strategies and goals, directly aligned to their mathematical standards, conducive to their Individualized Education Plan. Students are **prompted** to question any aspect of the mathematical lesson that is not clarified. **regularly.** . The students **are given several opportunities** to express knowledge of mathematical content to their teacher and peers.	Students are **granted unlimited opportunities** to question strategic intervention. The educator **never fails to** promote mathematical trainings for students who are struggling with certain concepts. The educator **perpetually exemplifies** how to fill in the gaps, both mentally and emotionally, during project completion **on a regular basis.** The educator observes acquired content knowledge **through several assessment avenues,** accommodations are always taken into account, before, during and after each math lesson, **all the time.**	During small group time, most students are **always encourages** to hone in on their favorite part/s of the mathematical lesson. **All** students are **reminded** to focus on one strategic intervention, during academic completion. The educator **always** uses math games, videos, reteach strategies and personalized problem solving techniques to reinforce all skills. The educator uses **numerous** interactive strategies, aligned with specified accommodations, in order for students to complete mathematical tasks.
3 **L** **E** **A** **R** **N** **I** **N** **G**	Students are given **a detailed break-down** of each portion of the state standards, **before and after most** mathematical activities. Students are given **certain** materials, strategies and goals, directly aligned to their mathematical standards, conducive to their Individualized Education Plan. Students are **often prompted** to question any aspect of the mathematical lesson that is not clarified. . The students **are given certain opportunities** to express knowledge of mathematical content to their teacher and peers.	Students are **granted several opportunities** to question strategic intervention. The educator promotes mathematical trainings for students who are struggling with certain concepts, **regularly.** The educator **exemplifies** how to fill in the gaps, both mentally and emotionally, during project completion. The educator observes acquired content knowledge through **several assessment avenues, ac**commodations are always taken into account, before, during and after each math lesson, **most of the time.**	During small group time, students are **encouraged** to hone in on their favorite part/s of the mathematical lesson. Students are reminded to focus on one strategic intervention, during academic completion, **regularly.** The educator **often** uses math games, videos, reteach strategies and personalized problem solving techniques to reinforce all skills. The educator uses **various** interactive strategies, aligned with specified accommodations, in order for students to complete mathematical tasks.

2 L A T E N T	Students are given **a semi-detailed breakdown** of each portion of the state standards, **before and after selective** mathematical activities. Students are given **selective** materials, strategies and goals, directly aligned to their mathematical standards, conducive to their Individualized Education Plan. Students are **sometimes encouraged** to question any aspect of the mathematical lesson that is not clarified. . The students **are given certain opportunities** to express knowledge of mathematical content to their teacher and peers.	Students are **granted A low number opportunities** to question strategic intervention. The educator **does not address** mathematical trainings for students who are struggling with certain concepts. The educator **exemplifies** how to fill in the gaps, both mentally and emotionally, during project completion, **sometimes.** The educator observes acquired content knowledge through several assessment avenues, accommodations are always taken into account, before, during and after each math lesson, **at selective times.**	During small group time, students are **encouraged** to hone in on their favorite part/s of the mathematical lesson. Students are reminded to focus on one strategic intervention, during academic completion, **at times.** The educator uses math games, videos, reteach strategies and personalized problem solving techniques to reinforce all skills, **occasionally.** The educator uses **a low amount of** interactive strategies, aligned with specified accommodations, in order for students to complete mathematical tasks.
1 L A G G I N G	Students are given **a vague explanation** of each portion of the state standards, **before each** mathematical activities. Students are given materials, strategies and goals, **indirectly aligned** to their mathematical standards, conducive to their Individualized Education Plan. A small number of students are **encouraged** to question any aspect of the mathematical lesson that is not clarified. . The students **are seldom given opportunities** to express knowledge of mathematical content to their teacher and peers.	Students are **granted minimal opportunities** to question strategic intervention. The educator promotes mathematical trainings for students who are struggling with certain concepts, **occasionally.** The educator **exemplifies** how to fill in the gaps, both mentally and emotionally, during project completion. The educator observes acquired content knowledge through several assessment avenues, accommodations are always taken into account, before, during and after each math lesson, **one to two times.**	During small group time, students are **encouraged** to hone in on their favorite part/s of the mathematical lesson, occasionally. Students are reminded to focus on one strategic intervention, during academic completion, **at times.** The educator uses math games, videos, reteach strategies and personalized problem solving techniques to reinforce skills, **rarely.** The educator uses **little to know amounts** interactive strategies, aligned with specified accommodations, in order for students to complete mathematical tasks.

| O L O S T | Students are given **no explanation** of each portion of the state standards, **before each** mathematical activities.

Student**s are not given** materials, strategies and goals, directly aligned to their mathematical standards, conducive to their Individualized Education Plan.

Students **are not encouraged** to question any aspect of the mathematical lesson that is not clarified.

. The students **are never given opportunities** to express knowledge of mathematical content to their teacher and peers. | Students are **grants no opportunities** to question strategic intervention.

The educator **never** promotes mathematical trainings for students who are struggling with certain concepts.

Under no circumstances does the educator **exemplify** how to fill in the gaps, both mentally and emotionally, during project completion.

The educator **never** observes acquired content knowledge through several assessment avenues, accommodations are always taken into account, before, during and after each math lesson. | During small group time, students are **does not encourage** to hone in on their favorite part/s of the mathematical lesson.

Students **are not reminded** to focus on one strategic intervention, during academic completion. The educator **does not use** math games, videos, reteach strategies and personalized problem solving techniques to reinforce all skills.

The educator uses **little to know amounts** interactive strategies, aligned with specified accommodations, in order for students to complete mathematical tasks. |

Individualized Education Social Studies/Science Individualized Rubric **Grades K-12** (Rate the content of each individualized lesson, based on the following)		
S c o r e	**Lesson Objective & Goals (4-point Rubric)**	**Evidence and Elaboration (4-point Rubric)**	**Historical/Science/Social Studies' Connections in the REAL WORLD**

| **4 L E A D I N G** | The educator **focuses on all** relevant material.

The educator provides **an adequate amount of time for students** to convey their personal relational value between the lesson's content and their personal goals/objectives.

The educator provides **extensive** insight on each aspect of the science/ S.S. lesson.

The educator monitors the student's progression/regression, based on personalized Individual Education Plans, **carefully .** | The educator provides **an extensive explanation** of the social studies/ science assignment for both the student and parent/s.

Students **are encouraged** by the educator to utilize avenues to gain content knowledge, **all the time.**

The educator will receive **constructive feedback**, from the Exceptional Student Education Specialist. Based upon the information received, short and longterm goals, will be modified.

All students are encouraged to convey what they learned about the daily lesson, through various means of communication. | The educator **always** uses songs, poems, cartoon expression and several other means to explain the lesson's content, according to each child's Individual Education Plan.

Students are **always** encouraged to convey historical/scientific content relativity, while using their five senses.

The educator **provides extrinsic motivation, before, during and after all parts** of academic completion.

The educator formulates assignments, including realistic transitional time, clear subject insight and vast experiences, **consistently .** |

3 LEARNING	The educator provides focuses **on all relevant** material. The educator provides a **sufficient** amount of time for students to convey their personal relational value between the lesson's content and their personal goals/objectives. The educator provides **extensive** insight on each aspect of the science/S.S. lesson. The educator monitors the student's progression/regression, based on personalized Individual Education Plans, **carefully** .	. The educator provides **an extensive explanation** of the social studies/science assignment for both the student and parent/s. **Every student** is encouraged by the educator to utilize various avenues to gain content knowledge. The educator receives **consistent constructive feedback**, from the Exceptional Student Education Specialist. Based upon the information received, short and longterm goals, will be modified. **Most students** are encouraged to convey what they learned about the daily lesson, through various means of communication.	The educator **always** uses songs, poems, cartoon expression and several other means to explain the lesson's content, according to each child's Individual Education Plan. Students are **always** encouraged to convey historical/scientific content relativity, while using their five senses. The educator provides extrinsic motivation, before, during and after all parts of academic completion. The educator formulates assignments, including realistic transitional time, clear subject insight and vast experiences, **consistently** .
2 LAGGING	The educator assists **selective students with** focusing on all relevant material. The educator provides **a small amount** of explanatory time for students to convey their personal relational value between the lesson's content and their personal goals/objectives. The educator provides insight on each aspect of the science/S.S. lesson, **on occasion.** Every so often educator monitors the student's progression/regression, **semi-based** on personalized Individual Education Plans.	The educator provides **a vague explanation** of the social studies/science assignment for both the student and parent/s. The utilization of various avenues to gain content knowledge, **was taken into account by the educator, rarely.** The educator receives **little to no constructive feedback**, from the Exceptional Student Education Specialist. Based upon the information received, short and longterm goals, will be modified. **Students** are **encouraged** to convey what they learned about the daily lesson, through various means of communication, **inconsistently.**	The educator **courages students to** use songs, poems, cartoon expression and several other means to explain the lesson's content, according to each child's Individual Education Plan, **every now and then.** Students are **not** encouraged to convey historical/scientific content relativity, while using their five senses. The educator **provides** extrinsic motivation, before, during and after **certain** parts of academic completion. The educator **places little to no emphasis on** formulating assignments, including realistic transitional time, clear subject insight and vast experiences.

1 L A T E N T	The educator **inhibits students** from focusing on relevant material. The educator does not provide a **sufficient** amount of explanatory time for students to convey their personal relational value between the lesson's content and their personal goals/objectives. The educator **places little to no emphasis** on providing insight on each aspect of the science/S.S. lesson. The educator monitors the student's progression/regression, **semi-based** on personalized Individual Education Plans.	The educator provides **an extensive explanation** of the social studies/science assignment for both the student and parent/s. The utilization of various avenues to gain content knowledge, **was not the main focus for the educator.** The educator receives **minimal constructive feedback**, from the Exceptional Student Education Specialist. Based upon the information received, short and longterm goals, will be modified. **Certain students** are encouraged to convey what they learned about the daily lesson, through various means of communication.	The educator **encourages students to** use songs, poems, cartoon expression and several other means to explain the lesson's content, according to each child's Individual Education Plan, **some of the time.** Students are encouraged to convey historical/scientific content relativity, while using their five senses, **inconsistently.** The educator provides extrinsic motivation, before, during and after some parts of academic completion **on a selective basis.** The educator formulates assignments, including realistic transitional time, clear subject insight and experiences, **a low percentage of times.**
O L O S T	The educator **inhibits selective students** from focusing on relevant material. The educator does not provides students with an **unreasonable amount** of explanatory time to convey their personal relational value between the lesson's content and their personal goals/objectives. The educator **places no emphasis** on providing insight on each aspect of the science/S.S. lesson. The educator monitors the student's progression/regression, **unrelated to their** personalized Individual Education Plans.	The educator **provides no details** regarding the social studies/science assignment for both the student and parent/s. The utilization of various avenues to gain content knowledge, **was not the main focus for the educator.** The educator receives **no constructive feedback**, from the Exceptional Student Education Specialist. Based upon the information received, short and longterm goals, will be modified. **Students are not encouraged** to convey what they learned about the daily lesson, through various means of communication.	The educator **refuses to encourage students to** use songs, poems, cartoon expression and several other means to explain the lesson's content, according to each child's Individual Education Plan. Students are **never inspires students** to convey historical/scientific content relativity, while using their five senses. The educator **does not take into account the importance of** extrinsic motivation, before, during and after all parts of academic completion **on a selective basis.** The educator **never** formulates assignments, including realistic transitional time, clear subject insight and vast experiences.

Special Education Parent Self Evaluation
(Score points based on individualized gifted characteristics.)

S c o r e	**School to Home Implementation (Rubric)**	**My Child's Individualized Gifts (Rubric)**	**Conventions of a Special Needs Parent-Frequent Reminders are Crucial (Rubric)**

4 LEADING	The parent **makes certain** the standards/goals/objectives, assigned to their child(per their I.E.P.), is reinforced, **daily.** The parent **attains specific insight** on the social, academic, longterm and short term goal progression/regression, **frequently.** The parent monitors assignments, sent home making sure they reinforce all state standards, **all the time.** The parent **remains abreast** of **all** changes to state standards, curriculum and field trip to academic correlation.	The parent **makes a conscious effort** to reinforce skills taught to strengthen skills, covered conducive to all Individual Education Plan Goals. The parent **encourages** their child to freely express details, about academic content, in various ways, **all the time.** The parent seeks resources to utilize at home that appeal to **all** senses, in order to exemplify their academic gift/s. The parent **observes** the individualized methods of learning for the student and helps them discover new aspects of their learning style, **carefully.**	The parent asks the student about all field trip experiences and **strongly encourages** the student to elaborate. The parent **establishes and maintains** a healthy relationship with all contributors to their child's academic road to success. The parent **asks sound questions to ensure** their child is not experiencing bullying from any individual. The parent attends academic awareness trainings, meant to enhance the student's learning experience, **frequently.**
3 LEARNING	The parent **ensures most** standards/goals/objectives, assigned to their child(per their I.E.P.), is reinforced, **every other day.** The parent **attains specific insight** on the social, academic, longterm and short term goal progression/regression, **most of the time.** The parent monitors assignments, sent home making sure they reinforce all state standards, **continually**. The parent **tries to remain up to date** on all changes to state standards, curriculum and field trip to academic correlation.	The parent **makes several efforts** to reinforce skills taught to strengthen skills, covered conducive to all Individual Education Plan Goals. The parent **encourages** their child to freely express details, about **most academic** content, in ways. The parent **seeks** resources to utilize at home that appeal to all senses, in order to exemplify their academic gift/s **on a regular basis.** The parent **observes** the individualized methods of learning for the student and helps them discover new aspects of their learning style, **most of the time.**	High School Student Training Programs-The parent asks the student about all field trip experiences and **encourages** the student to elaborate, **most of the time.** The parent **establishes and maintains** a healthy relationship with all contributors to their child's academic road to success. The parent **asks sound questions that address** their child is not experiencing bullying, from any individual, **most of the time.** The parent attends academic awareness trainings, meant to enhance the student's learning experience, **frequently.**

2 L A G G I N G	The parent **reviews** the standards/goals/objectives, assigned to their child(per the I.E.P.), is reinforced, **a small percentage of time.** The parent **attains general insight** on the social, academic, longterm and short term goal progression/regression, at **least half of the time.** The parent monitors assignments, sent home making sure they reinforce all state standards, **some of the time.** The parent **addresses** changes to state standards, curriculum and field trip to academic correlation, **marginally.**	The parent reinforces skills taught to strengthen skills, covered conducive to all Individual Education Plan Goals **to some extent.** The parent **encourages** their child to freely express details, about academic content, **in selective ways.** The parent **seeks** resources to utilize at home that appeal to all senses, in order to exemplify their academic gift/s, **in some measure.** The parent **observes** the individualized methods of learning for the student and helps them discover new aspects of their learning style, **occasionally.**	High School Student Training Programs-The parent asks the student about all field trip experiences and **encourages** the student to elaborate, **minimally.** The parent **provides** a healthy relationship with **some** contributors to their child's academic road to success. The parent **asks general questions that address** their child is not experiencing bullying, from any individual. The parent attends academic awareness trainings, meant to enhance the student's learning experience, to **some extent.**
1 L A T E N T	The parent **barely reviews** the standards/goals/objectives, assigned to their child(per the I.E.P.), is reinforced, monthly The parent **addresses** social, academic, longterm and short term goal progression/regression, **rarely.** The parent **monitors** assignments, sent home making sure they reinforce all state standards, **inconsistently.** The parent **places little to no importance on** changes to state standards, curriculum and field trip to academic correlation.	The parent **reinforces** skills taught to strengthen skills, covered conducive to all Individual Education Plan Goals, **a minimal amount of time.** The parent **addresses** their child's freedom to express details, about academic content, **scarcely .** The parent **uses** resources to utilize at home that appeal to all senses, in order to exemplify their academic gift/s, **some of the time.** The parent **observes** the individualized methods of learning for the student **but does not help them.**	High School Student Training Programs-The parent asks the student about all field trip experiences and **encourages** the student to elaborate, **minimally.** The parent **provides** a healthy relationship with all contributors to their child's academic road to success, **some of the time.** The parent **addresses** their child is not experiencing bullying, from any individual, **some of the time.** The parent **does not** attend academic awareness trainings, meant to enhance the student's learning experience.

O L O S T	The parent **does not address** the standards/goals/objectives, assigned to their child(per their I.E.P.), is re-inforced. The parent **places no emphasis on** social, academic, longterm and short term goal progression/ regression. The parent **does not monitor** assignments, sent home making sure they reinforce all state stan-dards, The parent **does not address** changes to state standards, curricu-lum and field trip to academic cor-relation.	The parent **never reinforces** skills taught to strengthen skills, covered conducive to all Individual Educa-tion Plan Goals. The parent **never addresses** their child's freedom to express details, about academic content, in various ways. **Under no circumstances** does the parent monitor resources to utilize at home that appeal to all senses, in order to exemplify their academic gift/s. The parent **does not observe** the in-dividualized methods of learning for the student and helps them dis-cover new aspects of their learning style.	High School Student Training Pro-grams-The parent asks the student about all field trip experiences and **never encourages** the student to elaborate. The parent **does not provide** a healthy relationship with contribu-tors to their child's academic road to success. The parent **never addresses** their child is not experiencing bullying, from any individual. The parent **does not invest time** at-tending academic awareness train-ings, meant to enhance the stu-dent's learning experience.

My Individualized Capability Reflective Log

	Articulation of My Struggle	**Math Time**	**Science/S.S.Time**
T o d a y	My name is Brandi. I am fifteen years old. My mama says, I am re-ally dumb. Ever since I was a little girl, letters look like numbers. It hurts my eyes to read. Today my teacher is talking about _____. I never really pay at-tention, because my mother says, I will pass, no matter what. Dumb kids, don't really matter. Me and my friends, have all been in the same classes, since elementary school. My teachers never ask me to do to much. They can't! Mama says, I can't do too much but this teacher is different. At first I did not understand if she knew how dumb I really was, but she will see.	We are learning how to do new things, in math! Some new things we learned are_____ _____. This teacher is so different. She is really helping us use different things to understand taking away numbers. My little sister takes away numbers. She is not fifteen. My little sister is five. My friends from other classes say me and my other friends, are in special classes for being dumb. I al-ready stayed back for one year. This is the first year, a teacher made subtracting numbers, fun for me. Even though I am way older than my sister, learning is starting to be fun. I don't care what my other friends say.	Science reminded me of my uncle. We are learning about sexy stuff. This is not fun! My teacher talking about stuff that is not cool. My friends think it is funny but I told them it is not a game. They don't know my uncle got me pregnant be-fore. My teacher don't understand. I don't like this class or the teacher. She is not teaching me, I could teach this class. If she talk about this again, I am leaving and never coming back. My mom didn't sign a form saying I can't learn this stuff.

T o d a y	My name is Tella. I am eight-years old. I don't talk, like regular people. My ears always feel clogged. That made me have to wear Hearing Aids. I also don't have two legs. My mom says, this makes me different but I don't feel good, about it. I was caught in a fire and it made my leg go away. My friends are really nice, at this new school. They help me with my book bag and other stuff. My teacher helps me to understand different things. Today she taught us, about nouns. This was a really great lesson. Sometimes when my teacher is talking, I step outside of myself. My latest report card has a lot of A's but my teacher says, if I don't get better, my grades are going to drop. It is really hard to explain, why my feelings take me over, when she reads certain books. I just wish, there was someone who looked like me.	Today we learned about counting and the terms less than greater than and equal to. My teacher asked us to split into groups. She lets us sit, however we want. I can't sit on the floor, though. It is hard for me. I wish everyone in the class could sit in regular chairs, like me. I tried really hard to pay attention but it was hard. Also, my teacher likes to use us to explain different things. She said, Larry has two legs and Jessi has two legs are the number of legs they have, less than greater than or equal to. This made me very sad. How could she use this example? Maybe she forgot, I have one leg. What did I do to deserve this? This really hurt my feelings. I didn't say anything, because I love my teacher. It was just hard to pay attention, after that.	Science is my favorite subject. My teacher says, this week I am the number one student. That means I get to pick one subject to teach my classmates, about. This is good and bad. I really want to teach my classmates, about science but I don't want everyone looking at my leg. Mommy says, my missing leg makes me special and she is right, but special to me is humiliating. Every time my special teacher and I walk down the hall, we get all these looks. People don't see me, they see my disability. Mommy says, never to use the D WORD, BUT I CAN'T HELP IT. I wish my hearing was normal and both my legs were on my body. I would tell my teacher about this but I do not feel comfortable. So … this morning, she asked me what my favorite lesson was about and I told her … what we learned in social studies everyone is special. I really want to teach about this because it spoke about special kids who are not just like their friends but are very unique, in many ways. I spoke about this with my classmates and everyone clapped, at the end. Maybe they understand me, after all.

T o d a y	My name is Eunique. I am twelve years old. My favorite shirt is yellow, my favorite lunch is peanut butter and jelly with the crust cut off and my favorite drink is milk. If I don't see my favorites, everyday they really miss me. This does not make me sad but worried. When I am worried I call for my favorites to come back. I don't say what is wrong, I scream. My screaming will bring my favorites back. If my favorites are not seen, they are alone. I know what it is to be alone and it does not feel good. Since this is the case, my favorites need to be here, everyday … otherwise, they feel alone and empty, like me.	I count one, two, three, four, one, two, three, four … one, two, three, four … one, two, three, four … one, two, three, four … one, two, three, four … my teacher says, Eunique you need to count to five but she doesn't know … I can count all the way to one million. I just can't leave these four numbers. They help me finish my worksheets, at home. Everyday, my tutor comes to help me. Mommy says, "Finish your worksheets and listen to your tutor." I always listen to mommy. I count all the way up and do addition, subtraction, multiplication and division with my tutor but that is with her. At school I count … one, two, three, four … one, two, three, four … … one, two, three, four … … one, two, three, four … … one, two, three, four … … one, two, three, four … … one, two, three, four … … one, two, three, four … … one, two, three, four … … one, two, three, four	Red patch, white patch, green patch … before I get angry, at the end of the day, during science. I need to rub my green patch, if I am still mad, I need to rub my white patch, if I feel out of control, I need to rub my red patch. Rubbing my patches help me to stay in touch. They help me, today my teacher is not here. Today my teacher is not here, what if, something goes wrong. I rub my white patch, I rub my green patch, I rub my red patch. I look around and everyone is loud. Even though people are only close by, It is like they climbed inside my ear and are playing the drums. The drums are getting louder and I can't rub my patches. I need to get away! With my hands over my ears, I decided to run home to a safe place. The bus driver doesn't know, I know the way home. I started to run and these men really hurt me. What did I do wrong? Why do they want to stop me? I do not understand!
T o d a y	My name is Gren. I am nine years old. My teacher says, I need to use my words. Words are not my friends. Whenever I use words, they use other people to hurt my feelings. When my teacher cals on me, in class she asks me questions to see if I know the right answer. I write the answer down, but she says, "Gren, use your words." Why won't everyone leave me alone? My dad, teacher and the speech lady, keep saying … "Gren, use your words. I have some not nice words to say to them. I hate words! The other kids use words to make people cry, and laugh but when they make the people around me laugh, I end up crying. I don't like words. All I hear about it words. I am sick of it.	Everything in math is fun, except when my math teacher says, "Use your words." I hate it! Otherwise it is great, when she asks the class to do experiments to prove they understand certain things, in math. When I use my words, sometimes I forget to say the first/last letter, the whole word or the word just comes out funny. My mommy, the speech lady and my teacher want me to use the really hard words to talk about things I learn. It is hard. Okay … could the teacher talk to the kids from my math class and tell them not to make fun of how I say certain words. If she focused on not making kids make fun of me, like she focuses on my words, there would be no more word bullies, in the school!	My teacher made up this really cool thing, called S.S./Science Calendar Math. She uses our time, at the end of the day to teach the lesson and we review our numbers, from calendar math. I love this times of day, since we all sing all the words, together. I don't need to feel shy, about talking or learning new things. Today, we were singing the Blast Past Historical Days and I forgot, one. I really hate when this happens. Sometimes the sounds and words from my brain are like an incomplete peanut butter and jelly sandwich. Sometimes I just have the bread or the jelly or just peanut butter, but everything does not smash together to make the sandwich. Nobody wants a sandwich with missing parts. I hate days, like this!

T o d a y	My name is Li. I am ten years old. I really love to read but math is really hard. Sometimes I forget the number of letters that are in certain words. I call these special words. People don't understand, math is all around us. They do not get the fact that I miscount how many letters go in some words. Other than remembering the right count of letters, I love to read and write. I really love to write creative stories and share them with my classmates and family. Today my teacher wanted us to do an activity that made us count as we read. It was from a really cool book. The activity was not as fun for me, since solving math equations, is confusing. My teacher wanted to know what my attitude was about, she just doesn't get it. Tonight I will write her a letter, explaining how sorry I am. My words just won't express it. Dear Ms. H. I do could not tell you about my attitude, yesterday … because my words fight, before they leave my mouth. A lot things get jumbled up but being rude to you, was not on purpose. I think math should be saved for math time. Doing math is really hard for me. Could you let me know, if this is possible? Thanks, Your Student Li	I hate dyscalculia! No matter how many times my teacher tells me to memorize five times five, I always think ten. It is really hard for me to add instead of multiply and vice versa. Unfortunately, this will never go away. I am really worried. My math teacher says, multiplication is a major foundation for a lot of other math problems. What should I do? When it is time for math, I put my head on the desk and start to cry. Lately, my teacher helped me make special cards to remember which symbol belongs to each problem but it is still so hard for me. I like my extra time with Ms. U. she picks us up and helps us by using math games. Mommy said, she may need to go away, if the school does no get more money. This would make me really sad. Someone needs to redo the math equations to put more money for our school and keep one of my favorite teachers! Anyway, I will try my best to do the math. Even if it makes me cry. These number	Science time is awesome! I really love everything we learn. Today we learned about observations. We observe a lot of things, in my family. We took a long nature walk with our class, today. It was amazing! In my science journal, I wrote about this amazing garden, my family and I visited. The nature walk … reminded me of our visit. The thing that stood out the most was _____ _____ _____. If I could change one thing about the nature walk, it would be_____ _____ _____. Using my words was not important, during the nature walk.Our teacher told us to use our sense of hearing and sight. In order to really hear everything, we could not use our words. My teacher helped me understand how to observe different parts of nature by_____ _____- _____ _____ _____ _____ _____My teacher is

The teachers were intrigued by the rubrics and content of the chapters. They enjoyed discussing the content. Casey was overjoyed to experience all the love in the room ... and then she spotted one hater, seething with jealousy. Shaking her head, she headed toward the auditorium stage to check on Friendmanship.

"How are you guys, doing," said Casey.

"They were a little nervous but we danced to shake it all out," said Lyric.

"Mrs. C. what if they don't want to get us," said Polly.

"If they don't want to they won't," said Lyric.

"People with their minds set on lock, may never get you, be you—regardless," she said.

"Stop thinking and just say what you need to say," said Don.

"Yeah, you think too much," said Bernie.

"If they don't like it, oh well," said Gesa.

Lyric and Casey glanced at each other and laughed. Lyric came such a long way from their initial encounter, in the restroom. She witnessed how much these kids changed, in less than a month. She knew Casey noticed how much they changed her, as well. They smiled and hugged each other.

"Um ... do y'all need a moment," said Na'tess.

"We will be fine," said Mrs. Coper.

"Let me get on stage and introduce the best supportive writing club on the planet," said Casey.

It's the moment you have been waiting for," said Casey.

"Please give a warm welcome to Friendmanship," she said. The students wrote their skit with a little help from Lyric my right-hand writing club leader and myself," she said.

"Please enjoy ... the skit We Have Something to Say," she said

Students enter stage right and start to fight. Student 1 records what is going on and gets the entire fight on video.

Instigating Crowd: Go! Go! Go!

Narrator: Students don't feel like we are heard. Teachers always want to tell us what to do and talk to us funny. It makes us feel some type of way. We want you to know when you talk down to us, talk about us, and misjudge us it hurts.

Mrs. Brye: Break it up animals. Do you need to go back to your pen? Crowd: They were fighting, but you can't talk to them any time of way.

Mrs. Brye: I can talk to them however I feel like, what is anyone going to do, fire me.

Narrator: Mrs. Brye felt comfortable, until the video of her saying mean things to students, leaked. She found herself moving to another school, never to be seen, again. This was one time, Don and Irv felt like someone did something good for them but it was only because Mrs. Brye was caught on video. How many other times do teachers talk down to students and nobody does anything? Let's keep watching to see.

Na'tess: (walks in singing with headphones on)

Mrs. Rich: (asks the class a rhetorical question) Don't you hate it when students know the rules and still don't follow them, I can't stand that.

Natalie: Don't you hate it when teachers see you do something and call you out to other people. If you got something to say, just say it.

Mrs. Rich: (approaches Na'tess) You think I care if you are good or bad. I got my degree. It's stupid of you to act like this. Your mother must be proud of such a "genius."

Narrator: Na'tess bit her tongue and said nothing. She was so hurt by what Mrs. Rich said, Na'tess thought about it, the whole night, into the next day. A whole week went by and she stayed out of Mrs. Rich's way but never forgot how she talked to her. Let's see if there are any aftereffects from what Mrs. Rich said.

Mrs. Rich: Good afternoon, Na'tess.

Narrator: "Na'tess chose to say nothing. There was no small talk that would make up for an apology. Her teacher talked to her crazy and it wasn't right."

Na'tess (enters class quietly): I have nothing to say to you.

Class: Oh ... she tried you.

Mrs. Rich: You'll say something.

Na'tess: Says who? You.

Mrs. Rich: Get out of my class.

Na'tess: Fine. I'll just tell the principal.

Principal Champel: Get in my office, now. You don't disrespect a teacher, under any circumstances. Do you understand me?

Na'tess: But you don't understand, she—

Principal Champel: I don't want to understand, he interjected.

You don't disrespect your teacher, do you understand

Na'tess:(placing her head toward her chest, she started to cry)

Narrator: I guess Mrs. Rich did not like feeling embarrassed. Maybe she should have taken notes on the way she felt, the day she was so cruel. She was sent to the principal's office for being disrespectful. She understands he is a busy man but figures he will hear her side of the story. When the principal comes out, she can tell he was talking to Mrs. Rich. She already won, because she is an adult. It hurt her badly and she started skipping school because she thought no one heard her.

Narrator: Let's meet Polly. She was only seven when Mr. Links almost crushed her spirit. She wasn't perfect but neither was Ms. Links.

Mr. Links: Polly, be quiet.

Polly: I wasn't talking.

Mr. Links: Girl, you better stop yo big mouth from running.

Polly: But I wasn't talking.

Mr. Links:(walks over and approached Polly) Now stop talking back.

Polly: Man ... Polly had to hold her reaction, inside.

Narrator: The talking incident stuck with Polly, a while. She could understand her teacher telling her to stop talking if she was but that wasn't the case. Why did he speak to her that way? Things may have been different if he asked her, but she accused her of talking when she wasn't. Think of how mad adults get when people lie on them. Why do they feel kids don't have the same emotions? Oh well ... maybe someday they will listen to us.

Narrator: Could you explain, why some teachers talk about students like they are not there. Here is another crazy scenario. I would not tell a lie. This is one of Gesa's stories. Check out her journal entry.

Dear journal,

I want to know, why my teacher doesn't respect me.

I wish she didn't yell at me, in front of my friends. Could she pull me to the side, sometimes? Also, another teacher came in and she started talking about me, in a bad way like I wasn't there. It's so obvious, when teachers are gossiping, about you, they glimpse at you and go right back to talking about you with the other teacher. My teacher doesn't understand what I am going through. It's hard sometimes not to talk back. She calls me out, in front of my friends and that is so embarrassing. Does she know, what it feels like to be embarrassed? Teachers have been doing this to me, since second grade. I want it to stop. Well, I guess my teacher will never know, my true feelings because of fear. Until next time ...

Love,

Gesa.

Whole cast: (all join hands) We are ... Friendmanship and Friendmanship is fabulous, exclaimed the students.

The crowd applauded.

Allow us to introduce ourselves,

"My name is Ivory, I'm in seventh grade, I was the narrator," she said.

"My name is Polly, I'm in sixth grade, I played Student 1," she said.

"My name is Sarah, I'm in seventh grade, I played Mrs. Rich," she said.

"My name is Na'tess, I'm in sixth grade, I played Student 2," she said.

"My name is Loreel, I'm in sixth grade, I played Mr. Links," he said.

"My name is Don, I'm in seventh grade, I played Student 3," he said.

"My name is Nescai, I'm in sixth grade, I played Principal Champel," he said.

"My name is Irv, I'm in seventh grade, I played Student 4," he said.

"My name is Rose, I'm in sixth grade, I played Mrs. Brye.," she said.

"My name is Gesa, I'm in sixth grade, I played Student 6," she said.

"Just in case you didn't know, we love Mrs. Coper And Miss Casanova," said the students.

An emotional crowd of educators stood up and gave the cast a standing ovation. Friendmanship achieved its goal of making an intimate connection with the educators. They made history. Casey and Lyric were beyond proud. They walked the students, backstage.

"Why didn't you guys tell us, you planned on saying that, in the end," said Casey. "Cause it was a surprise," said Rose.

"Who tells anyone, about a surprise," said Ivory.

The group started laughing.

"Naw real talk, we love you guys," said Irv.

"We know everyone was paying attention to what we had to say," said Gesa. "Thanks for giving us the chance to," said Polly. "We love y'all," said Don.

Nescai why you so quiet said Lyric.

He didn't say anything. He just got up and hugged Lyric with every last bit of energy he had left, after the performance. The students stayed and ate when they were finished. They got the chance to speak with several educators who complimented them on the performance. The students reaped the benefit from their monthly group meetings but their performance in March, really set the tone, causing leaders/educators to view their communication style, differently.

During the refreshment segment, several educators approached Casey and Lyric to tell them what a fabulous job they did with Friendmanship. The duo made it clear, the students worked hard to make it perfect.

"Great performance, how are you superstar," said Mr. Wu.

"Don't call me that, how are you," said Casey.

"I've been great, I hear you're doing the biggest and best things here, " he said.

"You class or should I say ... my class is doing big things, too, " he said.

"Scores are up and this year is looking amazing,

"Keeping up your Motiv'Plication, I hope," she said.

"So, how's your vote, looking," she said.

"I think ... we should all get equal compensation," he said.

"Oh ..., what made Mr. Judgement change his mind," she said.

"Check your tone, " he said.

"Sorry, this was the best thing that happened for us," she said.

"Man primary teachers do work hard," he said.

"You see how hard elementary teachers work," she said.

"Yes," he said.

"Well, we made history and will continue to make it," she said.

Let's take a picture of the first champs of "The Teacher Switch."

They were a part of making history. This would change the climate of education, forever.

Good Standing

Ding! Ding! After Casey entered her car(to drive home), the phone rang.

"Hello," she said.

"Monarch, daddy, and I are concerned," said Mrs. Peinst.

"Here we go, again," she said. Whatever happened to how are you, she thought.

"I know you're doing this challenge thing—it's called The Teacher Switch," Casey interjected.

"Yeah, that," she said.

"No-one tried to attack you, right," she said.

"Of course mom, all the students trampled me like elephants, part of my body is in my class," she said.

"Why are snide remarks your defense mechanism," she said.

"Because speaking without them doesn't penetrate your eardrums," she said.

"We don't want you falling the victim of fights or—this is my passion, I'm serious about it, please respect that," she interjected.

"We had a conversation before me calling and I vowed not to argue with you," she said.

"I hate having disagreements," she said.

"Please say monarch we support you," she said.

"Okay, monarch we support you," she said.

"Now your actions need to line up with the words," she said.

"I understand, well I hope you had a great day," she said.

"I did, we had a productive meeting," she said.

"Daddy and I love our monarch," she said.

"I love you guys, too," she said.

"Let's talk soon," she said.

"Okay," she said.

Casey knew if her mother lost control the conversation was over. Mrs. Peinst continued to express her concerns, via text/calls.

She ignored her sentiments. Whenever she felt there was a lack of her dictatorship, she distanced herself. Although the bond between them was not severed, affirming her decision created indirect resentment.

Nine
The V.

The next day as Casey and Lyric prepared for a special event (in her classroom), she pushed the conversation with her mother to the back of her mind.

"These videos are amazing," said Casey.

"For real," said Lyric.

"You've done such an amazing job with the club and the kids love you," she said.

"Thank you ... Achoo!" Lyric kept sneezing and had the cough of an eighty-year-old emphysema patient. Casey noticed she wasn't herself.

"Hey, when was your last checkup," she said.

"What's wrong Mrs. C., you don't speak mucus," she said.

"That's gross, seriously, when was the last time, you saw a doctor," she said,

"I don't know ... oh naw ... I remember, years ago that's when I got my inhaler," she said.

"Really," she said. She was not surprised.

"You need a checkup, I'll take you to my doctor," she said.

"Why ... I feel aight; it's a little cold," she said.

"Achoo!" She looked exhausted and proceeded to sneeze, incessantly.

"I'll be aight," she said.

"Hold on, give me a second," she said.

"Hi, this is Casey Coper, I would like to set up an appointment for a special girl," she said. She looked at her and smiled.

"Yes, her name is Lyric Casanova, hold on please, do you have Medicaid," she whispered.

"Yeah, I know where my auntie has my card, too," she said.

"Shh ...," she said. As she set up the appointment, Lyric marveled. She felt a sense of belonging for the first time—since she was in charge of Friendmanship.

"You're good to go," she said.

"Your new name is ma," she said.

"No, you have one mother," she said. Why did Casey encourage everyone else to be honest, while she continued to stifle her true feelings? Lyric's mother was an indifferent pseudo parent. Correcting her felt hypocritical.

"You my ma," she said.

"Lyric ... I—Naw, listen, you the only person, who gives a damn about me. Not even my step daddy cared bout me goin to no doctor," she said.

She was confusing abuse with adoration. Why did she refer to this horrific man as a hero? Of course ... it was the only perception of what felt like love. She reminded herself, this impressionable teenager had no baseline of true love. This is the norm, in several relationships. Abuse feels normal when it merges with lies.

"I ... I-Yes, what is it," Casey interjected.

"Nothin, just thank you," she said.

The two words were a cheap substitute for what she wanted to say ... I love you. Lyric never experienced true love. She knew, what to do to get attention, unfortunately, it earned her a discounted version of lust. Anyone will cherish a cheap imitation if they have no contrast.

Friendmanship's Finale

"I can't believe it's the last meeting with the kids," said Lyric.

"I know, we covered so much, do you think they will forget what we taught them," said Casey.

"Nope, kids don't forget what you teach, if you know how to teach it.

"That's so real," she said.

"You can't say that, no more," she said.

"What, I can't be down," she said.

"I don't know what that is, some old thing y'all say," she said. They enjoyed spending time together.

"Let's get ready for them," she said.

"Remember how scared I was, in the beginning," she said.

"Yes, you came a long way," she said.

"Everything gotta be perfect," she said.

Casey could tell she was not happy about the club coming to an end. Although she taught the students, a lot, they provided her with an opportunity to feel, again. She was numb for so long.

"I don't want it to be over," she said.

"It's time for the cocoon to transform, into a butterfly," she said.

"Here we go with the fortune cookie communication," she said.

"No, seriously … think of all the great skills you helped the group with," she said.

"They entered as caterpillars and are leaving as butterflies," she said.

"I didn't think about metamorphosis but okay," she said.

Final Thoughts

"Hey Mrs. C. & Ms. C.," said Rose.

"Where's everyone else," said Lyric.

"Down the hall, they come-in, close your eyes, please," she said.

"Oh … we have a little surprise for y'all," she said.

"Wow, what is it," said Casey.

"Don't peek, open on three, one … two … three," she said.

"Surprise," exclaimed the group.

"We made y'all some cards and here go some flowers," said Gesa.

"You helped us, so much," said Ivory.

"We want to say thanks," said Don.

"Awe … you didn't have to do that," said Lyric.

Casey was silent. In under five-seconds, she was balling.

"Mrs. C., you okay," said Lyric.

"Yeah, I get emotional," she said.

"It's aight, girls be like that," said Don.

"Boys too," said Polly.

"It's okay," said Na'tess.

"Let's sit down and talk about the meetings we had," she said.

"Yeah, we enjoyed helping you, with how to deal with hardships, in life," she said.

"It ain't … I mean it's not easy to come from where we stay or be around people we know are no good," she said.

"Now it's time for you to let us know, what you learned," she said.

"Please start your intro with We learned_____ being a part of Friendmanship," she said.

"Oh … I wanna go first," said Polly.

"Okay, just go in the order you're sitting," said Casey.

"We learned to respect ourselves and others with y'all Friendmanship," said Polly.

"We learned how important writing is to tell how you feel while being a part of Friendmanship," said Sarah.

"We learned we are special, no matter what while being a part of Friendmanship," said Na'tess.

"We learned to be the example we expect others to set while being a part of Friendmanship," said Loreel.

"We learned regardless of what people say, we are the best while being a part of Friendmanship," said Don.

"We learned when we face our fears, it helps us not be angry and nothing can hold us back while being a part of Friendmanship," said Nescai.

"We learned to not look down on others if we want the same thing while being a part of Friendmanship," said Irv.

"We learned to be good, even when other people are being bad while being a part of Friendmanship," said Rose.

"We learned selling or doing drugs won't help us and buying guns off the street won't solve anything, while being a part of Friendmanship," said Ivory.

They started to get emotional.

"Awe ... the best teachers bout to start crying," said Rose.

"Why not, didn't I teach you emotions need to be exercised," said Lyric. I won't apologize for crying or laughing there's a reason, emotions need to be expressed.

"You right, Miss," she said.

"We love both of y'all, as teachers," said Sarah.

One by one, the students approached them. Their tight hugs were a small expression of their gratitude. They would always remember, the values and strategies they were taught. Casey and Lyric would never forget the times they shared with the students. There was a precise and meaningful exchange. Friendmanship would impact them, forever.

Doctor's Visit

When the bell rang, Lyric rushed to Casey's room.

"It's time to see the doctor, now," she said.

"At five," she said.

"We can head there, in a few," she said.

"Of course, ma," she said.

"Lyric, I don't feel comfortable with you calling me that," she said.

"Fine, I'll keep calling you, Mrs. C. but on the inside, you my ma," she said.

"I don't know, what to do with you," she said.

"Why are these empty juice boxes in the back of the class," she said.

"Oh, Sanrell must have forgotten to throw them, out," she said.

Lyric frowned and avoided eye contact.

"Hey, you okay," she said.

"Achoo! Yeah, I just keep sneez--in and my throat is on fire" she said.

"Have a seat, you aren't feeling well," she said.

As she graded papers, Lyric placed her head down and fell asleep. Ding! She received a text notification.

Rye: Hey sweetheart! I got off early. Let's grab dinner.

Casey: You can pick it up. I have something important to do. I won't be home, until around seven.

She knew he would try and talk her out of taking Lyric for a checkup. She wasn't in the mood for rationalizing.

Rye: That's kind of late. Can you talk, now?

Casey: No.

Rye: Okay, please call me later.

Casey: Okay.

Rye: I still and always will love you!

Casey: I still and always will love you, too.

After texting him, she continued to grade papers. She noticed how much the student's writing improved. Finally, she was finished.

"Hey, wake up," she whispered. She shook her gently.

"I'm still sleepy, it was lights out for me," she said.

"It's time to go," she said.

"Aight," she said. Lyric was in a daze, as she entered the car. Casey's concern increased.

"Dang we finally, here, no offense—you young ... but drive so old," she said.

"Oh please," she said. The duo laughed as they entered the doctor's office.

"Hello, we're here for an appointment for Lyric Casanova," she said.

"Sure, have her fill out this paperwork," said the office attendant.

"I can't stand this, all these questions for what and it's so cold," she said.

"They need to know, background information, fill out what you can," she said.

"I got my Medicaid Card, from my auntie purse," she said.

"How did you know to bring, it," she said.

Lyric smiled.

"Here go my S.S. Card if they need it, I don't know if—Put that down, ever heard of identity theft," she interjected.

"You know how easy it is to steal this stuff, offline," she said.

"That doesn't mean you make it easy for people," she said.

"Yeah, my momma be steal-in people's information, even mine," she said.

"I had seven credit cards and a new car, at three," she said.

Although she made light of the situation, she knew Lyric was hurt. How could her mother stoop so low?

"Here go the information," she said.

"Thanks," said the nurse.

"I hope we don't wait, forever," she said.

"I don't think so, they move quickly, here," she said.

"Lyric Casanova," said the nurse.

"Man that was fast, come on ma," she said.

"Excuse me, you'll need to wait outside," said the nurse.

"No, she coming with me," she said.

"No issues, I can wait—," she said.

"I said no," she said.

"Shouldn't her mother be here," said the nurse.

"That's her—my mama," she said.

The nurse heard Lyric's cough and saw how adamant she was about Casey going into the examination room. She didn't press the issue. They entered the cold room that smelled like alcohol. She changed out of her clothes and sat on the examination table.

"I hope the first thang she look at is my head, Lord knows it needs some help," she said.

"You're so funny," she said. After a few moments, there was a knock at the door.

"Good afternoon, I'm Doctor Narsh, hello Casey," she said.

"Hey," she said.

"Before we start, I'm going to ask Mrs. Coper to wait, outside," she said.

"If she wait outside, I wait outside," she said.

"It's standard policy that a minor must be accompanied by a parent/guardian," she said.

"Lady, you want me naked, in the waiting room," she said.

She didn't know, how to react.

"I already told your hard of hearing nurse lady, my mama ain't goin nowhere," she said.

Achoo! Achoo! Achoo!

She frowned, looking at the confused yet ill teenager(sitting in front of her).

"Okay, let's start by reviewing your paperwork. I see you haven't had a checkup, in a while," she said.

"Achoo! Achoo!"

"God bless you," she said.

"Thanks, you right it's been a minute," she said.

"You indicated on the form, you would like to get tested for everything, could you be more specific," she said.

"Just test for everything," she said. Lyric wasn't sure what was going on with her body. She wanted to be positive it was not pregnancy symptoms.

"She has a really bad cough," she said.

"Yes, I hear it," she said.

"Okay, there's something else, confusing. You don't have the number of sexual partners on the form," she said.

"I did, I just don't know, that's why it's so many scratches, at that part," she said. Casey's heart started to pound. Please don't say anything judgmental, she thought.

"Do you know, an approximate," she said.

"Lady, just please"—she said.

"Could we get on with this," she said.

Dr. Narsh cleared her throat. The stethoscope felt cold, against Lyric's chest.

"Your lungs don't sound clear," she said.

"Duh … dough dough dio, say something we don't know," she said.

"Lyric, please … be respectful," she said.

"Sorry ma …," she said. The doctor frowned. Why was she calling her mom? Why didn't she correct her?

"Let's draw some blood, we also need a urine sample," she said.

"Should I go right here," she said.

"The restroom is down the hall to the right, there are cups in the holder for the sample," she said.

"Aight, I'll be back," she said.

"What's the deal with you and this girl," she said.

"What do you mean," she said.

"She seems ill and you're a little too comfortable, did you contact her mother, about this visit," she said.

"Look, I appreciate you squeezing her in but please just finish doing what you're doing," she said.

"This isn't healthy," she said.

"She's a special student," she said.

"Special enough to compromise our relationship and my license," she said.

"It's not that serious," she said.

"It is Casey," she said.

"This can't be allowed, in teaching, either," she said.

"Could you just help her, you know me," she said.

"Fine, the nurse will be in, soon," she said.

"I'm back, here go your cup, all warmed up," she said. Casey smiled.

"The nurse will be in to get it, I'll be back, soon," she said.

The nurse came in and drew blood, they were able to process everything, in the office.

"Please open your mouth and place this stick, inside" said the nurse. She smirked at her verbiage.

"Please wait a few seconds, I'll tell you when it's time to take it out," she said.

She looked a Casey, with an anxious facial expression.

"Time's up," she said.

"Good that was weird," she said.

"The doctor will be back, soon with all your results," she said.

About thirty minutes passed. Lyric and Casey talked and laughed, as they waited for the results. Eventually, there was a knock on the door.

"It's Dr. Narsh—may I come in," she said.

"Come in, we wait-in on you," she said.

She approached Lyric with a straight face. Casey knew the facial expression, she made— when something was wrong. She experienced it, each time they were not pregnant.

"Aight … doc. lady what little pill you got to give me, I'm sick of cough-in," she said.

"There's something important we need to discuss, privately," she said.

Lyric's beautiful eyes grew dim.

"I think it's best you wait outside, Casey," she said.

"Naw this lady my mama," she said.

"I can go, it's not a problem," she said.

"No, stay wit me, whatever it is, I can take it and she can too," she said.

"I wanna know, how many months, cuz if I'm pregnant, I want my mama to have the baby," she said.

Casey looked at her in disbelief. She would love to have that honor. It would be perfect. She started to imagine how cute the baby would be but was snapped back into reality by Dr. Morph's temperament.

"You're not pregnant," she said.

"For real, man cuz I been sleep-in a lot," she said.

The temperature of the room grew colder. Slowly, she delved into her large white lab coat and pulled out red and white pamphlets.

"Why you fumbl-in, whatever you gotta say, say it," she said.

As the doctor came closer, a shudder went down her spine. Her apprehensive look was disturbing. Each minute triggered a new level of anxiety. She wanted her to hand over two or three square-shaped blue pieces of paper with illegible writing that would make the symptoms subside. It was just another cold. Why was she lingering?

"Lyric, you're HIV Positive, the acronym stands for The Human Immunodeficiency Virus. Not only that the virus has transformed to AIDS," she said.

"What ... lady," she said. Each syllable dug a deeper level of reality. She sped off like she was hosting an informative t.v. special on the matter. Did she remember Lyric was human? Casey tried to stay strong, but could not help crying. She held her hand, in shock.

"Your compromised immune system caused you to develop the symptoms of diarrhea, fever, chronic coughing, and swelling in your neck, you described on the intake form," she said.

"Compromised immune system, what," she said.

"You'll need to inform anyone you engaged in unprotected sex with," she said.

"Inform anyone, naw you read the test wrong, I'm pregnant and I know who the daddy is," she said.

"Please listen, certain people infected with H.I.V have what's called a low viral load, it means they aren't necessarily symptomatic, but that doesn't mean the virus is not in their system," she said.

"What ... naw ... let's just be real, doc., ain't nobody got the V.," she said.

"I have no idea, what that means, but you do have A.I.D.S.(Acquired Immune Deficiency Syndrome)," she said.

She disconnected from her comment.

She fought to breathe as lumps of distress clogged her throat. She sifted through the doctor's words to find reality but came up short. How could she formulate a rational response out of an irrational state of mind? This was not happening.

"Based on the results, you have five months to live," she said.

Casey held her hand. She was in denial. How could this happen to her? She already went through so much. What could she say?

"We have clinics that provide support groups for teens who are HIV Positive. Please read these pamphlets, explaining the next steps to take and why they are important," she said. As the doctor explained details about HIV Lyric checked out. The unbearable words clenched her ears and seeped down into her soul. Reality did not set in. She yearned for anger or sadness to consume the state of shock. Instead, the words amplified shame and disbelief that permeated the room.

"Hell naw and I ain't got no AIDS," she exclaimed.

In disgust, she tossed the pamphlets in the air. The information landed on the floor as she ran to the restroom. Casey grabbed her clothes and ran after her. She knocked on the door.

"Lyric, here … your clothes," she said.

"Give me a minute," she said.

As her voice cracked in pain it brushed an unhealed wound. The sound was familiar, Rye would hear it, every time, she tried to mask her cries, while they attempted to have a child.

"Your clothes are right out here. I'll be in the waiting room," she said.

"Aight," she said.

In shock and disbelief, she headed to the waiting room.

"You're way too involved with this girl's life," she said.

"You don't understand, she needs me," she said.

"I do understand, I've been your fertility doctor for years," she said.

"You don't need to remind me," she said.

"This girl can't be your stand-in child replacement," she said.

"Shut up, you don't know, what you're talking about," she said.

"It seems as if you're taking on the role of a mother, it's not your place," she said.

"Who are you to say that," she said.

"Who am I, your doctor who knows you," she said.

"Not well enough, otherwise you would understand the huge part we play in each other's lives," she said.

"Technically, I compromised my license by allowing you to sign in a minor without parental consent," she said.

"Her mother is around but doesn't care," she said.

"That's not the point—Casey," she said.

"It is the point, I'm all she has," she said.

"That can't be true," she said.

"It is … she doesn't have her aunt, working two jobs or her mother, strung out on her weekly drug of choice," she said.

"Here's the information for coping with HIV/AIDS, the prognosis would be hard for a fifty-year-old to handle, much less a teenage girl," she said.

"Exactly, that's why I'm here to help," she said.

"Please talk to her. Ask her to reach out to whatever partners she engaged in intercourse if their status is the same, we can prevent an epidemic," she said.

"Please get rational and please encourage her to inform her sexual partners," she said.

"Sure, whatever you say," she said.

"It's not a joke, HIV spreads it's a fact," she said.

"You ready, please take me to the beach, mama," she said. Lyric's face was red and her voice sounded strained.

"One more thing, I hope you know what you're doing," she said.

"I ain't got the energy or time, mama, please … let's go, leave the lady alone," she said.

"Thanks for seeing her," she said.

As they headed toward the parking lot, Lyric kept reciting her poems. Quickly, they entered the car.

She tried to feel pain but shock numbed her. It was time to go back and erase memories of Stilt's fake smile and ingenue compliments. Life should give us a chance to go back to see people in a genuine state. She wanted to believe these boys cared but they didn't. Voices of regret were reprimanding her for every decision. As they parked she put down the window to take in the ocean air. The beach was always a place of peace. She opened the door and ran full force toward the ocean.

"Lyric ... wait," she exclaimed.

Falling to the floor, she grabbed her stomach and vomited. Casey cried as she consoled her. The time to pump the breaks on suffering was now. Lyric had too many things to live for. It was time to trade places. She would give anything to be in someone else's shoes.

"This ain't real," she said.

Her eyes were wide and Casey's shoulder was drenched in tears. Eventually, she focused on the waves. They were therapeutic.

"I know it hurts," she said.

"Killa boys stung me," she said.

"What if the boys don't know," said Casey.

"They know, they just don't give a damn, same as my stepdaddy, same as my mama and everyone else," she said.

"Awe ... I want to take the pain away," she said.

"You the only one who cares," she said.

"I wanna tell my mama, but she won't care," she said.

"You should tell her," she said.

"Why for her to laugh in my face and say I knew you would kill yourself," she said.

"If you don't do it for you do it for me," she said.

"No mother should have no idea her daughter is dy— I mean ... What, say it ... dying," she interjected.

"Aight I'll do it cuz you said, but you gotta be there with me when I tell her," she said.

"Okay, I'll be with you," she said.

They sat by the ocean, watching the waves, in silence.

"Reality be so real, it's just so damn real," she said.

"I know," she said.

After they watched the ocean for a while, she drove back to her aunt's house. As they pulled up, she saw a beautiful woman smoking, standing outside the door.

"Guess who that is," she said.

"I don't know," she said.

"We look just alike, how you don't know," she said.

She pulled up and rolled down the passenger window, slowly.

"May I help you? Oh, you gettin in here, late," said the woman.

"Where should I park," she said.

"Anywhere, this ain't no palace," said the woman.

She parked, on what was left of the grass. Slowly, they approached the beautiful woman. She was tall, thin, and had the perfect smile.

"My name is Casey, I'm Lyric's mentor, nice to meet you," she said.

She held out her hand, expecting the woman to do the same, instead, she rolled her eyes and flicked her cigarette.

"I'm Lyric's Mama, Dawn," she said.

She started to feel hot and cold at the same time. She never anticipated meeting her.

"I'm going to sit in the car," said Casey.

"Naw, she gonna stay here," she said. She started to cough, again.

"Oh ... you calling shots now, fast fish," she said. The words were sickening. Fast fish ... really ... she recalled her sharing Dawn's view of the molestation. This woman was twisted.

"Don't tell the pretty lady in the nice car what to do, you ain't run-in nothin," she said. Lyric looked like she was going to be sick. Fear gripped her attempt to speak. She looked at her mother's expression. Maybe it would finally happen. This was the moment she would rock her baby girl and say, everything will be fine, I love you. She had five months of care, love, and empathy in store. Why was she hesitant? The news was devastating. How would she react? She looked at Casey with bulging eyes.

"Whatcha lookin at her for, I carried you, not her, —-," she said.

"Mama ... I got AIDS, I got five months to live," she said. Casey didn't know, what to do, avoiding eye contact with Dawn, she started fidgeting and moved closer to her.

"I ain't the only one, other boys at the school got it too," she said. It seemed like saying the words quickly, would make things easier.

"Ain't you got nothin to say," she said.

"I ain't got no words for thieves," she said.

"How is she a thief," said Casey.

"Ain't she stole those baby boys lives, I know she gave it to them," she said.

"What," she said.

"She steal men, stole my Dylain from me—she was a little fast fish," she said.

"She's not to blame," she said.

"Yeah right girl, I see that rock, don't take her round yo man," she said.

She looked at Lyric. Her mother's words sliced what was left of the hope she had. How could she be so callous?

"Get in yo car and leave, stop acting like you care," she said.

"I do care," said Casey.

"I know she care," said Lyric.

"No, she don't," she said.

"Careful, don't get close," she nasty a nasty ... rotten ... fast fish," she whispered.

"Excuse me, that's enough," she said.

"It ain't never enough with this rotten girl," she said.

"If you have nothing positive to say, be quiet," she said.

Dawn started laughing, uncontrollably.

"Leave," said Lyric.

"I ain't goin nowhere, this my sista house," she said.

"You want yo mama to leave, my Special Doll-a Hoe," she said. She had a weird smirk on her face. It seemed as if she was either under the influence of something or had a mental imbalance.

"Get out the way," said Lyric.

"Oh ... so you push-in mama, now," she said.

"No, don't do it," Casey exclaimed.

"You gonna hit yo mama," she said.

"Lyric, please sweetheart don't do it," she said.

"The only thing Imma miss bout you, when you six feet under, is that check," she said. One tear trickled down her cheek, as she entered the car.

"Stay the hell outta my face, forever," said Lyric.

"You nothin, you nothin and ain't gonna be nothin. You dead to me and soon you dead to the world," she said.

As Casey drove, Lyric burst into tears. She pulled over and held her, tight.

"I told you, telling her was a bad idea," she said.

"My auntie just texted me, Yo mama left and won't be back," she said. She started coughing, uncontrollably, again.

"You sure, we could get you a safe place to stay for the night," she said.

"No, you go home to yo husband, you wit me all the time," she said.

"Okay, if she comes back I'll come and get you, no questions asked," she said. She drove her back to her aunt's house. Lyric looked like her soul was broken into tiny pieces that were too small to put back, together. As she drove home she thought of all the great times they had. Quickly, she pulled over in intense pain, placed her knees to her chest, and bellowed. She thought of all the ways Lyric made an emotional indentation on her heart. How could she envision life, without her? Ding! Just then, she received a text.

Rye: Hey sweetheart, where are you? I'm worried.

Casey: No need to be. I'm around the corner.

Rye: Okay, I still and always will love you.

Casey: I still and always will love you, too.

Casey wanted to be alone. She shared everything with her husband but this subject was off-limits. Slowly, she pulled into the driveway.

"Where were you, are you crying," he said.

"I was working late," she said.

"You're lying," he said.

"Please don't start this," she said.

"Look! I thought we were on the same page with trying to get pregnant," he said.

"I'm begging you, don't bring that up, now," she said.

"When then," he said.

"You have no clue, what happened today," she said.

"Of course not, you don't talk to me," he said.

"Stop, please," she said.

"I'm not pressuring you, but how are we supposed to have a baby with you stressed out like this," he said.

"I'm asking you nicely, leave me alone," she said. Her time was always accounted for, in the past. Things changed when she switched work locations.

Ding!

"Why'd your phone just go off? Are you cheating," he said.

"Is this a joke," she said.

"Give me your phone," he said.

"No, stop acting irrational," she said.

"Case. I'm not stupid, just tell me, be honest," he said. She rolled her eyes and went to take a shower.

"You need to trust me," she said.

After she finished. she laid down.

"Why are you acting so clandestine," he said.

"Again, you need to trust me," she said.

"What if it was me, you would freak," he said.

"I'm tired, go to sleep, please," she said.

"I still and always will love you," he said.

"I still and always will love you, too," she said.

"I'll let you sleep but you need to tell me what's going on," he said.

The silence was so loud. She tried to register everything that happened. He was right. If it were him, she would blow a fuse. This was the first time, she felt like a hypocrite but keeping Lyric's secret was worth it.

Reality

Lyric laid with her head facing the bottom of the bed, as an erosion of disbelief set in place. It was a miracle, no one was home. She waited for Dr. Narsh to call and say the whole thing was a joke or the results were wrong, but it never happened. At this point, the person who infected her was dying and possibly spreading the virus to others. Whoever it was, needed to understand they were sentenced to a five-month living window. Each time she engaged in unprotected sex, resurfaced in her mind. What was taking precautions? Her stepfathers never used protection. A few boys she was with insisted on it but she hated that. Did it make sense she contracted AIDS? The pain prompted her quest to feel numb. She ran to her aunt's room, looked under the bed, and pulled out the hidden liquor stash. Among the bottles were some pills. Quickly, she grabbed them and two bottles of liquor. She wanted to drink her status away. With each gulp, she hoped to drown out reality. People lied without blinking to have their way. Stilts would say, "I don't want nobody but you" then she saw him with another girl.

"If you were mine I would never hide you." Do's friends would ask when he was going to claim her and the answer was ... claim who?

What about times she had unprotected sex with different guys, at school and still felt empty. Every disturbing thought prompted another sip. Finally, she started to let the pen flow:
Every time you touched me
I thought the world would never end
but over time I realized despite sex you were not a friend
The funny part is we were always so tight
Until I gave it up to you and friends for a cheap amount that night … As she continued to write, sorrow filled the room. She was scared to press send.
#Anfel322##Swoondub590# #DennyJalllove368##Rat-G-O-D—M-A-K-E-M-O-N-M-A-K-E-I-T566# #MyMoney903##Lakesbakesbabycakes222#

#Nazear873##Doforyou234# #StandStilts4up782#Mr.G-R-A-T-E-S-T-isgreaterthenyou568#
Lyric went to her aunt's closet partially blinded by tears and stared at the solution to her problem.

She reached her breaking point, her whole life was an uneven exchange. She offered sex to people to fill an emotional void. Her perception of love was exchanged for a distorted reality, ever since she was little. Thanks to several horrific experiences, her innocence and trust were exchanged for hurt, bitterness, and low self-esteem. She vowed to never let it happen, again.

Tik ... Tik ... Tik

The next morning, was in disbelief.

"Good morning, ADORATION," said Rye.

"morning," she said.

"Up extra early for me, again," she said.

"Your face does not look billboard friendly, right now," he said.

"Could we talk about what happened, yesterday," he said.

"Oh no ... what time is it," she said.

"It's 5:15," he said.

"Okay, I have a meeting, tonight, I'll text you, when I'm done," she said.

"Here we go again with the weirdness," he said.

She planned on spending every waking minute with Lyric.

"Hello ... come in Casey ... Is this another daydream," he said.

"I need to get out of here to beat traffic," she said.

"I still and always will love you," he said.

"Love you," she said.

If he wan not sure before, he knew something strange was going on. No matter how tired, hurt or disengaged she was, they always expressed their love with the same words.

"You sure everything is fine," he said.

"Yes, bye," she said.

As she rushed into her car, she heard a text notification.

Mama, everything was going good. I gotta get my life, back. Love the best part of your favorite song, Lyric.

What did she mean, get her life back? She tried calling, her but the phone call kept going to voicemail.

"Good morning," said Casey. She finally made it to her destination.

"Morning, is everything okay," she said.

She noticed Casey looked frazzled.

"Hopefully, it will be, could you get me coverage for first hour," she said.

"Sure! Whatever it is, I hope it gets better," she said.

"Thanks," she said.

She rushed to Lyric's aunt's apartment and the corner store but she could not find her. She decided to send her a message.

Casey: Lyric where are you, I've been looking, all over. I need to know, you're okay. Please text or call me.

As the clock ticked there was no time to waste. She decided to visit her aunt's apartment, again.

"What you want, fancy lady," said Dawn.

"Have you seen Lyric," she said.

"No, even if I do, the answer will stay a mystery," she said. She started laughing.

"Okay, bye," she said.

She drove away in disgust, how could anyone be so callous? Treating Lyric like a plague, was not okay. She drove everywhere Lyric liked to visit—the grocery store, the beach, the park, even Get Down Middle, she was nowhere to be found. The last time they spoke, she did not look or sound the best. This was a horrible feeling. Where was she?

Security …

After searching everywhere, Casey decided to head back to The Best High school. She entered the cafeteria, it was loud and reeked of old mop water.

"What's up, I thought you were going to sell out, it's our day to do lunch duty," said Mr. Zee.

"Have you seen Lyric, the freshman," she said.

"No," he said.

"Are you sure," she said.

"Pretty sure, if I see her, I'll let you know, everything good," he said.

"Yeah," she said.

The worried expression and the sweat trail on her forehead contradicted her claim. Something was going on.

"You sure everything's good, you look worried," he said.

"It's nothing you can help with, I'll keep looking around," she said.

"Okay," he said.

Lyric slept on campus, the night before. Circumstances were in her favor.

Mr. Veftel was the only security guard, on campus. She knew where all the cameras were and every hiding place in the school. She snuck around the back entrance of the cafeteria, during the first lunch period with everything set to go. The workers were completely oblivious to her presence, they were busy gossiping. She peered through the serving doors, into the cafeteria at the culprits, who played a part in her status. She thought to herself look how happy they are … just wait 'til I send this mass message through the school notification webpage. Principal Waggenport encouraged students to use the page for updates and special events. Her fingers shook in fear. Ignoring them, she updated her status.

Untitled

Every time you touched me,
I thought the world would never end!
Over time I realized despite the sex you were just a friend,
The funny part is we were always so tight!
Until I gave it up to you and four friends for a cheap amount that night,
Funny how life can be, crazy and cruel!
When I walked by in my skirt, your friends would drool,
but all of a sudden I wasn't so grand!
So you told your friends to take me off your hands,
I barely talked and never bothered you!
But now I realize two halves don't equal two,
so you pushed me to the side!
While five other friends took a ride,
I didn't feel any pain!
A relationship was never on my brain,
you did what every man I ever knew would do!
Chew me up and spit me out after you split me in two,
but now I have some news for you!
This is not to brag or show out,
please believe that's not what this is about!
This news is very serious, you see,
it can't just stay between you and me!
I bet you never realized when
you passed me from friend to friend!
Your life at that moment would end!
I'm HIV positive you see,
but not just that, I have AIDS written all over me!
I don't know when I got it,
but I'm in a bottomless pit!
Y'all were real big on sharing,
But no part of AIDS is endearing!
So I suggest you get checked sooner than later!
Anfel, Swoon, Denny, Rat, Money, Lakes, Zaire, Do, Stilts, and Greater.
Your "friend,"
Lyric

Immediately, everyone looked down, at their phones. She was not interested in the reaction of anyone else, only the perpetrators. They needed to feel the same hopelessness, she felt after hearing "you have AIDS." she searched for meaning, in this hopeless situation. Yet again, there was no answer. The void caused the grip around her solution to get tighter. Anxiously, she crept into the seat of retribution, as she peered through the window. Holding an AR 15 she burst through the double doors. As she entered, screams permeated the cafeteria.

"I played everybody's way for a long time, it got me HIV that led to AIDS," she said.

"Yo, chill put the gun down," said Sanrell.

"Shut yo lyin infected behind up," she said.

"Every last one of y'all infected killaz gonna do what I say," she said.

"Aight … aight," he said.

"Hands up now, I need all palms on deck," she said.

The students listened carefully to her. Their lives depended on it.

"I saw everyone check they phones, hold em up high and smash em on the floor, now," she

said.

She watched as the students followed her command. "Control is great for the soul," she exclaimed.

"Ahhhh," exclaimed several students.

The rifle provided a sense of euphoria, she never anticipated.

"Shut up and stomp em, and toss em to the middle of the floor," she said.

The students were horrified.

"Now, If your name was in that message as a killa, get on stage and sit down," she said.

Shaking the boys fought not to pass out. Fear penetrated their thoughts and actions, as they walked toward the stage. The thought of what could happen made some of them want to pass out.

"Sit down on yo hands and don't say one word or a bullet in the head will be my last gift to you," she said.

They all sat in a line on their hands.

"If you have a walkie-talkie radio, turn it off and toss it, toward me," she said.

She pointed the gun at the boys.

"Don't even think about acting sideways or I'll shoot everyone, in here," she said.

They followed her directive.

"Mr. V. get on stage with the killaz," she said.

He felt impotent. What could he do? The title of the security guard was one he was proud of. How would this end?

"Stop thinking and get on the stage, or I'll shoot every person in here," she said.

After he obliged, she fired the gun toward the ceiling.

"IF YOUR NAME WASN'T IN THE MESSAGE & YOU AIN'T NO SECURITY GUARD, GET THE HELL OUT BEFORE YOU GO WHERE THEY GO," she bellowed. The veins in her eyes began to pulsate. She disassociated herself from reality. Quickly, survival mode dictated the mass amount of students, administrators, and teachers, as they ran for safety.

"Let's get out of here," said Mr. Zee.

"I can't leave," said Casey.

"What are you trying to do, get super teacher of the year," he said.

"She needs me, I can't leave," she said.

"Earning a trophy for bravery isn't worth your life," he said.

"Just go ahead without me," she said.

"You're hardheaded that girl looks out of her mind," he said.

"Just go," she said.

Lyric scanned the area and kept a close eye on the captives. She had to be vigilant. This was her moment of control.

"Mr. V. where you goin," she said.

He was about to run out with the crowd.

"All y'all get in a straight line," she said.

"Man this ain't even right," said Denny.

"Shut up, get in a straight line with your backs facing the door, now," she said.

"You doin the most," said Lancell.

"Shut up, now, lock arms and face me, keep your legs wide, too," she said. As they obeyed her commands the captives wondered if she would let them go. She did not look stable.

"Mr.V. Put extra locks you hide in your draw, in and outside on the doors, and give me the keys," she said. He could not afford to look noncompliant.

"I... I ... I ... can't do that," he said.

"That's the problem, y'all sit up here eat-in donuts and talk-in not pay-in attention, you never do yo job," she said.

"I have to say no," he said.

"You know how many times I skipped class to see yo greedy donut lov-in behind the vending machines, doin nothin," she said.

"Now you want to act like you care, this ain't yo business, keep it that way, do what I say," she said.

"Please don't hurt these boys," he said.

"Do what I say or you'll have early blood on yo hands," she said.

"Oh and if you even breathe to any cops, it's on, oh yeah, you ain't doin nothin with no phone, anyway," she said. She smirked.

Mr. Veftel left the line. Quickly, he went out and placed extra locks on the doors, from the outside. Lyric was extremely observant, he had no clue how she knew about the extra locks but she did.

"Good, now hand me the keys, slowly," she said.

"Here, now let us go," he said.

"Yeah right, you served your purpose, y'all don't move, Mr. V. follow me," she said.

Lyric led him to one of the cafeteria doors.

"Unlock it," she said.

"But you just said—I don't care, you tryin to live or die. Unlock it and leave," she said. She double-checked each lock was placed correctly.

"The rest of y'all better not move," she said.

As she slammed the door, he did not feel like a security guard. How would he live to tell the tale of running away from the victims? Why was he so scared? Sadly, he took one more look back and ran. She was in an intense zone and didn't realize Casey stayed behind when everyone else ran out.

"This is Officer Gant, we have the place surrounded, let the hostages go," he said. His voice echoed loudly, from the intercom.

"This is crazy," she said. She shot holes through the connectivity box that controlled the sound. Although the officers continued to try and give directives, it was difficult to hear, through the stormproof glass.

"This is Selah Sight, reporting live from, Max it Out News. Based on an anonymous tip news reporters were informed.

"I'm here in front of The Best High School. We have reports of a fifteen-year-old girl holding people hostage. There have been several tragedies, in the district, over the past few months. The victim's names have not been released," she said.

"Officer Gant as our police chief, would you care to comment on what's going on, inside," she said.

"We arrived on the scene and have been trying to correspond with the perpetrator but there's no response," he said.

"Aren't you professionals, from what I hear, this is a dangerous situation," she said.

"We're doing our best to secure the area, you can see we have the place surrounded," he said.

"Aren't speakers in there or some other way to speak with the person holding the hostages," she said.

"Leave this to the professionals, lady … please, we can't force a response," he said.

"Care to comment on any promising negotiations," she said.

"No comment," he said.

"Okay, that was the leading officer making attempts to deescalate the situation, hopefully, no one is hurt or worse," she said.

"Yo … lady we was in there, we could help," said one of the students.

"Okay, let's hear from two students who escaped the hostage situation. What are your names," she said.

"Yo my name Ayson and my name Yandell," said the students.

"Could you tell us what went on inside," she said.

"Well, everyone was at lunch and we got a school notification, through our main page and a mass text chain," he said.

"I just want to shout out my crew, right quick, all y'all ysons 2's and 3's shout out to the 4's and 5's,—" he said.

"Man shut up, anyway, we was eating at first lunch saw this message about this girl letting some boys know she got the V.," he said.

"Excuse my ignorance, what's the V.," she said.

"You know ... HIV, she said she ain't have long to live or somethin," he said.

"Sounds intense thankfully you made it out," she said.

"We shook cuz we know them boys inside, they in our grade," he said.

"The girl a freshman, I mean ... we see her around but don't know her, like that," he said.

"Really," said Reporter Sight.

"So then, she ran in the cafeteria yelling—if you not in the message get out and don't come back or I'll shoot up yo mama, grandmama, and granddaddy," he said. "Everyone like the teachers and students and everybody in the cafeteria ran to the doors to get out and run off-campus and we heard gunshots," he said.

"I thought people would run us over. We heard one teacher stayed and I don't know why," he said.

"It's crazy," he said.

"We was thinking, where was Mr. V. the security guard and where was the cops now they all here," he said.

"Could you tell us more, about the shooter," she said.

"We know she real quiet and was doing all types of stuff in the bathroom with guys, but she not in our grade," he said.

"She made us smash our phones and everything, it's like she was planning this for a while," he said.

"In your opinion, you think the people inside are in grave danger," she said.

"The way that girl look, heck yeah," he said.

"Hey, baby, I'm happy y'all okay," said a concerned parent.

"Good afternoon, what's your name," she said.

"I'm Yandell's mom, don't worry bout my government name," she said.

"As a concerned parent, do you have any words to share, regarding this situation," she said.

"It's been a while. I'm happy my baby and the other students made it out okay, but how these kids get guns, easier than candy, in these streets," she said.

"You believe there is an issue with gun violence and security, correct," she said.

"Of course, it's crazy, I can't stand the mental health laws they got, neither," she said.

"Have you voiced your concern, regarding these issues, before," she said.

"Of course, a bunch of parents did. We always get the same answer, these things take time, what the heck, it takes months to fix things. Think I not," she exclaimed.

"Would you say school security needs to get better," she said.

"Ma'am they got one donut-filled security guard for thousands of kids cuz of budget cuts but got all the money in the world for sports, uniforms, and other things not more important than keeping these babies safe," she said.

"I see, you're aware this same issue was brought up, during a protest, led by teachers," she said.

"Yup saw it on t.v. pretty lady with the big mouth (Ms. Zebedee) been trying to stand up and do something but every meeting, it's the same answer," she said.

"What answer is that," she said.

"Due to budget cuts ... blah ... blah ... blah. You think that girl would have got in if security was tight. I can't even blame the man, it's only one of him. What you want him to do, magically multiply," she said.

"Interesting, everyone watching the news segment is hearing your concerns, including stakeholders," she said.

"Good, hear this ... we can't cross the street safe hoping the people inside don't die, it ain't right," she said.

"I hear your concerns," she said.

"Over the past months, we had too many shootings, something needs to change," she said.

"Thanks for your comments," she said.

"One more thing, ain't nobody take-in away the second amendment, the laws around illegal guns and these babies gettin them need to get changed," she said.

"Thanks for sharing your perspective," she said.

"Well, that was the input of a concerned parent, regarding gun regulation and safety, stay tuned for updates. Again this is Reporter Sight with Max it Out News," she said.

Crazed to Retaliate

As Lyric continued to hold them hostage, her eyes bounced from them to the clock.

"Ops is useless," she said.

"I ain't doin nothin," said Greater.

"I guess you tryin to die," she said.

"Boy better not move," said Deider(Do).

The duo barricaded the door and made sure, no one could get in or out.

"Mama, what you still doing here," she said.

"I've been here, you were distracted," she said.

"Lyric, honey put the gun down, please. These boys are already suffering, they just learned their status, " she said.

"Dr. Narsh said AIDS, we got death in our veins. What's the difference between now or later," she said.

"I don't know which one did it but one of them did. I was only with them," she said.

"Real talk Mrs. C. she ain't have no gun to her head to bang us, unprotected but now she wanna put a gun to my head for her choice," said Stilts(Sanrell).

"Please stop talking," said Casey. She feared for his life.

"Naw, you taught us, bout choices," said Stilts.

"What part of shut up you not gettin," she said.

"Boys, I need you to be quiet and let me handle this. Lyric please put the gun down," she said.

She smirked. Casey noticed she was in shock and a bit inebriated. She stared at the boys and wondered, which one infected her. She turned and looked at her.

"Ma I didn't want none of this," she said.

"Nothing bad has to happen, it's not too late, put the gun down," she said.

"It's late, everything is wrong, I got four months and twenty-nine days to my last breath," she said.

As they spoke, Denny nudged Rimez. Looking at each other, they read between each bloodshot vein bulging in their eyes. This was not a joke. Lyric was serious. Quickly she redirected her attention, back to the boys.

"I don't know why y'all so quiet," she exclaimed.

"I'm the quiet one," she said.

"You just said shut up, make up yo mind, crazy," said Denny(DenJ).

"Denny please just don't say anything," she said.

"They just received news about their status and the entire school knows, isn't that enough," she said.

"Naw ... it's ... not ... enough," she exclaimed.

"Did these killaz care, when I screamed silently in the bathroom to stop and get off me," she said.

"So we dyin today," said Anfel.

"Finally, you get somethin right, slow dough," she said.

"Anfel ... not now," she said.

Rat refused to take his eyes off of Lyric. He placed his left arm down, he propped his right knee forward. Now, the plan was in motion. As he watched her, he moved, slowly. Using the last of his adrenaline and ran full force toward her. Boom! Boom! Boom! Without thought, she fired three bullets into his chest.

"Rimez no ...," exclaimed Casey. Large sweat bullets mounted on her forehead. As she watched him hit the ground. A loud bellow drowned out the sound of blood, running down the cracks of the cafeteria floor.

Compassion caused her feet to stumble, as she dove to cradle him. Her clothes were drenched in blood from the oozing bullet wounds, he received.

"Ma, move back, he ain't listen, he wanted it," she said.

"Please, no more, put the gun down," she said.

"Anyone else wanna try yo girl," she said.

The boys turned their faces away and some started to sob. Casey turned her head, in disbelief and continued to cry. This person was someone new. It wasn't even her shell. Who was she?

"Please put the gun down and let the boys go," she said.

"No, so they could kill other people with the V.," she said.

"Let us go, I ain't deal-in wit this crazy dirty ***," he said Do.

"Crazy," she said.

"I never tried you, but that one time," he said.

"Cause I never offered again," she said.

"Dog, shut up," said Nazaire.

"I was doin good, right ma," she said.

"That lady ain't yo mama, she our teacher," said Do.

"It's the bullet countdown, I helped Rat out, who next," she said.

"Deider quiet," said Casey.

"You're doing good we are not speaking, in the past tense, you can still do good, just put the gun down," she said. Her fingers shook, in terror. Where was everyone? Where were the cops?

"We ain't far from the other side! I won't be on Earth, no more," she said.

The rest of the boys remained quiet, standing side by side in front of the chained doors. Casey tried to get off the floor, but could not leave his lifeless body, alone. No one else could die. She was a writer. Why couldn't she come up with the right words to trigger remorse, in Lyric? She needed to think fast.

She attempted to get up and slipped on Rimez's blood.

"You okay, mama," she said.

"No, please stop, I will be, just let them go," she said.

"They gotta pay," she said. Casey was weak, she crawled closer to the boys.

"Each one of y'all better tell me why you shouldn't die, based on how you treated me, if it ain't good enough, you end up like Rat," she said.

"I ain't got nothin to say," said Money.

"You goin talk when I say talk," she said.

Casey continued to cry, intensely.

"What's wrong mama, I need to do this to teach everyone not to be killaz," she said.

"I'm begging you, please put down the gun," she said.

"Greater or should I say, Lesser, don't let me catch you puttin your arm down," she said.

Quickly, he got back to the original position, she demanded.

"You first Lesser," she said.

"I dunno nothin," he said.

She stepped forward, two inches.

Don't let me get closer," she said.

"Haaaaaaa!"Lyric started laughing, uncontrollably, her face was emotionless. There was no flicker of light shining in her eyes. The hope she once knew, died in seconds. She watched as the boys stood, arm in arm, petrified. Her eyes slid to the back of her head, about twenty seconds later, they refocused. Anger from her childhood kissed her gently, granting permission to act. Slowly, she looked up.

"People be so funny," she said.

"I—Boom! Boom! Boom! Boom!

She fired another round of bullets, killing Lanson(Lakes), Nazaire(Zaire), Stilts(Sanrell), and Garnell(Greater).

"Stop … no … no … no … please, oh stop, why," exclaimed Casey. She crawled over to the lifeless bodies. Blood drenched her pants.

"Why tell them to explain and then start shooting," she exclaimed.

"Same reason they lied to me," she said.

She let out another loud cry as she saw their bodies on the floor.

"Oh well, guess they won't be lying no more," she said.

"Lyric let's reason with each other," she said.

At this point, she barely knew who she was. Her blood-drenched clothes were unrecognizable.

"Why not be an example," she said.

"Example, how you want me to be that? I'm living on borrowed time," she said.

She started coughing and sweating, uncontrollably.

The remaining boys were crying, intensely. They gazed into Lyric's disconnected eyes and started to worry.

"You're fortunate, I love you ma, you keep tryin to negotiate, it's start-in to irritate me," she said.

"I'm trying to help you and the boys," she cried.

"You can't help yo child's killaz," she said.

Her mind went blank, as she tried to process what happened.

"It's aight you scared," she said.

"Remember our first meeting, I taught the kids so much oh … no, you remember when I had an asthma attack," she said.

She wasn't making sense, word she attempted to string together, turned into babbling.

Slowly, she took a close scan of her gun.

"Aight, shoot … lol no pun intended Deider you go, why you think you should live based on the way you treated me," she said.

He started to shake. The sight of blood and the smell of death caused a trickle of urine to run down his pants onto the floor. The shots raised the volume of his heartbeat.

"Man, just let us go," he said.

"Did you just have an accident, where we eat, shame on you, nasty," she said. Boom! Boom! Boom!

"No," exclaimed Casey.

Do and Money's listless bodies joined the other victims. Casey observed Lyric was not in her right state of mind, and had a clean break, from reality. She had no more energy to scream.

"I just love how shots come out of nowhere, kinda like the shock of hearing you got AIDS, it's gangsta," she said.

"Then there were three and me, any last requests," she said.

"Man, I need to talk to my people let me call them, " said Anfel.

"Should we let him call," she said.

"Nah, pass on that," she said. They watched as she spoke to herself.

"You crazy," he said.

"Whatever name you wanna call me it don't compare to me having THE V.," she said. "You takin long, I guess yo life don't matter," she said.

"Not again, no more," whispered Casey. She sat on the floor, rocking back and forth. Trying to avoid hearing any more gunshots.

"Oh well, gave you a chance, it's ova," she said. Boom!

Casey remained in an upright fetal position, clogging her ears, as the bullet killed him.

"Both of y'all make me sick," she said.

"I ain't dying like this," said Swoon.

"I ain't dying like this," she said ... mocking Swoon.

"You ... have .... no .... choice," she said.

She walked toward him overshadowed by grief. Each sway of her hips represented another second of borrowed time. Raising her arms slowly, she pointed the gun at his head.

"I'm dead you see me standing but I'm dead, just remember this ... YOU ... KILLED ... YOURSELF," she exclaimed.

Casey tried to move her numb legs. She finally gained enough strength to jump in front of Denny. She had to stop this. Even if her life was the price. Besides, this wasn't real. Any minute the cops, Principal Waggenport, or somebody would come in and say this was all a misunderstanding. Leaders were good at putting bandaids on gunshots. Where was everyone?

"This is the police, we have the place surrounded," said officer one.

"Great, here we go the cops, now they wanna try to talk, again, why they always late, security need to tighten up," she said.

"I can't let you kill Denny," she said.

"Oh ... so you love him more than your daughter, why you switch-in out," she said.

"Nah man," he said. He turned and tried to push the double doors open, out of fear. At this point, her trigger finger twitched. He was her last problem. The vein in her head started to pulsate, as she shook. She pointed the gun. "Stop," she exclaimed.

Boom! Boom! The bullets missed her by less than an inch. He was dead. Falling to the ground she held him.

"No more! Who are you, you aren't the girl I knew, where's the Lyric, I knew," she exclaimed.

She sobbed, bitterly.

"The Lyric you knew, disappeared when she heard the words you have AIDS," she said.

"I never thought I would disappoint you, but I guess I did," she said.

Time seemed as if it was going backward. She gazed out in space for about a minute, slowly, she raised her right arm. Click … click … the sound was familiar. She heard them, more than once. Looking at the pool of blood, she realized this was the starting point of the end. She recalled all the times she was told what to do and how it should be done. This was the moment of power she waited for. She was ready to cross the finish line of full control. At this moment, no one could tell her anything.

"Lyric ... no ... what are you doing," she said. She watched as she pointed the gun toward herself.

"I'm doing everyone a favor, goodbye mama," she said.

"We can talk about it, please don't hurt yourself, please ... I'm begging you," she exclaimed. She ran to stop her, but the last round of bullets won the race. Boom! Boom! Boom! "Why ... no ... why ... you're just a baby," she said.

She held Lyric in her arms and rocked back and forth, sitting in the middle of a blood bath. Finally, the police entered and Rye followed them. They pulled Casey away from her tiny lifeless body.

"Oh baby, I thought you were hurt or worse," he said.

"I can't feel my legs, maybe I got shot," she said. She wanted to be full of bullets to spear the pain of waking up to realize this tragedy happened.

"No, sweetheart, you weren't shot, It's okay," he said.

"Hey, we need a stretcher over here," said one of the officers.

She was experiencing an emotional flood. The words of each student, were on instant replay, in her head. When would she stop hearing the screams?

"This just in, police report ten lives were taken in the tragic event, tonight. The names of the victims still have not been released. This is a horrific end to hours of tension. It has been reported the teacher made it out alive; however, all students including the shooter are dead" said Reporter Sight.

As Casey was brought out on a stretcher, she saw bright lights and several people, standing outside the school. Among the chaos, something strange happened.

"Rye, it's Lyric, she's waiving," she said.

"No, sweetheart, you're upset, it's sad she's no longer here, just rest," he said.

"No, I see her," she said.

"It's okay, sweetheart, I'm here, relax, " he said.

"There's the witness, now, excuse me, could you answer a few questions, please," said Reporter Sight.

"Are you kidding me, get away from us," he said. His looks repelled her.

"Unfortunately, the teacher is not available to comment, at this time," she said.

"Here's our city's police chief— Officer Gant could you tell us what happened, I thought everything was under control," she said.

"This was a very disturbed young girl, who came from a distressed home and felt she had no hope, based on recent information she received about her health," he said.

"That's unfortunate, please continue," she said.

"We had the place surrounded but it was tricky, I mean ... she locked the doors, inside and out, we aren't trained snipers," he said.

"Do you think you failed in your attempt to save the victims," she said.

"I mean look ... there was no way to enter the cafeteria or try to negotiate, the shooter made sure, the security guard and the other victims barricaded the doors," he said.

"I see," she said.

"We also went inside to find the connectivity box(for us to communicate with her) was full of bullets," he said.

"This new information is unfortunate," she said.

"It is, what were we supposed to do," he said.

"I'm sure that's the question several people are asking, now, especially the parents of the victims," she said.

"This is such a tragic event. Parents and students are wailing, at the loss of their friends and relatives, how do you suggest we fix this," she said.

"We need more manpower and changes to the system," he said.

"Any idea where the shooter retrieved the gun," she said.

"We don't know, but gun accessibility is a major problem in, several recent shootings," he said.

"Do you have any updates on the name of the victims or the shooter," she said.

"The names of the victims and the shooter will not be released, at this time. All families have been informed of the event, we are happy to report, at least one hostage survived," he said.

"Who would that hostage be," she said.

"Lady, we said no names yet," he said.

"Thanks for the information," she said.

"We will continue to keep you updated, as new information arises, this is Reporter Sight, reporting live, from Max it Out News," she said.

Home Safely

The ride to the hospital seemed surreal. Casey was in a state of shock. "Where are we," she said.

"Finally at the hospital, you passed out," said Rye.

"Was it real, there's blood so much blood," she said.

"Try not to move, ADORATION," he said. The paramedics transported her upstairs. The doctor checked her vitals and she was under observation.

"Rye, what's going on," she said.

"Get some rest," he said. As she tried to close her eyes, she heard a stern familiar voice.

"My sweet monarch," said Mrs. Peinst(Casey's mother). As her parents entered the hospital room, their cheeks were drenched, in tears.

"Hey, M.I.L.," he said.

"How are you F.I.L," he said.

"Fine now that my monarch is safe, not in that rat's nest mess we saw on social media," said Mr. Peinst.

"I hate she had to go through that," said Rye.

"We do too," said the Peinsts.

"Stop talking like I'm not here," she exclaimed.

"We know you're here monarch," she said.

"I'm so sorry for our fight," she said.

"Don't think about any of that," she said. Her mother sat in the hospital bed, cradling her.

"It was so bloody, all I see is blood," she said.

"Shhhh, try to relax," she said.

"Hello Casey, I'm Dr. Morph, I'll be your therapist," she said.

"Hi, I'm not crazy," she said.

"Monarch the doctor knows that," she said.

"I know you're not crazy, this was a traumatic event and it will take time to heal," she said.

"It was bloody, so bloody doctor," she said.

"I know there are things you witnessed, we couldn't fathom," she said.

"All the blood and my sweet Lyric, she was only a freshman, who loved to write," she said.

"Monarch relax and let the doctor speak," she said.

"Should I leave," said Rye.

"Of course not," she said.

"Casey do you grant permission to disclose my recommendation, in front of your parents and husband," she said.

"What … yeah," she said.

"She needs to take a year off of work," she said.

"You mean … take a lifetime off," said Mrs. Peinst.

"ADORATION we need to focus, the doctor has important info," he said.

"Yeah um … go ahead," she said.

"Please sign this disclosure form and I will continue," she said. She wrote two lowercase C's that were barely legible.

"I recommend you take a sabbatical, as a result of the tragedy," she said.

"The kids … The Teacher Switch and the kids," she said.

"Hush love, let her finish, why you want to go back makes no sense to me," she said.

"Actually, may I speak with your husband, outside," she said.

"What about us, we need to know what you recommend," she said.

"Casey, may I speak with Mr. Coper, alone," she said.

"Yes, I'm tired," she said.

As they left the room, her parents scowled.

"Thanks so much, doc., this is what we go through," he said.

"No worries," she said.

"Will she be okay, doc., " he said.

"She thinks she saw the girl who killed those boys and herself," he said.

"Yes, she's suffering from mental aftershocks, also know as Post Traumatic Stress Syndrome," she said.

"I'm somewhat familiar with PTSD, from things I read and my friend serving in the military, what should I expect," he said.

"She may feel depressed, anxious, and want to be alone," she said.

"I'll write some scripts for her,"she said.

"Okay," he said.

"Please avoid loud noises, overcrowding, or leaving her alone for extended periods," she said.

"Thanks," he said.

"You know, I wasn't supposed to be in town, but I'm happy it worked out this way," she said.

"I definitely am," he said.

"She's going to need a therapist, I take her insurance, call me if you need anything," she said.

"Okay, thanks again," he said.

"Also, remember our minds are intricate works of art, the way we think the brain works, can hinder the healing process," she said.

"What does that mean," he said.

"Try to get away from time limits, don't expect she'll be back to normal, in six months," she said.

"Oh … that's unrealistic," he said.

"I know but some people believe it's feasible," she said.

"Anything [including smells, colors/sounds] could trigger her to cry, scream, act violently or not speak," she said.

"I hate what she's going through," he said.

"Reliving clips of insignificant memories, doesn't compare to seeing pools of blood, " she said.

"That's so true," he said.

"She also had a special connection with the shooter, correct," she said.

"Yeah ... I guess ... she would talk about her," he said.

"I also had the chance to meet her, seemed like a sweet girl," he said.

"Was she her student," she said?

"Come to think of it, she told me the girl Lyric was freshman," he said.

"I wonder how they made a connection," she said.

"Um ... something about a group ... it was a club," he said.

"Her classes had juniors that I know," he said.

"We'll discuss it, once she gets stronger, in therapy," she said.

"Try to limit her social media usage and if possible, she needs rest, without her phone," she said.

"She's attached to it," he said.

"Okay, you'll be taking care of her, so ... please limit the phone usage," she said.

"Here's a doctor's note, mandating she not return to school for the remainder of the year," she said.

"Perfect, her long needed rest, is the silver lining to this horrible cloud," he said.

"Here are some prescriptions for her to stay calm and lessen anxiety," she said.

"Why does she keep saying the same things, over and over," he said.

"Repetition to rationalize is what you're witnessing," she said.

"Oh ... is that normal, what do I say," he said.

"Sometimes you can disregard comments that make no sense, she's thinking out loud," she said.

"I keep saying the situation wasn't her fault," he said.

"That was my other suggestion, she needs positive reassurance," she said.

"Okay," he said.

"Whenever a witness to a crime or veteran feels they had control and could've acted differently, they relive the moment, several times," she said.

"Sounds like torture," he said.

"It is, that's why she keeps shaking and can barely function," she said.

"The situation is so hard, I need to be strong for her ... for us," he said.

"You're so supportive, that reminds me ... here's another script for sleeping pills," she said.

"Is it safe for her to take all of this," he said.

"Yes, I'm a therapist, trust me," she said.

"Also, a side note, her parents don't mean to be hurtful, they are just controlling," she said.

"Tell me something, I don't know," he said.

"So, don't take anything personally, work as a unit to help your wife," she said.

"You're right, I'll push my feelings to the side and focus," he said.

"She will need one caretaker, not three, I'll tell your in-laws if you want," she said.

"Sounds good, although I'm happy about your recommendation, why can't her parents stay," he said.

"She already feels out of control, having people around to undermine everything, will hinder the healing process," she said.

"That makes sense," he said.

"Her parents are welcome to call but they'll need to step back and allow her to feel a sense of control, no matter how small it is," she said.

"Thanks so much for your help," he said.

"No worries, I need to run, she opted out of staying the night for observation," she said.

"Yeah, she did," he said.

"Again, keep a close eye on her," she said.

"One more thing, before you go," he said.

"Go ahead, quickly please," she said.

"I know there'll be a service for the victims, she's going no matter what I say, what do you recommend," he said.

"I wouldn't recommend she go to the service, it could cause her emotional wounds to deepen," she said.

"How will I stop her," he said.

"Monitor her phone and block correspondence, regarding the incident on social media," she said.

"That won't be easy but I'll try," he said.

"I need to run," she said.

"Thanks, doc.," he said.

Before Dr. Morph left, she called Casey's parents, outside and let them know the plan. Since her parents did not want to hinder the healing process, they adhered to the doctor's request.

Bloody Flashbacks

Rye drove slowly, as she was in a state of shock. She kept repeating the same words, "Why did she do this," she said.

Finally, they were home, when he parked the car, she started screaming. He ran and held her, tightly.

"Baby, it's okay," he said.

She was triggered by the door slamming. The doctors said certain sounds could bring her back to the shooting scene. As a result, she could not walk. Rye had to pick her up and take her inside the house. Slowly, he walked her upstairs and laid her down on the bed.

She kept saying the same words, over and over. He was deeply disturbed to see her, in this state. Whatever the cost, he signed up for richer or poorer, through sickness and health, as long as they lived. This was not the time to default on marriage vows. She was his one true love. Since she wouldn't be herself for a while, he had to be her strength, during the aftereffects of this unbelievable event.

Thankfully, he had the support of her family.

That night Casey woke up, screaming to God, why this horrid thing, happened.

"ADORATION, I'm here," he said.

"Why ... why did this happen, there's blood, everywhere, look down," she said. He listened to make her feel better.

"It won't be better," she said.

"Yes, it'll," he said. Gently, he placed her on the couch and went for a glass of water.

"Please drink this," he said.

Her hands were clammy and no matter how much water she drank, her thirst was not quenched.

She searched for solidarity, in the depths of her soul but found none. The pain gnawed away at her emotions. Sometimes in suicide, blood baths, and unanswered questions, emotions get rewired. Fear of circumstances only get worse can paralyze the potential to change.

The next morning, Casey woke up, in shock. She remained this way for a while. Rye took time off from work to take care of her. She couldn't eat or sleep, peacefully. She just wanted to get answers. If Lyric never went to the doctor, this would not have happened. She tried to outrun the thoughts in her mind but they were winning the race. He took her phone, due to the nonstop text messages and Dr. Morph's recommendation. He replied to each one and thanked her coworkers, friends, and family for their concern. While scrolling down, he saw a picture of the flyer for the memorial service. It was one week away. He followed the doctor's orders and hid her communication lifeline. After a few days of silence she started to repeat the same words, again. He kept in contact with her therapist, who assured him, the pattern of behavior was normal.

"I'm going in the shower, sweetheart," I won't be long," he said.

Laying in the fetal position, she nodded. Five minutes later, she decided to check her phone. This time he forgot to take it with him. It was on silent.After entering her passcode, she did not see any notifications, from work or her friends. It was odd. She went to her settings and saw several numbers on mute. Quickly, she changed the setting and saw a slew of text messages and emails. One message stood out, from the rest.

"Rye …" she exclaimed.

Quickly, he ran out of the shower.

"You okay, what's wrong sweetheart," he said.

"How could you," she said. She turned to show him the message.

"I didn't know if you could handle it," he said.

"I need to go," she said. She sobbed intensely, as he held her.

"Right now you're sensitive to everything," he said.

"She needs a voice, she can't die for nothing," she said.

"We'll go if it'll help," he whispered.

"Those families need to know, their kids matter to me," she said. She yearned to bring everyone, back to life.

"My minds made up, it's the only way, besides prayer to have peace," she said.

"Whatever you need, I'm here to support you," he said.

As despair clouded her pupils. He wondered if she would ever heal.

"It was horrible. I can still smell the gun smoke … blood … panic, and fear," she said.

"Try not to think about it," he said.

"You keep saying that, these texts say that, it makes no sense," she said.

"Please calm down," he said.

"When I breathe, it smells like blood and fear," she said.

"Fear can't have a smell," he said.

"I'm not debating this, it goes, along with torment, hatred, and anxiety, they smell rancid," she said.

He wanted to kick himself. Why in the world, did he forget to take her phone, in the bathroom?

"The sweet Lyric I knew, was substituted by a monster, she checked out," she said.

"You did your best, it's not your fault, none of it," he said.

"It was like trying to reason with the gun she was holding, she wasn't there," she said.

"I should've read the signs when she left my car," she said.

"What she needed was beyond what you could give," he said.

"Why didn't I say the right things," she said.

"You're coming down, hard on yourself, she was a girl with so many problems," he said.

Her soul breached. This was a significant loss. She hoped the night terrors, lack of appetite, depression, and shock would stop running a relay race, in her mind. No matter what anyone said, it would not bring back the person, who touched her life, significantly. Rye prayed she would start to heal. Would she ever go back to functioning in a normal way? He wondered if the upcoming memorial service would provide closure or add salt to her open wounds.

Ten
Sad Endings *Should* Strike Change

Once again, Casey Coper found herself dazed, sitting next to a podium, only this was no graduation. The result of the unforeseen shooting at The Best High School drew a large crowd of news stations, anti-gun protesters, students, teachers, principals, superintendents, mental health professionals, and police officers gathered together, in pain, shock and disbelief. The air was filled with bloodstained torment. There were pictures of each victim, along with large clear bins for memorabilia/flowers to be placed on the platform.

"Case.," said a familiar voice.

"Hey," she said.

"How are you," she said. Her friend sat in disbelief. Casey's face was drained, she looked frazzled and Ava did not recognize her.

"Hey Rye," she said.

"Ava," he said.

"I tried to text but—she decided not to elaborate since Rye's eyes triggered a warning cue.

"These are yours," she said. There was a beautiful bouquet, in her right hand.

"Oh … thanks," she said.

"You okay ADORATION," said Rye.

"Yes," she said.

As she attempted to get up, her legs wobbled.

Slowly, Casey placed the flowers in front of Lyric's picture.

"I … I … don't know what to say … well—don't say anything, she taught me that," Casey interjected.

"Who," she said. Quickly, she started gazing, again.

"Right, I'm here, I'm here if you need me," said Ava.

"Let me get to my seat, they're about to start, I think," she said.

"Nice seeing you, again and call/text me, anytime," she said.

"Okay," she said. As she walked off, Rye rolled his eyes and pulled his wife, close.

"Welcome. My name is Superintendent Ray. The shooting that took place at the Best High School, impacted each one of us. I am deeply disturbed by all of the acts of violence, over the past few months. The misuse of guns, lack of security, and mental health services are huge issues, throughout various states. We are working on policies to address these issues. The past couple of months were filled with written and verbal concerns, made by parents teachers, and students regarding the issues. I would like to inform you, we will address all concerns, at our next school forum meeting, after the service. I see hundreds of people either for or against gun policy changes. I'm sure both sides would agree, saving lives should not be protested against. The purpose of today's service is to remember the cherished lives that were lost. Today is not the day for violence or threats. Please make sure, you show a high level of respect to the people who plan on speaking. These families will never get the opportunity to see their loved ones, alive again. Robbing their moment of expression would be an act of cruelty. I do ask out of respect for everyone, we do not use foul language. We also have a one-minute moment of silence for each victim. I'll now ask Principal Waggenport to approach the podium; he'll be moderating the event, Thank you," he said.

"Thank you, Superintendent Ray. This was a tragedy. Certain words get lost in the pain. We must maintain composure and look forward to brighter days. That's what the school therapist says. I can't believe the shooting happened. Our thoughts and prayers are with each family, who lost irreplaceable people, in their lives. I want to apologize to any student, who feels like not addressing issues, is the answer. Mental health is so important. We may not see our brains, physically but without them, it is impossible to function. If you or anyone you know, is suffering from issues, please see our guidance counselor or social worker. There are support helplines for students and their parents. You're not alone," he said.

We will start the memorial service by inviting the uncle of Sanrell to speak," he said.

Tears streamed down Mr. Krill's face like an ocean. Slowly, he approached the microphone.

"My name is Mr. S. I had the privilege of helping to raise one of the sweetest boys on the planet, Sanrell(Stilts). Y'all knew him, as a great basketball player. He was more than how he played on the court," he said.

His voice started to crack. Tears were streaming down his face. This was not a good place to be. It felt distant and cold. The moments that formed a strong bond, between him and Stilts were gone.

"He was funny, smart, and very caring. My baby used to help out with the boys in the neighborhood, who ain't have nobody. Every Sunday he would be down at the park, telling the boys, they could make it, helping with their jump shot, and reminding them dreams do come true. Our family will miss one of the best shining stars that returned to the sky. Y'all leave the guns, alone. What you doin with guns, anyway? If you know anyone who ain't think-in straight and needs help, please tell someone. Our community thinks there is shame in seeing someone like a therapist. Ain't no shame in making sure your head is in good health. Thank you."

As the crowd applauded, he approached his hurting family. The painful look in Sanrell's family's eyes was unbearable. Casey had to face the other way.

"Thank you, Mr. S., your son was an amazing person. He will never be forgotten," he said.

"Next to speak will be Ms. S., the mother of Spenez," he said.

Ms. S. was so distraught she needed two family members to walk her to the podium. "My son Spenez(Swoon) is dead. My sweet, caring baby ain't com-in back. I want y'all to understand he in the grave, now. When y'all decide to buy a handgun off the street, think-in you got self-control when you get mad over stupidity, just remember my face. I can't stop crying and the most comfortable place I knew was in my son's arms. He's gone!" She could not finish speaking. She had to sit down.

Principal Waggenport approached the family, distraught.

"Hey, this is too much for you right now, have a seat, I got this, from here," she said.

"Okay, thanks, this is a lot," he said.

"Hello everyone, my name is Ms. Sledna, I'm an assistant principal. I'll be taking over, from here," she said.

"It takes a true leader to take initiative, during such a challenging time. Thanks so much for sharing such profound words, regarding Spenez. They were so touching, he is missed," she said.

"Rimez's aunt will now say a few words, in memory of her nephew," she said.

"Hello, my name is Ms. R. I am the aunt of Rimez(Rat). He was a very active and smart boy who loved our hometown, Jamaica. He was always wearing belts with Jamaican colors and telling everyone, how wonderful the island is. He was a very kind person. Since I work two jobs it was hard for me to attend to him, the way I would have liked but we made it work. He was an excellent cook and kept the house clean. I'll miss my nephew," she said.

She appeared to be in a state of shock. Casey looked at her face and started balling.

"Again, we are so sorry for your loss. A good number of us knew, how proud Rimez was of where he came from. He will be missed," she said.

"Next is Lanson's mother, Ms. L.," she said.

She could barely wait for him to move, from the microphone.

"Hello, I was Lanson's mom. You kids called him (Lakes). My son was my life. Slowly, she took a deep breath. Is all this violence worth it? How in the world, can we reason with anyone, from the grave? If you have a problem with yourself, please get professional help. Nothing is wrong with finding someone trained to talk to. Picking up a gun and shooting them doesn't make it go away. You swear the problem is the person but it's not. The problem is within you. You know why? If someone makes you mad-you try to hurt them because that's how you think it'll solve your issues. Guess what, you're wrong. I'm so hurt my baby won't be coming home. Look, I know what my son did. He was no angel but he loved his mother and always looked out for his little brother. Saying I'll miss him is an understatement. That's all I have to say," she said.

She walked back to her seat, enraged and distraught, as the audience clapped.

"Thank you, Lanson touched so many lives," she said.

"You mean infected the lives of so many," said a voice from the crowd. Quickly, she approached the microphone.

"May I remind you of the superintendent's request. Let's be mindful of the feelings of others," she said. The crowd fell silent.

"Mr. N. the father of Nazaire(Zaire), will now share a meaningful speech, regarding his son," she said. The crowd watched, as he wobbled to the podium. The bloodshot veins in his eyes attested to the four bottles of hard liquor, he ingested—before the service.

"My name is Naz …. Naz … Naz …(Nazaire) was one of the best kids who thank me and you all the time. He play for everybody and knew not to do wrong. We love him. Thank you," he said.

Although his speech was confusing the crowd understood, what he was trying to say. As he passed, Ms. Sledna looked deeply disturbed. Alcohol fumes were emanating from his breath.

"Um ... next to speak on behalf of Denny is his mother, Ms. D. Please proceed," she said.

"Denny(DenJ) was my star who was always singing or rapping. My boy lost his daddy at two. It was hard at first but we pulled through it. That boy loved to focus on sunshine. I don't know, where he got it—cause I'm not a positive person, most of the time but he was. He loved the new teacher, Mrs. C.," she said.

Rye comforted Casey as she continued to cry, after her statement.

"Denny had that natural spark that would brighten up the darkest situation. We were evicted one time and I almost lost my mind. He stayed happy and kept saying "ma, we will get an even bigger and better place and you ain't gonna know, what to do with all the space we gonna have. He was right," she said. The memories of Denny's first day of kindergarten, his middle school ceremony, and prom caused her intonation to rise and fall. Tears streaked down her face, in anguish. My baby ain't here to shine, no more cause of this security problem. Why y'all can't get enough people to help with this. These babies are too young to be gettin buried. They went from suckin on a bottle to the grave. This ain't right. We need to do someth-in in," she said. As she walked to her seat, the crowd applauded.

"Thank you for special words; Denny will always be missed.

" I would like to invite Mr. D. to say a few words, in memory of his son Deider," she said.

"Hello, my name is Mr. D., my son you know as Do, we raised Deider, will always be a very special boy. He did so much for everybody. That boy never said no. He was always tallying up girls—he was wit. I gotta tell you, after reading the crazy message on my phone and knowing it was the truth, none of y'all better be have-in sex unless you are ready for what comes with it. Protection is the best policy. I love my boy and always will, he just thought actin like a player was cool. Guess what, it ain't. We got press here and so many of y'all are listening. When you have people's attention, you gotta say someth-in that counts. I gotta keep it real. I'm a single dad of three boys who would trade my life for Do, in a second but that ain't an option. My boy had H.I.V., he's gone. We're here. Protect your hearts, minds, and souls from hurt. Remember, my boy paid the price for it. I know this probably ain't the norm but I have never been normal. I will always miss my boy who tried to be a grown man," he said.

"Thanks, Mr. D. Your son was cherished by us all. Next, we have Mrs. G., Garnell's mother, who will share a few words, regarding her son," she said.

"Good afternoon, my name is Mrs. G. Let me tell you about Garnell(Greater), he joked around, so much and found the punchline, in everything. He wanted to be an artist and professional ballplayer and everything else. He would always say, "Whatever you think you great at, I'm GREATER." She paused and held her head down. I can't do this," she said.

Quickly, she sat down as her husband(Mr. G.) approached the microphone.

"I would apologize on my wife's behalf but it makes no sense. Who apologizes for feeling distraught their son is gone? Anyway, Greater was such a special boy. He was a natural comedian, who liked to prank, everybody. When we saw the news, it was crazy. The police visit was even crazier. We kept waiting for our boy to jump out and say, "Pop, I was mess-in with you" but those words will never come until we get to Heaven. No shade to Officer Gant or the police force, we respect y'all but you said, " We have everything under control." You wanted to but didn't. If you did, all them boys would be alive. We watched and waited for the news update, live and in person, outside the school, it was torment. That sick girl needed help. Now, our boy and others, ain't never com-in back. He's tellin angel's jokes, in the sky. We'll never forget his one-of-a-kind personality and ability to make anyone laugh. We love our boy and something in this system needs to change. Thank you," he said.

"That was very touching. Garnell was such a sweet and kind boy, he will be missed," she said.

"We will now hear the words of Ms. A.," Anfel's mom," she said.

She approached the podium with anguish in her eyes. She was on a mission to change the perspective of the audience.

"I would like to share a poem, written for my son. He was a poet and a very sweet boy. I'll be releasing his book of poems, soon. He got poetry writing, from his mama."

I Ask Myself ... Why?

"Why oh why, did my son have to die?
Why do we let the cause of death wave and pass us by?
How do you know, your son won't be gunned down for fun?
When will the horrible policies be addressed and killings be done?
I can't lie ... the more time passes by
I ask myself why.
Why can't you set good policies in place?
Why does death continue to laugh in our face?
This mass shooting is the outcome of a horrible lie.
The lie of acting that we care, while others die.
Truth be told we can't care,
There are too many indifferent faces, everywhere!
I will continue to ask the question why,
Why did my wonderful son Anfel have to die?
In the meantime why won't take the place of how?
How you and I will help change the perspective of mental health here and now.
We can't let these eleven lives go,
Or the several other lives that counted, oh no!

We must fight before things remain the same,
If they do, we only have ourselves to blame.
Thank you," she said.

After hearing her poem, several people from the crowd stood up and cheered. Casey's tears formulated into dried-out streaks resembling two chalk marks on her face. She stood up and clapped, intensely.

"Go, Ms. A., Go, Ms. A. ... Go, Ms. A.," cheered the crowd. We will miss your talented son and deeply appreciate your heartfelt poem," she said.

"Next, we have Miken's sister who will share, a few words, in his memory," she said.

"My name's Treasure. I had such a wonderful and talented brother Miken(Money). I suffer from chronic panic attacks," she said.

She recalled the last time her lungs felt as if they would implode. The thought of her brother not running to help her, anymore was a lot to process. Memories of him fixing cups of water and consoling her—saturated every word. Streams of tears ran down her face.

"Like I was saying... I suffer from chronic panic attacks. My brother was very special. He used to press my hand and the attacks would go away. We need better gun violence regulation because the laws we have aren't working. The crowd began to yell and certain people started to get riled up."

She approached the podium and whispered in her ear.

"No, I won't save my comments for later, she said. We need better security and gun laws. One security guard for thousands of kids is crazy. Maybe if y'all would stop being so cheap, we could stop the horror stories. We deserve the same security as rich kids on the other side of town. I can't turn my back, anymore. How's my brother supposed to keep me grounded, from under the ground? Do something! That's all I have to say," she said.

"Okay, thank you, let's calm down, " she said. Several people from the crowd cheered and wanted her to keep talking, but Ms. Sledna had to cut her off. No one wanted a riot.

"Next to speak is Mrs. Coper," she said.

"My name is Mrs. Coper ... umm ... Casey Coper. Her roof stuck to the hole of her mouth. Rye stood next to her—helping her not to sway.

"Yeah ... I teach juniors, at The Best High School. All of the victims were my students, except one. They were amazing. I started the year, teaching fourth grade, at an elementary school. The Best High School is a new venture for me that started about four months ago. Mr. Wu(my former student's teacher) and I, decided to participate in The Teacher Switch. The purpose was to gain knowledge of teaching another level, we were not familiar with. This was the result of educators not being able to get on the same page, regarding funding, after the protest we took part in."

"Um ... it's ... so ..." her hands were balled up. She looked drained.

"Sweetheart can you handle this," whispered Rye.

"No but that doesn't matter," she said.

"Educators were protesting for N.F.L. Salary matches, a change in security policies, and expansion of mental health funding and changes of ineffective strategies not beneficial for educators, students or parents. On air, we embarrassed ourselves by arguing over pertinent changes that should have taken place, immediately. I would like to apologize. Time is crucial; we couldn't afford to prolong decisions. Out of my experience this year, eleven lives were touched. After listening to details from each parent/caretaker who knew their child, I was taken back. It's evident the gifts and talents each student had, was inherited and didn't go unnoticed. Fortunately, through teaching, I got to know, the victims on a deep level.

Each student who lost their life deposited memories in my heart that will never be forgotten. Here are some memories I shared with them. One day, Spenez asked me to go to the restroom. Before I called for security to escort him, he asked me to babysit. Naturally, I asked, babysit who? He said to babysit his basketball. He was quiet but a joker. His silence spoke volumes, during every moment, in class. My baby lived by positive actions. Although he made some mistakes, he would always turn things around."

"Miken was so sweet. His future was promising. He was so tall and a great basketball player. He would always joke around, about my high heels.

"Deider was such a champion. Despite bad situations, he always saw the positive, in everything and tried to help everyone hence his nickname "Do." I remember the first day of class, I asked him why his nickname was "Do" he replied, cause, ever since I was little, every one be ask-in me to do everything. All I hear is Deider do this and Deider do that so I ended up with the nickname Do. He said I'm a proud Do Boy, miss. I never heard anything like that, before. My life ain't all about me, it's about helping other people. This made me marvel. Denny loved music and was inclined to make a song about everything—music, food, and different life experiences. He played three instruments and loved to draw. Sometimes, in the middle of class, he would sketch a picture of me. Although I was tempted to get upset, he would flash that zillion-dollar smile that would melt my heart. He would say, you a good act to follow, miss," she said.

She held her head down and paused for a few minutes. Her husband rubbed her back.

"Excuse, me, give me a second," she said. Her throat was dry. As she envisioned his face, another tear fell—from her cheek.

"Adoration are you sure, you want to finish," whispered Rye.

"Yes, I'm fine," she said. Quickly, gathered herself and returned to the podium.

"Rimez was a lively student who was rough around the edges. Which one of us isn't? He was a hardcore Jamaican, who wore a Jamaican Flag Belt, all the time. He would tell me interesting stories, about yard which's a Jamaican term, meaning home. I never understood, his nickname but it isn't important.

Rye continued to rub her back. Her voice started to crack, from sobbing. She could not take a break, no matter how much she wanted to. The words needed to come out.

"Here's a story, about Lanson, Nazaire, Sanrell, Garnell, and I. One day, we had Eat N' Express. This was a privilege, students earned who accumulate points for trying their best, in my class. They came back to the room with me, watch a movie/listen to music, eat takeout and talk about things we can't cover, during class. I asked the boys what they believed they would be doing if they dropped out of school. After thinking about it for a while, Lanson said, "I would probably be in jail, like some of my homeboys." That's why I try so hard, here to be better. Nazaire, Garnell, and Sanrell said, they would be selling drugs and guns. When I asked how they would get guns, they said Mrs. C. are you serious? We can walk down the street and get a gun, easy. It ain't how to get a gun, it's when. Some of us need protection, in my neighborhood. I asked the boys why they didn't feel protected and they replied, Mrs. C. you don't feel protected, we protect you."

Some students were planning on disrespecting me, and they intervened. I'll never forget that. Every student has a voice and needs to be heard. What could I say, regarding security? The students were right. It remains a major problem. We need to implement effective strategies that wouldn't just provide some phony sense of security. Next, the gun usage comment was addressed. I explained, if they knew of anyone selling guns on the street, it needs to be reported, right away. One less unlicensed gun will impact the community, in a major way. We spoke about gun regulation and how so many innocent lives are taken, as a result of gun misuse. We all agreed that security needed to "tighten up."

"The students wanted to know, how to stand up for their rights, without getting violent. I explained the first step to truly standing up for peace is establishing an action plan.

"Anfel was a special student. He was a talented rapper. During my time teaching at The Best High School, I learned to appreciate all students. Each moment provided hidden access to a student's potential. He was very caring and always asked if I was okay. She was at an emotional pinnacle, after a brief moment, she continued."

"He had such an inspirational smile that could cheer the saddest person up. He would constantly write song lyrics and poetry, in class. I'll miss him, a lot. Although she wasn't my student, I want you to practice empathizing with someone who is not popular. This student impacted the lives of several students. She led Friendmanship—a writing support group, at The Best High School. Despite what you saw on the news, I refer to Lyric, as an angel," she said.

"Angel! You mean devil—Lyric wasn't no angel," said a familiar voice.

"Excuse me, please hold your comments," she said.

"I ain't hold-in noth-in, they go the cops they could check," said Dawn.

This was such an embarrassment. Two officers told Dawn if she did not quiet down—she would have to leave.

"I ain't gettin quiet and I ain't leavin," she said.

"She best tell the truth, how that girl was a neighborhood mattress.

I was a great mama that cared and turned into an H.I.V. Havin ...—-liar!" she interjected.

"Sweetheart stop," said Rye.

"You're a liar. That's why she gave up you sick psychopath," she exclaimed.

"That's enough! Calm down," Ms. Sledna. Memories of what Lyric shared at the coffee shop, low self-esteem, and the initial meeting(in the restroom) triggered dizziness. Rye knew that look. She made the same face—after her fertility treatment. In an instant—he ran to get a garbage can—right before she threw up.

"Casey, you don't need to finish, you just vomited," she said.

"No, I'm not done," she said.

"See ... you sick think-in bout that killa," she said.

"Let me remind you—no interruptions or you will be removed," she said.

"Shut up," she said.

"Officers please remove the woman in the back," she said.

As the police removed Dawn, she was screaming, at the top of her lungs.

"Oh you takin orders from her, who's she, I'm Lyric's mama," she exclaimed.

"Okay Miss, settle down," said the officers.

"You goin see me, again you in the field—I'm in the house—-slave—I'm too good for this room," she said.

Members of the crowd were disgusted.

"My apologies, there was a look of sadness on her face. Lyric was at a disadvantage since childhood. Maybe if she had the right opportunities, she would have handled things differently."

"Are you okay to continue, sweetheart," he whispered

"Yeah, I'm fine," she whispered.

She took a deep breath and nodded her head. She was on a mission and no one was going to interrupt her.

"I apologize. As I was saying, we need to take safety measures against people who fire verbal, emotional, and sexual bullets. When these people release deadly ammunition—it harms the potential of others. Lyric couldn't handle finding out, detrimental news. She had a lot of issues, no teenager should go through.

We need the funds to get all hands on deck, regarding emotional support. She was a special girl who had a hard life and little to no guidance. Everyone who claimed they would help her was a letdown. According to Lyric, I was the realist person she knew. I don't believe she intended to hurt anyone.

"What are we going to do about the safety laws? Should we all turn our heads—and act as if this misguided soul who claimed the lives of several young people and herself didn't exist? Certain students led down this path can handle tragic news, others aren't fortunate to have proper guidance and support when their lives are considered over. We need to increase support in the school system, from mental health specialists. This is one of many horrific occurrences that should shift our requests to demands."

"Song lyrics have the potential to reach into the soul and turn feelings inside out. She had this capability. Over time, I realized humans are constantly evolving, and to sum up, a person is a social detriment, this was a revelation from Lyric. She treated writing with grace and delicacy. That beautiful young soul had a crushed potential. We'll never know, her contribution to the world, since she died with so many unwrapped gifts, inside of her. I don't condone her actions. If she didn't shoot your children, they would be alive. I'll say ... she had a horrific upbringing. Some of you may not consider her as a victim—-I get it. According to the news—-she was the villain. Please understand they have a story to tell. It's a blessing to have anyone genuinely care about your well-being. We don't recognize support as a foreign concept, since people don't usually let blessings set in.

Please go to the meeting after the service. Thank you," she said.

After her speech, the crowd gave her a standing ovation. She left them with so much to think about. At that moment, she made an internal pact to never let the memory of Lyric die.

The Final Decision

The time for the forum meeting was here. Emotions were heightened and everyone united to make a difference. Ms. Zebedee decided to address concerns, at the forum meeting on behalf of herself and several others. Her speech went as follows:

"We waited. The wait had its benefits but the tragedy that emerged as a result of us not getting on the same page on time—-can never be undone. We need all final votes, regarding new policies and funding, today. Some of you never lost anyone close that doesn't warrant indifferent actions. Several families lost children, due to gun violence and security issues. The losses will continue unless we have people, willing to stand up for change. One hundred lives are too many. Let's not treat these students as if their lives were insignificant."

"Tragically, Lyric Casanova took her life and the lives of ten others. She was a very intelligent, caring, and innovative girl that wasn't given an equal opportunity to thrive. I believe the lesson from this tragedy is—you should never leave any aspect of who you are, unprotected. As a result of her decisions, she contracted H.I.V. that later morphed into AIDS. In her words, she was already dead. I want to shed light on this disease and let you know, even if you have three months to live, your remaining time should be cherished. Life is not over if you contract H.I.V. Emotionally, she was unprotected that's where the danger began. If you feel the same way, your self-worth doesn't exist. This doesn't excuse her behavior but if she had the help of counselors, it would have provided an additional outlet. Mr. Wu is a high school teacher who decided to participate, in the first official Teacher Switch. He and Casey learned the challenges educators face, at different levels, from the experience. I think we can all agree, increasing funding for security takes precedence over everything, else. Mr. Veftel wasn't to blame for this horrific event. We allowed selfishness to cloud our judgment. How dare we put security policies on hold, because our paycheck increases were not the same. We were supposed to make fifteen grand, all of a sudden the proposition of millions of dollars was not enough. How dare we complain. This only proves the financial increase with the wrong mentality, is non-beneficial."

"We will continue to feel the impact of those who left us due to crime if we don't kill the site of emotional cancer at its root. We learn cute acronyms reciting them to students when we feel like it but do we take the time out for true implementation? Certain educators are emotionally indifferent. How can we expect students to care about our initiatives, if we don't?"

"Perfection is no one's strong suit, we need to stop, pointing the finger, and take accountability for our actions. That is the first step to change. Gun regulation and cracks in mental health are two ferocious beasts, we need to slay. The voice of each one of the students who died tragically continues to echo, in my heart and the hearts of their loved ones. We'll never forget, each victim's kind gestures, jokes, and actions. To honor their memory. We need to ensure policies are changed and adopt an unselfish mentality. Who's with me on striking a change," said Ms. Zebedee. The crowd started cheering and everyone was handed iPads to vote in favor of or against the new policies.

The proposed policies were:

1.) All schools will have active security cameras with monitors.

2.) All schools will review security measures and procedures, in an innovative and fun way.

3.) All schools will maintain open communication with administrators, regarding possible threats/violent acts that may occur.

4.) All schools will be required to have metal detectors.

5.) All schools will have a one-way entry and exit.

6.) All schools will ensure security equipment is in working condition, daily.

7.) All schools will ensure students have the opportunity to voice their opinion.

8.) All schools will provide a way for students to inform personnel of possible harm their peer/s may carry out. The identity of students who provide the warning will remain confidential.

9.) All schools will carry out an extensive investigation to ensure Possible Harm Reports are valid.

10.) All schools will implement a No Tolerance Policy, regarding all forms of bullying.

11.) All educators who participate in each safety training, monthly will receive a one thousand dollar bonus, yearly.

12.) All teachers and students who implement safety procedures accurately will receive a five thousand dollar award for their school.

13.) All schools will provide positive reinforcement for every student, teacher/parent without it's not my problem mentality. The evidence provided will be rewarded and recognized by the superintendent of each district.

14.) All schools will have Security Resource Officers, full-time on campus. The numbers will be based on enrollment.

15.) All schools will pay everyone, helping to ensure students are safe, a yearly bonus for every safety measure implemented and proven effective.

16.) All schools will hire several individuals, specialized in mental health to check in, track and update administration and security personnel, regarding potential threats.

17,) All schools will implement a no-tolerance policy, regarding threats that include but are not limited to: threatening to harm another individual/their school

18.) All schools are required to have safety meetings both in the house and open to the public. Public safety information will be disseminated, at all Parent Awareness Meetings.

19.) All schools will hold safety and anti-violence training, monthly.

20.) All schools will implement strategies to reward students for making positive choices, despite what demographic the school is located in.

21.) All schools will implement a school-wide nonviolence plan that will correlate to the specified struggles of the population.

22.) All schools will implement the district's unified nonviolence plan and integrate aspects of it, during lessons, speeches, and activities. Teachers, students, and parents who prove the implementation of the plan will be rewarded.

23.) All salary increases contributed by stakeholders, as a result of the protest, will be equalized, bonuses and additional earnings are not included.

Casey ran to hug her.

"I told you, we would strike a change," she said.

"You did and we did, this feels amazing," said Casey.

Although this story is Realistic Fiction, aligns with events that took place. Readers must react! Change is not limited to the people, in this story. We lost several lives, due to people neglecting mental health relevance and gun violence, throughout the United States. This raw reality will always be with us. The question is ... where do you stand? Casey, Ms. Zebedee, and the protestors were not afraid to step on toes. Fight for things to change until they do. We are more than complaints without action. Motiv'Plication was written to help crush complacency. Please do your part to end mental health stigmatization and gun violence. We must press through, despite opposition. Never forget to **KEEP UP THE MOTIV'PLICATION! CHAMPIONS LIVE FOR CHALLENGES!**

Time to Reflect
Chapter One
Setting the Stage

Leaders

1.) What would you do to help support your staff, fight against the budget cuts?

2.) If you could make up an alternate chapter ending, what would it entail?

3.) Who was the strongest leader, in the chapter? Justify your response.

4.) Would Ms. Zebedee's method work, in your district? Why/why not?

5.) Which leadership style would you utilize, during a protest to eliminate fund displacement?

Teachers

1.) Compare/contrast your first-year teaching experience to Casey's experience.

2.) What aspects of Ms. Motivation's speech could you relate to? Why?

3.) If you worked with Casey, how would you help her?

4.) Analyze Casey's graduation speech and write the top three relatable points.

5.) Compare/contrast your teaching experiences to Caseys. Why are these experiences relatable?

6.) Was Ava concerned or negative? Explain your response.

Students

1.) What new details did you learn, about the teaching profession?

2.) Create a play, with an alternate ending for chapter one.

3.) Write a motivational speech, by using at least two reading skills.

4.) Write an Informative Essay on protesting and how you could protest, in a peaceful way.

5.) What was Ms. Zebedee fighting for and why was it so important?

Chapter Two
Teachers Aren't Bleachers

Leaders

1.) Compare and contrast the role of principal vs. assistant principal, in the game of education.

2.) In contrast to Ms. Zebedee's approach to resolving the issue, at the protest, if you were in her place, how would you handle it?

3.) What leadership skills/strategies would you utilize to organize the protest.

4.) Would you support The Teacher Switch, from a leadership standpoint? If so, provide examples of how the switch could benefit your staff, students, and parents.

5.) How would the mission and vision of your school, align with aspects of chapter two?

6.) Would you alter the football positions/roles? If so, how?

Teachers

1.) Did the assertion of the protestors help you feel courageous to take a stand for what is right? If so, how?

2.) Do you feel the teacher's demand for more funds, was reasonable, why?

3.) Write a reason/s you would want to participate, in The Teacher Switch.

4.) What was the most relatable aspect of Ms. Motivation's speech?

5.) Identify three ways to contribute to the healthy emotional climate of your school.

6.) Interpret the slogan "Teachers Aren't Bleachers."

7.) What position do you play, in the game of education?

Students

1.) What new information did you learn about Casey, in this chapter?

2.) Would you want to be Casey's student? Why/why not?

3.) Would you support educators by attending the protest? Justify your response.

4.) If you had to organize a protest, how would you try to change policies, peacefully?

5.) Compare/contrast issues of middle/high school/elementary teachers.

6.) Why is mental health important?

7.) When was a time you hit your lowest point, mentally? How did you cope with the outcome?

Chapter Three
The Switch

Leaders

1.) What steps would you take to ensure a divide between teachers, would not occur?

2.) Did lesson one demonstrate Casey's leadership skills? If so, what skills did she display?

3.) Discuss three of the most important aspects of chapter three that impacted you, as a leader.

4.) Use the aspects from question three and correlate them to your school's mission and vision.

5.) What suggestions would you provide Mr. Wu with, as a leader of We Will Thrive Elementary School, regarding The Teacher Switch?

Teachers

1.) Compare and contrast Mr. Wu and Casey's Teacher Switch Experiences.

2.) What obstacles(not stated in this chapter) do primary and intermediate teachers face?

3.) Which school would you prefer to teach in, We Will Thrive Elementary or The Best High School? Provide five details based on your answer.

4.) Do you think the way Mrs. Coper handled the fighting incident, was effective? Why/why not?

5.) Compare and contrast your roles of choice, from the NFL teacher correlation.

Students

1.) Write an Expository Essay on which teacher you would prefer to have, based on the information, from this chapter and why.

2.) Write three-five questions and answers, about the chapter.

3.) Compare and contrast your introduction to one of the characters from this chapter.

4.) What would you do, if a fight like the one from the chapter, happened in your class?

5.) Would you want Mrs. Batet, as a teacher? Explain your answer.

Chapter Four
Two for Five

Leaders

1.) If you were informed of the restroom incident, what steps would you take to address the matter?

2.) Did Casey violate ethics, while dealing with Lyric? Please justify your answer.

3.) What steps would you take to help Mr. Wu, veer away from discouragement, regarding his students' scores?

4.) What are Casey's greatest weaknesses?

5.) Who would be more receptive to explicit corrective feedback, from their leader, Casey or Mr. Wu? Provide details to support your answer.

Teachers

1.) Did Casey violate teacher ethics, in any way, in this chapter? If so, provide examples.

2.) Construct a sample email response to Mr. Wu, regarding the email that read, he was concerned about the students' test scores. Specify the steps you recommend for the students to improve.

3.) Do you think Casey should have taken Lyric's situation, into her own hands? If not, discuss the steps you would take, in the same circumstance.

4.) What did Lyric's poem reveal, about her state of mind?

5.) Explain in your own words, what the phrase "it's one thing to be good at a subject, it's another thing to help students get on that level," meant to Mr. Wu, during his reflection.

Students

1.) If you were in Lyric's shoes, would you recommend she join the peer writing club? If so, why?

2.) Critique Lyric's poem, is it relatable? If so, how?

3.) If you were asked to help Mr. Wu, what steps would you take to help him relate to his new students?

4.) If you knew Lyric's reputation, would you help or harm her with your words? Explain your answer.

5.) Interpret the meaning of Lyric's poem—Present but Not Here.

Chapter Five
Attention

Leaders

1.) Write steps you would implement to train Casey on how to lead The Big Wig State Test Training.

2.) Compare/contrast the rules from chapter five to the rules at your school?

3.) Would you alter your leadership approach, in dealing with Casey/Mr. Wu? Write a response with several details to explain your answer.

4.) On a scale of 1-10(one being the lowest and ten being the highest), how would you rate, Casey's delivery of the sequencing lesson? Based on your rating, what suggestions would you provide, if you were observing her?

5.) Which unethical practices did Casey engage in? Write alternatives to her actions.

Teachers

1.) Have you ever felt misunderstood, during an observation? If so, please elaborate.

2.) How did The Big Wig Statewide Test impact teachers?

3.) Did you think elements were missing from Casey's lesson on sequencing?

4.) Who would benefit from Eat N' Express from your school?

5.) Did Mr. Wu handle Kaz's mother(Ms. Beauty-Built), professionally? If you were in his shoes, how would you handle a parent like the character?

Students

1.) Out of the neon, sparkle, and shine group, which rule breakdown did you relate to? Explain your answer.

2.) Can you relate to Lyric's emotional state? If so/not please write steps of how you address feeling depression.

3.) Compare and contrast the rule preference of the neon, sparkle, and shine groups.

4.) Construct a student lesson plan, based on the information, from this chapter.

5.) Write an alternate ending to this chapter.

Chapter Six
Friendmanship

Leaders

1.) Name at least three ways you encourage teachers/staff to identify and conquer fear.

2.) Identify important aspects of what Lyric said, how would you use her advice to help students, at the school you lead?

3.) If Casey's bullying experience happened at the school you are leading, how would you handle it?

4.) What details would you document— if you completed an observation on Mr. Wu?

5.) Write a Professional Development Plan, addressing how teachers should deal with the circumstances, from this chapter.

Teachers

1.) If you helped run Friendmanship, what steps would you take to ensure the students understood all content?

2.) Do you think Casey's fertility issues, conflicted with her job? Justify your answer.

3.) Although Casey identified Lyric's mental state as an issue, she never made a referral. Was this right or wrong? Provide a detailed explanation to support your answer.

4.) Would you add anything to Casey's comments on "talking white" with the students? If so, what would you add?

5.) What suggestions from the chapter would you implement, in your class?

Students

1.) What are three suggestions you would provide Lyric with regarding Friendmanship?

2.) Identify and elaborate on five-chapter details that impacted you.

3.) Use comparison context clues for unknown words, in paragraph form.

4.) Interpret this statement, "Use your capabilities, as a mirror of your true reflection."

5.) What dreams would come true, if you were not fearful? What are the steps you take to get rid of fear?

Chapter Seven
Tracking Priorities

Leaders

1.) How many tests does your school administer, monthly? Write a proposal on why you feel students are/are not required to take an unreasonable amount of tests.

2.) If there were no statewide tests, how would your leadership style change?

3.) List ways you encourage teachers to support students and their parents, struggling with understanding elements of The Big Wig State Test.

4.) What steps would you take to address the way teachers communicate or demean the students?

5.) Write a detailed explanation on, who you would rather team teach with (Casey or Mr. Wu). Provide at least five details from the chapter to support your response.

Teachers

1.) Please write how your personal experiences, correlate to the following statement, champions live for challenges.

2.) How did Casey's positive attitude influence Mr. Wu's performance?

3.) Construct a Motiv'Plicational Plan for the members of Friendmanship.

4.) Did Casey's contribution(to The Number Ones) appear misleading? Provide details to support your answer.

5.) Construct a poem, based on the elements of this chapter that stood out. Dedicate the poem to students.

Students

1.) Write an essay about ways you would impact Friendmanship.

2.) Have you or anyone you know, failed a test, based on how a teacher treated you? If so, what did the teacher say/do that caused this behavior?

3.) Create a poem about why taking a U-turn back to the slavery mindset is wrong.

4.) Construct a character tree based on how you relate to each person, from this chapter.

5.) Do you feel schools give an unreasonable number of tests? Why/why not, provide an explanation(with several details) related to the question.

Chapter Eight
Student Genres

Leaders

1.) Analyze the training content and pinpoint aspects, you would implement at your school.

2.) Does your school have a gifted program? If so, what does it entail? If not, what are you doing as a leader to ensure the population is serviced?

3.) During observations, what elements do you look for, regarding the classroom's climate?

4.) How would you measure the consistency of the rubrics?

5.) Did Principal Champel handle the student, correctly? If not, what would you do, differently? Provide a detailed response.

Teachers

1.) Why do you feel the students felt comfortable, opening up during peer writing sessions?

2.) Do you share the same dynamic, as Lyric and the students, in this chapter? If not, what is preventing you from making students feel comfortable to open up, during class?

3.) Choose at least three student genres, write additional ways to deal with the types of students.

4.) Provide a detailed explanation of why you feel/do not feel the gifted population is not serviced, in low socio-economic areas?

5.) Why do you feel Casey would not give up on Lyric? Do you share the same sentiments, why/why not?

Students

1.) Provide three-five ways you or someone you know, could relate to the skit the kids performed.

2.) Provide a detailed interpretation of the following quote: "If you end up doing something, you don't want to, it gets to the point where you hate your reflection," said Lyric.

3.) Write a play, about drug misuse and why anyone would give up control, as a result of it.

4.) Pick three to four student genres to compare/contrast, which genre do you relate to the most and why?

5.) Do you feel, your teacher/teachers deal with you, uniquely? If so, why or why not? Provide a detailed response.

Chapter Nine
The V.

Leaders

1.) Construct a detailed school safety plan to address the deficiencies that compromised the safety, at The Best High School.

2.) If you were in Principal Waggenport's shoes, what steps would you take to help the hostages, in the cafeteria?

3.) What words of inspiration, would you say to the hurting staff at The Best High School?

4.) After such a horrific event, how would you keep your staff motivated to remain in the teaching profession?

5.) What type of grief counseling plan would you suggest for the hurting staff, parents, and students, at The Best High School?

6.) How does mental health play a key factor in the events that took place?

Teachers

1.) What are the three effects of PTSD?

2.) Was the way Casey(Mrs. Coper) handled her relationship with Lyric ethical? Please provide three reasons to justify your answer.

3.) Formulate five questions, based on this chapter.

4.) Provide alternate ways you would've handled the situation between Casey(Mrs. Coper) and lyric regarding her HIV/AIDS status.

5.) Describe Officer Gant's actions? Did you make the right decisions?

Students

1.) Describe Lyric's state, of mind, when she found out her diagnosis?

2.) If you were friends with Lyric and knew she planned to bring a gun to school, what steps would you take to tell an adult?

3.) Is this scenario farfetched or relatable? Provide details to support your claim.

4.) Use complete sentences to analyze Lyric's poem, about her diagnosis status.

5.) Write an essay on how you expect teachers/authority figures to set an example.

Chapter Ten
Sad Endings Should Strike Change

Leaders

1.) Would the proposed policies be effective in your district? Why or why not?

2.) What are some important aspects of the policies in this chapter?

3.) Compare and contrast the policies at your school to the policies that were proposed and adopted, from this chapter.

4.) What actions could the security guard have taken to avoid the shooting?

5.) Would you alter the memorial ceremony? If so, how?

Teachers

1.) What would cause the policy implementation to happen in your school?

2.) Which of the speeches inspired you to strike a change in your community and why?

3.) If you were in Casey's shoes would you have stayed in the cafeteria to try and negotiate with Lyric why/why not?

4.) Which teaching ethics(if any), did Casey violate?

5.) Create a skit to practice the safety plan, from your school.

Students

1.) Write an essay/skit on school safety?

2.) Would you like the policies from this chapter to be used, at your school? Why/why not?

3.) Have you or anyone you know, participated in a protest for change? If so, what was the outcome?

4.) What policies would you change, at your school/in your community to improve safety?

5.) If Lyric were your friend, what advice would you give to her?

Made in the USA
Columbia, SC
18 July 2021